Forms of Capital

Pierre Bourdieu

Forms of Capital

General Sociology, Volume 3

Lectures at the Collège de France (1983–1984)

Edited by Patrick Champagne and Julien Duval,
with the collaboration of Franck Poupeau
and Marie-Christine Rivière

Translated by Peter Collier

polity

First published in French in *Sociologie générale. Volume 2. Cours au Collège de France* (1983–1986) © Éditions Raisons d'agir/Éditions du Seuil, 2016

This English edition © Polity Press, 2021

Polity Press
65 Bridge Street
Cambridge CB2 1UR, UK

Polity Press
101 Station Landing
Suite 300
Medford, MA 02155, USA

ISBN-13: 978-1-5095-2670-3 - hardback

A catalogue record for this book is available from the British Library.

Library of Congress Cataloging-in-Publication Data
Names: Bourdieu, Pierre, 1930-2002, author. | Bourdieu, Pierre, 1930–2002.
   Sociologie générale. Volume 3. English
Title: Forms of capital / Pierre Bourdieu, translated by Peter Collier.
Description: Cambridge, UK ; Medford, MA : Polity Press, 2021. | Series:
   General sociology ; Volume 3 | "Lectures at the College de France
   (1983–1984)." | Includes bibliographical references and index. |
   Summary: "One of the greatest sociologists of the 20th century
   introduces a key concept of his approach"-- Provided by publisher.
Identifiers: LCCN 2020039954 | ISBN 9781509526703 (hardback)
Subjects: LCSH: Sociology--Study and teaching (Higher)--France. | Capital.
   | Capitalism. | Sociology.
Classification: LCC HM578.F8 B68213 2021 | DDC 306.3/42--dc23
LC record available at https://lccn.loc.gov/2020039954

Typeset in 10.5 on 12 pt Times New Roman by
Servis Filmsetting Ltd, Stockport, Cheshire
Printed and bound in Great Britain by TJ Books Limited

For further information on Polity, visit our website: politybooks.com

Contents

Second session (seminar): time and power. Acting on structures and acting on representations. – Symbolic action. – The reassuring role of the rule. – Time and the exercise of power.

Editorial Note

This book forms part of the ongoing publication of Pierre Bourdieu's lectures at the Collège de France. A few months after his final lecture at this institute in March 2001, Bourdieu had published under the title *Science of Science and Reflexivity*,[1] a condensed version of the last year of his course (2000–01). After his death, *On the State* was published in 2012, followed by *Manet: A Symbolic Revolution* in 2013, corresponding to the lectures that he gave in 1989–92 and 1998–2000 respectively.[2] The publication of the 'General sociology' lectures that Bourdieu gave during his first five years of teaching at the Collège de France, between April 1982 and June 1986, was then started. A first volume appeared in 2015, collecting the lectures given during the 1981–82 and 1982–83 academic years.[3] The second French volume collects the three following years. This English translation presents the first of those, 1983–84, with its ten two-hour lectures.

This edition of *General Sociology* follows the editorial options defined at the moment of publication of the lectures on the state, and aim to reconcile faithfulness with readability.[4] The published text represents a transcription of the lectures as they were given. In the great majority of cases, the transcription used in the present publication relies on recordings. However, for some of the lectures the recordings could not be found and the text published here is based on the literal transcriptions that Bernard Convert made for his personal use. He kindly sent them to us, and we are very grateful to him. Finally, in one case (part of the lecture of 7 March 1985, in a forthcoming English volume), lacking any recording or transcription, Bourdieu's argument has been reconstructed using the only material available: Bernard Convert's notes from the lecture.

As in the previous volumes, the passage from the spoken to the written word has required some minor rewriting, which scrupulously respects the approach applied by Bourdieu himself when he revised his own lectures and seminars: making stylistic corrections and emending oral infelicities (repetitions and linguistic tics, etc.). On one or two exceptional occasions only, we have curtailed the development of an argument, when the state of the recordings did not allow us to reproduce it in a satisfactory manner. The words or passages that were ambiguous or inaudible or that reflected a momentary interruption in the recording have been signalled thus [. . .] when it was impossible to recover them, and have been placed between brackets when their accuracy could not be guaranteed.

Acknowledgements

The editors would like to thank Bruno Auerbach, Amélie and Louise Bourdieu, Pascal Durand, Johan Heilbron, Remi Lenoir, Amín Perez, Jocelyne Pichot and Louis Pinto for their collaboration. They particularly wish to thank Bernard Convert and Thibaut Izard for their continual and often essential help.

Lecture of 1 March 1984

First session (lecture): preamble on the teaching of sociology. – Lector and auctor. – *The field–habitus duo.* – *System, field and subfields.* – *The field of the fields.* – *The structure of distribution of specific capital.* – *The institutionalization of the functioning of the field.*
Second session (seminar): the hit parade of the intellectuals (1). – *A symbolic coup.* – *The overrepresentation of fuzzy categories and the question of competence.* – *Instituting the judges.* – *Adopting a standpoint on the standpoints adopted.* – *The universalization of individual judgements.* – *Producers for producers and producers for non-producers.*

First session (lecture): preamble on the teaching of sociology

Beginnings are always an occasion for anxious reflection, and I have been led to ponder over the meaning of what I am teaching and the significance of what I could achieve in the conditions prevailing here. Without revealing all the reflections that this anxiety inspired in me, I would simply like to give some idea of my manner of teaching and the conclusions that I have drawn. In fact, sociology, like all the sciences, can be taught in two ways: you can teach either its principles and formal procedures, or examples of these formal procedures at work. My intellectual temperament leads me to prefer the second formula, which consists in showing the science at work in research situations, but since the conditions in which I am placed obviously prevent me from doing this in practice, I have sought a kind of compromise between the aim of conveying the formal structures and the aim of communicating examples of these formal structures in operation. For this reason I shall divide my two hours of teaching into two parts: in the first, following the logic of what I did last year and developing its arguments,

I shall present theoretical analyses; in the second, I shall try to give an idea of what a seminar might be, by showing how we can construct an object of study and elaborate a problematic, and above all bring these theoretical formulae and formal structures to bear on actual operations. Which is what seems to me to be the essence of the scientific profession, that is, the art of locating scientific problems in the most specific and banal facts of everyday life, and making practical use of this theoretical apparatus by transforming the object from something perceived superficially into a truly scientific object. Obviously, this is not a common procedure and what I shall present will always have a slightly artificial air. It will take on the appearance of an *ex post* experiment, reconstructed after the event. It may perhaps lack the essential, which is – to be honest – the tentative, hesitant and clumsy nature of real research. I shall of course myself make genuine blunders, because I cannot eliminate all the uncertainties and weaknesses that are part of any exercise in research.

To return to what I aim to discuss during this first session: a development of the arguments that I put forward last year. Here again, the conditions provided for my communication are not entirely suitable and I shall offer a kind of compromise, however unsatisfactory, between this kind of abstract aim and the material conditions in which I have to accomplish it. I would like in passing to make a remark that is not earth-shattering, but that I still believe to be important. The essence of an act of communication of any kind is to connect the aim to express with what I call a market – that is, a demand;[1] what happens in an act of communication is the outcome of a sort of negotiation between the original intention and the conditions of its reception. Even if every speaker uses metadiscursive strategies in an attempt to control the conditions of reception of their discourse, in practice they are never completely in control of the results of their production. A scientifically controlled pedagogical intention should be able to master the conditions of its own reception. I offer this reflection to those among you involved in the world of teaching. Yet it is not at all certain that reflecting on what we are doing makes the practice any easier. In fact, it is rather the opposite – I think that my own hesitation at this very moment bears witness to this – but nonetheless there is a pedagogical principle, which is that we need to know that what we are doing is trying, however minimally, to adapt the conditions of the production of a discourse to the conditions of its reception. One of the causes of my hesitation is the gap between my aim to produce a discourse whose coherence will become apparent over a period of years, and the fact that I know my audience will fluctuate: how do I reconcile a continuous discourse with an intermittent audience, or worse, with an audience that is partly regular and partly intermittent? For those who are regular, what I have to say may seem to be full of repetition, recurrence and afterthought, contradiction even, some of which I am aware of, but not always. And those of you who come and go will risk finding the logic of my discourse difficult to follow, all the more so since the arbitrary timetable of the lecture slot does not necessarily match up with logical, easily self-contained units of theory.

Lector and *auctor*

Therein lies one of the contradictions analysed by sociology: the contradiction between a priestly role – administering communion at given times – and a prophetic situation. In granting me your intermittent presence, you place me in a prophetic role, for the prophet bursts into the space 'outside routine', at moments or hours unforeseen, to produce a 'deroutinized', as it were miraculous, discourse.[2] The pedagogical situation in this institute [the Collège de France] elicits a deroutinized and therefore prophetic status, but at the same time its weekly, regular and repetitive aspect calls for something that is not at all prophetic. The prophet must be able to choose his moment: he does not want to speak when he has a migraine or when he is tired, he prefers to speak in periods of ferment or crisis, critical moments when the world teeters on the brink, when nobody knows what to think, when everyone falls silent and he is the only one left speaking. The scholastics already signalled this contradiction by contrasting the *auctor* who produces a creative discourse with the *lector* who pronounces what are essentially readings and commentaries.

There is a problem with the status of the pedagogical role: situations that are ambiguous, being half-charismatic and half-bureaucratic, like the one I find myself in, are very difficult to live with once we become aware of the contradictions that they imply, and especially once we wish to avoid exploiting one or other of the options. These are sociological analyses without seeming to be so: such ambiguous situations and propositions solicit and encourage a double game, which can be very fertile. But many dual situations allow us to benefit from both situations without paying the price – which I believe to be the case with many pedagogical situations in France, and explains the status of pedagogy in France. For example, the dual situation of 'research professor' allows us to take advantage of being a professor in virtue of the fact that we are also a researcher, and allows us to take . . . there is no need to continue the analysis, it would lead to some possibly quite tragic reflections . . .

If we are sensitive to the constraints imposed by the two positions and we attempt to deal with them, we find them practically impossible to handle, which creates considerable anxiety. Let me reflect on this a little longer. Teaching sociology today is a considerable task. For detractors of sociology – who are often recruited from among sociologists, since those who struggle to fulfil their role have an interest in discrediting it – sociology appears confused and uncertain, as a newborn science. But if we look at sociology differently, constructively, making the slightest effort, however inconclusive, to understand its development, we get the feeling that sociology has achieved so much that the simple role of *lector* or commentator could already enable us to transmit its achievements clearly and coherently. This is the role of the *lector*, the person who forms a canon: the jurists were the first to accomplish this kind of task. For a century now, sociologists have been producing a corpus of acts of jurisprudence. Every day produces its quota of studies, concepts, experiments and research; journals founded and published, and so on. Another role for the *lector* would be to create summaries – which would be synthetic, but not reductive and destructive as ordinary pedagogical acts so often are – which would in their way help advance our knowledge by making it more clearly cumulative. This formidable task would not be the burden of a single man, but the work of a whole team.

It is characteristic of France that this work of canon formation and coding, which seems to me to be one of the conditions of scientific progress, is something that we do not undertake. For sociological reasons that I could explain, we do not have manuals, or 'readers'. These procedures for summary and synthesis require modesty and competence, and this tradition is not rewarded in France, where it looks better to cobble together an essay based on third-hand research and give interviews to the weekly press. We lack the means of summary and synthesis that modesty and competence would provide. We lack translations: Max Weber is still either not translated, or only partially and very badly.[3]

Contrary to the role of the *lector* would be the task of pursuing knowledge and presenting the latest results of research or the latest state of our science, at least on one or other particular question. This task is not any easier, because sociology, like any science I think, has antennae: it puts out feelers in very different directions. This common core of competences shared by people of apparently opposing views – but mainly driven to oppose each other by the prevailing Parisian doxa – does give rise to discoveries and progress. But can we communicate these discoveries without assuming that the founding body of knowledge acquired is already known to all? Reflections of this nature are not merely a rhetorical preamble. I hope that they will help guide you to make the best use of what I have to say.

The field–habitus duo

I am going to settle for something of a compromise: I shall continue to develop the analyses that I presented of a theoretical system and a body of concepts that seem to me to be coherent and important in constructing social reality and objects of scientific study. These concepts were not based on a theoretical presumption.[4] For the most part, they were elaborated through a process of practical research before being established as concepts. Often, they function almost independently of me and escape my theoretical control; so that the logical control that I shall exercise in these lectures will lead me to indulge in a certain amount of self-criticism, or quite simply make corrections to the concepts that I have been presenting. If the analyses that I offer are to be useful, they will be insofar as they will also function for research purposes, and, without being sure of accomplishing this very difficult task, I shall attempt to do my best as far as possible to make the examples that I offer in the second session match the theoretical analyses that I offer in the first session. This is to prevent you from feeling that this is an abstract conceptual exercise, and also to avoid the trap that I inevitably fell into previously, of launching into vast digressions where the concern to provide empirical illustrations caused the theoretical discourse to lose its coherence. For those of you who were here last year, I recall the example of the literary field that I used:[5] in that example, you could hardly see the wood for the trees, and you might easily have lost sight of the main thread of my theoretical discourse.

What I have to offer now follows on from last year's argument. I shall recall the broad lines of the argument without entering into detail. First, I set out the theoretical uses of the notion of the habitus. I tried to show in what way this notion enables us to avoid a certain number of traditional philosophical alternatives, in particular of mechanism or purposiveness, which I found lethal to any realist analysis of social activity. Second, having argued that the inseparable notions of habitus and field must function as a pair, I started to analyse the notion of the field understood as a space of positions. Let me take a moment to discuss the relation between habitus and field in order to dispel one kind of misunderstanding that I find very dangerous. My readers, or those who use the concepts of habitus and field, tend to dissociate these two concepts. For example, when it comes to explaining a practice (such as placing one's children in such and such a school, or following a particular religious practice), sociologists tend to divide – more unconsciously than consciously – between those who draw attention to factors linked with the trajectory, and the social conditions producing the producer of the practice, that is the habitus, and those who emphasize factors linked with what we might call the 'situation' – although I showed last year that this is not the best word – that is, factors linked to the field as a space of relations imposing a certain number of constraints at the time of the action.

For example, the analysis of teaching relations that I mentioned earlier drew attention to the field rather than to my own properties, whereas, in order to give a full account of my anxieties and hesitations, we need to take into account not only the situation as I analysed it but also the properties specific to my career and the social conditions, among others, that produce me. Depending on the object studied, the moment of research and the intellectual inclinations of the different producers of sociological discourse, we may tend to emphasize one aspect more than the other, whereas in fact what is at work in any action – and this was the principle behind my analyses – is always the relation between, on the one hand, the agent socially constituted by their social experience and the position they occupy in social space, and endowed with a whole series of given properties (dispositions, inclinations, preferences and tastes), and, on the other hand, a social space within which these dispositions will encounter the social conditions that govern their implementation. In the perspective that I propose, action in the widest sense (which may just as well be the formulation of an opinion as the delivery of a speech or the execution of an act) is always the product of the implementation of two virtual systems: on the one hand, the virtual possibilities associated with the producer; on the other, the potentials inherent in the situation and the social space. Which means that there are within each one of us potentials that will never materialize because they will never find the social conditions of their implementation, that is, a field in which they could be implemented. Thus, as we see for instance in writings on the 1914–18 war, which was a kind of collective shock that permanently haunted the thoughts of all the writers of the 1920s, a situation like war is the occasion for revealing potentials that, without it, would have remained buried in the dispositions of the agents. And part of the stupefaction that situations of crisis provoke arises in fact from the effect of a revelation that they may have in leading to or authorizing literary expression, the revelation that potential is hidden, because it is repressed, by ordinary situations.

This is one example that illustrates this relation and which also shows how the fact of thinking in a profoundly relational way – the habitus and the field being systems of relations, with any action being a relation between two systems of relations – leads us to think in terms of a logic of imaginary variation: if such a system of dispositions produces such an effect in such a field, we can wonder what effect it would have produced in another field, and we can proceed with a sort of experimentation. The manuals tell us that sociologists and historians cannot conduct experiments, but the possibility of virtual experiments is always available; we can very well envisage proceeding by imaginary variation, as Husserl called it, but on the basis of real experience.[6] Thus we may wonder how the dispositions of the first generation parvenu intellectual are made manifest in the intellectual field in France in 1984, what form they assumed in a differently structured field in the 1830s, how they appeared in the artistic field and in the literary field, how they arise today in France, or in Communist China. We do then have the possibility, within the fields of reference, of varying the potentially different manifestations of the supposedly constant habitus. This enables us to substantiate Durkheim's formula associating sociology with the comparative method;[7] the comparative method is the sociologists' mode of experimentation. Obviously, putting this comparative method into practice has taken very different forms. Max Weber, for example, could not write a single sentence without immediately adding, 'But for the Phoenician Greeks . . . but for the Australians . . . but for the Bambara', whereas Durkheim preferred a much more statistical mode of variation.[8] Yet the fundamental intention – which is part of the common corpus that I referred to at the start of this lecture – is basically the same. Simply, given the limits of human capabilities, it materializes in different forms according to the specific expertise of the different producers of sociology.

System, field and subfields

The relation between the habitus and the field is primordial, even if, in the interests of an expository argument, I was led last year to proceed in stages, analysing first what affected the field and then what affected the habitus, and subsequently how the two function. Having set out this fundamental relation between the habitus and the field, I proceeded in the first instance to analyse the scientific functions that the notion of habitus performed, and the problems that it enabled us to consider. Then I moved on to the notion of the field. I tried to present its properties, following the same procedure as for the notion of the habitus: I showed the theoretical functions that it performed, the problems that it enabled us to consider and the false problems that it was able to dispel. I shall first recap the provisional definition of these notions that I arrived at, giving further details, and then continue with what I have to say this year.

I defined the field as a space of positions, a point that I should like to qualify immediately by explaining the difference between field and system. I could spend some considerable time developing this argument, but since it is not central to my analysis I shall restrict myself to the aspect that some of you might find useful, insofar as there is in sociology a whole current using the theory of systems to study the social world. This projects onto the social world a mode of thinking in terms of a theory of systems,[9] which in my eyes runs the risk of importing the organicism that is implicit in the theory of systems, and in any transfer of modes of thinking inspired by biology in general (effects of self-regulation, homeostasis, etc.).

When we speak in terms of fields, it means that we are considering the social world as a space whose different elements cannot be considered outside their position in this space. The social space will then be defined as the universe of relations within which any social position will be characterized. To give a simple idea of what I mean, we could say that the issue facing the sociologist studying a social world (the universe of, say, journalism, medicine or the university) will be to construct the space of relations in which the positions occupied by each of the agents or institutions considered is articulated. An issue that immediately confronts those who use the notion of field – something that I did not discuss last year – is the question of the boundaries of the field and the conditions that govern attempts to locate and define these fields concretely. In fact, this issue arises in practice itself. For example, last year I referred to a literary field, but also sometimes to a field of cultural production, into which I subsumed it, along with its writers, journalists, critics, and so on. I also referred in passing to a field of critics as a subfield: you would be justified in asking me if this procedure was not somewhat arbitrary, and how I was constructing these spaces and their boundaries in practice.

On this point, the distinction between field and system stands out very simply and clearly. A system is defined by its finite and closed nature, and it is impossible to define a system other than as a system of relations linking a finite set of elements, each of whose relations is completely defined as a part of that relational reality by its position in the space of the system. On the contrary, the notion of the field is defined by the fact that it is open; a field is a space whose very boundaries are actually called into question in the space considered. (At this very moment, I am illustrating the embarrassment that I announced at the start of the lecture: it would need only one concrete example to make everything blindingly obvious, but this concrete example would take ten minutes and you would completely lose the plot. I think that a certain number of things I am saying at this moment will become clear right at the end of the lecture). A subfield is not a part of a field. There is, when we pass from a field to a subfield, a leap, a qualitative change, and this is the case at every level of division. For example, the subfield of criticism obeys a different logic from that of the literary field. Its laws of functioning are different, they cannot be deduced from a knowledge of the surrounding field: its stakes are different, as are the forms of capital that operate within it. The subfield, then, does not function as a logical part of the whole.

Furthermore, the question of the relation of the subfield to the surrounding field will take the form of relations of domination, of struggles between partisans of autonomy and partisans of heteronomy. I shall illustrate this point briefly, and I shall give an example later (in the second session) of a concrete analysis, where one of the issues is the relation between the field of journalism and the intellectual field. We could say that these two fields are themselves subfields of the field of cultural production. We will see straight away here that the relation between the two universes cannot be defined in terms of juridical boundaries and that one of the fundamental issues in each of the subfields is precisely the struggle to define the boundaries between the fields.

Consequently, the sociologist does not arbitrarily construct his fields, and a change of fields is not simply a change of scale. In a constructivist, idealist perspective, we might say that the construction of a field depends on the level at which the analysts place themselves. This is fair enough: when I place myself, for example, at the level of the critic, I am operating on a smaller scale than when I move to the level of the field of criticism as a whole. In changing scale, the sociologist transforms the status of the elements they are dealing with: things that might appear as wholes become parts. For example, having established the literary field, we might change scale and move on to the field of a genre – for example, the genre of the theatre – where we will find oppositions homologous to those that we found in the field as a whole.

But this functionalist and constructivist view fails to include a property of the notion of the field that seems to me fundamental, as I said
several times last year: the approach in terms of field leads us in each
case to raise a certain number of general questions on the relations at
stake in the social space, but it is the particular case that will allow us to
answer these questions. In other words, the notion of the field enables
us to put general questions about each field, but it is experimentation
and detailed study that will provide the full set of answers, in particular
concerning the borders and boundaries. To take one example: one
principal source of the differences between the fields is to be found in
the fact that certain fields have clearly defined, fixed boundaries, with
a *numerus clausus* very tightly controlled by the people who dominate
the field, whereas others on the contrary have very porous, ill-defined
and fluid boundaries. For example, the struggles within a field may at
some points have as their goal the dissolution of a subfield within a
field, or, on the contrary, the recovery of the autonomy of the field.[10]
In passing, we see that autonomy, which is one of the properties defining a field, cannot be taken as given once and for all: the autonomy or
heteronomy of a field is constantly at issue in a field. There you have
the very example of the universal question: you can raise the question
of the autonomy of any field and the only answers are historical and
particular. In fact, the principal virtue of this method is to raise universal questions that can only be answered by investigation, historical[11]
and empirical experimentation.

The relation between autonomy and boundary seems to me important: it is rare for the limits of a field to be a juridically sanctioned frontier. Most often – and this is another universal question to be asked
about any field – they are only temporary fronts or places, *loci incerti*,[12]
where the struggle is particularly fierce. We could for example take the
history of the academic disciplines and refer to the relation between
psychology and sociology in the nineteenth century, or the struggles
for the division of labour among the biologists of today. The boundaries are the places where the very definition of the field is decided.
The functionalist posture that consists in saying 'I am entitled to say
that criticism is a subfield since in fact the notion of the field is a pure
constructum, a purely theoretical construction, and I construct and
change scale however I wish', is therefore only partly true: although it
is certain that any scientific concept is a construct (in the sense that it
is not extracted from reality by induction), the constructivist operation
formulates a valid general question only if it draws its reality from
a scientific labour of empirical construction and confrontation with
scientific observation.

In other words, we might say that one of the ways of deciding the question of the limits of a field is to find the place where what we might call the 'field effect' is weakest. I am thinking of an article in *Actes de la recherche en sciences sociales* on the relation between centre and periphery in Italian painting,[13] which raises the question of whether we are justified in placing the Avignon painters in the field of Italian painting in the fourteenth and fifteenth centuries, for instance. First, there is no universally right answer: Avignon painting may be in the field at one moment, and then no longer be there – which gives us information about the field and its scope. At the same time, whether it is present in the field or not is itself in a sense a function of the power of the field and its domination effects. Today, for example, we could say that French painting is present in the field of American painting: field effects are evident, for instance, in the fact that our painters are obliged to exhibit their works in the United States at least once. This means that I could only answer this question of the limits of the field through empirical research that will inform me of the scope of the effects of the field.

That having been said, let us return to the issue of the field as opposed to the system: we may suppose that in any field there is a tendency to close and set itself up as a system or, more precisely (for I am committing an error that I constantly criticize: I am establishing an abstraction as the subject of a proposition), that in any field those who dominate tend to close the field, that is, transform it into a system. It would take hours to flesh out the details of this proposition: the *numerus clausus* is a manner of establishing a juridical obstacle that is a boundary in the strongest sense of the term, a porous frontier that people may pass through, to leave or, if they can afford the entrance fee, to enter and be admitted to become agents in the field.[14] The tendency to form a closed system, to close down, is then always present as a possibility of the field, and is all the stronger, I think, when the agents who dominate the field have more power to exclude new entrants, that is to raise what economists call barriers to entry, to render the cost of inclusion higher, as it were. Here again, the notions of relative autonomy, of boundary and field effect are absolutely inseparable. These are, in fact, general questions.

The field of the fields

Another question has been put to me in relation to my lectures last year: is there a kind of field of the fields? Here I must spell out, for those of you who do not have them in mind, the presuppositions of my argument: the notion of the field is born of an effort to account for the fact that within the complex entity we call 'society' there are sub-universes that we may think of as resembling games, within which things happen differently from the way they do in neighbouring games. One important thing is that this is in no way a universal property of societies; there are historical and social conditions that govern the possibility of social entities taking the form of fields. For a long time now, sociologists have noted and given different names to this process, which is also referred to in the Marxist or Weberian traditions (I shall return to this in a moment),[15] which we follow Durkheim in calling 'differentiation';[16] it is the process that leads the 'social world' to divide up into sub-universes with their own autonomy, their own laws of functioning relatively independent of what surrounds them. But then, does speaking of a field not lead us to negate the notion of a 'social world'? Are we still justified in speaking of a 'social system', as so many people do? I consider this to be an important question. I shall answer it once again on an abstract and theoretical level, which may seem arbitrary, but can be justified. It is not a simple metaphysical choice, although most of the people who write about the social world answer it without realizing that the question is badly put – I may sound arrogant, but I am right.

So I shall answer this question: I think that the social space, as space of spaces, field of fields, is even less closed than each individual field. It is precisely the sort of place open to all the social fields. It is difficult to think of this for a number of reasons. As I keep repeating (since I find that repetition is rather helpful in this case), just as Bachelard argued for a psychoanalysis of the scientific mind to be applied to the natural sciences,[17] so we need to argue constantly for a psychoanalysis of the scientific mind to be applied to the human sciences. If the psychoanalytical cure is long and difficult and if it is true that sociology is not a science like the others – despite my opening declarations – it is to a considerable extent because this psychoanalysis is formidably difficult.

We all have a philosophy of the social space that we would find very difficult to articulate discursively. If I gave you a sheet of paper and asked you to describe 'what I understand by society', you would either be reduced to silence or you would want to write a whole essay, as you have certainly done before on this kind of topic. Having said that, in our everyday choices, as in the scientific choices made by sociologists when they construct their object of study one way or another, using sentences like 'French society is . . .', we cannot avoid engaging a philosophy of the social world. This philosophy too has its coherence and is not the same as it was fifty years ago. Our philosophy of the social world is linked to the state of the social world that we inhabit, but I think one of the obstacles to thinking scientifically about the social world and providing an adequate construction of it is the architectural type of philosophy of the social world that Marxism, with its infrastructures, superstructures, procedures and apparatuses, so powerfully underpins. In other words, we have what Durkheim called 'prenotions',[18] spontaneous schemes that are constituted and reinforced by the scholarly vision of the social world bequeathed to us by past generations. If the question of the space of spaces or the field of fields that I have just raised is difficult, it is largely because it upsets the structures of our social unconscious, which tends to represent the social world as a house where there are foundations (the infrastructure) and then superstructures. The social world then is construed as something well structured, something we could draw: society is like a pyramid with an elite that is necessarily narrower than its wider 'base' (our vocabulary being redolent of our social philosophy . . .). It is thus something finite and closed, it is a set of individuals – which is nonsense.

The notion of the field calls all this into question. It is already an improvement to speak of a 'system of systems', or a 'structure of structures', as was current in the structuralist period of the 1960s. But we then had to wonder how to 'articulate' the structures (for the metaphors of 'articulations' and 'bodies' appeal to a form of organicism), and when we say 'system of systems', we are thinking of a head, and feet, and we end up with infrastructure and superstructure, etc. We are pleased to find that Bachelard said that there is a polemics of scientific reason, and we write it up in our theses – but if I develop my analysis much further, and make you suffer, you are going to find me mean, so I prefer to let you continue your self-analysis and the analysis of your own representation of the social world by yourselves. You might amuse yourselves with the salutary exercise of taking a sheet of paper and asking yourselves how you would draw the social world. I advise you to do this; but now that I have warned you, you won't draw a pyramid, will you? [*Laughter*]

Speaking of a 'space of spaces' is to say that there is a universe of spaces whose boundaries are not very clear – which is a nuisance: we like to draw lines around things, we like things to stay in their place – and with no obvious hierarchies, since the hierarchies are in a state of constant flux. One property of these sub-spaces is precisely their struggle for their position in the space. We might see them as a sort of artistic construction like mobiles, which move either very subtly with a kind of imperceptible shift (by the time we have detected it, it is already over) or, sometimes, with an abrupt change of position.[19] But it is something open and indefinite both in the moment and in its evolution, which is very important: among the various social fantasies that we draw from our surrounding culture, there is also this idea that things have a meaning, that we are heading in some chosen direction. I would also point out that saying that the universe is unfinished and indefinite, and that constructing it raises questions which seek to impose definitions but can only be answered in confrontation with reality, is to call into question a whole set of comforting assumptions that underpin ordinary scientific operations.

You will see in the example that I shall use in a moment that we are confronted with these problems in an absolutely concrete way, but there too the whole process of scientific research leads to resolving them without really posing them: if I am an empirical sociologist, I need a population, and so I need to define the population; if I study professors, what do I take a 'professor' to be? Any scientific operation calls on me to return to the slippery slope that leads me to think in terms of limits. I shall stop here, but we should also consider the notion of 'the last analysis',[20] which is a magnificent metaphysical notion; everything that I have been criticizing could be summed up by the phrase 'in the last analysis': if we argue that the field of fields is open, this means that we will have to wait for a very long time before we are able to say 'in the last analysis'.

The structure of distribution of specific capital

I want to take this a little further. The fields are spaces. Their logics contain invariants, but are also defined as much by their variations, singularities and specificities as by these invariants. These variations are linked to historical junctures and in particular to the state of relations between the different fields at a given moment, which to some extent governs the relations within each field. You will say that I am drawing on a notion of a 'field of the fields' here, but remembering that at every moment the notion of relative autonomy implies that all the other fields act to a certain extent – which we need to measure – on every field in no way means that there is at every moment a sort of ideal and measurable integration of all the fields.

There are then invariant properties in all the fields, the principle invariant of all the fields being that the structure of each one is determined by the distribution of what I call specific capital, which – as I shall explain in more detail in the lectures to come – defines the lines of force in the space under consideration. Each of the spaces has the property of defining the conditions of the efficiency of the action designed to be exercised in this field. For example, 'Let none but geometers enter here'[21] is a field slogan. It means that to enter there you have to know your geometry; it provides a definition of the mathematical field as characterized by the imposition of an entrance fee at a given moment. If you want to start an argument, you cannot say 'Schwarz's theorem is right-wing',[22] whereas in sociology you can say, with some chance of finding approval, 'Bourdieu's current argument is right-wing' – this marks the difference between the two fields. Any field, then, tends to set its terms of entrance, that is, the properties that the new entrant must possess to produce effects in the field. Without these properties, he may enter, but he will produce effects that are not those of the field, he will be inefficient, excluded and covered in ridicule, except in an institution where the autonomy of the field has become very weak.

Let me give an example. Marat was a very poor physicist who had written violently polemical invectives against Lavoisier. Here is a social fact: revolutions enable people to settle accounts in alternative ways. In an autonomous field ('Let none but geometers enter here'), Marat would be simply ridiculous; but with the help of the Revolution, the relative autonomy of the scientific field was weakened seriously enough to threaten Lavoisier, whereas Marat, on the other hand . . . such is the effect of a field. Each field then sets its entrance fee, which will take very different forms, whether explicit or implicit. 'Let none but geometers enter here' is an explicit formula, a canon law, the codification of a tacit principle, but many fields are defined by the fact that the entrance fee is tacit: nobody says 'Let none but capitalists enter here', but if you have no capital, you are quickly bankrupted and sent back to the drawing board. There is an implicit or explicit entrance fee, and once you have entered, you are defined by the fact that you can create effects.

To return to the question that I raised at the start of the lecture (is defining the limits of a field a kind of functionalist constructivism, or is it an objective observation?): only through observation can I learn the principles of constitution of the space that I shall call a field. To know how the field is differentiated, I must observe empirically what produces the differences. In an empirical enquiry (for example, if I construct a population of professors in higher education),[23] I shall use statistical procedures to try to reveal what it is that makes the significant differences. One of the aims of an empirical research will be to find the two or three principles – there are obviously universal economic and scientific laws – that when rationally detailed and articulated allow me to reproduce the universe of constitutive differences that are its characteristics. When I enter a universe, I am asking both the question of difference and the question of the principles of differentiation. That having been said, I must establish in each case what the principles are, with their relative strength and importance. If I can say that the three principles of differentiation among the bishops are this, that and the other,[24] make a numerical evaluation of the relative importance of these three principles and show that they enable us to account for all the pertinent differences, I will have made a contribution to science and constructed both the field and the principles that produce the differences within the field. It follows that I cannot construct the field without at the same time knowing the forms of capital at work in the field, and it is the same operation that makes me construct both. To make a rather risky analogy: you cannot construct a card game without knowing what the trumps are: so you construct the rules of the game and its trumps simultaneously.[25]

One thing that defines belonging to a field, albeit, as you will see, to varying degrees, is the ability to produce effects in it. For example, one way of entering a field, that of heresy for example, and confirming one's entry is to produce effects there that establish your existence – this is very important in the fields where the capital is essentially symbolic; to be the object of a riposte by a major holder of symbolic capital means that you have been granted existence. One strategy for the new entrant to a field is to invite attack by a major holder of symbolic capital in order to manage to produce an effect there, and the choice facing the major holders of symbolic capital is to decide whether it is better to let them speak without answering them, or to counterattack and, by the same token, grant existence to the person who is calling into question your symbolic capital and the domination that it implies.[26]

To conclude briefly with this point: field and capital being interdependent, we cannot define a field without at the same time defining the capital that is at work in it. Consequently, all capital is specific, and there are different kinds of capital – I shall return to this. Capital is a form of power that is effective within a certain space, where it produces effects – in particular effects of differentiation – and the differentiation linked to the unequal distribution of capital is the principle structuring the field. Finally, the structure of the field is essentially the structure of the gaps between the capitals present, and this means that the structure is the motive force of the field – which negates an opposition prevalent in the 1950s, structure versus history.[27] The structure of the field is, at the same time, the motor for change, since it is the system of differences which gives the field its structure that generates both the movement of the field and the struggle in the field aiming to preserve or transform this structure, a struggle that owes its properties to the structure.

The institutionalization of the functioning of the field

One last thing, which I shall also return to later: in the past I have often insisted on the structure of the distribution of capital, while omitting one important thing: the institutionalized aspect of this structure. One property of any state of the field at any particular moment is the degree to which the acquired strengths that make the difference in a field are legally recognized or not, that is, made explicit, rationalized and codified. I shall return to this crucial notion of coding, which marks the moment when a linguistic code becomes a juridical code, or the moment when a canon of traditional rules becomes a canon of juridical rules. One of the universal questions to be asked of each field is to what degree the state of its forces is canonical, codified and sanctioned by explicit rules of a legal nature; the degree to which the game is formulated through explicit rules with a deontological code, implicit or explicit entrance requirements, and the like.

This is something that varies considerably over time: for example, there have been periods when the economic field has not always had the degree of coding that it enjoys today: the relation between economics and law – magnificently analysed by Max Weber, as I shall remind you[28] – is extremely variable. Within the constituent fields of the same given period, the degrees of institutionalization are very unequal. The literary field that I took as an example last year was not typical (which is why I am taking another look at it today) because one of its properties is to be one of the least institutionalized fields possible – which I think has important consequences for anyone engaged in the sociology of literature. It is one of the universes where the benefits acquired have very little juridical guarantee. The legal guarantees are disqualified (see the role of the academies today) and the benefits acquired are very poorly guaranteed by the law, which gives rise to all sorts of properties. This means then that, for every field, we should question the degree of institutionalization of the procedures of struggle, success, consecration, accumulation, reproduction (which is very important for the capital) and transmission (with the laws of succession, etc.). For example, the symbolic capital of the literary field is not transmitted by heredity, as is the case in some other fields. We put the question in universal terms, and in each case we investigate the degree of institutionalization and the effects associated with the greater or lesser degree of institutionalization of the benefits previously acquired.

Second session (seminar): the hit parade of the intellectuals (1)

I shall now change register entirely, but at the same time I hope to continue to discuss what I have just been referring to in rather abstract terms. My idea is to present you with something that I found while rummaging through my notes: I had written a commentary on a ranking list that appeared in the journal *Lire*[29] in April 1981, which was the result of asking a certain number of people who, according to them, were thought of as the three leading intellectuals[30] – unfortunately, I do not have to hand the exact formulation of the question, which is very remiss of me, since it is very important in the way that it structures the replies.[31] This enquiry by *Lire* was reprinted in all the newspapers – which is already a social event in itself: it became a topic for debate; people said: 'Here is a list of the forty most important intellectuals.' The interest is not so much the list itself, but, as I hope to demonstrate, the significance of putting this question and producing some sort of order of merit or, as it would be called in the world of the popular song, a 'hit parade' of intellectuals.

Here we have an event that was broadcast to the public, and accepted as gospel truth, whereas it was in fact a social intervention and even, we might say, a social invention. If you reread Max Weber (his analyses of the evolution of the law, or again, the very fine text that forms the introduction to *The Protestant Ethic*, where he shows how the procedures that we consider as rational were gradually constructed), you will notice that when he refers to what he calls the 'process of rationalization', he very often applies the word 'invention' to things that we would not normally associate with this concept. For example, he says: 'The jury is an invention of the kings of England.' In the case of the square of the hypotenuse, we accept the notion of invention, but we don't apply the word invention to social techniques. The kind of parlour game that *Lire* offers us is, I believe, an invention, but an invention that doesn't appear to be one, for it looks self-evident. We have the impression that we are familiar with this sort of thing. The first question to ask then is: why do we accept this? Where does this invention come from? Which universe has produced it? And why at some historical moment can it be applied to the universe of the intellectuals?

The second question to ask is: what class of social actions does this invention belong to? As soon as you start to think about it, you see that the weekly papers, especially those devoted to the arts, often resort to what I call the 'ranking effect': a considerable number of articles take the form of a balance sheet. The 'bilan de la décennie' ('balance sheet of the decade'), published in *La Quinzaine littéraire*[32] of January 1980 under the title 'Tous les essais' ('all the essays'), is an interesting example of such a document. It is a series of 'best of' lists signed by writers of 'best of' lists: thus we have Catherine Clément[33] from *Le Matin de Paris* (who opts for *L'Anti-Oedipe* and *Dialogues* by Deleuze, *Télévision* by Jacques Lacan, etc.), then Max Gallo, Jean-Marie Rouart, Jean-Paul Enthoven, Jean-François Kahn, Robert Maggiori, Christian Delacampagne, etc. Ten named personalities, which is one of the issues at stake in the account that I am about to give, simultaneously propose their ranking of intellectual productions in the light of an entirely arbitrary criterion – 1980, a round number: 'What has happened during the last ten years?'

A symbolic coup

Situated in the same class, that of actions, in a relatively more discreet form, we also find what we might call 'the prophecy of the end of history' or the 'prophecy of times to come' – that is, all the propositions where the word 'new' figures: 'new philosopher', 'new economics', or again, 'the end of structuralism', 'the end of Marxism', 'Marx is dead', etc.[34] These propositions are most interesting from a sociological point of view because they are presented as descriptive, or 'constative'[35] utterances: 'We have seen the last of . . . .' Recently, someone announced 'the end of the social sciences' – which may be what alerted me to the problem. [*Laughter*] Another property of these procedures is their decisive impact on all the producers of such affirmations. I believe that it was Catherine Clément (we can often pin down the origins of an act of prophecy) who was the first to say 'We see the end of the social sciences', and the other prophets hastened to follow suit. That is one of the properties of the field: if Catherine Clément (who happens to be the first on the list) says 'We see the end of the social sciences', we can be sure that Christian Delacampagne and Jean-Paul Enthoven will follow suit shortly afterwards. These propositions are presented as 'constatives'. They say 'The sciences have finished', without defining what the social sciences are.

But are these constatives not performatives that are also saying: 'Let's see an end to the social sciences!', [*laughter*] 'Death to the social

sciences – and scientists [*which includes people like me!*] too'? Why are
these performatives disguised as constatives? What are these acts of
aggression all about? One property of symbolic acts of aggression is
that they come in disguise. This is one of the properties of the symbolic
order: symbolic violence is violence that people wield without appearing to do so. Consequently, the fact that a performative can take on the
appearance of a constative is extremely important. But why is it able
to take on the appearance of a constative? And in whose eyes? I have
conducted these analyses a hundred times and I hesitate to repeat them:
all symbolic authority supposes a social space within which this authority has been accumulated – and I believe that this is what the theorists
of the performative argue. We will say: 'These people are informing
us, and if we think they are informing us, it is because they are well
informed themselves.' Yet we could in fact say: 'But, actually, isn't this
a performance? Might they be taking their desires for reality?' This
would be a most healthy reaction – but we would then be dismissed as
ignorant, particularly if we are, for instance, quite provincial (because
we live far away, we are not in the know, and the well-informed inform-
ers, that is, the Parisians, are there to tell us in advance – to prophetize
– what everyone in well-informed circles knows already).

You might think that I am indulging in gratuitous polemics, but it
is a very important effect: behind this type of utterance, which we find
everywhere in the press, there may be an act of aggression, and an effect
of authority, whose foundations we must investigate. I have started to
describe the mechanism: what does 'well informed' mean, and 'well
informed' in whose eyes? A paradox with the 'well informed' is that
the more you are addressing people who are less well informed (this
is a general proposition, whose application to politics you will soon
see), the greater your chance of being recognized as 'well informed'.
The ranking list published in *Lire*, which is edited by Bernard Pivot,
is generally considered to be written by the 'well informed'. But what
does this 'well informed' mean? 'Informed' of what? When I said 'well
informed', you no doubt thought that it meant 'well informed about
the topic in question, that is, the state of the social sciences, or philosophy'. But there is a second level of meaning: 'well informed' of the
relation between the informed informer and the topic in question, in
other words 'well informed of the specific interests of the well-informed
informer and his interest in appearing to be informed of the issues'.
Symbolic strategies of the kind that I am describing will be all the more
effective when they affect people far removed from the place of production of the message and from access to information on philosophy,
but also from information on the conditions in which information

on philosophy is produced. In other words, if you don't have pals in journalism, you have no chance.

I am stating all this baldly to make sure that it is clear. I am reminded of the famous comment which says that one Roman soothsayer cannot look at another soothsayer without laughing.[36] These soothsayers (the journalists) are not very amusing, but they ought not to be able to look at each other without laughing, for they know they often speak of books that they have not read; the conditions of their profession dictate that they cannot read them all. We could draw an analogy with the relation between the priesthood and the laity – to which Weber has devoted some very fine analyses that I shall return to: the effect of closure of the field, the effect of esotericism and the effect of secrecy (of which the *numerus clausus* is a mechanical form), all help to produce the conditions that favour the symbolic efficiency of action by the people belonging to a relatively autonomous field against the people excluded from the field. We are therefore faced with the problem of the relation of the clergy to the laity: we need to ask ourselves what is the position in the field of these clerics [the writers of the ranking list] and ask (using a Marxist approach), whether the standpoints they adopt, which claim to be universal, are not the universalization of particular interests. Does the specific symbolic efficiency of these seemingly universal standpoints not depend, first of all, on their position in the field and, second, on the fact that, in this field that tends towards closure, the relation between the position held and the standpoint adopted, that you are bound to guess if you have the notion and method of field to hand, cannot be traced by the reader, or at any rate cannot be substantiated? Which means that the provincial reader of *Le Nouvel Observateur* may either have no idea of it – this is the effect of authority – or say 'I smell a rat – there must be something in it for them', but be none the wiser.

The overrepresentation of fuzzy categories and the question of competence

What is to be done with the ranking list ('1st Lévi-Strauss, 2nd Aron, 3rd Foucault', and so on), which we even hear broadcast on the radio? Should we criticize it? Are you expecting me to say: 'It's not right, So-and-so shouldn't be third'? [*Laughter*] No, we need to study the social conditions of production of this list. What this list is hiding is what is tacitly contained in the hidden conditions of its production. In the magazine, they give you the list and the commentaries as well:

'Sartre is dead, he has no successor.'[37] This is interesting . . . It is always very difficult to analyse something where you feel too involved – just now you didn't feel involved enough – because you understand too quickly. I feel authorized to say this because I think that the whole difficulty with a phenomenon like this is to manage to be surprised by everything, even by something that we understand too quickly, as our laughter shows, because when we laugh it always means that we have understood too quickly – we could not say why we laughed, but we have understood something.

I don't have the issue of *Lire* to hand – I hope that you can obtain copies – but I shall attempt to describe it. There is the chart, with photos and biographies of the top five, then the list of names, followed by commentaries produced by the producers of the questionnaire, that is, the inventors of the technique. To the question 'Is Sartre still with us?', they say they don't know how to reply, that it's a shame, or that if there were someone, it would be So-and-so. These commentaries seem to be inspired by the ranking list, but it would be a salutary reflex to ask whether or not they are the unconscious principles of the production of the list. And in a corner right at the end, we have a list of the 448 people questioned.

If these people are cited by name, it is not in the interests of science (so that Bourdieu can analyse them . . .), it is because these people deserve to be cited: they are people who have made a name for themselves, and this is why they have been questioned and why they are justified in giving their opinions. There is even a hierarchy in this composition. Very important names are allowed to have their reactions quoted. We read: 'Yves Montand – poor man! [*laughter*] – tells us that he was very embarrassed' (I am making this up . . . so as not to quote real examples that you can find [*laughter*]). His reply is very interesting because it comes close to asking the key question: 'But what right have I to judge?'[38] If they ask him, it is because they grant him the right to judge: you don't put a question to somebody if you don't grant them the right of reply. So Yves Montand feels legitimate because he has been asked the question, but he finds that it is a hell of a problem, because, although he has been judged legitimate, he does not feel competent – the word 'competence' is interesting: it is a legal term; he feels incompetent, that is, not only incapable of replying (lacking the 'capacity'), but also lacking the statutory entitlement and right to reply that would make him a legitimate judge.

This is the fundamental question: who is invested with the right to judge questions of intellectual performance? *Lire* gives a list of the people who replied, and, for the most eminent, their reactions and – it is here I think that sociology produces its effects – the question that is tacitly raised by this ranking operation is in fact the following: who is to judge the matter of intellectual production? Who has the right to judge? Who has the competence to judge? *Lire* gives the list both of those elected and of the electors. To understand the principle of selection at work in the list of those elected, you have to look for the principle of selection at work in the list of the electors. The electors have been chosen according to an unspoken principle which is unconsciously reproduced in the list of the elected. Let us look at the list of the electors: they are classified by category – 'writers', 'writer-academics' or 'academics', 'writer-journalists' and 'journalists'.

When we look at the lists, the looseness of the taxonomies is striking. For example, some people are classified as 'journalists' where, using the criteria that have led others to be classified as 'writers', they could have been writers. Thus, Max Gallo is among the journalists, whereas Madeleine Chapsal is in with the writers.[39] I don't want to upset either of them; I do not judge. Another example: Jean Cau, Jean Daniel, Jean-Marie Domenach, Paul Guth and Pierre Nora are considered to be 'journalists'. They are alongside Jean Farran, Jacques Godet and Louis Pauwels, which must be quite uncomfortable for some of them. And we find among the 'writers' people like Madeleine Chapsal, Max Gallo, Jacques Lanzmann, Bernard-Henri Lévy, Roger Stéphane. This betrays a typical looseness of categories. A sociologist would proceed otherwise; they would choose an objective indicator of the degree of participation in journalism, such as the frequency of appearance in a precise number of newspapers, or the fact of being appointed by a newspaper – which would be a better criterion – or the average income from journalism. Here the taxonomy is loose, so clear it is that all writers are journalists and all journalists are writers in the eyes of *Lire*. The same thing applies to the writer-academics;[40] people who clearly write frequently for newspapers are classified as 'writer-academics', whereas some who no longer contribute to the newspapers are classified as journalists.

The looseness of the taxonomies leads to a list where, for a good proportion (more than half) of the people, the distinction between journalist and writer is inoperative. In detail, practically half the list is made up of people who cannot really be classified as journalists, writers or academics. We are in the order of *metaxu*,[41] the intermediate, the loose or the fuzzy. The corpus of judges has been recruited largely from among people who characteristically escape simple classification. Above the list of journalists, the review editors state: 'Note that many journalists are also writers.' They don't write this above the list of

writers, which indicates that there is a hierarchy: they think that a
certain number of the people whom they have classified as journalists
may be offended to see themselves classified in this category, which
they tacitly recognize as inferior by this act of warning. The categories
are loose and there is an overrepresentation of people with fairly inde-
terminate properties.

Now it is sufficient to match the list of names, as just described briefly,
with the body of judges in order to understand the principle behind
the ranking – which is to be biased in favour of the journalist-writers;
if you read it, I think you will be convinced. In reality, the writer-
journalists are overrepresented, as if the principle behind ranking them
had been their score on a scale of lovability, to put it crudely – a bias
towards the most journalistic writers or the most writerly journalists.
That having been said, things are not so simple: Lévi-Strauss is not an
ambiguous case.

Instituting the judges

To understand the procedure, it is important first of all from the point
of view of social philosophy to note that social techniques may not
be the inventions of a single subject: if it takes hours to disentangle
what is happening in this ranking, it is largely because it is a much
more intelligent invention than the sum of all the individual intel-
ligences, since the subject behind the enterprise is a field. It is the field
of journalists – here I am anticipating the conclusion of my analysis
before developing all its considerations – that has invented this institution, by transposition or transfer of a technique analogous to that
employed for politicians – but when we are looking at politicians we
are on the outside; as intellectuals, we share the same universe, we
are judge and jury without appearing to be so (at all events we would
like to plead the cause that we want to judge). Through the transfer
of a technique used elsewhere, it is the collective interests that are
manifest in the field – but not at all in the sense used when we speak of
'collective interests' in the trade unions, for they are not an aggregate
of interests. The ranking list is a ranking list, but a collective one; it
expresses a collectivity. Simply, the symbolic effect of this list depends
on the fact that the collective it expresses is not the collective perceived
by its readers. In fact, this list presents itself as universal: 'These are
the forty best writers', insinuating that this is 'according to the writers
themselves'. It is a judgement that presents itself as the product of an
autonomous self-selection of the intellectual field, whereas an analysis

of the electors reveals that the body of electors is dominated by people who are actually the subjects of the list – it is dominated by people whose social role consists in establishing such orders. If we read the small print, we discover that the writers of the enquiry themselves say that they wanted to seek the opinion of people who wield power and influence in the field. I quote: 'Men and women who, through their professional activity, do themselves exert influence over the movement of ideas and wield a certain cultural power.' They interviewed people, then, according to an implicit criterion. They offer a ranking order that aspires to the absolute and universal, but to constitute it, they in fact interviewed people who have real power to constitute the social, who have the social 'competence' (in the legal sense of the term) to produce ranking lists and thereby to produce the ranking effect as a universalization of the collective interests of a particular category of agents who are basically the non-mandated delegates of the whole community of journalist-writers and writer-journalists.

To recapitulate, we have a judgement, we have judges, but the question that is evaded and yet arises every time we have a judgement is that of the legitimacy of the judgement: in the name of what does someone formulate the judgements? Weber has answers: someone may formulate a judgement because they are legitimate, because they are charismatic[42] ('I incarnate the eternal legitimacy of France, I am therefore legitimate'). They may be legitimate because they have been mandated: the teachers who draw up a syllabus have been mandated to include X in the syllabus. Someone may also be legitimate because, as Weber would argue, they inherit a tradition: it has always been done like this ('from time immemorial writers have been expected to . . .') and these people from *Lire* could have said that, in 1881, Huret[43] asked people what they understood by literature, and what they thought of Naturalism. The comparison is interesting: Huret asked the writers what they thought of Zola, or of X or Y, he did not ask them to rank Zola, Hennique, Mallarmé, Céard et al.

We can, then, call on several principles of legitimation. Here, the principle of legitimation tacitly invoked is one that we might call technical-democratic. For example, below the title of the enquiry is written 'referendum': there is therefore a collective basis, which is significantly different from the individual ranking list or the chart prophesying the end ('we see the end of Structuralism'): we pass from a singular judgement, where the agent is engaged as a singular, individual, non-universalizable *idios*, a judgement valid only for the person professing it, to a collective judgement, *koinos*, that acquires the status of a consensus among the collectivity, but a collectivity of those who are competent, that is, those who possess the competence to judge. It is then as if in order to find whether something is legal we were to democratically consult a body of judges. But this has a considerable social effect: in consulting a body of judges in a case where no judge has been mandated, we constitute the body of judges. In other words, we appear to be composing an order of merit, whereas we are appointing a panel of judges – this is an important sociological effect. This is why the list is so important: they have published the list – which I said just now jokingly was not designed in order for Bourdieu to analyse – because the list is important, but the whole process was quite unconscious. To constitute the list was to make it official, like some index published by Rome. One juridical effect is that of publication: we draw up tables that everyone may read. We thereby render public and publishable, we grant publicity and official notoriety – as publishing banns is a juridical act par excellence – to a body of judges, and we have a judgement both democratic and competent: the hierarchy established by the community of competent people who, beyond the factional conflicts dividing the intellectuals squabbling among themselves, form a body of judges who are both partisan and yet detached.

I have said several times that the analysis requires us to draw conclusions. As I drew up my plan just now, I said in theoretical terms that the notion of the habitus had the advantage of enabling us to avoid the alternative of mechanism and purposiveness, and, in particular, the conspiracy theory that in this case is to say that this has all been deliberately contrived or that it is 'Pivot's fault'. The famous denunciation of Pivot is a scientific error of the first order. One of the things that I want to demonstrate is that this chart is not at all 'Pivot's fault', as some people, even in the upper echelons of government, might think.[44] He surely has nothing to do with it, which doesn't mean that he is not the subject of the matter insofar as he holds a dominant position in the field of the agents who produced it.

It is because the orchestra has no conductor that it plays so well. If three *polytechniciens* specializing in operational research had been appointed to conduct it, it would have been a catastrophe. There is no conductor, no individual intention. In fact, the people concerned form a subfield within a subfield; they have their solidarity and their rivalries, but there are limits to their rivalry; they have hidden agreements as there always are between rival firms; they have tacit rules – 'we don't finish them off', 'we don't use lethal weapons'. It is as stupid to say that 'it is Pivot's fault' as it would be to say that 'it is the fault of the cultural journalists'. There is then a field of cultural journalists who happen to be bearers of the collective interest of the journalists, but without being mandated to do this.

The important political effect is that, on the pretext of establishing an order of merit, they establish judges, which is one of the most fundamental issues at stake in any symbolic struggle: in any field, the key question is to know who has the right to be in the field, who belongs there (and who does not belong), who says who belongs to the field, who has the right to say who is a real intellectual. By saying who the real intellectual is, I say who really is intellectual. Nominating Lévi-Strauss is not the same as nominating Bernard Henri-Lévy. By choosing an exemplary and paradigmatic formulation of the intellectual, I am affirming in universalized form my own definition of the intellectual, that is, one closest to my own specific interests. The question will be to find what is the principle of the definition of such specific interests (why, in my case, as you can tell from the way I am speaking, am I in favour of Lévi-Strauss rather than Bernard-Henri Lévy?). We might suppose that there is a relation between a position in the space concerned and the standpoint adopted towards that space.

Adopting a standpoint on the standpoints adopted

Does this mean that there is no objective position left in this space? This kind of scenario was much used in the years around 1945, based on readings of Max Weber. In the somewhat depressive atmosphere of the period, people wondered whether the historian caught up in history could deliver historical judgement on history, whether the sociologist caught up in society could speak objectively of society.[45] In our present surroundings the question is raised in the most dramatic fashion: can we in an officially authorized *ex cathedra* lecture speak of these things without committing an act of aggression or an abuse of symbolic power? Does what I am doing at this very moment obey the same logic as what I am in the process of describing? In other words, is it possible for someone who is part of the intellectual universe to engage in a sociology of intellectuals? Is a scientific sociology possible? This is a massive question, and the source of some of the most virulent attacks on sociology.

What matters is being able to tell the difference between what I am doing as I sketch a description and what it is that I am describing. First, one difference, as I have just explained, is that I am making explicit the practical principles behind what is happening, which means that as I do so I am obliged to apply them to myself – I cannot declare that the principle of each and every standpoint adopted towards the intellectual field should be sought in the position occupied by the agent in the field without giving my audience the possibility of questioning the relation between what I am saying and my own position in the field. Second, I am at the same time giving myself the possibility of checking the effects that my own position has on the standpoint that I am adopting towards these standpoints. In other words, I am taking the opportunity to objectify the viewpoint from which I am speaking, in the same way that I objectify the viewpoint from which my discourse is produced. I can therefore objectify the basic strategy, which consists in transforming a spatially located viewpoint into a free-floating viewpoint. The ideological strategy that I described at the outset, which consists, according to Marx's original formula, in universalizing the particular,[46] becomes much more concrete. It means, if you have followed what I have been saying about the notion of the field, that all sociology is produced from a subfield that is itself placed within the field. It illustrates Pascal's famous dictum: 'By space the universe encompasses and swallows me up like a mere speck: by mere thought I comprehend the universe.'[47] The sociologist who claims to comprehend the world within which he is encompassed has no chance of comprehending it scientifically unless he understands that he must include within his comprehension the fact that his own comprehension is produced in a given place, like other people's, with this difference that comprehending the viewpoint from which scientific comprehension is produced has scientific effects.

This is not a criticism. The fact that people confuse the sociology of the intellectual with what I call 'Marat's point of view' is a severe difficulty and even extremely tragic. I learned Marat's biography through a book on science recently published.[48] I then went on to analyse some studies where he was presented as the precursor of the scientific sociology of the intellectual, which is lamentable. People are confusing sociology with a slightly bitter critical vision, with an anti-mandarin discourse and resentful vision that is most typical of people holding a dominated position in the field of cultural production. I also call this 'Thersites' point of view', from the name of a character in Homer, a simple soldier who spends his time observing things from his angle.[49] People in editorial offices and university common rooms constantly identify sociology with Thersites' viewpoint of the Greek army and Marat's view of the Academy of Sciences, that is, a vision from below, like looking through the wrong end of a telescope. But the viewpoint adopted by the sociologist is not that at all: he must take as his object of study the game in its totality, that is the field, in order to render explicit the rules that govern the operations of the game and the specific interests that are engendered in it, and, in so doing, the specific interests that are expressed in such and such a standpoint adopted towards the game.

What makes sociology unlike physics is the fact that the fields can be described in the first instance as fields of forces; these forces affect the people who have a viewpoint of them and who can therefore work to change them by changing our vision of them, changing our vision of the field of forces, but always from a particular viewpoint.

The object of sociology then is both to describe the field of forces and to describe people's visions and struggles to impose their vision, the struggle for the monopoly of the legitimate vision of the field of forces, defined as orthodoxy – *ortho doxa* means 'right opinion'. It is most interesting to see that in the intellectual field there is no genuine orthodoxy, there is no intellectual jurist to say: 'Here are this year's ratings, A is on the way down, B is on the way up.' Whence the temptation facing the sociologist: 'There is no jurist, we need one, so I shall state the true order.' One riposte to Pivot's analysis would be to say: Pivot is not a sociologist, his sample is ridiculous, it is meaningless and badly constructed, it is not representative, there is no writer from Éditions de Minuit – this observation is true [*laughter*], but it is related to my position – although there are some among the people elected, which is interesting (I shall explain why). A temptation for the sociologist, then, is to be what the Romans called the censor, the killjoy who denounces an 'illicit practice of sociology'. This is very important: we constantly find illicit sociological practices. Yet sociology cannot defend itself, for social reasons that it would be interesting to study. The case of opinion polls is not very different.[50] Faced with the illicit practice of sociology, I may be tempted to reaffirm the legitimate authority of science by providing counter-expertise. I shall say that the sample is faulty, that journalist-writers and writer-journalists are overrepresented. I shall then contest the criteria for the selection of the judges. If it is true, as I said just now, that one of the issues at stake is establishing the judges, I shall then establish different judges. But if it is the criterion for the selection of the judges that governs the judgement that I pronounce, I fail to escape the vicious circle. I can say that we need to start with Nobel prizewinners and then run on down through all the indices of consecration. This is a technique employed by the American sociologists who work on the elite[51] and that Pivot unwittingly reinvents: you take the top twenty as determined by what we call reputational indices, such as the number of citations, and you ask these top twenty to say who the others are; and you end up with a list of 100 or 150 names that you can take to include all the people who matter. Here we have a technique of social selection that has scientific backing and people could say that sociologists are unscientific because X says that something is good, but Y says it is bad.

This enquiry then has a social basis. There are several criteria. The academic criterion is not good if we want to draw up a ranking order of the people who have the most social influence in the media – it is a criterion that I have heard used in some editorial offices (for example, when wondering which book out of those received should be discussed this week). If it is to measure the impact in the media, there is nothing better than asking the people who are both the best judges of impact in the media and those who produce this impact. One property of these circular universes is that it is the perception that produces the phenomenon. Here we have the perfect circle: we ask people to produce something that they are helping to produce. What science can do in such a case, rather than counter with a scientific criticism, is describe the social conditions and mechanisms producing the object, since the truth of the enquiry lies not in its result but in the enquiry itself. In this particular case, the objective of science is not to say who is the greatest French intellectual, but to find out how this question is produced, what it means, and why they are not asking who is the best French judge.

There is then the question as to what is a field, and what the degree of institutionalization of the field is, since one of the properties of the intellectual field is to lack any legitimizing agency. But this raises the very general question: are there legitimizing agencies that judge the agencies of legitimacy? In other words, is there a judge of the judges? I shall return in a future lecture[52] to this problem, which is, I mention in passing, one of the problems raised in Kafka's *Trial*:[53] is there a judge to judge the judges? This is a very general question that may seem to be resolved in fields where competences are institutionalized and distributed: there is a chief judge, and a tribunal that sets out the hierarchy of the judges. In the case of the intellectual field, where institutionalization is not very advanced, there is no judge to judge the judges. The question may then be put, as long as we know how to put it.

The universalization of individual judgements

I was saying that the people in *Lire* staged a coup, because they universalized the judgement of one particular category, the writer-journalists and journalist-writers, who are a dominated category in the intellectual field but dominant from the point of view of their power of short-term consecration (they have effects on publishing and so on). Through this use of *force majeure*, that is through the universalization of a biased collective judgement, these agents help to transform our vision of the field, and in so doing, the field itself. If I may formulate another very general proposition, the less organized the dominant vision of the field is, the more chance the transformation of the vision of a field has of transforming the field. It would have little chance of succeeding in a field where the dominant vision of the field is very institutionalized, that is, recorded in statutory form: if the rankings of the official intellectuals were published every morning and measured with objective indicators (such as the Citation Index),[54] it is likely that such a coup would be self-destructive, and it would not even occur to people to try. For the possibility of attempting such a coup to exist, the relations between the intellectual field and the field of journalism have to be such that attempting to stage such a coup would not seem an act of madness.

The coup having been staged, how does it achieve its effects? Through the effect of codification, which consists in its ability to replace what Arab jurists called the 'tacit consensus of all'. For jurists, the question of who has the right to judge is also raised, but they pretend that it has been resolved. When I judge, do I judge in the name of the interests of the dominant, or of those of the dominated? They say: 'It is the consensus of all.' For the intellectual field, we could say that there is the tacit consensus of the doctors, which can be manifested in the process of co-optation, in references, in manners of citing or not citing, for instance. This is a tacit consensus of all. In the case of the ranking list in *Lire*, we are looking at a list. It is not tacit at all, it is a one-off list, which has, as they say, the merit of existing, it does not show doubt: in place of an extremely vague whole, they substitute something that everyone will discuss ('it can't be true', 'they left So-and-so out', 'they must be blind', and so on.) That having been said, it does exist, and it exists in the shape of the objectification of a universal judgement.

This means that there is a *vis formae*, a formal force:[55] there was an informal set-up – when we say of a dinner or of the relations between X and Y that they are 'informal', we are saying that there is no etiquette, no deontological code, no objective rules – whereas now we have an effect of formality. I believe that it is very important to understand this, for its juridical effect,[56] for example: the formality effect is the kind of effect produced by the fact of rendering something objective, written, published and public. What is public is universal, it is official; we are not ashamed of it. In this case, the fact that the journalists can publish their judgements with no shame is surprising and interesting. They could not publish a list of the best mathematicians; that would be shameful. The fact that they can publicize themselves as qualified to publish and judge is most interesting. The people who have replied, and who are listed, have been chosen as qualified to respond, and they have responded as being worthy of this choice – some more reluctantly than others. There were also people who did not reply[57] because they refused to play the game, they refused to be granted legitimacy: there are systematic absences that we may observe, without prejudice. For example, none of those ranked best according to the internal criteria of the field of production for producers replied to a questionnaire designed to choose the most eminent among them. In other words, this series of small individual choices ('Shall I respond or not?', 'I have my doubts', 'I'll wait a couple of weeks', 'Shall I send it, or not?', 'Why did they choose me?', etc.) produces a sense of objectivity, with all the effects that I have described.

Producers for producers and producers for non-producers

To take this a little further: this ranking exercise blurs the boundary between the field of restricted production (the field of production for producers) and the wider field of production (the field of production for non-producers). Obviously, these are subfields of the field of cultural production and this opposition may be found within any field of cultural production – but in our current state of affairs, it is not true of every field: there are producers for producers (as with avant-garde poetry) and producers for non-producers, with all the intermediate shades, of course. If you remember what I have been saying, the people overrepresented in this population of electors, and thereby in the list, are those who are situated in this neither-fish-nor-fowl, bastard zone, *metaxu* in Plato's terminology[58], where we don't know whether they are one thing or the other. The interest of the bastard is to legitimize bastardy, to erase the distinction that designates them as bastards. The unconscious interest of the people who are on the borderline between the field of restricted production and the field of production for non-producers, that is the journalists – who typically publish for the general public – is to say that 'at night, all cats are black', to abolish the *diacresis*, the critical division. One of the issues at stake in symbolic struggles over the social world is the principle of division, and orthodoxy is the power to say: 'This is what we should see here, and that is what we should see there', 'Don't confuse the sacred and the profane, the distinguished and the vulgar.' Confusing the taxonomies, or imposing a taxonomy that does not discriminate between things that were previously differentiated, means changing the balance of power within the field. It means changing the definition of the field (who belongs / who does not belong) and thereby the principle of legitimation.

You see the difficulty that arises in this description: the analysis cannot avoid becoming purposive. We should not say: 'they wanted this', 'they fought for that', 'it's a revolution', 'they belong to a category that is dominated from one angle but dominant from another, and have seized power through the revolution of imposing an order of merit'. No, we should talk in terms of what I call *allodoxia*, after Plato's *Theaetetus*. We see someone in the distance, and we ask: 'Who is it? Is it Theaetetus?' 'No, it was Socrates'; we mistake one thing for another.[59] The interest of this concept is to indicate that the mistake has been made in good faith. It is an error of perception linked to the categories of perception of the person who employs them: they have insufficient powers of discrimination and they confuse things that someone endowed with greater visual acuity would discriminate between. *Allodoxia* designates what happens to people who perceive things for which they lack categories, and often they lack these categories because it is not in their interest to have them. If you take into account all the information I have given you, you will admit that they do not wish to see this difference, and so they are unable to see it. This is a very general social law; we do not desire what we cannot attain, we cannot attain what we do not desire. Each contributor perpetrates his own little individual act quite innocently, but nonetheless plays his part in placing Dumézil[60] alongside some journalistic writer or other in the list.

The plot thickens, however, because at the same time, as well as the law of interest well understood, there is another law that encourages *allodoxia*. If I claim that my alter ego is the equal of someone I know I am not equal to, I am comparing myself to someone I know I am not the equal of. In voting for my alter ego, it is in my interest to say: 'He is the greatest, because he is me.' This is valid only up to a point: if, like Proust, you say, 'Mme Verdurin's salon is great', you show that you are not very great, not very distinguished; saying that X, whom everyone knows to be not very good, is very good, condemns you out of your own mouth. The classifier is classified by his classifications. Our lists, then, are a compromise between our alter ego and the incomparable. If we say 'Dumézil is a sure value', we do so in order to classify the classifier: I classify myself in the act of classifying – and alongside, who do you have? Look at the classification, I don't want to name names, you might see it as meanness, whereas it is scientific. (If I were working on the Nambikwara, everyone would think this to be a good thing, not ethnocentric at all, but humanist; but the idea that I work on my closest fellow citizens makes people's flesh creep in a way that it doesn't when they read *Tristes Tropiques*.[61] They think that dealing with our close contemporaries is not really scientific, whereas I think that they are much more complicated to analyse – and with my experience of having studied both, I am well placed to tell.) We have our interests, of course, but there are limits: we cannot without disqualifying ourselves seem to be unable to discriminate between the things that are the very stakes to play for at the heart of the game.

The list thereby produces another symbolic effect that was not intended by any one individual: it starts with Lévi-Strauss and continues with Foucault, Lacan, and the like. If the list had been completely free from what I see as the 'judge-is-judged-by-his-judgement' effect, it would have been different. I have in mind an assessment obtained by the calculation of judgements in a freer situation, where we would have asked for ten names rather than three. As I saw immediately, by asking for ten names the dispersion is greater, the big names are more submerged, they disappear because there is more freedom. We can still produce the 'I do know how to judge, I know that the great book of the decade is Such-and-such' effect, so we do it for the first entry, and then we can put down nine of our 'best friends'. 'Best friends' is misleading: you might think 'they are in this together, it's a conspiracy'. Whereas there is no conspiracy at all, these things happen quite innocently! Moreover, that is another property of this universe: the symbolic attacks are all the more effective, the more their perpetrators believe in them. If they were petty, cynical manoeuvres ('I like Delacampagne so I'm going to say that he is the greatest contemporary philosopher'), they would lose much of their efficacity. Whence the expression *allodoxia*: in *doxa* there is belief – they believe in it, poor things.

In my next lecture I shall return for a few minutes to the difference that I briefly mentioned, between scientific judgement and indigenous judgement: scientific judgement knows what its statements are based on, and therefore produces a standpoint that is no longer in the field. This I do believe. I shall return to this and try to show how this reflexive analysis on the position from which I was producing my discourse on the positions enabled me to find in the ranking list things that I had not at first seen. One last point: this error of the badly constructed sample is very banal in sociology: if I want to study the writers of the nineteenth century, I draw up a list, and then ask what defines the writer, without seeing that my list has answered the question in advance. It is then not an innocent error, and this is why it has such symbolic power. If it were a clumsy blunder that any sociologist and *a fortiori* any individual unversed in sociology would spot outright, the ideological effect would fail, but I venture to suggest that it is a much more sophisticated error.

Lecture of 8 March 1984

First session: the hit parade of the intellectuals (2). – Wrong questions and right answers. – Models of the market and the trial. – Concrete individual and constructed individual. – The issues of visibility and titles. – Inventing the jury. – Position of the journalistic subfield within the field of cultural production. – Defining the rules of the game.
Second session: the hit parade of the intellectuals (3). – The model of the trial. – The model of the market. – Value judgement. – Establishing differences. – Producing the producers.

First session: the hit parade of the intellectuals (2)

I shall return to what I was discussing during my second session last week, that is the analysis of the *Lire* enquiry into intellectuals, starting with what I did not want to give you last time, namely the wording of the question and some details of this 'hit parade'. It appeared in *Lire*, no. 8 (April 1981) and was titled 'The forty-two top intellectuals', with, above it, the word 'referendum'. This is very important. I think in fact that one of the virtues of what I have to offer you is to draw your attention to the unconscious processes at work in reading: the *Lire* ranking list was read by thousands of people who, I venture to say, saw nothing in it, which does not mean that they did not experience the effects of things that they were unaware of. We often say that one of the functions of modern education is to teach people how to read, but this supposes that those teaching the reading do themselves know how to read. One of the functions of my approach is to teach you how to read between the lines, that is, to read what is being said while being filtered by a social censorship that works on discourse through euphemisms and overtones, overtones that an old-school rhetoric did in fact tune in to and interpret. The neo-rhetoric that nowadays rejoices in the name of semiology does sometimes analyse this kind of social technique, but in very naive terms, because the specifically social dimensions of this communication relation are often ignored.

The question put by the panel of *Lire* was: 'Who are the three intellectuals writing in the French language (*this detail is extremely important, it is an extraordinary coup de force*) whose writings (*this is important*) seem to you to exercise the strongest influence (*another word that needs analysing*) in depth on the evolution of ideas, literature and the arts and sciences?' The words stick in the throat as soon as we start to question them. For example, because many people use it in everyday contexts, the word 'influence' is bound to go unnoticed, whereas it is in itself a whole social philosophy of the relation between the sender and the receiver of a message, a social philosophy that is part of our teaching of literature. We could also comment on the hierarchy of 'literature, arts and sciences'. We might think it is a verbal automatism, we often speak of 'art and literature', but this is not the same thing; here, there is a whole implicit hierarchy at work. The sciences would not have been mentioned in the 1930s. In the heyday of the *NRF* [*La Nouvelle Revue Française*], it is likely that they would not have mentioned the 'sciences'. We note that several scientists appear in the list and it is perhaps because some of them appear there that the word 'sciences' appears in the question, rather than the other way round. In short, there are so many questions. But I obviously cannot deal with them all.

Now I need to return to an earlier point. I should have commented on the formula 'the forty-two top intellectuals': why 'forty-two', 'top', 'intellectuals', etc.? These are absolutely formidable presuppositions: why draw the line at forty-two? Why is number thirty a *normalien* and number thirty-one not.[1] These are very important questions from a sociological point of view: who decides on the boundary? Is number forty-three not an intellectual, or is he simply not one of the 'top intellectuals'? Moreover, do intellectuals aspire to be 'top'? They are presupposing that intellectuals join in a race to be top. Another presupposition is formulated in the headline: 'Are there still masters of thought? (*We need to think about this expression*). Is there a Gide or a Camus or a Sartre?' Here they are presupposing that those three were intellectual masters. (I am taking advantage of the fact that there are not many people here today, to mark a kind of pause and proceed at the slower rhythm we should adopt in order to work really well, that is in a non-pedagogical way – but I am still going faster than I should.)

'*Lire* questioned several hundred writers, journalists, teachers, students, politicians, etc.' There too the essential has been said, according to the paradigm of the purloined letter commented on by Lacan:[2] they blind you with the obvious; they tell you what is essential. Here the essential is said in a phrase that goes unnoticed because the person who produces it does not see it and does not know what he is saying. This is important: the best symbolic effects are those that the senders produce without realizing what they are saying, although they are saying something very important. They are saying something that they are unaware of, and, speaking in ignorance, they engender a relation of shared misunderstanding which is perhaps what I call symbolic violence.

'*Lire* questioned several hundred writers, journalists, teachers, students, politicians, etc.' (Here there is a gap that is filled in later: 'The questionnaire was sent to 600 people. By 11 March, 448 had replied. We are grateful to them. Here are their names.') They replied 'en masse' (the 'en masse' would be interesting to study). You are starting to have the right reactions: the order is important: 'writers', 'journalists', 'teachers', 'students' (I think these were an afterthought), 'politicians'. We ought to think about the significance of the placing of these people. And then, 'they replied en masse'. As you have already read 'referendum', it is self-evident ('en masse', 'referendum') that it is going to be a plebiscite – that is, a mass consultation to which a mass of people have replied. You are treated to the numbers effect: the judgement that they are going to produce for you – the word 'produce' can be taken in several senses – is socially sanctioned by a collective that seems to be specified ('writers', etc.) and numerous. It is then the mass effect, the consensus or consensus omnium effect – but they never say who the omnium includes. Here we find an implicit definition of the role of the population participating. You are being told: 'You are going to read the result of a referendum in which the sum of the parties concerned, almost all the judges competent to judge what is to be judged – except for a few odd characters who found the question too complicated or who couldn't find time to reply – responded.' And the headline adds: 'They replied en masse. Admitting their doubts. Without clearly endorsing any particular individual, but recognizing the influence of Lévi-Strauss, Aron and Foucault.'

Wrong questions and right answers

This 'without clearly endorsing any particular individual' is important. You have to read between the lines: one question underlying this ranking list is whether there is a successor to Sartre, a typically journalistic question, which is a product of the unconscious interest of the journalists and their unconscious structures of perception of the social world. The journalists transfer to the intellectual world a problematic that belongs to the political world, and which concerns the problem of succession, a sociological problem of the first importance. Those among you who are familiar with Weber know that he investigates the mode of succession that characterizes each form of domination.[3] There is nothing more characteristic of a world of domination than the form of succession that is typical to it, and one of the most interesting properties of the intellectual field is precisely that there is no successor. In other words, they are asking the wrong question, which immediately attracts the wrong answer, or rather the right answer. For this is an effect that sociologists continually produce: they obtain the right answers to the wrong questions.

This effect is classic: respondents to an enquiry are worthy people who, despite what we tend to say, do always reply – there are some non-replies, but if we insist, they will always respond – but you only need to forget that the question they are meant to answer was the wrong question, producing a genuinely wrong answer, which becomes right for the sociologist himself. Not knowing that his question was by definition wrong, the sociologist is the person least well placed to see that he has produced an answer that did not really exist, or more precisely an answer that exists for someone who was not asked the question that he answered.[4] The sociologist must then factor in the fact that the person who replied had not been asked the right question, which does not mean that once the question has been put the answer does not exist – it is very complicated. A sociologist must question the status of the question that he puts.

Of course, this also applies to those who write histories of literature, the sociology of literature, or the history of philosophy, for instance: 'Why don't I ask my author, my authors and texts, and so on questions that they couldn't ask themselves?' Which does not mean that they do not answer these questions – we can always make them answer – but it is important to know what we have done in asking this or that question.

The headline then is laden with presuppositions. But I must insist on the fact that these presuppositions are unconscious. We need to think a lot about this word 'unconscious'. I am using it in a strictly negative sense to say that it is not a conscious strategy: it is not intended, it is not done 'on purpose', and it is not the product of an individual intention. If the authors of this enquiry were in the room here, they would probably be astonished to hear what I am saying. They would jump up to deny it: 'But whatever is he trying to prove? We are not so perverse.'

One difficulty with sociological analysis – I mentioned this briefly the other day – is that the simple fact of making implicit strategies explicit changes the status of the strategies and transforms the product of objective intentions into something intended. In other words, everything that I can discover in this list, in its order of merit, appears to bear witness to an objective intention, and as soon as we analyse it, looks as if it is orientated towards certain ends, as if it possessed a kind of immanent purposiveness, as if all was intentional. Whence the 'it all looks as if . . .' that I often use in my phrases, and which is not a rhetorical flourish, but a manner of constantly reminding you (as mathematicians use quantifiers) that everything looks as if it is aimed at an end. But it would be a fundamental theoretical and political error to think that all these intentions that we discover in what people are doing are the product of deliberate intent. In the case of the ranking list here, we are presented with an ensemble of objective intentions, and in fact I could almost sum up everything that I have been saying in one sentence: 'This all looks like the result of an objective intention to promote journalists, and especially intellectual journalists and journalist intellectuals, to the status of judges of intellectual production.' This summary covers everything that I could say, even if I went on for hours.

The problem is that in explaining and communicating the results of an analysis, we are often obliged to use the expression 'in the last analysis'. We might say, for example, that 'Kant's *Critique of Judgement* seems to conform to the objective interests of a certain group at a certain moment in the eighteenth century . . .'. We are obliged to put it like that. People who cannot tolerate scientific objectification will immediately jump on this kind of phrase, saying 'How stupid to say that the *Critique of Judgement*, one of philosophy's most sacred writings, expresses the objective interests of a category of the German bourgeoisie!' (I can say this because that is what they said about my analysis of the *Critique of Judgement*.)[5] In fact, things are more complicated: since these objective interests coincide with the interests of the commentators on the *Critique of Judgement*, who are professors of philosophy at a certain moment in time, the *Critique of Judgement* is, so to speak, read and not read: people are so at home with it that they don't see that they are involved. If I wanted to resume in a sentence my analysis of the *Critique of Judgement*, that is what I would feel obliged to say. Similarly, if I were to resume in a single sentence my analysis of the hit parade, I should be obliged to say what I have just said. (In truth, the mystery of social facts and social logic[6] – although I am not keen on using the word mystery – for me is that formidably complicated things are at work, a kind of labyrinth of intentions appears, which can be grasped and summarized in the sort of proposition that I formulated just now: 'There is an objective intention to . . .', 'Everything happens as if . . .'. The problem is that very often in political polemics, people have got into the habit of using very rudimentary sociological analyses and saying things like: 'This is only the interest of the upwardly mobile petite bourgeoisie.' One of the major problems of sociological analysis, as I conceive it, is that it often takes an enormous effort to reconstruct this kind of extremely complex network of relations, with their minor mystifications, petty prejudice and personal attacks, to reach conclusions that in the last analysis boil down to something relatively simple. Obviously, opponents who receive this complicated analysis and suffer from it – because it is true that the scientific analysis of social actions can hurt – hasten to construct a system of defence based on the idea that 'these sociologists are stupid and primitive and are peddling vulgar Marxism'. This parenthesis allows me to say something that I hold dear and to attack one of their defence mechanisms, among others).

Models of the market and of the trial

I now turn to the list itself. I am not going to read it out in its entirety, but I shall give you the beginning. In first place, we find Claude Lévi-Strauss with 101 votes – for each entry, we find the number of votes beneath the name. 'Votes' makes us think of a plebiscite or an election. It is something that occurs to me as I speak to you: I shall try to show you that the logic of ranking is either that of a trial, in the legal sense, or that of the market, as a process of setting prices; in either case, the people will judge. Sociologists would like to know how a market works, and here we have a chance to see a kind of small mechanism or machine, a miniature scale model of how prices are set: we have cultural products (such as a book by Raymond Aron) in a bookshop window, these cultural products are on offer, and people will take them or not. Obviously, literary prizes contribute to this process.

When I say that things can be described in terms of the market or of trials, these are neither metaphors nor analogies, but possible models. (I say this in passing, for it is often said that the language of economics is metaphorical, whereas it is not.) These two possibilities, homology with the trial and the market, are confused by homology with the electoral market, which is not absurd either: it is true that an election also operates in this manner. In a moment, I shall attempt to demonstrate the principle factors that affect the act of judging a cultural product, and I think we shall find the same factors as those affecting a political product (a member of parliament or a president, for example). That having been said, the analogy with the political product confuses the issue through its very obviousness: it is once again the paradigm of the purloined letter; there is no better way of making things invisible than presenting them in a way that we are so used to seeing that they are blindingly obvious and we don't think about them at all. I can say this out loud, so to speak: I noticed that the word 'votes' is important, and yet I had not realized that it is one of the little subliminary signs that place us within the logic of the referendum.

Claude Lévi-Strauss, then, gets 101 votes, Raymond Aron 84, Michel Foucault 83 – they are almost *ex æquo* –Jacques Lacan 51, Simone de Beauvoir 46, Marguerite Yourcenar 32, etc. The six winners earn the right to have a portrait photo and an intellectual portrait whose every line needs a commentary – you would find this unbearable, and so would I, but it is interesting to see what has been recorded for each of these people.

Concrete individual and constructed individual

I just need to briefly point out one thing: I shall try to reflect with you on what it is to be an individual. God knows, it is something that everyone believes they know – there are even people who construct their sociology around the notion of the individual,[7] I think they must know what an individual is. I came across the problem in very concrete form in an enquiry[8] where the characters were displayed in a factorial analysis – that is, distributed as points across a space. I wondered, and I still wonder, whether I am entitled to publish this space with the names of the individuals that correspond to those points. Am I entitled to write 'Lévi-Strauss' beneath the point placed top left, and 'Deloffre' beneath the point placed below right. Am I entitled to name these names? What happens when I write a proper name on a point in a theoretically constructed space? To put it briefly, without revealing too much of what I shall go on to argue, the question is how to tell whether the Lévi-Strauss that I find in this space is the same person as the Lévi-Strauss that you know in your minds. Several good philosophers have spent their time studying this (I allow myself a value judgement here, once more to dissipate a form of resistance organized by poor philosophers to defend poor philosophy against good sociology) and some of you will know their reflections on 'The king of France is bald'.[9] Speaking of the bald king of France is acting as if a bald king of France existed. This is also a classic political strategy. Speaking of things ('The

people think that . . .', 'Intellectuals think that . . .') makes us forget
to question whether they exist. Our attention is drawn to the predicative judgement and diverted away from the existential judgement that
underpins the predicative judgement. They forget (and get us to forget)
to ask whether the subject concerned exists. For the individual, things
are just the same: does this point exist in the same way that the real
Lévi-Strauss exists?

I shall not take this argument further, since it would create an impression of déjà-vu and you would switch off when I came to talk to you
about the concrete individual and the constructed individual. I believe
that our research studies the constructed individual, who is not a concrete individual. One difficulty in assimilating scientific argument lies
in the fact that its readers are always thinking in terms of the concrete
individual, whereas what is represented is the individual constructed as
a sum of properties within a space of properties. This problem is not
raised in any deliberate attempt to be esoteric, but because it is a very
difficult problem for sociological discourse, and it arises for me today:
for example, I am spending some time with this list, but I hesitate to
read it all out and I will not pursue it to the end, because what I take
to be a detached analysis, with no aim other than scientific – which is
never completely true – runs the risk of being taken at face value, that
is, on the same level as the one where the people who have produced
the list are situated: 'Who really is the best?', 'What does Bourdieu
think?' 'Is he going to put the skids under number 1, 2, 3 or 4?', 'Is he
trying to tell us that the ranking list is wrong, that if we had the right
one it would not be this one?' I am saying all this because, even if you
have not formulated these questions explicitly, I think they will occur
to you unconsciously.

The issues of visibility and titles

To return to the list: as number one, Lévi-Strauss has earned a portrait, which is the longest (three columns). Aron is granted a slightly
smaller one (a short column). The size of the portrait is proportionate to the ranking. You would need to look at the details to see the
social image of each of these people. From the seventh person on
the list downwards, there is no portrait, but these people do merit a
professional title: '7th Fernand Braudel, historian; Michel Tournier,
novelist; Bernard-Henri Lévy, philosopher; Henri Michaux, poet;
François Jacob, biologist; Samuel Beckett, playwright and novelist',
etc. So these people are granted a professional title, which is extremely

important, as I shall attempt to show you in a moment, but I am telling you straight away, so that you can reflect upon it metadiscursively in relation to what I am in the process of saying: the mechanisms that I am trying to bring to light in this particular case are very general in that they operate all over the social world. Simply, I am dealing here with a microcosm within a microcosm where these mechanisms are particularly noticeable because, in a word, the principle issue in this universe is visibility – that is, what I call symbolic capital. The principle form of profit pursued in this field is visibility. Which means that it is a good terrain for studying the social conditions of the setting of prices when these are the prices of visibility. In fact I shall describe how, in the specific universe of the intellectual field, this particular form of struggle, the symbolic struggle, unfolds and how this particular form of capital, visibility, is accumulated.

This struggle is present all over the social world, but the relative weight in the universe of the visibility of social capital is greater or lesser according to the universe. For example, an OS too faces problems with their title: they want to be promoted to OP or OQ, for instance.[10] This is important for them, it has social consequences. In their case it doesn't sell books, but it does mean that they can benefit from collective bargaining conventions that protect their status; they can say: 'My title stipulates the limits of what they can ask of me, and I'll go on strike if they ask me to do something that is not required by the kind of social status that I am granted and which is encapsulated in my title.' The professional title then is very important. For example, if we say (this is quite nasty) 'Edgar Morin, sociologist and philosopher', it immediately arouses interest [*laughter*]; or 'René Girard, philosopher' (no comment! [*laughter*]), or 'Jean Bernard, doctor',[11] etc. We're not here to play games, you can go away and read it all for yourselves.

I have said as much as I can say in public, which is also an important part of my analysis: all the constraints regulating publication or publicity, and the conditions of rendering public the things that can be said publicly, in a public, official situation defined socially by implicit or explicit rules, are in play here. This publication effect is one of the most devious, hidden effects.

Inventing the jury

I shall now briefly sum up the main points of my analysis, and then try to take things a little further. What is at issue is what we might call a social technology, or a technique of action on the social world. I mentioned this briefly the other day: there are inventions in the social world, as elsewhere. For example, Max Weber makes a point of the fact that the popular jury, with which we are so familiar that we don't even think about it, was a great invention in the history of law. It completely changed the structure of the judicial field.[12] In this judicial field, there is always a problem of balance between the specific competence of the lawyers (if they had free rein, they would apply a law more and more coherently rationalized, but a law all the more divorced in a way from real life) and the requirements of their clients (for example, since the industrial revolution, the bourgeoisie asks the law to be, in Weber's terms, an instrument of prediction and calculation) as well as others (whose presence is symbolized – although perhaps not expressed – by the jury). Since the judicial field is one of the fields that I have studied the least, what I am saying is more of a second-hand academic commentary than a scientific report, but it does come from Weber (whom people have often not read): this invention of the jury changed the structure of the field.

In the present case, we have an invention of the same type as the jury. Compared with Proust's or Huret's questionnaire (Huret, a journalist for a newspaper that was the equivalent of *Le Figaro*, set out in 1891 to put questions to writers),[13] the *Lire* list presents something new: you get the impression that it really is a referendum. There is an objective intention which – as I made abundantly clear at the start of this lecture – is not a subjective intention, nor even a sum of subjective intentions, 'intention' being understood as a will directed towards explicitly stated ends. For it is the product neither of the individual intention of a kind of conspirator – Bernard Pivot – nor of the collective intention of a group of conspirators plotting together to say: 'How can we at last overthrow these dominant intellectuals and impose a journalistic vision of the intellectual?' I think this shows one of the properties of social inventions. We need to spell out the word 'invention' to remind ourselves that this is not self-evident, that there are breaks, gaps and changes.

As an example, and I shall return to this, the *Salon des refusés*[14] – we have all heard this said in lectures on the history of literature – was a formidable historical invention that was extraordinarily difficult: it really did need painters to die of hunger for twenty or thirty years in order to render this invention possible. There was the Academy, with its exhibitions, called the Salons, that were mounted each year, and then they created the *Salon des refusés* – the Salon for all those painters who had not been accepted by the Academy's official Salon. The *Salon des refusés* is an idea and a word; and people will turn this word into something that will later be perceived by people who will say: 'Oh yes, the *Salon des refusés*.' Very often, literary movements start – as has often been noted of the Impressionists – with an insult, which then becomes a concept.[15] But art historians forget this; they want to give meaning to concepts, they then find this very difficult and say some very silly things. It is extremely important to know that what we call 'baroque', for example, is a mixture of contemporary insults and academic categories, all dressed up in the paraphernalia of a doctoral dissertation. The 'baroque' is something ideal-typical; it doesn't even mean the same thing in Vienna. I am being naughty here, but my point is valid, I could substantiate my argument.

This social technique then really is an invention, but an invention lacking a subject, in the ordinary sense of the term, which does not mean that there is no intention, that anything may happen. This is in fact the paradox of the social. I think that our spontaneous vision of the social world oscillates between two visions: one vision according to which things just happen at random and we don't know why anything happens the way it does, which leads to a pessimistic view of sociology – this is what Hegel called the 'atheism of the moral world':[16] we suppose that the world of nature has it reasons, and when we move on to consider the social world, we say that things just happen (although I personally and professionally cannot hold this view); and on the other hand a vision according to which, if there is an order, it is because there are people who impose order, imposers of order (with conspiracy theories, and arguments that 'it was bound to happen', for instance). The spontaneous critical discourse on the social world that we read in the left-wing press is of the second kind: 'There is order, and there can be no order if there is nobody imposing order', those imposing order being 'the capitalists', who are the grammatical subjects but also the subjects in the sense of traditional philosophy, the philosophy of the subject: people who have intentions, understanding and will, who know what they want and know what they are doing. I say this is not true: there are objective intentions, meanings, ends, functions, goals and coherence, and yet there is no subject.

In my last lecture, I sketched a provisional and imprecise answer to the question 'But who is the subject of all this?'. I said that it was the field of cultural production. You may have thought that this did not take us very far, but it is in fact a great step forward. I think it is sometimes possible to make significant progress by changing our overall way of thinking about a social problem. In the present case you will grant me that the subject of the action is the field of cultural production, because we are talking about minor intellectuals, but think of the major intellectuals: who is the subject of Mallarmé's works? To what degree? Are all subjects the same kind of subject? Is someone a subject to the same degree whatever their position in the field, or is it the field that is the subject at all times, even if, sometimes, there are people whose position in the field makes them slightly more of a subject? I think this change of approach is very important. I tried to show last year, in the case of the literary field, that this move entailed quite radical consequences for the way we study cultural, scientific artistic or literary works: in any case-study we can always ask who the subject is, and in my opinion the subject will on every occasion be a field as a set of agents linked by objective relations, irreducible to the actual interactions that they may engage in. I must insist once more, it is the alpha and the omega: relations are not reducible to interactions; people who do not interact with each other, who have never met, may be in relation with each other.

The subject of what is happening here is the field, and the problem is to find out what the field is, how it is defined, how it functions and what its limits are. I remind you what I said last time about limits and boundaries: are there juridical limits? One of our goals here is precisely to challenge the limits, and it is through the definition of the competent judges in the list given that we shall find our definition of the field. In fact we might say that the whole work of 'deconstruction'[17] that is needed in order to find out what is happening in the four pages of the review (pp. 38–41) – which, I say for any philosophers among you, are as complicated as any page of Hegel – will consist in diverting your attention away from the pages giving the ranking list (what people have read, the list itself and all its associated comments) towards what is given right at the end as a kind of appendix: 'The questionnaire was sent to 600 people. By 11 March, 448 had replied. We are grateful to them. Here are their names.'

In fact our whole task boils down to saying that, behind the apparent object of the ranking list, the real object is the establishment as judges of these people who are listed, and who are worth many sessions of commentary. I don't mean personal comments like: 'Hey, that's odd, they've put Suzanne Prou in, and why did they put her with the writers?'[18] If I wanted, I could make more snide remarks like this, but you can do it yourselves. What I want to do is to comment on the body of judges constituted. A constituent body is a body assembled and named by an act of nomination: for example, the Conseil d'État [State Council]. This could be either a cultural or an artistic State Council. You would only need a decree by the President of the Republic, and imagine the consequences. This constituent body is disguised by the product of its action: your attention is drawn towards the ranking list and diverted away from its authors, for whom the very fact of drafting it renders them legitimate drafters of ranking lists. In other words there is an operation of self-legitimating by the list drafters, and this, it seems to me, is the real issue: it all looks as if the inventors of the social technology of the intellectual hit parade had in mind the project of nominating legitimate drafters of hit parades, like a *Gault et Millau* for culture [*laughter*].[19] That made you laugh, and it was intended to do so. If we accept what they are doing, it is because there are ranking list drafters in other areas too (for example, they tell you: 'These are the top ten films') and it is always the same operation; the judges are self-legitimized and forbid you to ask who has the right to designate the judges. This I what I have argued.

Position of the journalistic subfield within the field of cultural production

The subject is a field whose limits need to be defined. Does it have boundaries, or not? Does it aspire to have any? Is it inserted within a more important field? Is the position it holds dominant or dominated? Another move is to present the field designated by the list as coextensive with the field of cultural production, whereas it is roughly representative of a subfield of the field of cultural production – that is, the subfield of cultural intermediaries, mediators, distributors, journalist-intellectuals, and the like. These people inhabit the borderline between the field of producers for producers, the restricted field of those who write for other writers (which we often call the avant-garde, but this is not always strictly the case) and the field of mass distribution or mass production: they are borderline men. This subfield inhabits a dominated position within the broader surrounding field of cultural production, while still exercising a potentially dominant action, through the impact that it can have on its readers – the laity, as it were, to use the helpful analogy of the Church – on its clientele and, through the laity, on sales, through these 'offerings of the faithful', on booksellers, through the booksellers on publishers, through publishers on publishing, through publishing on censorship – which is important. This subfield then is composed of people holding a position that is dominated on the cultural plane – I shall give a whole lot of clues – but potentially dominant.

Through this subfield, another kind of cultural domination may emerge, an economic this-or-that type of domination. But in a cultural field domination can never be purely economic. This is a fundamental law that I have often repeated. It needs to be dressed in cultural clothes. They don't tell you: 'This is a list of best sellers', but 'These are the top forty-two intellectuals'. In other words (I have just thought of this as I speak), it is a struggle to impose a new legitimacy, which introduces the force of the economic. The economic is never absent from any field however autonomous – whether the field is religious, juridical or literary. It is present, but it cannot appear in its own name. This is important: in religion, they don't speak of the 'salary' of the priest, but of 'offerings'. In a relatively autonomous field, the economic constraints are always disguised, masked. But this is a purposive vocabulary: it sounds as if they have to wear masks, which leads into a Helvetius-type philosophy of religion – that is, a cynical, materialist vision of religion. So it is better to say that these constraints always appear euphemized (speaking of 'offerings' rather than 'salaries'). In the present case, it is the same thing: new judges impose themselves by a symbolic *coup de force*, they express their specific interests as dominated intellectuals exercising a dominant role through the intermediary of the press. This *coup de force* by which people express their interests is the mediation through which are expressed things that could be described in crude language ('domination by the market') and crude materialist analyses (the 'concentration of publishing houses', 'Hachette's monopoly', etc). With my way of working, I am able to forget these analyses. What seems important to me is understanding how these things work. We have spent so much time and effort denouncing the stranglehold of money on religion that in the end we forget to ask how it operates, which is the most important thing, I think.

The subject, then, is a set of agents, but not individuals. The word 'agent' is not elegant (we think of spies or policemen). It sounds awkward in a literary text, but it is important. It can easily convey a whole social philosophy: 'agent' is related to 'action' and 'practice'. It is free of the ideological overtones attached to the word 'person'. Nor is it a 'subject' – after everything that I have been saying this morning, you can imagine how much the word 'subject' implies. It is someone who acts but does not necessarily know what they are doing. And I think the word implies that the agent (here the connotations of someone working in law enforcement or some other institutional agency are useful) has functions, but not in a functionalist sense (which is another stupid misreading of my work). They are agents in the sense that they are socially constructed individuals: agents come preceded by their social definition. You are never dealing with an individual – an individual ultimately is a biological object that is of no interest to the sociologist (except insofar as biology does present the social with problems, as I might explain later). The agent is socially constituted, and comes to be provided with a social identity.

I said at the start of the lecture that the game I am showing you is a kind of scale model of the overall social game, and to generalize what I have been saying, I might simply say that the authors of the *Lire* list are concerned with their identity in the intellectual field, their visibility, their status as writers, their own name. 'Can I become a proper name, a "Jean-Paul Sartre" with surname and first name, or must I remain a generic title like "sociologist" or "writer"?' This is the challenge. For ordinary social agents, the issue is 'how do people describe me?' In many societies, you are Someone's Cousin's Cousin, or Someone, son of Somebody. In our own societies, it is the professional title that is at the heart of the social struggle. We fight to control the places where professional titles are awarded, that is the school system and the state. This is what I mean when I say that the state is the institution disposing of the monopoly of legitimate symbolic violence.[20] I keep saying this, but not for the sake of effect: all those people who speak of the state in phrases like: 'The state is . . .' are trying out 'The king of France is bald' on you. 'The monopoly of legitimate symbolic violence' means that object 'X', which we are accustomed to call the 'state', and which we should much reflect on to know what we understand by that,[21] exercises what I call a power of nomination, that is the power to designate the dominant identity. When I say 'The state is something that . . .', my subject is defined by its predicate. Clearly, I am provisionally naming this social agency, this social operator that tells people quite forcefully what they are, the 'state'. If I present myself as a qualified teacher, you know what that means (it corresponds to a salary, it defines claims I am entitled to make, and so on), whereas if I say, 'I plough the heavens and other spaces', I may win a prize for poetry. This is important, and it doesn't matter whether it applies to me or to someone else (if I tell someone, 'You are nothing but a . . .', it is the same). The game that we play and the stakes that we play for are particular cases of a much more general game, which is a whole aspect of the social world; in fact, what I have in mind is to show you one of the major ways of constructing the social world (which does of course lead us to miss some things), which has been dismissed as materialism by some unthinkingly gullible people.

Defining the rules of the game

This manner of constructing the social world, by constructing a profile or a powerful perspective, accounts for a considerable proportion of the social facts that other manners of construction do not enable us to see. It is not the last word, it is not the whole picture, but that does not mean that it is wrong. One manner of constructing the social world as the place where something much more important occurs than what materialism takes to be the issue (such as salaries) – in the sense that questions of life or death are involved, things that people are ready to die for, ready to sacrifice everything else for – is to grasp it through the problem of identity, which means having to answer questions like, 'What am I, deep down?', 'And who can tell me what I am?' Here in the ranking list, a certain number of people may wonder: 'Where am I in this list? Am I in it or not? Am I well placed? I can attack the ranking order, but I am obliged to take a position in the list.' The social world is made up of lots of questions of this kind: 'Am I (or is he) really a Christian or not really a Christian?' (you can die for such a reason . . .) 'Can I call myself that, can he call himself that?', 'Is he allowed to talk to us like that', 'And who has the right to tell me who I am?' I shall return to this point in a moment, but I think this is what is at stake.

The subject of the game that I am trying to study is the game itself, as a whole. I am faced with what is pretentiously called a hermeneutic circle: the better I know the game, what the stakes are and what its limits are, the better I shall know what the game is. Knowing that we need to question the limits enables us to save time, because I shall go directly to the polemics over 'so-and-so is not a writer' or 'the *nouveaux philosophes* who are not philosophers'. The polemics indicate that something is afoot, that there are hidden issues and covert definitions: if I take all the texts written by philosophers for or against the *nouveaux philosophes*, I shall find a hidden issue, the one that everyone must confront in order to define the game in such a way as to be a master of the game. This is what is at stake in every game: I must define the rules of the game so that I am left holding all the trumps. When we play with children, this is the kind of thing that happens: there is a sort of negotiation over the rules of the game so as to make sure that they win. Between adults, it is no longer child's play: we define the game and if we could we would change the rules whenever we could. Scientific life is like that: a good scientist changes the rules so that he can do what he needs to do, and everyone else might as well lose their job or go on strike.

What is at stake in the game then is the very definition of the game, what can be played and who can play, and each agent shares a common concern, which is the existence of the game. Imagine that the literary game were to be banned: a lot of people would be out of work. Which means that games played in relatively autonomous fields often have a hidden limit: people don't take their struggles to the limit because that would ruin the game, according to the rule that 'you should not saw off the branch that you are sitting on'. This is a rule of folk wisdom which is for once a scientific law: there is in any game a fundamental, but often completely unconscious, collusion (which has the same root as the game)[22] – this is the most unconscious aspect of the social game – with everything involving the actual existence of the game, with everything that makes me hold fast to the game, in every sense of the word, and keeps me hooked on the game. In a colloquium on philosophy, you can explore all sorts of variations on the interest of philosophy, but nobody mentions the very simple fact that you need to believe – especially when practising the *épochè*[23] and enjoining others to practise it – that the existence of philosophy matters. If, today, so many essays in defence of philosophy finish by supporting the ministry of education's definition of philosophy, it is because the existence of philosophy does finally depend on the existence of the general board of the ministry of education, for posts of lecturer and professor in philosophy. There is no harm in this: we all need to make a living [*laughter*]. However, it is better if we admit this, otherwise we run the risk of spinning endless arguments that are no more than a rationalization of that basic interest. For philosophers who make a point of peddling radical doubt, this ought to be very disturbing. I remind philosophers, therefore, that in any game there is a common interest, which is often its most hidden aspect: it is the interest of existing with a title, a label that states: 'I am a writer' – there are various ways of saying 'I am a writer', 'I am a philosopher', etc. Enough said.

Second session: the hit parade of the intellectuals (3)

I shall now try to discuss the problem of a sociology of the perception of the social world, a problem that sociologists hardly ever consider. And yet there is matter for reflexion on what it is to perceive the social world, for instance on the question of 'what it is to make a social judgement'.

Before continuing, I would like to answer a question that I was asked last week on the notion of the 'postmodern'. I was asked: 'Could you explain the process of fabrication of the notion of the "postmodern" and establish its validity in the field of knowledge? What caused the need to formalize this break and therefore bring it into being by naming it? [. . .] It seems to me that nowadays it is those who make the least use of historicity who are happiest to use the prefix post-, which is exemplified in the term "post-historical" [. . .].' I think this is a very good question, but as so often with good questions, it supplies its own answer, and I think everything that I am saying is an answer: one of the games that those who hold the monopoly of discourse on the social world – or at least struggle to gain it – constantly indulge in is a prophetic kind of game that consists in introducing breaks; they will say 'it is pre-this or post-that', 'it is neo- or paleo-'. In other words, one of the goals in the symbolic struggle that I am discussing today is to manipulate our principles of vision and division, to play with our categories of perception of the social world. To say that something is post-, ante-, neo- or paleo- [. . .], is to constitute reality after a certain fashion, and this act of constitution, in the traditional philosophical and juridical sense, will carry the weight and potency of the authority of the author of the constituent act. In the case in point it is the same. In my view, people who can say 'post-' or 'ante-' are not sociologists [. . .]. I can justify my definition of sociology, which like any definition takes its place within the framework of a struggle to define the limits of the field and the space of the judges therein. Any scientific struggle is a struggle of this kind, which does not mean that it is not scientific. The fact that the people who use this language exclude themselves from sociology may be fairly argued. I think they posture as prophets: they institutionalize themselves in a role that relies on using words to modify the world that they claim to study. More precisely, they attempt to modify the world, and thereby their position in the world of people trying to modify the world. A prophet is someone who, by modifying our representation of the world, hopes to modify their position in the space of people working to modify our representation of the world [. . .].

There is then an implicit definition of sociology that I have been promoting during these two sessions. In this particular game, my role is not to say what the real list should be (although, obviously, like everyone, I do as an individual have my own list, but I shall not tell you what it is); as a sociologist, I need to define the game whose goal is to give the right list, and therefore to understand its logic, which may in fact lead me to change my view of the right list, and profoundly transform my attitude towards what I saw as wrong lists, for example by making me accept humorously what I felt indignantly. Which means that I can keep saying what I have been saying so far, quite seriously and yet sometimes playfully: 'playing seriously' as Plato says.[24] (But in general the people who comment on these things are not a bundle of laughs. They make us forget that we can say very serious things humorously, that scientific study is tremendous fun if you go about it the right way. I can really discuss anything, which is one of the properties of the prophet [*laughter*]: the prophet is the man who says everything about all things, all there is to be said; once a year, on an exceptional occasion, in carnival time, on Mardi Gras,[25] you can say everything about all things, and then afterwards you return to things defined as socially serious.)

I believe that I have answered the question on 'the postmodern'. Not really, but I don't think this is a cop-out on my behalf, since, given the way that the question was formulated, I think the person who asked it can answer it themselves. In passing, I would like to express my gratitude (which is also an appeal): during the interval someone brought me a magnificent article taken from *Matin* magazine: 'After Sartre, who?'. You see, I couldn't make it up! The article dates from 25 September 1982 (which more or less corresponds to the time I have been discussing) and it was written by Catherine Clément[26] (we must always render unto Caesar . . . [*laughter*]). It is another ranking list, with overlaps and familiar friends, but there are more similarities than differences, because, obviously, she is someone who is at the centre of the space of production that I am trying to define.

The model of the trial

I would now like to try to describe – not in depth, because it is a vast subject – what the analysis of this social game contributes to a sociology of the perception of the social world. I said just now, rather too briefly, that we could describe what happens either through the logic of a trial or through the logic of the market and price setting. To specify what I imply by the word 'trial': I am thinking of the way that Kafka uses the word, and I shall continue today's analysis with a kind of reading of Kafka, which is not a reading in the literary sense; it consists in seeing in Kafka a model of the social world. I believe that we can read *The Trial* as the account of a procedure where the social agents are struggling in a way to discover their identity: this is the aim of the supreme court. This means that we may undertake either a sociological or a theological reading of Kafka's *Trial*: the two readings in dispute are in fact not antagonistic or incompatible. It is only because we have an excessively naive view of the social world that we fail to see how theological our society is. And yet Durkheim in his old age made the authorized commentators laugh when he said: 'Society is God.'[27]

Said by him, and given the way that he said it, it was sometimes difficult to accept, but I think that the theological question of God is raised in society through the question: 'Who am I?', 'Who can tell me who I am?' Step by step, faced with the last analysis, as a last resort, people say: 'It is God.' Now I have a reading of Kafka to offer you.

(I think that if there are a number of questions raised by sociology that find themselves expressed in a different guise, in what we call theological language, it is better to know this, unless we want sociology to be theology. This is what you might call my scientistic side: my profession is to engage in science and not to engage in theology by mistake, whereas sociologists do very often practise theology without realizing it. Although I have stated this rather brusquely and peremptorily, I do believe that it is relatively important, for it is important that you know why I am saying certain things – if I suddenly throw Kafka at you out of the blue, you might think that I have lost the plot.)

There is, then, a trial, a trial in the course of which a body of judges is constituted and at the end of which a verdict, that is *veredictum*, 'something spoken truly', is promulgated:[28] 'Who can tell the truth?' 'Who can tell the truth about the social world?' 'Who am I?', 'And who truly has the right to pronounce any verdict on me?' 'Who truly has the right to tell me who I truly am?' You would have to be truly blind not to see this in Kafka; the question keeps recurring. To define the relations between sociology and literature, which have themselves generated a whole literature, we could say that good literature (another value judgement) has a virtue that discourse claiming to be scientific cannot have, which is to dramatize a problem. In the case of the social world, one of the difficulties of science is how to turn the problem round so that it is presented as a real problem for people, rather than a demonstration. We want to make Kafka function like the dramatization of a social problem, with the theatrical pathos of an action capable of being acted on stage,[29] and inviting identification (as we often say of the theatre).

Scientific discourse enjoys a mode of comprehension of the social world which I think is of a different order from the mode of comprehension that we expect from biological or mathematical discourse: we only really understand if we are able to re-dramatize. I always quote this phrase by Sartre, who said of his readings of Marx in his youth: 'I found everything perfectly clear, and I really understood absolutely nothing.'[30] This is very often the case in a teaching situation: if we understand everything, we understand nothing. It is clear that sociology as I envisage it cannot tolerate a merely formal understanding.

Many people will say of what I have to say that 'it is not scientific' or that 'it is political'. No, not at all. I think that if we want to be actively productive in the social sciences in general, it is not sufficient to understand sociology as a set of theorems. It is an issue on which I can only repeat what I have just said. Sometimes I happen to suggest that I would have more to say, in order to avoid saying what I don't want to say, but here I have no more to say. I leave you to think about it.)

The model of the market

So much for the model of the trial. As for the model of the market, things are simple: we have products. Here is one advantage of using this language: I can say 'product' and 'producer', for instance. When Max Weber says that 'the Church is the institution that has the monopoly of the legitimate manipulation of the goods of salvation',[31] his argument may horrify true believers, but it is very important because the economic analogy that he uses helps to construct the object, and in constructing it, he severs our naive relation to the object, which is lodged deep within words such as 'worship'. Sociology is often so deeply ensconced in its language that it finds it almost impossible to make such breaks, particularly since those who practise it have not distanced themselves much from the object of their discourse. Sometimes it is important to change our language in order to change our relation to its object.

But the economic analogy has another function too. Saying 'producer' rather than 'artist' or 'artisan' may allow us to avoid creating historical anomalies and making breaks without bothering to analyse them historically. Speaking of an 'artist' in the case of a medieval woodworker who is not even a sculptor is historical nonsense, a monstrous anachronism. By saying 'producer', we avoid a gross error, and at least we avoid giving a thoughtless answer to the question as to whether the artist is not – just like the jury of *Lire* – a social invention that needed social conditions to make it possible, which took place over time, which was not invented once and for all time, and may disappear, although once it has existed, it is always possible to resort to it again. Resorting to the terminology of production is therefore not at all an arrogant display of a rather crude and basic materialism. It is to assume a provisional definition whose virtue is above all negative. To say, for example, 'producer for producers' is a kind of brain-washing, which allows us to see a host of problems that we don't see when we say 'avant-garde artist'.

There is then a market where prices will be set. In the interplay of the mechanisms or the balance of power, more or less forceful judgements will be articulated, more or less liable to be universalized and imposed universally in exchange relations, which can range from a meeting in the street ('Have you read So-and-so's latest book? It's hopeless.') to nomination to the Académie française, by way of the ranking list, or the list of best sellers in *L'Express*, for example. Thus there will be a series of acts of judgement and the intervention of a host of little judges, and that includes you and me: buying a book is committing an act of economic judgement, but one exercised in the space where economic action is not merely economic, but also a ratification and a consecration. Similarly, going to Mass is not only contributing to the collection, it is also ratifying, sanctioning and consecrating the place of worship as a place worthy of respect. Going to the theatre is not only paying an entrance fee, it is also voting with your feet, granting the sanction of consecration. Whence the ambiguity of the best seller – this is very important, I shall come back to this in a moment. I have heard – and perhaps you have too – people who ask the village newsagent: 'Can you give me the best seller?'; there is an effect of consecration for people who are not in the loop, who don't know that you shouldn't buy the best seller, that you should say best sellers are stupid, which is the tacit norm in the restricted field. People who transfer to the world of the economy of symbolic goods the laws of the economy of ordinary goods – 'It's selling well, therefore it's good' – are contravening the specific logic of the field. Whence the ambiguity of this sanction. At one extreme you have the most intimate, internal sanction: Blanchot writing on Robbe-Grillet[32] is in, it is relatively autonomous (note that I am taking a historical example, one that is twenty years old . . .) and, at the other extreme, you have people who buy the latest Goncourt prizewinner, and between the two you have all the intermediary stages.

I think the economic analogy is perfectly valid as long as we recognize the specific nature of this economy that I have tried to define by describing the difference between the best seller and the absolutely 'in' novel; I point out that these acts have an economic dimension, as Weber says, but that they are never wholly economic. To fully understand them, we should never forget – as I was tempted to do when I started talking to you this morning – the economic dimension. Through the verdicts of this group of taste-makers there is an economic effect at work, this economic effect is also able to a certain extent to operate within the more restricted field. This is true, for instance, in the case of poetry published at the author's expense.

Value judgement

These are actions with an economic dimension, but at the same time they are not economic actions, and we need to question their other dimension in order to discover the specific logic that they obey and that I have been constantly trying to capture: it is the logic of the value judgement that consists at one and the same time in perceiving and appreciating, using categories of perception that are simultaneously categories of appreciation. I think this is one of the properties of social perception, whatever the type of society: the categories of perception are inseparable from the categories of appreciation.

Thus in many societies it is as a function of categories of kinship that people measure distance in the social world, the principal and the secondary, the genuinely true and the false, the truly good and the bad, and so on. I think the categories of kinship are inseparable from the categories of perception and, simultaneously, appreciation: you cannot say of someone that 'she is your sister' without saying 'it is good or bad' – as in the case of incest – or 'it is good or bad to do this or that', 'it is good or bad to love or not to love'. This is true of all of the categories of perception of the social world: to say 'It is vulgar / distinguished' (there it is clear), 'It is hot / cold', 'It is dull / bright' or 'It is constructed / shapeless', etc., implies a value judgement. There is no classificatory term that does not imply a value judgement. Which renders very difficult any discourse that tries not to be normative: the only non-normative discourse on a social world is a metadiscourse on normative judgements, like the one that I am currently engaged in. The content of the perception, the verdict, will be the 'product' of the relation between something seen and an agent seeing it.

To understand any judgement of whatever nature, to understand a phenomenon and what the papers say about it, to understand a newspaper and what its readers read in it, to understand a book and what its readers read in it, to understand a reading as the act of reading something, we must then enquire into, on the one hand, the social conditions of production of the perceiving subjects, and in particular their categories of perception and the conditions of the exercise of their act of perception (where are they placed? What do they see?) and, on the other hand, the social conditions of the production of the producer of the product as well as the objective properties (in the sense of 'those that are placed before the perceiving subject') of the product, in which the social properties of the producer and those of the field of production are expressed, through the properties of the position of the producer in the field of production.

In my opinion, all this is at work in every instance. The theoretical apparatus that I bring into play to perceive some detail – four pages in a magazine – could apply to hundreds of things. If tomorrow you told me that I needed to understand the Centre Pompidou at Beaubourg, I would proceed in the same way: social conditions of the producers, social conditions of the consumers, and I would be able to predict quite a lot. I know in advance that everyone will be thinking the same thing, and I can predict by and large what people will think, who will be in favour, who against, and to what degree, as a function of the determining properties of the receiver. What we have then is a kind of general theory of the perception of the social world that enables us to put general questions, which will obviously have to be specified on each occasion: on each occasion we will have to assign values to the variables. When we perceive a social thing, our perception – in the sense of *perceptum* (what is perceived) – will be the product of a relation between the properties of the person who sees and the properties of the thing that they see.

A very simple verification is provided by cases where something goes unnoticed, so to speak. In literature this is obvious. For example, for my generation Bachelard went unnoticed by most people, except for a small minority who were well aware of him, and who afterwards brought him out into the open.[33] But if these people who saw Bachelard had not seen him or if, having seen him, they had been dominated and had not been in a position to impose their vision in the struggle, we would still be unaware of Bachelard, who would not be a great man. He would be invisible, dead and buried once and for all time, until someone came along who had the categories of perception needed to see him and the power to make him visible and rehabilitate him. This can happen for a monument, a person or a work. We call it a 'discovery' or a 'rediscovery', for instance. But to make this discovery the person needs special properties: he must have the capacity to see, to impose his vision, and have a particular interest in rehabilitating.

The sociologist will immediately formulate the hypothesis that if the discoverer rehabilitates something, it is because in rehabilitating it he rehabilitates himself. In other words, we rehabilitate our alter ego, or more exactly, our homologue in a neighbouring field. The famous preface to Mauss by Lévi-Strauss[34] is for example a manner of self-celebration by proxy. It respects the law of the field that prohibits self-celebration, first because it is not right, and second because I have done it myself [*laughter*]: you disguise it with euphemism, using a person that you are in fact inventing. As I am sure that someone will be thinking of it, I had better own up [*laughter*]: I did this once myself, with Panofsky. Obviously, since 'the man who has will always be given more',[35] you can attribute so much to Panofsky, and you then run the risk of people telling you: 'You have taken all that from Panofsky',[36] which is one way of compensating for what I was going to say about Lévi-Strauss – it is obvious that Lévi-Strauss finds a lot in Mauss that is only there for Lévi-Strauss.

It is a very demanding task to analyse the strategies of the preface, rehabilitation, consecration and celebration, including centenaries, anniversaries, and the like. We can do it for the history of philosophy as we can for the history of literature and painting, and so on. These universal mechanisms just take specific forms according to the structure of the field and the laws of the game. One example of verifying the proposition that perception is always a relation is the case where there is an object to perceive, but no subject to perceive it: the object goes unnoticed, until those who have an interest in perceiving it perceive it.

The word 'interest' is interesting: 'interested in perceiving it' means 'capable of telling the difference'. To say 'It's all the same to me' is to be like Buridan's ass,[37] to be blind and not tell the difference. Contrary to those who make a reductive reading of what I say about the word 'interest', what I do have to say is that to take an interest is basically to tell the difference ('For me, they are not the same'), which supposes categories enabling us to make the *diacrisis* or division between this and that. If I lack the categories of sweet and sour, I can make no sense of the cuisine of many civilizations. To have no taste is to be unable to tell the difference. Of children who eat canned baby food we say 'they have no sense of taste'. Sure enough, these children are going to be like the journalists that I am studying [*laughter*] . . . This is a very good image [*laughter*]: they have not acquired the principle of differentiation between sweet and sour. To take an interest means two things: to want something, and to want to tell the difference. 'Taste' is a splendid word because it expresses both: to have taste is to have a propensity to consume and at the same time the capacity to discriminate. Which is at the heart of what I was saying just now: taxonomies are always both positive and normative. To say that 'men are different from women' is to say that men are better. I can never say that 'this is different from that' without saying that one is better than the other. This proposition is universally applicable in society. Whence the great difficulty of sociological discourse: as soon as you say: 'the school system reproduces', people hear 'it's a good thing' or 'it's a bad thing'. The judgement of taste or preference is then a judgement of difference and of distinction that at the same time implies a value judgement.

Establishing differences

To prolong the analysis a little further, I would like to introduce this example: the perceiving subjects help to create the thing perceived. If we put the question of classes, it would be the same: the perceiving subjects help to create social differences: 'That's chic / that's not chic', 'He's a prole / he's a bourgeois', 'That's the Balzar[38] / that's a bistrot', they note the differences and thus help to create them. One of the paradoxes of the social world is that it is always perceived as already perceived. Already constituted, firstly by perceptions, which then become things perceived. Past generations discriminated between for instance a *juge de grande instance* [county court judge] and a *juge de petite instance* [local magistrate], and for us the former becomes someone with three stars to his epaulette, or who makes us wait another three sessions – as in Kafka's *Trial* – someone established as different. The law is a great institution for establishing differences, for instituting them as things in a world of things. It reifies perceptions. The differences constituted are accompanied by acts of differentiation. People who are different 'make the difference felt', as the saying goes; distant people are distant, they keep their distance and insist on it, avoiding familiarity. But, as we know, you have to be able to assume this difference: distant people are precisely those who are distant from us (otherwise they would just be 'pretentious'). There is a difference that is a symbolic difference produced by symbolic acts of differentiation, but reified and naturalized. The difference has become a thing: that's how it is, it is natural. This is the objective aspect of the thing perceived, which is perceived as already established.

For the perceiving subject, there are categories of perception – here I must speed up for otherwise it might take forever – which are mostly the product of the internalization of objective differences. The difference between sweet and sour is not an invention, it exists objectively. In the case of science, for instance, we ought to reflect on the number of problems that would never have been raised if scientific tradition had not raised them. Why do we study leisure without studying culture?[39] There is an institution, the Congress of the International Sociological Association,[40] where those who study culture sit in one room, those who study leisure in another, and those who study education in yet another. They each have their little set of problems and fail to see that the simple fact of being in one room rather than another imposes one method of problem solving rather than another: social boundaries are transformed into mental structures. Think also about the difference between sociologists and philosophers and of the number of problems that, at any given time, cannot be faced socially because of the institutional differences between the disciplines. The disciplines are our tables of the categories of understanding.[41] Which means that a whole lot of things cannot be thought. Obviously, when we have as our categories of thought the structures structuring what we need to think about, everything works like clockwork; they are bound to match up. I could go on for hours, but I won't.

Producing the producers

After this aside about the perceiving subjects, I return to my specific object; I shall apply my little machine to the case in point. The first question is to ask how the producers are produced. We shall then ask if these people are intellectual-journalists, journalist-intellectuals, writer-journalists, journalist-writers, academic-journalists or journalist-academics, where they have come from, how they were produced. Our first reflex when faced with cultural producers is to think of their family. What we nearly always tend to forget in the sociology of cultural works is the school system that has produced them. What I want to say is not exactly what we say when we recall that Descartes was a pupil of the Jesuits. Let us say that what the school system transmits is less important that its action in attributing places, saying: 'You are literary', 'You are scientific', 'You are an option C', 'You are an option D',[42] which may mean all sorts of things. In other words, the school system works less through what it teaches than through the classification that it produces and the effects of that classification. There is an effect of 'You are this', 'You are only a . . .', an effect of *fatum*, of consecration, effects of stigmatization ('You are good / no good', 'You are gifted / not gifted'): how many philologists are people who spoiled their exam papers at the age of 18?

In the present case of the ranking list, the relation of the producers to the school system is obvious. One of the characteristics of the journalistic milieu is a sort of rampant, covert anti-intellectualism. It's a kind of revenge. Writers have always said it and there are some terrible pages in Zola: the anti-intellectualism of academic-type critics is linked to the division of labour and the objective hierarchy between teachers and writers. What Zola says about the pupils of the École normale,[43] their mixture of arrogance and modesty, humility and mediocrity, is the effect of the social conditions of their production. The relation of the writer to the writer-journalist will be quite different: the writer-journalist does not have the statutory arrogance endowed by the fact of being the consecrated critic of an institution; he has accounts to settle with the intellectuals. I shall say no more, because it would look too polemical. And yet it isn't, it's just one of those things that we need to know, that I would like to be able to say but that I don't. (Several times just now I may have avoided saying things; it was not that they were unpleasant, but they would seem so to you if you heard them. It is in the relation between what I am saying and the categories of perception that you are likely to apply to it that the unpleasantness could arise.)

We need, then, to consider the conditions of the production of the producers: their families, their original milieu, their studies, and so on. For the studies, it is not so much their scientific bent as whether they were successfully completed or not. There is, for example, a form of hostility to science, a neo-mystical ideology that emerges not only in certain sectors of the scientific field, but also in the journalistic field. This sort of irrationalism, or anti-rationalism, was flourishing in Germany around 1933 and it is obviously prevalent among people who have accounts to settle with the sciences. It is no accident that the bad scientist often becomes a good revolutionary, as I suggested last time in the case of Marat, or a good national-revolutionary. I am putting all this quite crudely and bluntly, but I refer you to my study of Heidegger[44] and the context within which National Socialist thought arose, thinking that it helps explain quite a lot of things.

We need then to consider the social conditions of the production of the producers, their social origins, the education system, and the relations between the two: their way of assuming academic failure will be very different depending on their origins (and their relation to the education system). Effects of resentment, for example (and their bitter, unhappy, hostile, submissive, dominated relations – none of these is exclusive), will be linked to the relation between their starting point and their point of arrival, mediated by the education system. All this is very complicated. Building on this, we can return to anti-intellectualism – for example: it is plain to see from what I told you just now that 'Who is the successor to Sartre?' also means: 'There is no one, thank goodness, free at last!' I am saying this naively, but it is what they are saying. I could give you twenty examples (please bring me any documents you have – I appeal to you to contribute . . .), for these things are hidden in a host of journals, yielding small clues here and there. The more documents I can collect, the more clues I shall have. There comes a time when, for historical reasons (a very important consideration), these permanent drives – for example the anti-intellectualism of the intellectuals – are likely to find an audience, and express themselves.

We need to ask what these conditions would be, what the chance causes were that meant that, in 1933, anti-intellectualism was particularly able to express itself; might it not be linked to the surplus production of diplomas, to the fact that professors' assistants had long and slow-moving careers, and also to the context of political crisis (you could say virtually nothing and appear to be saying something meaningful)? There would be a whole analysis to be made here of something that is very difficult to grasp sociologically but that the sociologist, or at least myself, is very often obliged to hypothesize: the existence of a sort of confused awareness of the conditions of acceptability of what a person can do or say. At every moment, for everything that we do there is a sort of vague reference: 'We can do that', 'We can say that', 'That is wrong, but it is acceptable', 'It's unthinkable', 'It's impossible', 'It's not on'. It is very difficult to know how this sort of evaluation is made up. I think it is composed on the basis of a kind of semi-conscious, practical statistical calculation. In any case I think it is very important to understand phenomena of literary revolution, or everyday manners of acting and behaving, to know that this sensitivity to an objective index of acceptability of practices exists.

After the conditions of the producers, we need to analyse the social positions of the producers in the space. The field is the subject of actions mediated by the position occupied in the field as expressed in the practice of the agent, the agent having in relation to this position a disposition partly preceding their holding the position (it is shaped by the family, among others), but partly constituted by the position, in particular by what the position renders possible or obligatory. To tell the truth, a position is a post, with its functions; and the post of the writer since Zola and Sartre includes the function of signing petitions. To say that there are social inventions is to say that there are functions. We talk of the function of the turner or the fitter, for instance, and it is the same thing for intellectuals, even if obviously it is not so strictly defined. One of the properties of these functions is that the higher they are, the more vague is their definition and the more it implies that we can and should play with the definition – this is a very general law – and the more interest we have in the position being vague, whereas, unless I am wrong (I haven't checked, I'm not sure), the lower we go down the social scale, the more interest we have in the definition being rigid and juridically defined. Of course it is a nuisance, but at least it is a protection, a safety net: there are things that they can't make you do. But the function implies duties ('You should do this'). It also creates an objective potential: assigning functions to someone engenders a very complex psychosociological process that psychoanalysts would have a lot to say about. I shall leave it there.

One aspect of the position of journalists is very important. We call them 'the press': things are pressing and urgent, they don't have time to read but they are paid to speak of books they don't read (this is a verifiable social fact, I say it without ill will; any journalist will admit it, and in any case there is no way that they could). Consequently, they read what the other journalists say about the books they have to comment on, and the most typical effect of the field (verified ten times over; I don't have the statistics to hand, but there are other ways of penetrating the social truth) is that there are books that you cannot not discuss, and the editor says: 'You have absolutely got to talk about So-and-so's book.' The people on that list, although we ask from a normative viewpoint why they are on the list, cannot publish a book without unleashing this phenomenon: 'You absolutely must talk about his book.' However, the combination of this very strong constraint with a rampant anti-intellectualism has the consequence sooner or later that they start to tear someone to pieces. Again, this is not a deliberate decision, but it is very embarrassing when you are top of the hit parade, for you are structurally exposed. The actual or potential victim may feel it as a plot ('They resent me', 'They are out to get me', 'It's the right / left who are out to get me', 'It's the government', and so on), but I think in fact, in the cases I have studied, that it is an effect of the field combined with an effect of the habitus: 'We absolutely have to discuss So-and-so, but he's a pain in the arse, he could become the new Sartre, better shoot him down first . . .' [*laughter*].

(Obviously this is not conscious, but it prepares the ground for what will come later – Durkheim said that religion is a well-founded illusion.[45] I think this statement applies to a lot of social phenomena: the sociologist so often has to destroy things in order to construct his object. For example, I have just spent the morning destroying an analysis of the type 'they meant it', but we need to know why this illusion gains a collective social status. A good scientific theory – which is one of the differences from the natural sciences – should include and integrate a theory of what is there with a theory of the reasons that prevent it from being perceived as such; it should comprise a sociology of what things are and the reasons why we fail to see this. That is, I think, one of the great breaks, which is explicable for strictly historical reasons, between what I am doing and our founding tradition, Marx above all, but also Durkheim. They had to work so hard to found a social science – it is no accident that it was the last of the sciences to emerge – they all said that it was very hard, that they had to expend so much effort, for example in destroying the representation of labour and replacing it with the theory of surplus value, that they did not have the energy to think why they needed so much energy to understand it.[46] If it had been obvious that labour is the production of surplus value, they would not have found it so difficult and they would have been able to incorporate the reasons why the theory was difficult to construct and not so easy to transmit, and met with so much resistance.)

I have wandered away from my particular case. I was speaking of the illusion of simultaneity which is a fundamental objective of conspiracy theory. The conspiracy theory is really an elementary form of the perception of the social world. The likelihood of its arising varies depending on the social class, the milieu and the historical moment: it will be particularly strong in the declining petite bourgeoisie. That having been said, it can meet with objective conditions. Here, if I am right, there is an effect of the field. At any given moment, one person is at the top of the hit parade of intellectuals. Now that Aron (number 2 on the list) is dead,[47] it is easy to tell who will be the next target for character assassination. Effects of the field will provoke the obligation to celebrate, in a context such that the legitimacy of anti-intellectualism is enhanced, and there is a good chance that we may see . . . I shall say what I was thinking: for example, they might pick on Foucault. This is an example of a well-founded illusion: the effects of the field combined with the effects of position linked to the habitus can engender simultaneous forms of invention at many points in the field, from *Le Point* to *Libération* we can see things emerging that we may perceive as a campaign. Now there are many kinds of campaign, and the best ones in terms of dissimulation and symbolic violence are those that have no subject.

I think it is time for me to stop. But I would like very briefly to add the fact that the objects of perception will have properties of visibility and readability. Everyone feels this: given the categories of perception of journalists, who are people in a hurry (here we should detail their social education and training, their categories of perception, what they are interested in seeing and not seeing), there are people who are going to be more visible and readable and there are also people who will have a greater propensity than others to be seen and appreciated: there are, then, people who will be better seen and better appreciated. *A priori*, all this is easy to deduce: the people who are better appreciated are those who have the habitus closest to that of their judges. There are complicities between the judge and the judged: the intellectual-journalists will obviously appreciate the journalist-intellectuals and vice versa: there will then be a kind of structural love match that has nothing to do with 's/he's my pal', although it can be enhanced by personal acquaintance.

We tend to seek out the small causes, and our explanation, taking a historical perspective, will place the accent on the role of women in history or the role of the salons in the history of literature. It is very important to take these small causes into account, but they are not accidental at all, they are structural: they are affinities of habitus ('we are comfortable together'), which are nothing to do with conscious manipulations of the market. We have, on the one hand, affinities of the habitus and, on the other – and it is here that things become complicated – strategies of condescension. One factor that we should take into account in the relation between intellectuals and journalists is the structure of the field of production and the particular position occupied by the field of the critics – writer-artists, artist-writers – in the field of production. I defined this position just now: it is culturally dominated and temporally dominant. One of the strategies through which the desire to be noticed will be expressed is a particular category of the class of strategies of condescension. Intellectuals anxious to be recognized as intellectuals must – because of the definition of the intellectual at a given moment in time, as established since Voltaire, Zola, Gide or Sartre, for instance – go beyond the role of simply writing books. So they depend on journalists. It is part of the definition of their role because, ultimately, being an intellectual is to be a great scholar (for example . . .) plus something else, and this something else is what journalism gives. Since this is the case, the intellectuals who want to be appreciated recognize by that very fact a certain legitimacy in the verdict of these judges, and they can acknowledge it through strategies of condescension that may flirt with cynicism. For indeed, the strategies of the social world are not all unconscious. They are much more so than we think, but they are not absolutely so. I need to return to this point. Let us say that if these people are granted legitimacy, it is because they receive recognition even from those who feel least qualified to judge.

Lecture of 15 March 1984

First session (lecture): preamble on social understanding. – Does a field have a starting point? – Rules and regularities. – The process of objectification. – The interest of following the rules. – The spontaneist position and the continuist position. – The passage from discontinuous universes to continuous universes.
Second session (seminar): the hit parade of the intellectuals (4). – The margin of liberty of symbolic action. – The duplication effect of symbolic power. – The specificity of symbolic action. – Political prediction.

First session (lecture): preamble on sociological understanding

I propose to start today with a brief preamble on the meaning of 'understanding' for sociology. In my last lecture I indicated that, in my opinion, one of the functions of my exercise in presentation was to try to make you understand things differently from the way in which you usually would: for there are in fact different ways of understanding any message, and in particular a sociological message. I would like to return to this point, first by quoting a statement by Wittgenstein that I read in a book by Jacques Bouveresse, *Le Philosophe chez les autophages*,[1] which I strongly recommend you read, because it is immediately relevant to the problems that I am raising here. In his (rather demanding) book, Bouveresse quotes the following text:

What makes a subject difficult to understand — if it is significant, important — is not that some special instruction about abstruse things is necessary to understand it. Rather it is the contrast between the understanding of the subject and what most people want to see. Because of this the very things that are most obvious

can become the most difficult to understand. What has to be overcome is not difficulty of the intellect but of the will.'[2]

This very clear text expresses extremely well what I often say about
sociology: practising sociology would not be so difficult if the will to
understand were not so fraught; the social object is to some extent
something that we do not wish to understand.

I shall continue with a text by Freud on laughter that one of you
has handed in to me. I think the person who brought me this text was
thinking of the laughter that I inspired in you on some occasions and
what I had tried to say about this laughter.[3] This well-known text from
Jokes and their Relation to the Unconscious seems extremely relevant:

> Many of my neurotic patients who are under psychoanalytic
> treatment are regularly in the habit of confirming the fact by a
> laugh when I have succeeded in giving a faithful picture of their
> hidden unconscious to their conscious perception; and they laugh
> even when the content of what is unveiled would by no means
> justify this. This is subject, of course, to their having arrived close
> enough to the unconscious material to grasp it after the doctor has
> detected it and presented it to them.[4]

As the person who communicated this to me said (as you may imagine,
I am very pleased with this kind of communication, which shows
genuine understanding), laughter could then be a form of practical
understanding preceding what we might call theoretical understanding (although these words are not very meaningful): there would be
a practical understanding preceding understanding through words or
expressed in words.

To say a little more on the subject of words: words are one of the
obstacles to a true understanding of the sociological object and one
part of our task consists in working on them. This is obviously a task
that has been much practised, notably in a certain type of philosophical tradition – and in different genres: the Hegelian tradition and the
Heideggerian tradition do not use words in the same way at all – but
I think that, working on words, saying the same things in different
ways, and replacing one word with another, is very often a precondition of real understanding, both for the producer of sociological
discourse and for its receivers. If oral communication has some virtue
– otherwise, you might as well just read, it would be more economical
for all concerned – it is precisely because it shows words being tracked
down, found and replaced. To follow this work of struggling for words

is, I believe, a part of true understanding. I have myself, for example, had the experience of realizing that we never come to the end of understanding what we say: rereading texts that I had written some time earlier, I am sometimes surprised to see things there that I have only just now really understood; I then say to myself that my verbal automatisms had anticipated me. This means that you can say certain things without really understanding them, whereas very often, to undertake scientific work in sociology, you have to try to really understand what you are saying.

This preamble is a means of justifying the exercise that I was engaged in last time and the rather unkempt or 'liberated' aspect that I gave my argument: I wanted to liberate a certain number of repressions and show that we may speak of this intellectual universe in a totally free manner, with a Nietzschean laugh, although I think it is very often experienced as suffering. I shall return to this problem in the second session to try to show how social universes are places of suffering. There is suffering, and our approach may invite an analogy with psychoanalysis.[5] I always handle this analogy very cautiously because it is often used impressionistically, but also because the psychoanalytic discourse, insofar as it constantly touches on reality without ever grasping it, is one of the most dangerous screens filtering our understanding of the social world. However, in this particular case, the analogy seems to me to be well founded. (You may sometimes think I am saying things that are trivial or that I am repeating myself: this may certainly occur, but it may also happen that it is a deliberate intention based on a certain idea of what it means to transmit ideas in sociology.)

Does a field have a starting point?

I shall now pick up the strands of the analysis that I undertook in my first lecture, that is the analysis of the notion of the field (and I shall return in our second session to what I was saying about symbolic struggles and the intellectual field). In my first lecture, I was saying that a field is a space that contains its own motive force. The central idea of what I want to say today might in fact be resumed as follows: since a field is a structured social space, it can be described, by analogy, in the language of topology but, insofar as its structure is produced by antagonistic forces, the field may also be described in the language of dynamics, as a field of forces. In a way, a social world, or a social game, contains its own motive force – I think the analogy of the motor is rather crude, but we need to bear it in mind in order to understand.

'Setting up a field' has no sense: there is no beginning, a field does not start out with a contract, although, *ex post*, when we analyse it, we discover something that looks like a contract, one of the properties of a field being precisely that it bears within itself an axiomatic; a certain number of rules, whether practical or explicit, define its functioning. But nothing could be more false than to imagine that social worlds or fields start at a certain moment with a contract, and one of the major problems of the scientific analysis of the field is to describe those intangible processes that constitute its developing function as a field. For example, when we study literary history we may start by saying: 'Well, yes, there was a literary field as early as the twelfth century.' Yesterday, for instance, I was reading an article on treatises on art in the Middle Ages that compares three classical discourses on the world of art in the twelfth century, and these people were speaking in terms of a field, which is liable to surprise art historians who would situate the beginnings of the functioning of the artistic world as a field in the *Quattrocento*.

One of the major problems then is to find at what moment a field is initiated as a kind of little machine that will go on to generate its own problems and perpetuate itself, which will become autonomous and, dare I say, 'auto-mobile'. There is then nothing more false than to imagine that at a certain point in time there is a sort of creator's *'artifex'*. Another sociological illusion is artificialism, the illusion of a contract or a God as watchmaker who at a certain point in time would construct something like a social game. I think that the sociologist's scalpel has never discovered an entirely constituted social game. This is even true of the parlour games that we constantly use as analogy – I think they are one of the least bad analogies for studying the social world: we can always find their antecedents, but we don't know if even these might not be the reproduction, in an imaginary and rule-governed space, of social games that pre-existed them – like, for instance, all the games that mimic warfare. We could develop research into this topic.

The field, then, is not something that started at a certain moment by contract or decree. There is no absolute beginning. Even if sociological analysis performs the function of extracting a sort of *nomos*, or originary law that is at the same time a division, of extracting *nomoi* and rendering them visible, there is no reason to think that there is some 'nomothete' who at a certain moment might have posited and constituted the *nomos*. Ethnologists, who discover the laws immanent in a social space, will say that in Kabyle society, for example, we find a certain number of fundamental oppositions between wet and dry, east and west, hot and cold, and the like.[6] They thus make explicit the principles of division of a world that are at the same time the principles of vision of this world; they exist both in things (for instance, in the space of the house there is a masculine part and a feminine part) and in the minds of the people who inhabit the house and who perceive it according to the very structures that are immanently inscribed within it. But discovering this *nomos* or law does not oblige us to think that there is a constituent act underlying it. I think that the artificialist or nomothetic illusion is reinforced by all the theories of a social contract and a whole tradition of the philosophy of history and the history of society.[7]

Rules and regularities

That having been said, a field is by analogy a kind of game that has immanent rules, which may be mechanisms producing regularities or explicit norms engendering rule-governed practices. We should avoid confusing mechanisms and rules, these two principles of order that we find in the social world. On the contrary, we need to keep in mind the opposition between regularities and rules, the confusion between the two modes of regulation of the social world being one of the most persistent and fertile errors in sociological thought. This error – to repeat a sentence by Marx on Hegel that will serve as a slogan: 'Hegel takes the things of logic to be the logic of things'[8] – consists in believing that a regularity has its origins in a rule. Although the social world is full of regularities, of things that constantly recur, these regular links between cause and effect, events and consequences, are not necessarily produced by a rule. Paul Ziff, a linguist, remarks that there is a gulf between these two sentences: 'The train is regularly late' and 'As a rule the train is late'.[9] Quine makes this important distinction explicit when he says that when we construct a model, we must distinguish between to *fit* and to *guide*:[10] a model can be adapted and adjusted to fit the thing that it accounts for, or, on the contrary, it may guide and orientate what it names. Since what we say about the social world is always situated somewhere between these two positions, the confusion is endless.

For example, what do ethnologists mean by phrases of the type: 'The Dobus people do this or that'? Do they mean that it is the rule to do it or do they merely note that people do it regularly? Between these two meanings lies a whole anthropology. Everything that concerns the notion of the rules of kinship turns on this distinction, which may seem to be a pointless quibble. I shall not insist on this any longer here: admitting that my oral discourse cannot include everything, I refer you to my book *The Logic of Practice*, where I have made a long analysis of this distinction and pointed out its importance for understanding a certain number of things in anthropology, and in particular the rules of kinship (consult the index under 'rules' and you will find precise references that will enable you to appreciate the coherence of the argument).

There are countless reasons why this gap between 'as a rule' and 'regularly' is, so to speak, constantly glossed over in sociological discourse. First, respondents spontaneously use the language of rules; as soon as we ask an informant: 'What do you do?', 'What do people do on these occasions?', 'What do your people do?', 'Is it polite to do that?', we invite him to be his own theoretician and to reply as a nomothete. He will say: 'Yes, our people will not . . .', or 'On the first day of spring, we must . . .'.

Something that I would like to emphasize today is that one of the great problems in social science and the evolution of societies is precisely the passage from the things we do to the things we must do, from practical regularities to constituent regularities or norms. You might say that there is no difference: Paul Ziff's remark is unimportant because the train is late in either case and if people strew their threshold with flowers on the first day of spring it makes no difference whether their practice is really a practical submission to permanent, semi-conscious dispositions, or whether it obeys an explicit rule. But the distinction that I am pointing out here is not a simple theoretical and anthropological point of honour.

In this case as in others I have found Quine very helpful, and this philosophical nicety is important if you want to follow the logic of social evolution, and if, for example, you want to compare different societies. One of the things that interests me today is to understand how social universes endure and prolong their existence: how to account for the fact that social worlds reproduce themselves and perpetuate their existence, perpetuating themselves as a normative existence, as a place of a self-reproduced necessity. If we place ourselves in this perspective, we find there are basically two answers to the questions that I have raised: our spontaneous philosophy of the social world (when I say 'we' and 'our', this includes ordinary individuals but also scholars who claim to study the social world systematically) oscillates between a philosophy of spontaneity and a philosophy of mechanism. This is a crude opposition (it is obviously not the most proper kind of scientific communication, but this is the way we need to teach), but we could oppose the great scientific traditions in this light. Some sociologists are more open to the emergence of the new. They see society in the light of its spontaneity, unexpected creativity and novelty – to use Bergson's terms. Others, on the other hand, are more aware of society's regularities, and its self-perpetuating, self-reproducing character.

In fact, what is often described as a sort of ethical, existential or political choice – there are those who are for reproduction and those who are for change (very often these so-called theoretical debates are no more than confrontations between quasi-aesthetic world-views) – hides the very important problem of the logic of the functioning of social spaces, which I do not think we can answer by choosing one of the alternative terms. We can see why this apparently sociological problem is so fertile: it overlies a social programme of the opposition between movement and conservation, progress and repetition. A very strong social dichotomy (conservatism/progressivism) thus tends to be reproduced in the guise of a seemingly scientific dichotomy. In my experience, these sociological problems, which are no more than the euphemized and transfigured form of social problems, are false problems, or at least badly formulated problems, that need to be undone if we are to find the real problems. In this particular case, things seem relatively simple. I would like to show that we cannot limit the comparison between a pre-capitalist society and a society like ours to the confines of the alternative that I have outlined: all societies tend to ensure their own duration, even if they may use extremely different means to attain this end; this implies that we will find varying answers to the problem that I have raised.

To return for a moment to the problem of rules: one of the most considerable historical changes, powerfully described by Max Weber, is the passage from something diffuse (in its practical stage) to something codified, objectified, public and official. It seems that as we advance in the history of societies, the proportion of practices based on explicit, legal, constituent rules, and the proportion of institutions charged with guaranteeing those rules, increases. Which, contrary to the evolutionary schema that most people – including Max Weber – harbour, does not mean that this progress seen in terms of Weber's 'rationalization' (which I shall explain later, since it would be better to say 'this progress seen as an objectification of the principles of a practice') is a general progress and that all sectors of a universe are subject to this process to the same degree.

The process of objectification

How do social universes last? How is it that social fields, which are a product of history, are organized in such a way as to perpetuate themselves? Or perhaps – I have given several definitions of the notion of the field, and I shall give even more – there are two aspects to every field: on the one hand, mechanisms that are not necessarily constituent and institutionalized, and, on the other, institutions. I would like briefly to emphasize this distinction between field and institution: not everything in a field is institutionalized and fields are not all institutionalized to the same degree – this is important. It seems to me that the notion of institution, which the Durkheim school identifies with the social,[11] should be much more strictly circumscribed: in my view, what is institutionalized would be the aspects of social mechanisms that are raised from a state of regularity to a state of rule; it is the product of a process of codification or an act of institution, which is in itself an act of codification. I mention once more the theme of nomination that I have referred to on several occasions previously: we can talk of an institution when actions no longer just happen, but someone in authority says how they should be performed, and the proper form of their performance is objectified; it is important that this should be expressed in writing – that is, explicitly stated and subject to logical control. This is how we arrive at the notion of rationalization; the passage from the implicit and practical to the explicit and objective implies the possibility of logical control and challenge, which is a prerequisite for coherence.

In a game, a space or a social field, there are, then, things institutionalized and things not institutionalized; to take the game as metaphor, there are trumps, and a pattern of distribution of the trumps is one of the structuring principles of any field. Thus, one of the structuring principles of the intellectual field that I mentioned last year is the unequal distribution of what I call symbolic capital, which we may for the time being identify as roughly equivalent to reputation, renown, celebrity. This structure of the distribution of symbolic capital, although invisible and not codified, is very active (I remind you of what I was saying last time about the rough justice dispensed by codification as an order of merit: like honour in pre-capitalist societies, the structure of distribution of symbolic capital is in fact something impalpable, intangible): despite being diffuse and impalpable, it governs people's practices, interactions, exclusions and circles of acquaintance. Moreover, the field contains things that are institutionalized, in the guise of rules and those who implement them. There are laws: they may be more or less elaborate, more or less systematic; they may simply be customary laws, that is sets of partial rules representing an invisible system and consisting in the application of principles that are fundamental but never formulated, because left in the world of the 'it goes without saying' in the unwritten constitution. This is true of pre-capitalist societies, but also of a field like the intellectual field where there are hosts of rules that you need to know on pain of exclusion or excommunication, as in primitive societies. Often more important than the written rules, these unwritten rules are the pillar on which are based some written rules – a painter cannot exhibit wherever he fancies, and so on. This codified part, this institutionalized aspect, is extremely important: the passage from the diffuse to the institutionalized marks a qualitative change. For example, in the literary field, which is a very under-institutionalized field, the institutions are all the more powerful for lacking an arbiter.

In any field, then, things bound by rules coexist with things governed by a combination of mechanisms and dispositions. A social universe will owe its longevity to the conjunction of these two types of principles. The rules will produce regularity because a rule generates predictability. A lawyer will apply the rule every time the occasion, or 'case', arises: the rule is a means of producing predictability and calculability. This is even the definition of rational law for Weber: rational law, which is that of capitalist societies, is a law that provides the economy with what it needs, that is, calculability and predictability.[12] One property of the rule is to assure the person who knows it that he will know what he has to do, and to assure the person who knows it and who sees it at work that he will know what he will do. The rule is a sort of explicit law that ensures a kind of predictability. It is no accident that social science has always been tempted by what I call the legalistic. There are historical reasons for this – the social sciences were often founded in law faculties that generated a very particular form of social science – but there are also more fundamental reasons: looking for regularity, the scholar is predisposed to find it wherever it is announced, in particular by nomothetes, rule-makers or legal experts who tell him that 'as a rule, what happens is . . .'. Anthropologists too are often spontaneous lawyers and it is no accident that ethnology was pursued partly in colonial countries by people of legal training; they were in a way the legislators of pre-capitalist societies that lacked writing and so had not codified their codes of practice. That having been said, we should recognize that the simple fact of transcribing into the rule of law things that existed as practical principles is a radical change. Legalism is a permanent temptation for the social scientist in search of regularity; if we find rules, we are going to describe the world as obeying those rules; if we don't find any, we will translate what we hear – 'On the first day of spring we go and pick flowers in the fields' – into a rule that generates a 'must'.

The interest of following the rules

This temptation will moreover be all the stronger if the social agents still have extremely complicated relations with the principles of their practice: as soon as a rule exists, the interest of following the rules exists. I am tempted to say that if you work on pre-capitalist societies, you find that very few actions have a rule as their principle. Since they are universes where objectification has made little progress, it is better, in explaining practices to look into the habituses, the permanent dispositions and the micro-mechanisms that may exist. Having said this, you may say that there are some rules, nonetheless. Such as those governing marriage with a first cousin.[13] But should we say, as anthropologists often do, that it is the rule that drives the practice, and that if people marry a first cousin it is because 'it is the rule'? In fact, first of all, it is a rule very infrequently applied – at a rate of 4 per cent – which makes us doubt whether it is a rule; then again, even in cases where people seem to be obeying a rule, it may be that they are simply obeying a desire to be in order, to be onside, which is extremely important.

If we applied this to our own societies, we would immediately see that morality has its advantages: it is very important, even when we transgress the rules, to appear to have obeyed them, which in this case enables us to combine the benefits of transgression with the benefits of conformity. Respect for the rules procures specific profits, the hypocritical profits of conformity. In pre-capitalist societies – in the case of Kabyle society, you will find some good examples if you look under 'rule' in the index of *The Logic of Practice* – a considerable amount of our social ingenuity is spent on producing behaviour that is a product of interest – in the widest sense, which I shall return to – but which may look as if its principle is obedience to the rule. This means that the two forms of profit may be combined: the group is not fooled, but – this is important, although phrases that have 'the group' as their subject are always dangerous – it willingly grants this supplementary profit because it finds a specific profit in behaviour aiming to 'follow the rules' because this has the virtue of acknowledging the group. I always like to quote the brilliant concept of *obsequium* (obedience)[14] which Spinoza uses to designate the basic respect that we pay to the social order as such: it is a sort of fundamental respect, lying deeper than any conformity, that is a basic requirement of the group demanding respect for its formalities. Groups often say to you: 'But what does it cost you to dress like everyone else, show good manners and not transgress these insignificant formalities, why not allow that to the group? In exchange, the group would grant you so much, with its recognition, and so on.' I think the strategies designed to put ourselves in the right are a kind of *obsequium*, a formal recognition of the formalities.

What groups demand is always that we should conform to the forms and formalities, that is, the explicit regularities. There are people who produce form; creating form is their specific task: the writer, the poet, the aesthete, the artist and the jurist, of course. We might say that cultural production is to a large extent a production of forms. The difference, which we can all sense, between politeness of the heart and formal politeness or good manners, is the opposition between form and formlessness. Some splendid pages by Rousseau, who was ill at ease in the Parisian intellectual universe, describe this kind of conflict between sincerity – springing from the depths of the heart – and the formal, the formalism of polite Parisian society.[15] In fact, it is something really profound; it is no accident that this opposition between the formal and the formless or informal is to be found between societies as well as between classes: there are interests at stake, and people have a greater or lesser interest in respecting formalities, insofar as people quite simply don't all have the same capacities.

And in fact, respecting formalities is sometimes all the competence it takes. For example, in my study of Heidegger,[16] I have tried to show – if I may put it as simply as possible – that he formalizes a certain number of themes that were the creed from which Nazism drew its ideas. Obviously, the work of imposing form so successfully that we can read Heidegger today without realizing that it is Nazism transformed supposes a formidable specific competence: you have to have read Kant and Heraclitus; the task is tremendous. This imposition of form, which allows you to say whatever you like through these forms and elude censorship, is euphemism: it is the art of speaking in conformity with the group's requirements. The group is always grateful when we observe formalities: the flesh is weak, but in respecting formalities, we are agreeing to do all that we can to abide by the norms, and play by the rules. We show our gratitude, as opposed to the attitude that would be to spoil the game, which is the worst possible attitude, especially when practised by someone whom you can see could easily observe the formalities but doesn't want to: someone who has the necessary capital, is able to do it, but refuses. We may think of prophecy, one of whose properties, according to Max Weber, is precisely to be extraordinary and thereby to spoil the game by breaking with the legitimate forms upheld by the priesthood.[17]

This opposition between the formal and the formless, between what is objective and what is regular but lacking form, is to be found in every social space: in pre-capitalist societies and in societies like our own, where it is also to be found within every space, from the most codified – like the world of the law, for example – to the least codified, like the intellectual field.

The spontaneist position and the continuist position

This opposition is very important insofar as it corresponds to two manners of ordering the social world. There are two quite different principles of order and it seems to me that, to make a comparative sociological study of different types of society – as we constantly do unwittingly in our daily lives, and as sociologists nearly always do more or less shamefacedly – the approach that I shall adopt is not at all bad. I shall attempt to compare the different societies in the light of their manner of ensuring their duration, of governing their relation to the passing of time and to the future.

Now, without wishing to overemphasize its importance, I shall refer to something that may seem rather eccentric to you, but which I think will be meaningful for those of you who know the cultural context. We could say, if you like, that the social world is very often viewed in two diametrically opposed ways: one, a vision of the social world that I call spontaneist, instantaneist and discontinuist, seeing it as a place of permanent emergence and eruption; and the other vision seeing it as a place of constancy, reproduction, and the like. To explain, I shall quote from Durkheim's famous lecture on Montesquieu and Rousseau: 'For Hobbes, it is an act of will that gives birth to the social order and it is a constantly renewed act of will that underpins it.'[18] This statement is interesting and I recommend you read the rest of the argument. For Hobbes, according to Durkheim, the social world is a kind of continuous creation. There is a nomothete who creates, and at every moment the world is recreated.

The analogy with Descartes's continuous creation is, I think, quite valid. A distinguished authority on Descartes, Jean Wahl, said: 'Creation is continuous because duration is not.'[19] The Cartesian God must recreate the world from moment to moment because the world does not contain its own energy and principle of continuity. Leibniz, who was severely critical of physics, including Cartesian metaphysics, said: 'What is this world, and what is this God who is not capable of creating the world once and for all time?[20] He said, more or less: 'He is like an artisan who keeps having to return to the start because he wasn't able to fit in a motor, he made a world with no motor.'[21] On the subject of motion, Leibniz made a very fine observation that anticipates what Bergson said about the cinematographic vision of duration:[22] 'He (Sturm) says that motion is only the successive existence of the thing in different places.'[23] Motion is a series of static photographs where the place of things has changed: it was there, and now it is here, and the motion is only an appearance produced by the serial arrangement of instantaneous visions.

In our contemporary sociological universe, or in the social world, there are people who speak the language of this instantaneist vision whereby the world starts anew as it were from one instant to another. The ideologies of May 1968, for example, were spontaneously spontaneist: they had this idea that the world is something that we can create *ex nihilo*, that we can rebuild from scratch. Against this vision, there is the continuist vision, embodied in philosophy by Leibniz, according to which the social world, and every one of its sub-universes, or fields as I call them, has its own immanent law inscribed within it. This *lex insita*, as Leibniz called it, is at the same time a *vis insita*, which means that the field contains within it its own force its own motor, and when the field is transformed, it is *motu proprio*: it is so constituted as to engender its own future and it has therefore a sort of *conatus* – the term common to Leibniz and Spinoza – it possesses its own motive force: it does not advance at random, it has tendencies. You can find the language of tendency in Weber. Discussing the Church, he refers to the 'tendencies' of the priestly body.[24] When sociologists describe a body – which is different from a field[25] – such as the priestly or the professorial body, they must grasp these immanent laws, this tendency of beings to persevere in being, this *conatus*, this tendency to perpetuate a position that is what constitutes an agent, a group of agents, or a body of agents. Sociology must grasp these immanent tendencies. We could develop this analogy further, but I shall merely quote Leibniz, when he refers to this force as a *'lex insita'*, an 'indwelling law', a 'permanent impression'.[26] The expression 'permanent impression' is significant: it is in a way a permanent trace – in a clearly theological vision, there is a first beginning, whereas in the sociological vision there is no first beginning – a sort of inbuilt necessity which defines both the world considered in the instant and the world considered in its claim to duration.

The passage from discontinuous universes to continuous universes

The fact that I have used a philosophical reference may lead you to believe that these two visions of the world, which we might call mechanist and instantaneist as opposed to continuist and dynamist, are two ideal types or ideal models, which social science would have to choose between. Whereas, according to the societies and subspaces within a society, do we not rather find some sort of combination of these two forms?

In the first instance, I would like to say that I think it possible, without running the risk of falling back on a simplistic evolutionary schema, to describe the passage from pre-capitalist societies to capitalist societies with their immanent logic as a passage from a discontinuous Cartesian-type universe to a continuous Leibnizian-type universe. Likewise, we can describe the establishment of a field and the process of objectification that accompanies it as a move towards replacing discontinuous universes with continuous universes where social relations tend to be self-perpetuating without needing the constant intervention of the social agents. To translate this into very simple terms: one of the properties of pre-capitalist societies, at any rate those like the Kabyle society that I have described – I refer you once again to *The Logic of Practice*[27] – is to require social agents to make a permanent effort to maintain social relations. They are societies in which – like the God of Descartes who must perpetually rework his creation at every moment – social relations must constantly be refashioned anew; there are no social relations if you do not maintain them. The task of establishing social relations requires a permanent investment of effort.

I would like to immediately correct any impression of linearity I may have given: the more we move towards societies achieving a high degree of objectification in many areas, the more institutional places we find that are self-perpetuating, but even in the most rationalized societies (in Weber's sense) we will find entire zones where the work of establishing, maintaining and restoring the institution is still to be undertaken. For instance, in the economic universe, although the objectification, formalization and codification of relations will be very advanced in the major capitalist societies, family-type models are still very much alive in so-called 'paternal' small businesses, whose labour relations can only perpetuate themselves insofar as both parties maintain them through a whole lot of basically non-economic activities. Of course, one of the places where this type of non-capitalist relations is perpetuated is the household economy, where, as we know, everything depends on a whole enterprise of maintenance and care and consideration.

But although there is no linear schema, the contrast nonetheless remains valid. Relations in pre-capitalist societies require the social agent to engage in a permanent effort of maintenance; relations can only be constituted and maintained by this work of creation, of which the exchange of gifts is one example: the exchange of gifts assumes the guise of a form of continuous creation, since at every moment things could come to a stop if one of the partners so decided, which does not mean that he is not constrained by the series of gifts that has been launched.[28] When you make someone a gift, you leave him no choice. Whatever he does, he responds: if he does not respond, he gives offence, and if he does respond, he is choosing to continue. That said, the game could stop at any moment. We could describe the same process at work in the relations between masters and servants, and there is an important tradition of analysis of the difference between the domestic servant and the agricultural worker. In a very fine text, Max Weber shows how the replacement of the domestic servant by the agricultural worker is absolutely capital for the foundation of a rational economy with its formally free working men, etc.[29] The economy based on relations with domestic servants relies precisely on this type of enchanted relation, both charming and mystified, that we designate by the term 'paternalism'; economic relations can only be perpetuated here at the expense of the symbolic labour needed to mask the reality of economic relations: transforming a salary into a gift is quite an undertaking. We have only to think of a doctor's fee, or 'honorarium', and the relations between family doctors and bourgeois families, or the relations between doctors who do not charge fees, which makes a lot of work for those who have received the service, because they have to invent an honourable, that is a euphemized, manner of paying the honorarium.[30]

In very formalized societies, structures of an informal type do subsist, but they do not have the same weight, and are not dominant. Pre-capitalist societies do not have legally constituted institutions with powers of coercion, like police and prisons. They do not have constituent economic mechanisms, even for services like the construction of a house. They must therefore constantly work at creating durable relations in a universe where there is nothing to guarantee them. There are contracts, but they are very complex contracts of confidence. We need to draw on the notion of *fidēs* as explored by Benveniste in the *Dictionary of Indo-European Concepts and Society*.[31] there are economies of good faith and *fidēs*, or fidelity. As with the household economy, they are economies of confidence where everything relies on what may appear to be people's good will.

Although the basic question, which is to find how to bind someone to a long-term commitment, is faced by every society, it is resolved in different fashions. One way of committing someone to you permanently is to make them hold you dear, that is to establish relations of dependency that may be affective. An affective relation is one of the mechanisms on which household economies and politics are broadly based. Quite simply, maintaining this kind of relation supposes, on the part of the person who has no other way of exercising his power durably, a work of maintenance that may well go as far as exhausting all his energy. Duby has a luminous comment to make about this. I may be simplifying (I always hesitate when I quote someone, for I am always afraid of traducing them – not through lack of respect, quite the contrary), but I believe Duby argues that emerging from feudalism supposed that a certain number of people were freed from the effort required to maintain a symbolic capital.[32] As long as people are spending so much energy and ingenuity maintaining these complex relations, they have very little in reserve to make economic investments. Maintaining lasting economic relations is very costly: these relations – between the landlord and the sharecropper, the blacksmith and the farmer, for instance – are extremely complex and require enormous efforts of euphemism, misunderstanding, gratitude and transformation of economic debt into moral obligation. You should read Benveniste on this subject: the whole vocabulary of Indo-European institutions is ambiguous because it relates to a pre-capitalist economy where all the means of binding others are what we might call moral – that is, things are obtained only by means of moral gratitude and sentiment. Words like *fidēs* or *pretium*, that have become economic terms, were originally laden with affective and ethical connotations.

Imposing form obviously enabled a saving of energy: these ambiguous structures are formidably costly, and replacing the relation of hospitality – *philos* as Benveniste calls it[33] – with a contract of association makes life much simpler. One of the functions of the passage from regularity grounded in confidence in ethical dispositions to a rule-bound society, that is, regularity grounded in law, is to enable a considerable saving in time and energy and to establish relations that are clearly less ambiguous, more unequivocal. I should give you more detail, but I shall end the first session here.

Second session (seminar): the hit parade of the intellectuals (4)

During the break, I have been asked three good questions that seem important to me, but to avoid improvising now, I shall answer them next time. I would like in the present session to return to the analysis that I was engaged in last time, in order to conclude, and also to take the analysis of Kafka that I had started to outline further. My position involved describing the foundations of a sociology of social perception, distinguishing what is attributable to the object, on the one hand, and to the perceiving subject, on the other. I recalled that for the object, in the case of intellectuals, there were characteristic properties of the objects to be seen, that is, the propensity to be seen and well seen. Moreover – and all the more so the more we enter an institutionalized and codified universe, as I was saying just now – individuals are bearers of institutionalized signs: vestimentary signs (the green turban to show that they have been to Mecca, a moustache to show that they are men of honour as opposed to women, distinctive clothing, etc.) or titles (in many societies it is simply a proper name, which is always a family name, that is the indicator of a collectively owned symbolic capital.

In the case of intellectuals, there are things that recall pre-capitalist societies, in particular the determining role of symbolic capital, which is a very fragile capital. The Kabyle say that 'honour is like a turnip seed',[34] and we could say that intellectual reputation is just as fragile: a turnip seed is very small and round, it rolls around and slips through your fingers. Reputation and fame, and the like, are very fragile things, they are very weakly codified or objectified. You need to work at their upkeep, and when what is at stake is the reputation of an intellectual, which, given the historical definition of the intellectual, implies a political dimension: you need to maintain relations with journalists. You find yourself in a kind of pre-capitalist structure: you need to maintain lasting relations and transform them into charmed relations. Pre-capitalist societies are well aware that you need to work on maintaining relations *all the time* to be able to make use of them *from time to time*, because relations that are not maintained are of no use: if you revive them at the moment when you need them, they are exposed as interested and do not function as relations. These very simple things are important. A relation based on a contract is terribly simple. You know what payment is due on expiry, and that if you need it earlier, there is a forfeit to pay: everything is foreseen, there's no problem. Relations of the kind that have to be maintained are much more costly: you need to improvise all the time, to invent at every turn, and accidents are always possible.

To return to the markers. Intellectuals are branded products, but the markers themselves are debatable. You might think that membership of the Academy is one of the most ancient and widely acknowledged markers, although it may in some circumstances bring discredit rather than credit. But this varies over the years: there are a certain number of Academicians in the list that I read to you the other day, but, if you stop to think, it would have been unthinkable to have Academicians in a list of intellectuals fifteen years ago. Why is it possible today? I think that there are phenomena of marking, of 'labelling' as American sociologists call it:[35] cultural products bear a particular label. One of the properties of this field is to be weakly institutionalized and codified. There is no legal framework, no clearly accredited institution, outside the very important but invisible institution of the education system; this institution remains a holder of the power of canonization – here is another analogy with the Church (analogical thought linking one field to another is entirely legitimate because we need to link structure to structure and look for homologies) – even if it is a power that is only exercised *post mortem*. It is very interesting to note that, as you know, it is forbidden by law to register a thesis topic on someone who is still alive: very few statutory rules exist in intellectual and academic life, but this is one. It would be worth some research to find out when it was promulgated, why, and with what implications . . .

That said, this rule marks a break between the process of canonization *post mortem* by the education system and the process of secular canonization of living authors, which is prey, on the other hand, to much more confused and diffuse games. Whence the question of how far the anticipated canonization, of which the ranking list that I discovered the other day is one moment, prefigures or perhaps pre-shapes the canonization that the education system will perform. The answer to this question supposes some historical research. Depending on the period studied, it will not be the same, but the question itself is transhistorical: it can be raised in any field. The relations between the intellectual field and the academic field are central. The question requires us to find indicators, for example the number of academics in a ranking list established by journalist-academics. We could look up all the syllabuses of French teaching and look at the proportion of teaching devoted to living authors: it probably varies considerably from one historical period to another. That is a question we need to think about. That having been said, there are not many authorities authorized to legitimize, endowed uncontroversially with the legitimate right to legitimize, and these authorities are themselves open to criticism: the Académie française, the Académie Goncourt and the Goncourt Prize may confer more discredit than credit (depending on the person concerned . . .).

This universe of fiduciary economics is based on an economics of belief. This needs to be emphasized in order to counter the evolutionist schema that some people may have in mind. It is obvious that while the pre-capitalist economies rely on *fidēs* and belief in all their dimensions, including the most economic, the more formalized economies still harbour a considerable part of belief. A new wave of economists has at last started to realize that economics is based on belief and trust, and the like.[36] (Very often economists make a song and dance about rediscovering things that they have occluded in order to constitute their object – which does not simplify their relations with sociology . . . .) The economies that are most advanced in terms of objectification and formalization still have *fidēs* type foundations, for example the employment contract does not owe so much, nor in the same respect, to the *fidēs* as does the relation between the servant and his master, but it still owes much more to the *fidēs* than people believe. We discover it, for instance, when a whole generation starts to inaugurate an unprecedented relation to work. This becomes known as an 'allergy to work'[37] as if it were an illness: it happens quite simply that at a certain moment the social conditions of production and reproduction of the relation to work tacitly demanded by the economy – and so tacitly demanded that it is not accounted for in the economists' theory – being no longer fulfilled, a whole aspect of the economy can no longer function. We realize that in the contract of employment, as in any contract, all things are not contractual, as Durkheim said.[38] There are things implicit and unspoken.

The margin of liberty of symbolic action

To return to the properties that predispose the writer to be noticed. There is then the fact that he will be more or less marked by institutional markers. Belonging to one university institution rather than another plays a very important part in their perception, as does belonging to one publishing house rather than another. There is a kind of pre-construction through its covers of the book to be read, through what its covers signify as a sign in the space of signs. There is also the name of the author and its image in terms of his previous writings or what is known of them. There is never an innocent reading, even by the readers employed by the publishers: nobody reads a manuscript without a covering letter. Enquiring of publishers reveals that a book never arrives on its own, but is often introduced by an in-house author,[39] and moreover, when it does arrive, it is chosen in the light of a preconstructed representation by the publisher. It is the cover effect too that causes the manuscript to be sent to that publisher. The book is already preconstructed for that publisher: you don't send your manuscript to any old person (you wouldn't send a postmodern novel to Stock). So there is a sort of preconstruction of perception affecting the object.

As for the journalists, may I briefly recall some of the principles structuring their perception. I indicated their position in the space of the field of production overall: in particular, the ambiguous *metaxu* position of the cultural journalists, which is why their perception is equivocal and why they find *allodoxia* and mistaken identity to be in their interest. But I also argued that their inclination for mistaken identity enables them to produce an effect of consecration through contact. Just as we speak of 'contamination through contact' in primitive societies (two things that touch magically contaminate each other), so there is a consecration through contact: placing a minor author alongside a major one – as in the case of the preface effect – allows the major to symbolically consecrate the minor. Consequently, juxtaposing separate things in a list associates them, and since we tend to identify with the lesser, we identify with the greater by associating the lesser with the greater.

These entirely unconscious procedures are clearly at work in the inclination to produce these lists, which from the point of view of anyone who has their categories of perception properly constituted according to the real structures of the distribution of symbolic capital, display distributions that seem confused and barbarous. These lists that mingle sheep and goats may be the product of a series of more or less unconscious motivations, among them the inclination for *allodoxia,* but this cannot explain everything. In fact, we can make a guess at what would happen if the journalists let themselves go (because they are sometimes less censored, depending on the place where they publish, and do more or less express their 'personal favourites') – the consecration effect would not even operate, the list would be limited to their fellows. This is an obvious social property: we tend to like people with whom we identify. They would then tend to go for the absolute consecration of their like. I shall not give any examples, but if you want to amuse yourselves, you only need to follow the affair that I have just given you some elements of. If they let themselves go, there would be nobody on the list but people like themselves.

What holds them back is the fact that the position they hold in the field is culturally dominated, but dominant from a temporal viewpoint, through the power that their power over the press gives. But the temporal power that they wield would be null and void if they did not retain a certain cultural power, if they did not at least keep up appearances. In other words, for their cultural power to work as a symbolic power, that is as a misinterpreted and therefore acknowledged power, their judgements must appear to be legitimate. If they let their social impulses carry them away, they would lose the benefit of their acts of consecration. This is one of the reasons for these bizarre mixtures like Dumézil/Bernard-Henri Lévy.[40] Another reason is that, in order to affirm your membership of a field, you need to affirm your recognition of people recognized in the dominant section of the field in which you hold a culturally dominated position.

This leads us to a very important property of symbolic action, that it always enjoys a margin of liberty from real actions. The aim of symbolic action is to transform our principles of vision and division of the social world. It is always basically aimed at perception and categories of perception. To be effective, it must compromise with the categories of perception that it wants to transform: you cannot declare that it is night time in broad daylight. It is only in the sessions when all cats are grey that you can say: 'This one is black, this one is white.' Consequently, the fuzzier the objective structures of a social space, the better the symbolic power will be able to operate. This explains, among other things, that – as has been noted by anthropologists, ethnologists and sociologists of all periods – prophecy, which is one of the most extraordinary forms of action affecting the categories of perception, flourishes in times of crisis, precisely when the structures of the social world start to tremble. There are periods when all futures seem possible – for those of you who lived through it, it is enough to think of May 1968.[41] I referred this morning to those effects of benign continuity that are part of our ordinary, unconscious relation to the social world, this feeling that there tends to be a continuity of being, that there are probable careers and futures out there, that all is not possible, that we do not inhabit the universe of the game, where at any moment everything can change; all this can vacillate in times of crisis. We suddenly get the feeling that a host of possibilities is at hand. This terrain favours the intervention of the prophet. At moments when we have no idea what can happen, when, as the saying goes, we can't see what is round the next corner, the prophet intervenes. In pre-capitalist societies. he is a poet. In societies like our own, a politician emerges. He is no ordinary politician, he is Cohn-Bendit, he is the man who speaks when all around him are silent, who finds something to say when everyone else is struck dumb with stupefaction. I think the sociology of perception leads to a sociology of the power of perception, therefore to a political sociology that is, I think, largely a sociology of the power of perception, of the means of vision and the principles of division of the social world.

The duplication effect of symbolic power

This power over the principles of vision and division cannot operate in a vacuum. Here again, I shall offer a rather simplistic opposition, albeit to transcend it. We might say that there is a classic Marxist vision of the politician as midwife: the structures are there, and the politician consciously gives birth to these structures by stating them; this is 'awakening consciousness'.[42] The theory of classes amounts to saying that there are classes in reality that I discover. In fact, it is a Heideggerian theory of truth: I am the person who discovers the pre-existing structures and makes them exist.[43] In discovering them, I produce the effect of objectification and explanation that I mentioned just now, but this effect is only an effect of duplication of pre-existing structures. The opposite position – that I am almost inventing, but not entirely – would consist in a kind of radical and spontaneist subjectivism: I do not state what exists, but I state, and then it exists. This is political action as the magical action that says 'there are classes', 'there is a class', 'there is such and such a class', or which uses the demonstration – 'demonstration' is a formidable word – to make manifest the fact that there is a class and thereby makes it exist, makes it manifest. This leads to a completely subjectivist theory of the social world according to which there would be no classes other than those that people believe in, or persuade other people to believe in, so as to be recognized as credible when they say that they exist, or, even more crudely, when they say that they *are* the class.

The truth is not a compromise, but I set out these polar positions because they often correspond to political positions – this is yet another of the problems of sociology. This means that they become mental structures that are incorporated and entirely unconscious and continue to function in our scientific studies. It is for this reason that we must cast them out. As faith healers cast out evil, I have just cast them out without caricaturing them too severely (I would even say that I showed them in a good light and that they are actually less attractive . . . [*laughter*], whereas this morning, when I established the two oppositions in those terms, I did rather caricature them . . .). These two oppositions mask a crucial problem: what are the limits within which this power of perception can operate? Within what real limits can you say whatever you like and do whatever you like by stating it? Is it an absolute power?

Interestingly, we could say that the most important symbolic power is to say what really exists, for that changes everything. There is a poem by Ponge, 'You teach the fish how to swim'.[44] Many social activities, particularly educational ones, consist in teaching fish how to swim: we teach things that are only learnt by those who know them already, then we consecrate as being learned those who seem to have learnt. The consecration effect is a formidable and most important effect: to say that the Catholic Church consecrates the Christian family is not insignificant. Sociologists have debated whether it is the Catholic Church that sustains the Catholic family or the Catholic family that sustains the Catholic Church.[45] I could give you a bibliography with a thousand references. Much of the empirical literature seeks to disentangle cause and effect, but we are faced with a consecration effect whose characteristic is precisely to be invisible. You can delve as deep as you like, you will never manage to isolate the consecration effect from the previous effect, and obviously the consecration effect is all the more effective if it seems to merely affirm something that would have happened in any case. It is like the lad in *Jean Christophe* who wants to believe that he is all-powerful and tells the clouds to 'go to the right' when they are moving towards the right and 'go to the left' when they are moving towards the left.[46] A part of political action is of this kind. A great politician – albeit perhaps rather a right-wing one – is someone who can say 'I am telling you the facts'. He can make people believe that he is the efficient cause of something over which he will impose a symbolic efficiency that is not negligible and that is very difficult to define – as you see, I hesitate, I don't quite know how to define it, but it is already important just to name it.

Many social actions, particularly rites of institution, are of this kind: I call 'rites of institution' this kind of rite of passage.[47] They consist in telling a boy that he is a boy, and that changes everything, because the boy believes he is a boy, because the girls believe that he is a boy, and so on. It is a whole moral system. Then you have to make every effort to rise to the heights of your socially constituted definition. When you are told: 'You are a *normalien*', 'You are a *polytechnicien*', 'You are an idiot', 'You are an imbecile', 'You are illiterate', these are purely symbolic acts of repetition, where the problem that I have just raised is not questioned, because I am 'teaching fish how to swim'. But we need to think about the interest of the symbolic activity and ask who benefits from it: it is clear that the interest is conservative. If we find that the world is fine in its present state, it is best to give the impression that it is as we intended; it is even better because it is intentional.

The specificity of symbolic action

But the problem of symbolic action arises in dramatic form when we want to resist it: what freedom of manoeuvre do we have in such a case, where we can try to measure the specific efficiency of the symbolic, since we are attempting to produce a different effect? It is very difficult to explain, and I have started with the least obvious because it is the symbolic action of the very type that I have named that is the most difficult to see. It goes unnoticed by definition because it duplicates something that would exist in any case. We might think that it has no purpose, but this is not at all true. We can see this from the vast literature on the Catholic family and the Church: is the Church's family policy responsible for the size of the family or the inverse? The second case [resisting symbolic action] is much easier: the problem appears much more clearly but the empirical measurements and the description of its limits are not so evident.

I think political action has a mission to transform the social world by transforming the perception of the social world that goes to make up this world, insofar as, on the one hand, a large part of this world comprises objectified perception – as with the law, for instance – and, on the other hand, agents act in this world according to the perception that they have of it. One of the only means that we can resort to when we want to change the social world rather than conserve it – this morning I was placing myself in the logic of conservation – is to try to transform people's perception of it. How can we change a perception that is objectified, canonized and consecrated – the law, for instance, is an upright, straight and orthodox vision – and an incorporated vision, that is, the principles of vision and the categories of perception? I am speaking very generally, but the very minor case that I have taken as my pretext does illustrate my argument perfectly well.

Of course we can always persist in trying to say whatever we like, with the likelihood that people will listen varying according to the state of the social world. If we inhabit a Leibnizian type of world where the drive to self-perpetuate is very strong and immanent tendencies are very strongly felt, we know what the future will bring, and saying any old thing is sheer madness. Saying whatever you like has more chance of being listened to in situations where this type of order is in crisis, or in a society where such talk meets social structures that are less self-perpetuating and less stable. This seems to me to explain many things, even if I am saying too much or too little because this is not my main concern. In the case of a normal order, we can think of the problem raised by Kuhn for a scientific universe:[48] what is a scientific revolution? If you say whatever you like, you will be burnt. This has happened historically. There are even discoveries that were not perceived as such and that were discovered as discoveries 150 years afterwards. This means that the person who made the discovery was treated as mad or not even noticed: the categories of perception to perceive him were lacking.

The likelihood of a purely political action successfully transforming our categories of perception depends on a host of objective variables, but in any case someone who transforms objectified visions and objectified forms of perception (for example, the person, like the poet in some societies, who says that we need peace when people are tearing each other apart), the person who changes our vision, and changes our actions by changing that vision, must square the circle: he must use what he is fighting against in order to fight it, therefore he must be familiar with it. This is why the great transformers are masters: transformation supposes mastery of what they are seeking to transform. In a pre-capitalist society, for example, the way the transformer negotiates will be to use the structures that generate what he wants to fight in his fight against it: he will use a point of honour to fight against a dispute over honour, he will appeal to the values of ancestry: 'You are a Somebody, son of Somebody, son of Somebody, as we all know, and it is in the name of this fact that I appeal to you: you are big enough to grant yourself what would seem dishonourable to someone else.' You will see that these are very general models. If I say that Isidore Isou[49] is the greatest contemporary poet, I will find it difficult to get anyone to agree: it will show that I am out of touch, or otherwise that I am very perverse, but that will depend on my position in the very structures that I want to transform. This is another law: the higher up I am in the structures, the more able I am to transform the structures, but . . . the less likely I am to want to! [*Laughter*] This is not a joke, but a law to verify, and that is the paradox of the scientific field: to accomplish a great scientific revolution today, you need to have a large scientific capital.[50] In other words, the revolution tends to be the monopoly of the capitalists, it is not within everyone's grasp. This is one of the properties of highly objectified and highly formalized fields.

In the present case of the hit parade of the intellectuals that we see before our eyes, the problem is to know whether I have enough credit to transform the structure of the distribution of credit. If I act in all ignorance, that is, without knowing the structure of this distribution of credit and my position in the structure – which are two important things – I may say something that I believe but which sounds ridiculous. Second, if I do not know my position, I will not know my margin of manoeuvre. To play the game well, a cultural journalist, for example, must know his status. His status may be quite decent, but remain middling, his authority only recognized by those who do not know him. You need to have a realistic view that is not theoretical. This is what I call a sense of placing, to use a metaphor from sport. The sense of placing is what leads you to the spot where the ball is going to land, while the clumsy person is still at the spot where the ball was aimed or where it looked likely to land. The sense of placing is the fact of knowing where you are and knowing your margin of manoeuvre, your latitude of error and the degree of tolerance of your heresy conceded to someone in your position, the threshold between 'he is mad' and 'he is eccentric'. These are absolutely fundamental things, almost everyday currency. The sense of placing then reveals a certain number of limits. It also supposes a knowledge of the real structure of the distribution of symbolic capital: to know where I stand in the structure, I have to know the structure, at least in practice, and often I only know the structure by sensing my position. When we draw up the theory of a field, we must construct what we call the 'structure of the distribution of symbolic capital', and it is often a considerable task: you have to find indicators, calculate indices and aggregate them, and what you produce is a sort of artefact that does not correspond to real people, but which results from a process of codification of the same order as that undertaken by jurists.[51] That having been said, this structure is not merely theoretical; people have a sort of intuitive mastery: someone who has a good intuition of their place in the field, of what they can allow themselves and what they can't, so to speak, has a kind of rough feeling or practical alternative for the whole of its structure.

Thinking of what I was saying this morning, it would of course be a monstrous error to transform this practical alternative into a theoretical mastery, to situate in people's minds the theoretical construction that we are obliged to produce through instruments like statistics. Symbolic action and political action are limited by people's practical mastery of the structure, the position that they occupy, the liberties that they can take with the structure, exploiting its marginal gaps, weak points and vague areas. The link between objective and subjective that I distinguished for the purposes of explanation will now appear: a mixed enterprise like that achieved by this hit parade is only possible if there are foundations *in rei – cum fundamento in re*, as the scholastics said. It is a typical Durkheimian expression: for certain symbolic actions[52] to be thinkable and possible, they need to have an objective likelihood of success, and a foundation in reality. They exercise an effect of consecration by accentuating or reinforcing something that was made possible by objective properties. Consequently, if the French intellectual field – at the point in the 1980s that we are considering – did not enjoy a relation with the field of journalism allowing journalism to present itself as judge of intellectual works, I think that such a hit parade would not exist. If it does exist, it is because it is given the objective chance to do so, which does not mean that its appearance as an expression of symbolic will power adds nothing to this objective chance. This is the reason why the famous question 'if Napoleon had not existed . . .' is naive. It still often haunts historical discussions and it is resolved by saying that 'the glass is half full or half empty', with a kind of stupid common sense that liquidates the real problems. This is a very real problem, material to all human action, and political action does no more than bring it to a climax. The aim to transform a situation through action supposes an unconscious appreciation of opportunity, and I think the aim to transform things correlates with the likelihood of success of the operation – while there are other variables concerning the dispositions of the person appreciating the situation. Which does not mean that this aim does not help to accelerate and reinforce the transformation; the symbolic has its own efficiency.

To return to the problem of classes that I mentioned before (but more rigorously and didactically now): I set up two positions, one spontaneist, the other determinist. The problem is of the same order: if you say, 'Bosses and workers of all lands, you are united, unite!', I don't know whether you would feel very motivated. You can always say whatever you like, but the likelihood of a discourse on the social world becoming socially effective are proportionate to its objective nature, that is, the nature of the relation that it enjoys with the objective reality on which it wishes to act, and in an extreme case, it consecrates. If I say, 'You must be what you are, be yourself!', I have 100 per cent success rate – and this does not mean that I am doing nothing. If I say, 'Change your life, have a radical *metanoia*, die a death, develop and become someone other!', it is very different. Totalitarian institutions accomplish social actions of this type: such as entry into the convent. I refer you to Goffman's *Asylums*, which is an absolutely crucial book, one of the founding texts of sociology. Total institutions in some cases say, 'You must change from top to bottom', which supposes very special conditions: the concentration camp, the barracks or the convent, for instance. Political action – thank God! – is not always able to summon the very special conditions required to produce the new man.

Political prediction

Political action lies somewhere between these polar opposites. It is a negotiation with the probable. I have, after a fashion, described the impulses of people, starting from a description of their position. I have shown what they would like to see and what they would like to say. But there are limits to what they can say if they want to be effective and credible, which are more or less the same thing: they need to preserve their symbolic capital, which for a journalist amounts essentially to being credible, to being considered worthy of being believed. If I say the first thing that comes to mind, I lose credit – there you have a word both pre-capitalist and capitalist: 'credit'. If they want to preserve their credit, there are limits, so to speak. They are incorporated limits. They may also be limits of a legal kind, but only in certain cases, for example where there is a professional deontology. If we issue a decree stating, for instance, that a journalist may not say that Lévi-Strauss and Bernard-Henri Lévy are exactly the same, this changes everything, such an act becomes a transgression of the rule. But in a universe with no rules, the only limits are incorporated limits. I keep returning to this argument because I believe that its importance goes beyond this particular case.

I shall give just one example, which I shall not develop because it would take too long: the particular status of prediction in politics.[53] If you think about it, you will find a whole lot of things: prediction doesn't have anything like the same status in politics as it does in science. That doesn't mean that there isn't prediction in the social sciences: you can predict, but prediction is a political act even in the case of a scientific prediction. If I say: 'This is bound to happen', it is the *fatum* effect. If I say: 'I'm sure that So-and so is the greatest, just wait and see', I already have a line on the graph that shows him rising. The prediction effect is a political move, and in societies where social science (or, to put it more modestly, the idea of a social science) exists, prediction becomes an absolutely crucial issue. Social science, whether we like it or not is a political science: even the most neutral statements (such as 'Cultural capital is attracted to cultural capital') are predisposed to function as predictions (for example designed to demobilize: 'There is nothing to be done, since it's a given law'). In any case, prediction is one of the most common strategies. It remains the case that there are different forms of prediction. If, for example, I am a politician, I can say: 'I predict that on 1 May there will be a demonstration at the Bastille', or 'France will be forced to leave the currency snake'[54] because I have the power to make it happen. But in the name of what authority do I say it? Am I not helping to make the prediction come true? This is a very complex problem, but you may see it as a good way of considering the true status of the social sciences. Popper had some very interesting things to say about it,[55] but I think we can go still further. If you find that fun, I can say more about it, but today I would like to briefly outline one last point.

Those people who designed the hit parade of the intellectuals were accomplishing a political strategy – I intend to use the word 'political' in its widest sense: any action aiming to transform our categories of perception, etc., is political. They have accomplished this political action by imposing a vision charged with a principle of vision, and they have imposed this vision in the shape of a list that is a classification implying a principle of classification – any division implies a *principium divisionis*, as the Ancients said.

(A parenthesis here: among the more subtle principles that these people have imposed is the principle of 'mixture'. At the same time, a whole epistemology of mixture is developed and affirmed. It is a negation of the break between science and non-science, the scholarly and the non-scholarly, the historical history of the historians and our own common-or-garden history. Moreover, the person who develops the epistemology of the mixture is very well placed in the classification we are considering[56] – which makes us pause to reflect, and I am not saying this for a laugh.)

They have imposed constituent principles of vision, a class list, a code in two senses: a linguistic and a legal code – a code is also something that enables you to discriminate, to separate and to distinguish between sounds. They have imposed a code and exerted the social force that jurists call *vis formae*.[57] It is the force of form. Form exerts its own kind of force as form, as something formally constituted, in opposition to the formless. The formless is what is indifferent and undifferentiated: you can say whatever you like, that 'at night all cats are grey', whereas form has contours. It is opposed to content. It is designated, distinguished and framed, for instance. This constituent form is itself linked to a constituent body that decides what is the right form: 'This is what you should see', 'This is the Gestalt', 'Here you think that A is different from B, but it is not true, they are all of a piece, and you think that he is like C, whereas he is not, he is different.' They have created a kind of legal effect, an effect of objectification, codification, clarification and rationalization. I shall analyse this effect elsewhere and this is why I chose this example.

Just one final point: the deepest secret revealed by this game is that it required a social universe in order to exist. In fact, what I would like to communicate through this series of lectures is the permanent need for a sociological metadiscourse. As I say this, I have my doubts – it is in any case the way that I experience things; I don't know if I have the right to universalize. But for me, in my experience, I think that what we normally call epistemology, meaning a discussion of discourse, is in general engaged in by people who have no idea of the science that they discuss. This leads them to make *ex post* codifications, without really knowing the fundamental legislation, and they invent a law with no object and above all with no subject. I cannot say that I appreciate this epistemology. At the same time, my experience is that in scientific practice, people never reflect enough on what they are in the process of doing. I am not saying anything brilliant here, Saussure said it much better: 'We need to know what the linguist is doing.'[58] We can never question ourselves too much about what we are doing. For example, in the case of the ranking list, I had the impression that I had finished my little exposition, but at the last moment I said to myself: 'Hang on! There is something else that matters: what this game reveals about the space in which it is played.' In other words, what must the social space, the intellectual field and the place of journalism in the intellectual field be for an action of this type to be possible, and for my investigation of this game and my report of my study to be possible without spoiling the game.

For me, this is a habitual way of thinking that makes for good scientific practice in the social sciences. But is it specific to the social sciences, or is it true of all science, with the difference that scholars fail to mention it, or if they do mention it, do people fail to listen? I leave the question open. In any case this type of reflection seems to me to be absolutely constituent: it is not in my opinion a luxury inherited by a nostalgic philosopher; it plays a vital part in making scientific choices of samples and parameters. It is a crucial foundation of the whole scientific enterprise.

Lecture of 22 March 1984

First session (lecture): responses to questions. – Interest in the wider sense. – Is the subfield a simple change of scale? – Is business a field? – The field as subject of social actions.
Second session (seminar); Kafka's The Trial. *– The Trial and the search for identity. – Recognition in weakly objectified fields.*

First session (lecture): responses to questions

First of all, I would like to thank those of you who have sent me questions: this contact is very important for me because I sometimes have doubts about whether what I have to say is communicable. In fact, you give me very pleasant proof that I have been understood much better than I thought. As what I have to say is often complex and I may not always have all my wits about me (there may be stage fright in some situations), I tend to feel that I have not always said what I wanted to.

Now for the questions: the first deals with the notion of interest, the second with the notion of the subfield and the third with business firms. I will try to answer these three questions succinctly. They seem important to me, and they may enable me to nuance or complete some parts of my argument.

On the first point, the notion of interest, I expounded my views last year,[1] but I constantly need to return to this issue because it is a notion that causes misunderstandings, to a great extent because most people who use the term do so in an ahistorical way, lacking the historical culture that you should have in order to know what you are talking about when you pronounce the word 'interest'. On the history of the concept of interest, you can for example read Albert Hirschman's book, *The Passions and the Interests.*[2] Hirschman studies the social genesis of the concept of interest as used by economists.

In the sense that I use it, the notion of interest does not have the restricted sense that history, through the evolution of the social world and the constitution of the economic space as an autonomous space, having its own laws, has gradually conferred on it. The development of this notion is historically linked to the process of differentiation between social universes which leads to the constitution of those separate social spaces that I call fields, and one thing that I would like to talk about today is the kind of historical process whereby separate universes are gradually composed.

Among these universes there is one that we tend to treat as the alpha and the omega: the economic universe, where people say: 'Business is business.' (The fact that it has to be stated means that it is not self-evident: tautologies are always very significant, they are acts of constitution and affirmation. Saying 'This is what this is', 'This is your sister', 'Business is business' – or 'There is no place for feelings in business', which simply develops the tautology – is to establish, through an act of constitution, a universe within which certain things will come into play, and come into play in a certain way.) This law of interest has a history: it is linked to the existence of spaces where, as Weber splendidly says, it is no longer family relations that provide the model for economic relations, but economic relations that tend to provide the model for all relations, including relations of kinship.[3] This universe, which we all swim in, and which is so self-evident that we do not see the axiom that governs its functioning, therefore has nothing universal to it.

This is why the notion of interest gives rise to some misunderstanding: when I say 'interest', I use the word in the sense of a universe of interests relating to the universe of social universes, but people immediately read it in Bentham's limited, utilitarian, economic sense. Economists then rush to say that we are adopting an economic model, without seeing the absurdity that lies at the heart of their unconscious universalization of the economic model. This is very important, in relation to the current debate surrounding the economics of interest, which is what the member of the audience here has referred to. Carried away by the hubris of a dominant science, economists take it upon themselves to apply one particular axiomatic based on one particular social universe to absolutely everything. I am thinking, for example, of a form of the economy of interest that is in fact most interesting as an example of teratology: Gary Becker's work on marriage.[4] In complete ignorance of the topic and its context, including work by anthropologists on kinship, this distinguished economist launches into a model of marriage considered as a kind of economic enterprise. It is true that marriage is, among other things, an economic enterprise, but only in forms more or less strongly denied depending on the society.

The word interest is polysemic and you might well wonder why I use it if it is so ambiguous. The first reason is that we cannot keep on inventing new words (I am already reproached severely enough with doing this, being told for example that it would be so much simpler to talk of 'habit' rather than the 'habitus', whereas the 'habitus' has nothing to do with 'habit'). Then again, concepts sometimes have a polemical function – in Bachelard's terms,[5] which has nothing to do with ordinary polemics – and the concept of interest is thus extremely useful when applied to universes whose logic is apparently one of disinterest. There is, for example, an interest specific to political delegates.[6] As they exist in a universe where agents are inclined to think of themselves as disinterested, devoted militants, saying that they have specific interests as delegates (to read me correctly, please note that I always say 'specific interests' because these are interests linked to a particular universe) is to lend this concept a critical charge and to recall that here, as elsewhere, there are interests at work. Each of the fields described by sociological analysis has its own interests, and paradoxically there do exist universes where people can be interested in being disinterested, 'disinterested' being implicitly defined as relating to economic interests. For instance, to write pure poetry today, you must be totally 'disinterested' in the sense that a banker would use the term. Using the concept of interest in this way is to use it as the means of a break, as concepts are so often used.

In addition, we should note a distressing tradition of scientific communication in France where people do not bother to understand: they prefer to criticize first. (I am not a fan of national characteristics, but some historical traditions do relate to objectified social forms and in France these historical traditions are clearly detrimental to scientific communication: what we call 'criticism' is often a very naive defence of the specific interests of the critic who is more concerned to draw attention to his opinion and reputation than to understand what he is criticizing.) The notion of interest is thus very risky, but I think science sometimes requires us to use risky and vulnerable concepts, because they enable us to make progress, even through the criticism and shock that they provoke, or the fact that they provide rods to beat us with. Using risky concepts is particularly risky in a country that prefers to avoid taking risks and finds comfort and reassurance in a certain kind of superficial overview of the work of others. Interest in the sense that I use the term always runs the risk of seeming to espouse a utilitarian vision, and there is a danger of forgetting that the notion of interest as used by economists is only one particular instance, a historical creation, an institution ultimately associated with the invention of economic fields whose ruling principle is interest as such, interest in its own right.

If you had understood this already, excuse me for insisting, but this notion of something 'as such', 'in its own right' is correlative with the notion of the field. A field is a place in which certain things are done in their own right, as of right, *'als'* to use a word renowned among philosophers, who do for once have something important to say.[7] The economic field is a place where people will act in conformity with interest in its own right, in conformity with calculations of interest considered as such, rather than repressed, denied or shamefully assumed – as in the exchange of gifts. We can describe the exchange of gifts as a kind of credit, but it is a credit that is denied, in the Freudian sense of denial: it does not accept itself, it is not accepted as such by its own author and it is not recognized as such by onlookers. The existence of an economic field and economic contracts, or the existence of what Weber calls a rational law linked to economic practices, supposes, on the one hand, agents able and inclined to establish an economics as such in its own right, and, on the other, a social game where they can manifest themselves overtly as calculators: the accredited agent may officially claim to have interested objectives, which, in many societies, and even in many of the universes that make up our societies, would be enough to lead to his downfall. If you think of the exchange of gifts, it is obvious that to say 'I am inviting you so that you will be obliged to invite me back' or 'I am making you a gift so that you will use your contacts to help me . . .' would destroy the whole point of the action. Some exchanges are repressed economic exchanges. Saying this does not mean that they are only economic. In fact, it is the denial that is important: objectively, they are economic exchanges, but they do not function like economic exchanges, they achieve their ends – for example protection, reward or profit – only by denying them, which sometimes requires conviction, because for denial to succeed, you have to experience it as such – 'you'd better believe it', as the saying goes. These economic actions succeed only as long as their economic aspect is denied both subjectively and objectively, and this obviously changes everything. Interest as operated by societies that are rational (for Weber) or capitalist (for Marx), that is, calculating societies where economics is established as an autonomous field with its own laws, is one particular case in a universe of possible interests, within which may be found scientific, literary, political or charitable interest, among others. We might for example look at the economics of charity and ask a series of questions: why should people volunteer? Why do welfare and charity exist? In my logic, we shall postulate that there is a particular type of interest, which may be an inverted form of what we take to be an ordinary form of interest, the one that governs the economy.

But this 'ordinary' logic governs the economy only up to a certain point, and one of the advantages of my own analysis is to reveal how even the economic world established as such is far from functioning according to interest in Bentham's restricted definition.[8] I refer you to my article on employers:[9] even in those relations most subject to rational economic calculation, involving *homo economicus* par excellence (I doubt if there is any *homo* more *economicus* than a banker), we find that, even in taking economic decisions, there are relations that have nothing to do with economics in the strictest sense of the term. The kind of generalization of the notion of interest that I activate when I use the word is therefore most helpful for understanding not only the forms of interest lying outside the limited concept of interest as defined by economics, but also for understanding the specific logic of the economy, which is not as interested, in the strict sense, as people outside those circles like to claim, which happens when intellectuals comment on economics.

To sum up, briefly: interest in the sense used by economists is a special case. It is a historical creation linked to a particular space in which economic interest is established as such, in opposition to feelings and to family-based models such as matriarchy, patriarchy or brotherhood, for instance. It is nearly always these social models that govern pre-capitalist economics. In these societies, the kinship model extends beyond the limits of the family and, up to a point, even affects the market too. For example, you don't buy an ox from just anyone: if you can buy it from a brother it is great, but from a cousin it is already slightly less good; you always look for a relative as a guarantor. There are still societies where you wouldn't buy an airline ticket without involving your cousin (I am exaggerating slightly . . .). In short, the universal model of economic calculation is not as universal as all that and it has not established a very sure footing in our societies: as soon as a slightly risky purchase looms, we look for guarantors and we try to transform a brutal, anonymous, impersonal relation, based on calculation alone, into a familiar, family relation, into a model we can control. This interest in the strictest sense is therefore only one particular historical institution, which was not born overnight. It is never finished, it always incomplete; it is never universal and it depends on the establishment of an objective space within which the appropriate rules of behaviour pertain.

Interest in the wider sense

The notion as I use it is obviously more general and it establishes economic interest as only one special case. In very general terms, I use it to imply that we do not act without a reason, which is a way of importing into sociology from philosophy the famous principle of sufficient reason:[10] we act when it is in our interest to act. You may say that this is as tautologous as the soporific quality of opium.[11] We may know it already, but this is not a reason not to say it: we act when it is in our interest to act, and action supposes a form of investment – which is already a synonym for 'interest' – in the economic but also in the psychoanalytic sense. (It happens that an accident of translation makes the same word mean both things in French,[12] and we should not draw universal conclusions, but in this particular case, I think it is valid. Interest is a form of investment in the game, and another synonym I could give is *illusio*. A field is a game and the *illusio* is the fact of being caught up in the game and investing in it: the etymology is suspect, but no matter.[13] The word is interesting because it reminds us that the *illusio* is an illusion that is valid only for someone who is involved: anyone who is not involved would see no interest in it. Interviews show this clearly: if, taking two extremes, you get an avant-garde poet to evaluate the game of the banker, it is likely that he will be very struck by the illusory character of the investment in the game, and vice versa. In other words, other people's games seem to us to have no interest. For there to be a game, in the full sense of the term, there has to be not only a game, that is a space of probabilities, a place where probable regularities are engendered, probabilities of a specific type of gain; it also requires people ready to take part in the game to play and be caught up in the game.

But is it the game that produces the *illusio*? Are games able to produce the desire to play, or do people have to be predisposed to take part in the game in order to take part in it? This is one of the big questions posed by the notion of the field: does being predisposed help your entry into the literary field? One aspect of professional heredity – as rather simplistic sociologists call it – is that you are caught up in the game before you have started to take part: you have inherited, essentially from your family, belief in the game, the inclination to invest in the game, as an economist would say. This is very important for understanding the economic game itself: to go down the mine is not an innate tendency, but it exists as an inclination under certain conditions at certain times. Today a certain number of social activities, like the workings of the education system, conceal various obstacles to the reproduction of the inclination to invest and this is called an 'allergy to work',[14] which is absolutely meaningless – that really is a soporific platitude.

This is extremely important because economists believe that economics provides its own foundations. Yet we may query whether the belief underlying so many games is not also the foundation of economics; which does not mean that the economy is not determining, but if it is going to determine, you need people determined to let themselves be determined by its determinations [*laughter*]. I don't think these games are simple. You can always withdraw: monasticism, for instance, is ultimately a rejection of the *illusio*, of investment; it is a flight into 'otherworldly asceticism'. Weber says that, at the beginnings of the capitalist economy, there is this historical invention linked to capitalism, which 'is asceticism within the world'.[15] He does not say that 'worldly asceticism' is the determining principle of the economy, but that capitalism owes its specific form to the fact that people made this kind of investment.

You might in fact say that interest = expectation. Getting caught up in the game does in fact mean expecting to get something out of the game. But then do those who have nothing to gain from the game have any chance of getting involved in the game? The question is important: to get involved in the game, don't you need to have at least some chance of success? You can see that it is not so simple, it is not a matter of radical subjectivity: the relation to economics of a subproletarian, who has nothing much to hope for from the economic game, is less than magical.

'Investment', 'expectation', 'hoping to gain', 'inclination to invest', and investment in the widest sense, including the psychological: these are the synonyms of 'interest'. Obviously, there will be as many interests as there are fields, as many forms of interest as there are games, and one man's interest will be another's disinterest. 'Interest' in this very general sense is of course the opposite of 'disinterest', but there will be as many disinterests as there are interests, since in each case the disinterest will be the category complementary to what is defined as 'interest'. Thus the concept turns to dust and, ultimately, interest is non-indifference. Here we touch on something important: non-indifference implies the capacity and inclination to make distinctions. When we say: 'I don't mind', 'I see no difference' or 'That's of no interest', we see quite clearly that this *illusio* is fundamental; it is the desire to play, and at the same time the capacity to play, to discern profit, for example. Anyone who lacks the *principium divisionis*, the principle of vision and division, sees no interest in the game because he doesn't detect the profits. Think of the problem of the diffusion of culture: today cultural politics postulates that culture is something universal that only has to be offered for it immediately to become an object of concupiscence, but what the prophets of cultural diffusion forget is that the inclination to invest in it is proportionate to the inclination to see the game. When you see only smoke, and no interest, when you don't see the difference, you are disinterested in a very special sense: you are indifferent – 'you have nothing to do with it', so to speak.[16] In the last analysis, you might say that interest is that kind of very general disposition that we could define as the capacity and inclination to draw significant distinctions. Obviously, the inclination exists only if the capacity is there: if I see only smoke, if all things are equal and everything looks the same, I am not going to invest in the undifferentiated universe. The principle that enables us to draw distinctions, engage in *diacrisis* and differentiate things, is itself adaptable, and works in a space only if it makes pertinent differences, those that really divide up the space.

To return to what I was saying last time: if in order to differentiate between intellectuals, we use success in an economic enterprise as our criterion, we will say that the victor is the one who sold 500,000 copies, and the greatest French intellectual is Alain Peyrefitte.[17] But this principle of differentiation is not pertinent from the point of view of those who are involved in the game. With this principle, we produce differences, but they are not the right ones, they are not *cum fundamento in re*, they do not correspond to the thing itself.

We can give another synonym: the notion of 'taste' is an interest. Taste is at once the capacity and the inclination to discriminate, and it may be applied to all sorts of objects: the dictionary will give 'have a taste for women', 'have a taste for literature', etc. In every case it is about discrimination and inclination, the two being correlated.

Another synonym – which may catch you unawares – would be the 'libido', in the sense of the *libido sciendi* (I don't say 'desire' because it is all too fashionable,[18] but I could use it as long as I endowed it with a meaning that it is rarely given). Obviously in both cases this *libido* is socially constructed, even if its foundations are infra-social. I don't mean that the *libido* discussed by Freud is a social product, but that it is always affected by the social, so that it has very little to do with what it was before the social got to work on it. The *libido sciendi* is one way of designating the specific interest of the scholar, which, from a banker's point of view, seems not very interesting.

One final synonym would be 'passion'. Although this may surprise you, I shall read you a well-known passage from Hegel:

> We assert then that nothing has been accomplished without interest on the part of the actors; and – if interest be called passion, inasmuch as the whole individuality, to the neglect of all other actual or possible interests and claims, is devoted to an object with every fibre of volition concentrating all its desires and powers upon it – we may affirm absolutely that nothing great in the world has been accomplished without passion.[19]

Since people know the end of this quotation, but not the beginning, they discuss this statement of the passions at cross purposes. In fact, the sense in context here is that 'passion' is a form of total investment, which contributes an idea that I had not given (as philosophers tend to do): why should the investment necessarily be total? One of the questions that we need to test empirically will be asking what the degree of investment is. Is there a relation between the objective investment and the objective chances? That was my first question in sociology. Does the inclination to invest, as postulated by the economists, and being persistent in doing so, depend on whether the economic conditions offer opportunities? Might I not be the more inclined to invest the greater my chances of success? Below a certain threshold, might I not be an investor at all? In other words, might there not be economic conditions, however neglected by economists, needed for economic investment? These are questions that the notion of interest confronts us with.[20]

Is the subfield a simple change of scale?

Now for the second question. It turns on the notion of subfield that I looked at rapidly last time: 'Why talk of a subfield? What are the criteria of discrimination? Does the term "sub-" indicate subordination to a field that would be defined by a certain number of effects – which is a very important question that I did not consider at all?' I shall try to be fairly brief, although there is much to say and it all follows on logically from what I have been saying. We can first of all take a subjectivist definition of the notion of field and subfield. Depending on his dispositions or opportunities, a social scientist could constitute as a field the whole of the field of cultural production and assemble all the people who produce things symbolic: the Church (if you say 'fields of cultural production', nine people out of ten will think of the Church), journalism, the press, education, and the like. It can be very interesting to construct the field of cultural production with its particular properties in this way. At another time we might take the Church on its own and consider it as a field or, within the Church, take the field of the episcopate or the field of theology. This leads us to say that it is a *constructum* and that there is something arbitrary about it, since the size of a space depends on the level of analysis adopted by the researcher.

I think this response is useful in the first instance, but quite inadequate. In the case of the literary field, the one that I have reflected on the most, it is possible to study the literary field, but we can also move down to the level of genre to study the field of the theatre, or move further down and consider the field of the *théâtre de boulevard*. Does this mean that we move from a field to a subfield through a simple change of scale? This metaphor of the change of scale is one of the most sinister in the social sciences. It underlies all the oppositions between the macro and the micro that I find economists manipulating indiscriminately[21] – but since I don't have the legitimate authority to pronounce on this terrain, I shall say no more – and sociologists transposing onto the terrain of sociology, in general to create scientific or scientistic effects. They say: 'macro/micro', 'change of scale', 'we construct it differently', etc, and we get a sort of micro-positivist, relativist philosophy. My notion of the field is defined in opposition to this manner of thinking, and the field is not something to be constructed *ad libitum*: thinking in terms of the field obliges us to raise the question of the limits of the field, and to do so in empirical terms. We need to use as principles of research those that I have indicated: the field stops at the point where here are no more effects to be observed. Starting out from general questions open to empirical verification or falsification, we set our task as looking for the boundaries of a field. We are not going to work in the dark by simply carving things up. We are not going to draw arrows on the board. If sociology conducted in terms of the field may draw up schemas, its lines are question-marks: how far does the field extend? Is the line continuous or discontinuous? Is it the fringe of a cloud or a precisely and juridically traced frontier (I have already discussed that)?

Then again, the question of subordination raised by someone in the audience is important because it adds a point to my argument: to speak of a subfield is to suppose that the field enclosing it dominates the field enclosed. This raises empirical questions. I could say for example that the theatre is a subfield of the literary field if we observe effects in the theatre that we cannot explain without drawing on the literary field in its ensemble: for instance, the position of the theatre in the hierarchy of genres. In fact, the problems of hierarchy among the disciplines, genres and styles (I constantly refer to these, and discussed them in last year's lectures),[22] can only be treated in terms of the logic of the field and the subfield, while remembering that a subfield is a space relatively independent of the space enclosing it, this relative autonomy being contained within the limits of the effects that the surrounding field exercises on the field that it surrounds.

Here is a very precise example: in my first studies of the intellectual field, I was inclined, through an inevitable intellectual-centrism, to think of that field as relatively autonomous, and, following the traditional literary-historical model, I did not look for the source of its heteronomy anywhere other than in the wider social space enclosing it. So it was an important discovery for me to see that one part of the properties of the intellectual field derived from the dominated position of the intellectual field in what I call the field of power, which is commonly called the dominant class. Thus there are properties in the intellectual field that we cannot understand if we look only at the intellectual field. We could look at the intellectual field, or *a fortiori* an intellectual like Flaubert, for thousands of years, but there are things we will never understand if – like Sartre[23] – we fail to see that he held a dominated position in the field of power. Subordination manifests itself in visible effects like the intellectual/bourgeois relation, as traditionally portrayed in nineteenth-century literature, with its symbolic denunciation of the bourgeois and the ambivalent fascination felt by the artist for the bourgeois. These are effects that we note in the intellectual field but which don't have their source there, even if these effects are retranslated through the logic of the intellectual field – otherwise you could ask me why we should speak of the intellectual field. This is what is implied by the notion that relative autonomy signifies relative dependence: the intellectual field is relatively independent of the field of power, and its relative autonomy is manifested in the fact that the external effects of domination are always retranslated. We shall not say: 'Working men of all countries, unite!'[24] but speak of 'Artists against the bourgeois' – so that the effect of domination of the subfield by the field will find its expression in the specific logic of the intellectual field. There, I believe that I have more or less answered the question.

Is business a field?

Moving on to the third question, which would also merit a long discussion, and also suits the logic of my argument. It is about business. This question [from Mr Georges Tiffon] is very elaborate. It gives me great pleasure because I was naive enough to believe that the brief argument I had so far produced might be sufficient to produce this kind of contribution. It is not a sociology of the business enterprise, but it is already an interesting construction of a problematic to understand what a business enterprise is. I am tempted to read it to you, even if I can't read it all: 'Is the industrial or commercial or similar enterprise a field? Can we establish it as a relatively autonomous field with specific interests, etc.? Is it a subfield of a professional sector (*that is a very good question*)? Is it implicated in other fields, for example financial and other, or capital?'

I shall reply very briefly, referring you to an article on employers that I wrote with Monique de Saint-Martin.[25] In this article, the section titled 'L'entreprise comme champ' ['the business firm as field'] (pp. 57–60) seems to me to contain my reply to the question. To put it briefly, you can draw on my argument to construct the field of business firms as a space within which each firm will owe a part of its properties to the position that it holds in the space. In fact, economic enterprises, like literary enterprises, are defined by the permanent and lasting objective relations that, on the one hand, bind them one to another and, on the other, link them to their various markets. For example, in the article on employers, we first described the structures of the field of firms, the principal oppositions that we use in order to understand a certain number of properties of each of the sub-spaces. From here we could construct what [Mr Tiffon] calls subfields, and in particular those subfields that we call sectors or branches. There have been some very interesting studies of branches, in particular by people from INSEE who have analysed the historical genesis of divisions into branches.[26] Like all the social classification in use at the moment, for example the CSP [socio-professional categories], the forms of classification of firms are the result of an often strange and mysterious historical process, where theorists, that is creators of systems of classification, collaborate with social agents who struggle to be classified, to create associations, find titles and labels for themselves and mark their divisions.

To rehearse one of my epistemological hobby horses: every time that we have to make a classification, we should enquire into the historical and social genesis of this classification, on pain of becoming an object of the thought process that we think we are using as subjects. It is a socio-

Kantian precept: 'If you want to know what you think, take as your object the categories of thought.'[27] Our social categories of thought are the product of a very complex and confused historical process, with countless subjects in competition. Now the categories of INSEE that designate, for example, the textile sector have a history, which means that they are much less stupid than the categories that a technocrat in his cabinet could invent with a smattering of mathematical culture and what he sees as common sense, that is, a sense of class – they are also much more rigorous. They should be respected. The newly qualified young sociologist is proud to cast doubt on INSEE's categories, but these are much better than the new sociologist thinks – I can guarantee this, having followed twenty years of their publications. That having been said, we do need to handle them with care, because they have a social provenance: they are the product of complex negotiations, social struggles and more or less shifting mental structures, etc.

This gives us a branch or sector; Eymard-Duvernay and another economist, for instance, have published a study of the watchmaking sector.[28] They analyse as a field of production the particular business space that produces things called 'watches', 'clocks', and the like. They discover that these enterprises are linked to each other by permanent and lasting relations of rivalry for the production of the product and its distribution in the market. This kind of lasting relation is established on the one hand between the producers and, on the other, between the producers and their chosen markets – and all this applies just as much to the market of literary production. These businesses are characterized by the fact that they have a specific capital.

In speaking of 'specific capital' we are speaking of 'specific interest': the concept of field implies 'specific' capital and interest. I can link this to the thread of the argument of my last lecture, which showed how fields within which specific interests and capitals will function are constituted. I needed to go through the analysis of this process of differentiation of the fields and the constitution of relatively autonomous spaces called fields to be able to arrive at what is the main object of my lecture, that is the description of what I call species of capital. There are specific forms of capital and there will be as many of them as there are fields, and everything that I have said about the interest is valid for the capital.

Within the watchmaking industry there are specific forms of capital that economists describe as particular methods of production; for instance, manufacturing secrets belonging to a specific firm, procedures of manufacture, modes of man management – whether with patriarchal strategies inherited from a long tradition, rational strategies borrowed from social psychologists, or group dynamics, etc. – modes of enhancing the value of the products – modern-style advertising, but also all sorts of techniques that preceded it, such as focus on a proper or family name. This specific, properly economic capital is specified according to each field and a watchmaker's capital is not easily transferable to textiles: which leads us to define the existence of a subfield.

There is also a symbolic capital – there, things move of their own accord: the brand, the personal touch, 'in the family since the eighteenth century', for wines and perfumes, and the like. If you stop to think about it, the use of the name and advertising resemble the intellectual field: 'making a name for oneself' is also very important in the economic field.[29] This is why it is interesting to have a general theory of fields, because the scientific capital acquired in the study of one field can be transferred to another field. The symbolic capital of the brand or the reputation is often acquired through seniority (it is one of the great principles of the accumulation of symbolic capital that one of its properties is to be a capital of seniority). And then we also find effects of the field: for instance, the inclination of producers whose products are very similar to differentiate themselves as far as possible. This is very interesting: each firm tends to mark out its difference from the firms closest to it in order to minimize the competition: if you have a unique and irreplaceable product, you fear no competition. This is well known in the history of the scientific field (I can't resist making this analogy): a very fine article by Kantorowicz on Polish jurists shows that once jurists entered the picture in the twelfth century, they started to divide themselves up according to specialities; following this, the whole history of science is built on the specialization that is encapsulated in the law of being 'rather first in my village than second in Rome' (rather first in 'the epistemology of labour relations' than second in 'epistemology'). The inclination to differentiate is one whose effect is to avoid competition. Very often, the enterprise of differentiation is over-determined: the interest in differentiation has objective foundations because the product is different and the inclination to differentiate for differentiation's sake is limited by objective constraints. (What I am saying is very difficult to argue because I am obliged to say so many things so quickly, and I fall into the trap of saying things one-sidedly, whereas I counterbalance them in my mind.) Another analogy could be made with the political field, which, as we all know, is the terrain par excellence of the inclination to differentiate oneself from the products, most like one's own.

The field as subject of social actions

There is then the economic field and the 'branch' subfield, which we should call by a name yet to be invented, which is not easy: we need to take into account the product and the market, and there are overlaps. One problem is the autonomy of these subfields: an empirical study is faced with all sorts of problems, because a field can be autonomous while having one of its sectors partially overlap with other fields. Although these things are not simple, it does enable us to raise rigorous questions. I shall not develop it here, but there is at bottom the firm itself, which would be the subfield within the subfield of the branch. I refer you to the discussion in the article on 'Le patronat' [employers], which raises questions that are important from a theoretical point of view, since classical economics tends to treat the firm as an agent. When classical economics says that there are households or firms, this is taking firms to be acting like agents, and all sorts of psychosocial arguments (or the sort of amateur sociology that economists produce when they have got their concepts in a twist) lead to the conclusion that 'the firm is an economic subject'. One tradition in 'sociology' (although I place it in inverted commas, it does have a social existence) in the United States is the case study whose aim is to trace the historical genealogy of a decision.[30] This raises the question of finding out who makes the economic decision, who is the subject of the economic action, in the same way that I was asking who was the subject of the hit parade, who had made the judgement. For the economy, there is obviously a common-sense answer to the question 'Who decides?': 'It's Capital', 'It's Godot!' If I hesitate to say that these case studies are ridiculous, it is because their empiricism does nonetheless show a considerable progress from the simplistic totalitarian thinking of the 'It's Godot!' type.

For instance, in the case of the la Villette affair,[31] these studies investigate the problem of who decided. The danger of this kind of investigation is its simplistic political thinking in terms of people responsible.[32] Remember what I said about the hit parade; it would be the same for the la Villette affair, meaning that no individual is responsible. In fact, the question 'Who is responsible?' is more or less meaningless. The subject of the economic actions is a field. One obvious conclusion is that those who dominate the field are more responsible than those in the field who are dominated, but saying this is quite different from saying: 'So-and-so is responsible: he should hang.' The search for the subject of economic actions – which is what makes sociology a moral science whether it likes it or not – immediately dissolves the single subject, and the first lesson that sociology learns is that there is an infinity of subjects. Which makes things complicated: we speak in terms of influences, we use *network analysis* to reveal networks, we study diaries and address books to find connections; one thing leads to another and we find the whole social space filled with a network of objective relations where certain institutions or agents have greater structural weight and are therefore more responsible. But it is the space as a whole that functions as the subject of this space.

This part of my argument was not intentionally planned, but it is important: it runs counter to one of the spontaneous, probably sociologically motivated, inclinations of research. In particular, historical research is almost always inspired by the search for those responsible. It is no accident if history, as mediated by the media, is often a tale of 'scandals', and often the search for causes is no more than a way of looking for those responsible; looking for the causes of the French Revolution is not much better than asking, 'Whose fault is it that there were concentration camps?' One major advantage imposed by analysing in terms of fields is that social actions are subjectless actions – but not in the sense stated by structuralism in the 1960s – actions whose subject is an ensemble of structurally related agents, submitted to collective constraints. The least false solution is to say: 'The subject is the field' – that is, the whole set of agents is responsible. They may sometimes have their little *clinamen* and deviate from their allotted path, but they are all responsible, each one in their own place, in proportion to their weight in a structure that determines what they can see and what they can understand, and therefore the limits of their complicity and also their refusals. Sometimes their only responsibility may be the ability to say: 'No, I refuse to follow'; this may be only a grain of sand in the machine – but that is what morals are about. And I believe that this is important because the kind of moral judgement that overdramatizes the problem prevents us from making a rigorous construction of the object. If you open a history book, you will see that the search for those responsible – for the good as for the ill – is the principle behind much of what calls itself historical research. They say that 'The Louvre is So-and-so', whether architect or king. Seeking those responsible for art is the same: it's Giotto or Leonardo da Vinci, but someone must be responsible.

I have been a bit long-winded, but it is important in view of the sort of psychoanalysis of the scientific mind[33] that I propose to keep constantly in mind during these lectures. Now to return straight away to the question raised: yes, of course, the firm is a field, but who is the subject of the economic decision? We can always say that it is not the employer but some *éminence grise*, which is a way of 'shifting the blame', as historians often go to great lengths to do, for instance by saying that it is not Louvois, but Louvois's mistress who is really responsible, which is quite beside the point. Similarly, they ask: 'When did it start?' Here I am going to be rude to the historians (although it is certainly the discipline where I feel most at ease, more than in sociology); the law of the field of cultural production, which in its advanced form is always to move further on (as in the saying 'you are beyond the beyond',[34] 'I have gone beyond the most advanced guard of the avant-garde'), leads historians to seek the 'beyond the beyond' in reverse [*laughter*]; they seek out the author of the first journal and the first memoirs, then one says 'It's Rousseau!', another says 'No, it's Montaigne!', and they go back to the fourth century before Christ and . . . whoever goes back the furthest is the winner! [*Laughter*] An enormous part of historical study (I could give you bibliographies) has no principle other than what I have just described. You see, sociology is liberating (when people say that it is determinist, it is not true) because we see straight away the traps there are to avoid.

To finish with the notion of the field: the business enterprise, then, is a field of forces where there are positions. For example, in French businesses there are different areas of competence, and we can say, as the author of the question did, that there are marketing personnel, production workers, researchers, and so on. But there is also the position itself as motivating force: there are qualifications that are statutorily guaranteed, such as the diplomas of the *grandes écoles* and the clans linked to these titles (*polytechniciens*, etc.). These different forms of capital, wielding power in the field and over the field, will confront each other over any decision, but there will hardly ever (not never, mind) be an obvious author of the decision. This is why the social traps are particularly subtle. I think the subjects of social actions are nearly always fields.

To take another, quite different example: the family. It is a field, and the Kabyle know all too well that an important, say matrimonial, decision can only be taken by the man as subject, and the woman who has often decided everything puts all her efforts into giving the impression that it is the husband who has decided, because otherwise it would not be a decision.[35] This law prolongs what I was saying last time about the need to 'abide by the rules'. This is why the trap for historians functions so well: the subject may well be collective, given that it is the employer who decides and that it is crucial that, at one moment or another, someone seems to have decided. This does not mean that appearance is unimportant – things are never so simple. Sometimes we can say that the apparent subject is only an apparent subject, that the subject is a network or a field and that it is ridiculous to look for an *éminence grise* or to persist in looking for mistresses, but the literary field, for instance, is affected by very strong influences from one field to another, and if we realize that it is through the salons and women that the influence of the field of power is exercised on the literary field, we will have understood something important. To say that taking an interest in the problems of anecdotal history is pointless is then stupid . . . Fields are real subjects, but in many circumstances it is not without significance that the decision in its official manifestation appears to be taken by a man. Moreover, this last situation is socially controlled and varies according to the moment and the society: one of the properties of the fields that we need to investigate is the degree to which a field allows, or allows itself, self-government, or the degree to which it delegates a person to assume the guise of decision-taker. And what is the specific effect of this apparent concentration of decision-taking? And if these questions matter, it is because they relate to problems such as charisma, or Gaullism.

I shall stop there. I have used up my session, but I think this excursus was justified because it allows me to project certain analyses that I had developed in relation to the ranking list, and in speaking of a more distant and abstract reality I could say things that I could not decently say of a universe that you and I all belong to.

Second session (seminar): Kafka's *The Trial* (1)

If you like, the central idea of my argument is that in *The Trial* Kafka proposes a sort of model of the social world – although not obviously constituted as such, which is a problem. I should say straight away that Kafka functioned and continues to function as a projective test, and that those who venture to discuss Kafka must know that they are in danger of revealing much more about themselves than about him. It would moreover be very interesting to analyse what we call 'readings' of Kafka in this light. Indeed, I think that, whereas not all texts will act as projective tests, the more obscure texts lend themselves to it more than others. A history of the readings of pre-Socratic philosophers would also be exciting. The texts are both very ancient and very obscure: we have thousands of years of projective texts. It would be a very fine history of mental structures . . . (The expression 'projective test' is, I believe, a valid one: since socially constructed mental structures tend to project beyond themselves, the obscure and ancient texts have received a whole series of superimposed readings. I think each historical era is bound to deliver its collective structures, or at least their academic form – although the pre-Socratics have not been read only by academics, the readings started much earlier.)

It is amusing to read Kafka in this light. A kind of doxographic study might take as its object not the texts, but what has been said about them, assuming that the commentaries have not been written at random, but express mental structures and constitute a document, or rather a historically constructed social experiment. I must once more give the lie to the old wives' tale that 'there is no experimentation in sociology'. In fact, the social world is full of experiments, but you have to establish and interpret them as such. That is what I did with the hit parade in my last session: I took something that was given, and I tried to construct it so that it could be treated as an experiment, the only difference being that the experiment had already been carried out by people who had no plan and were not fully aware of what they were doing. There are so many operations of this kind that we might undertake.

Kafka has contributed considerably to the projection of the representation of the writer as *vates*, as prophet or precursor (which is a socially invented historical representation of the writer – it is not current in all periods or all societies); Kafka has been seen as a sort of prophetic reader of totalitarianism, the adjective 'kafkaesque' having become the common label for a certain number of phenomena. He has also been seen as the prophet of bureaucracy. The reading that I find most amusing, because it is the most probable, given the social chances of getting to read Kafka, is the one that consists in seeing in Kafka the spokesman of a sort of revolt by the free individual against all forms of repression. Only recently, I read a commentary that seemed to rehearse naively one of the most common readings, that is the moral indignation felt by people who feel important, who, when confronted with the powers of a bureaucratic order exercised by men without qualities, are socially consecrated as celebrities. One thing that I had never thought about but that I find very amusing and interesting is the indignation of the celebrity arrested by some gendarme or other. The self-analysis is interesting here: partisans of this reading point out that in Kafka powerholders are anonymous but above all base and crude: the painter likes little girls, the judge reads pornographic novels hidden in his legal textbook, and so on. In fact, this kind of revolt resembles that of the intellectual accomplishing his military service who rebels against the sergeant major, for instance. I see this as one of the projective tests, an amusing effect of projection. Obviously when we know this, it makes us wary: we start to be careful about what we say, for we know that we reveal a lot about ourselves when we make this kind of comment on literature, however brilliant it makes us feel.

'Kafka the prophet' enables us to say something important and I would talk about this if I had to deliver a long lecture on 'sociology and literature'. It is an issue that we are quite often asked about. In the 1960s, there was much discussion of the links between philosophy and literature: is the writer a philosopher? Is the philosopher a writer? Can he express a philosophy through writing? Today there are those who would like to investigate the links between the sociology of everyday life and literature. I think this is a valid subject. Talking of literature, I noted this problem of style last year, and I said that philosophers had established the specificity of their style in the field of cultural production by producing a certain ugliness of style as a guarantee of Kantian profundity.[36] Clearly, the sociologist has a problem here: if he writes too finely, that is, with style, he is accused of being unscientific; if he writes too unattractively, that is, clumsily, he is reproached with this, while he is struggling more and more with the specific internal constraints of the creation of concepts, and the like.

This is one way of putting the question. Another way is to say, as I did briefly last time, that literature can produce a key effect that a dispassionate analysis would fail to produce: it can dramatize a model. In fact, this is how I wish to make use of Kafka. I make no claim to be a Kafka specialist, I am using Kafka to say something about Kafka that I think is actually there in Kafka, and moreover I shall try to show that there is a link between my reading and the very existence of Kafka: so I shall, after all, be doing a sociology of literature. I shall respect the logic of scientific discourse that invites verification, confirmation or falsification, but I still expect this reading of Kafka to be productive. Kafka does offer a model, but it is a dramatic model. This means, however, that it is not a true model, and its pedagogic virtue depends on the fact that it is not completely objectified, and could not be signed by a sociologist worthy of the name, given that its production is driven, I think, by a form of moral indignation close to that expressed in the reading that I was talking about just now. As an educated Jew in a society very strongly marked by anti-Semitism, Kafka must certainly have felt with a peculiar intensity this experience that is very common among intellectuals who feel that their person is not reducible to their personage when they are confronted with bureaucratic authorities who reduce them to their social identity: 'You are just like the others.' Behind the production of Kafka's model, I think there is, then, a form of indignation that can explain a certain number of details. On the other hand, the

Kafka model still clings in some ways to Kafka's own experience, as shown in the tone of indignation.

Among other things, the sociologist must master, or at least objectify, the relations of non-indifference that link him to his object and are the source of an adhesion that prevents objectification in complex cases. Whence the precept that I have formulated more than once this year: you should always objectify the subject of the objectification to have some chance of knowing what you are doing when you objectify. In particular, you need to objectify the particular pleasure that you take in objectifying certain particular objects, since objectification is obviously at work in polemics (you are always an objectifier for someone: 'You are only a . . .'). There is then a slightly murky pleasure in the practice of sociology: the pleasure of objectifying and being guaranteed by the appearance of scientificity. If we don't know this and if we don't objectify ourselves objectifying and taking pleasure in doing so, we have every likelihood of objectifying badly or only partially, cutting corners and forgetting to objectify the place from which we are objectifying. This is what happens in Kafka's case. If his model is dramatic, it is of course because of his talent, his writing and imagination, and because his model is a story. The sociologist cannot do that. Unlike the sociologist, the novelist is a professional storyteller: he creates suspense and expectations, we get inside the work and identify with the characters, but in this way the model stays attached to its fictional motor and is only a 'model' in quotation marks (if I say that, it is not only to mark out the difference from science, for all the models that we produce for the social world are 'models' in quotation marks).

The Trial and the search for identity

Kafka describes a game where the goal is to reply to the question 'Who am I?', or more exactly: 'Am I?' The trial proceedings are a process, an intricate mechanism that is gradually set in motion. The principal character engages with it from the very first sentence: 'Someone must have been telling lies about Joseph K.'[37] So before the novel even gets going, there is a symbolic judgement, an accusation, an act of categorization, *categorestein*: he has been publicly accused. Calumny is a very special form of accusation. We need to see what separates it from a public accusation pronounced by a judge or a tribunal, the question being to know who has the right to judge. Slander is a covert accusation pronounced in unofficial form. It is to the verdict of a tribunal what magic is to religion, according to Durkheim – Durkheim said that magic belongs to the shadows and the night, outside the official space, whereas religion is public and official,[38] exposed to the eyes of the world and the consensus *omnium*: to be able to show yourself to everyone you need to be recognized and known by all. From the outset, we have a verdict that is like original sin, but has started even earlier: he has been slandered and he has that sort of label stuck on his back. The link with Jewish identity, that all the critics have picked up, is so obvious that there is no need to insist on it.

Once this process has started, the hero is caught up in the game: he cannot laugh it off, and for him the question becomes: 'Am I accused justly or unjustly?', 'Who can tell me if I am accused justly or unjustly?', 'Who can even tell me whether I am accused?', and then 'Who can tell me what I am, that is, innocent or guilty?', and, at a further level, 'Who can tell me who I am?'. Through this dramatized model of a game whose challenge is to find out what and who I am, Kafka gives us a one-sided vision – Weber would say an ideal-type – in which he accentuates one profile, one reality. Weber speaks of *Vielseitichkeit*, 'many-sidedness': the social world is many-sided; if I see one profile and favour it and enhance it, it is an ideal type.[39] Kafka proposes an ideal-typical vision of the social world as a world where what is at stake is to find out what I am and even who I am. Can someone who is not even told by the social world that he exists actually exist? Can I exist if the authorities charged with telling me what I am and who I am do not tell me, if I do not know where they are located and cannot find them? The mechanism is under way then, and *The Trial* charts the progress of this race to find the true tribunal, with the constant temptation to opt out of the game and say: 'I am only answerable to this judgement as long as I chase after it.' If I say: 'I don't care', I leave it, it no longer has any hold on me. The hero says several times: 'But after all, I am free.' This is very important: it reminds us of how all social games are founded on *illusio*. Ultimately, we might think of Hegel and the dialectic of the master and the slave . . . (I speak these metaphysical terms in a disenchanted and ironic tone because they have been spoken of too often in a tone that annoys me, but that doesn't mean that they are not true: this is very complicated, I have to say this, otherwise I am creating effects of clandestine persuasion that do not correspond to the effect that I want to produce. I can exercise a clandestine persuasion effect, but only when it matches my intentions.)

The key word of a game whose goal is to find out who I am, and thereby to find out who can really tell me who I am, is the word 'verdict', which means *veridictum*, 'what is truly spoken': who can truly tell me who I am? And who can judge the legitimacy of the judge? Who can judge the right to judge? Obviously, this game is a model of human existence. One of the things at stake in human existence is the symbolic capital that our identity basically is, which is how other people describe what I am. If they say 'You are null and void', that means that we do not exist. There is a way in which the social world can scotomize us, as psychoanalysts say, that is, annihilate us: 'I do not even perceive you', 'You are not perceptible for me, you go unnoticed.' Excommunication is thus a way of expelling you into outer darkness, of 'ruling you offside': 'You do not even exist in this game, there is no place for you.' You are a pariah. There would be a comparative sociological study to be made of the strategies that different societies use to symbolically annihilate people who do not conform to the dominant representations of what you should be in order to legitimately exist. The question is one of legitimate existence: it is about official status, the right to officially exist, to be known and recognized. In other words, it is a model of the social game as a game of truth, a model of the social game as a game in which the truth of my own self is at stake.

If some people are exasperated by sociology, especially the kind of collective work that has expanded considerably over the last twenty years, which I have tried to synthesize (the objective work by American interactionist sociologists, ethno-methodologists, and some socio-linguists and philosophers of language), it is because it reveals that what is at stake in the social world is not simply power or economic capital or economic domination. All those scholars who have drawn our attention to the determining role of symbolism in social exchanges ultimately reveal a much more vital challenge, something that affects the very existence of social agents. This is why this kind of sociology is particularly irritating for people attached to a philosophy of the individual subject. The kind of exasperation that my argument provokes is understandable enough in the case of someone who has a personalized vision of the world and is determined to exist as an 'I'. There is nothing more terrible for them. Moreover, these people are the most diligent readers of Kafka – but they obviously don't see in him what I see there. Their goal is precisely to exist as a person, and it is the social world that tells someone whether they are a person in the positive or the negative sense: 'Do you exist?' The definitive reply lies absolutely in the hands of the social world.

I shall now pass on to more specific matters, but I believe that I have said at the outset what is most important. A passage that exemplifies what I have just been saying is a conversation with Block, the travelling salesman – who, as all the critics have noticed, is Jewish. Block is permanently installed with the advocate, who is also K's advocate. With

K., the oscillations of the *illusio* are made manifest in his very complex relations with his advocate: when he enters the game, he starts to toady to the advocate, but when he has had enough, he says 'I'm going', and drops the advocate. Whereas Block is permanently alienated. He lives in a permanent *illusio*. He is *illusio* made flesh: he is a believer, he sleeps in the advocate's home, which is very symbolic. As in the quotation from Hegel just now, he gives himself over entirely to the game. He lives for justice day and night, he sleeps at the feet of the advocate, who rings a little bell when he comes in. It is alienation bordering on insanity, for what I am describing is an extreme form of alienation; the game of *illusio* also implies alienation. K. starts by despising him completely, partly because Block is caught in the clutches of his alienation, but then there comes a time when he starts to consult this perfect madman, who is quite well informed. Gradually, the status of Block changes: as K. starts to get caught up in the game, he comes to see him as someone 'senior' – as in the army, elders are betters. What I am saying is a model, it is not an amateur analysis. We could find many other analogies with the military world. Goffman says that the asylum exercises an 'asylumization effect': these grim totalitarian institutions produce an effect on those whom they assimilate, causing the agents to assimilate themselves to the institution, identify with it and finally feel quite at home there.[40] Block is an 'asylumized' inmate of the legal asylum, he identifies with it perfectly. K., who is still a newcomer, is a new boy due to be ragged[41] – the rites of initiation into the *grandes écoles* and their preparatory classes are rites of asylumization. He is just starting out in '*taupe*', it's his first term, and he is up against an asylumized '*bica*'. He rather despises him because he obviously sees the external signs of asylumization displayed as a kind of submission to the whims of the institution. The most absolute, most totalitarian institutions demand the total gift of the self to the institution. The newcomer, whom we might call the neophyte by analogy with a religious institution, sees these signs of asylumization clearly and is rather contemptuous of them, but as K. begins to be caught up in the game, Block becomes an important source of information: he knows all the habits of the institution, he knows that you can slip out unnoticed towards four o'clock, and so on. In fact, the more K. himself becomes asylumized, the higher Block is rated. But I digress.

There is a moment, I believe, when K. says that the master (I have forgotten his name)[42] is a great advocate, but Block puts him in his place:

He always refers to the Advocates of his own circle as the 'great Advocates', by way of contrast. Now that's untrue; any man can call himself 'great', of course, if he pleases, but in this matter the Court tradition must decide. And according to the court tradition, which recognizes both small and great advocates outside the hole-and-corner advocates, our Advocate and his colleagues rank only among the small advocates.[43]

For me, this sums up the whole thesis: everyone gives themselves an identity or assumes a persona, and the verdict on these individual verdicts is pronounced by the High Court, in the last instance.[44] The problem then is how to know who will have the last word on deciding who I am: who will be the judge of the hierarchy of judges? This is the myth of the last instance. This is why, as I suggested last time, sociology and theology are so similar. It is no accident if we can make a theological reading of Kafka at the same time as a sociological reading of the type that I am proposing (and which has been very rarely proposed because the image that we have of Kafka and of all literature is such that we cannot read him sociologically). I think sociological and theological readings are perfectly interchangeable insofar as our relation to the social world turns on a fundamentally theological question: how to know who can really tell me who I am? We could say that it is God, but we could also say, with Durkheim, that 'God is society'.[45] It is society that holds the power of nomination – the term is important. It is society that has the power to say: 'He is a writer', 'He is a great sociologist', 'He is a great theologian'. And this power is such that I may say: 'It is not I who say so, it is not I who consecrates me.' As I said last time, Napoleon placing the crown upon his own head represents the degree zero of legitimization: when someone says that they are the greatest, we are particularly disposed to doubt the objectivity of their judgement: they are too interested in saying so for us not to doubt that their judgement is interested. Verdicts are the more legitimate, the more distant their source. In the literary field, everyone knows that there are exchanges of book reviews, but short circuits (X writes on Y then Y writes on X) are hardly legitimate; the circuits that confer the most legitimacy are the longest. The supreme agency would be a sort of anonymous, collective agency, representing the consensus *omnium*: the absolute verdict is the *consensus omnium*, that sort of worldly incarnation of God as repository of absolute truth, with no beyond. The theological reading and the sociological reading are therefore not at all incompatible, but are absolutely interchangeable.

To continue more concretely with the play of identity that I have been discussing in very abstract terms, let us return to the games played by writers that I was describing last time. Who can say that I am a writer? Who can say that I am the best writer? Am I the person best placed to say that I am the best writer? More generally, in everyday life, who has the right to say who I am? Who has the right to say of others what they really are? This is the problem of the insult that I broached three years ago.[46] When I say to someone: 'You are nothing but a this, or a that', I am committing only myself, and they can reply: 'You are one, yourself'. It is reversible, or as Heraclitus said,[47] *idios logos*, that is an individual statement, with no social force, as opposed to a legitimate speech, which is *koinos*, common, sanctioned by the community, and which, being common, can be broadcast in the community, publicly announced, and sanctioned by the group. We have then an opposition between an individual accusation and a tribunal pronouncing a judgement in the eyes of the world, an opposition between individual judgements and judgements with claims to universality, between a curse – or accusation – and an official nomination.

Let me insist for a moment on these words 'curse' and 'accusation'. Sometimes it is important to be able to play on words. In 'accusing' we can hear an echo of 'cursing', yet we don't see the connection. I think in fact that a curse is an extreme case of an accusation. The curse is the reverse of a blessing. In both cases they are attempts to act through language – in Austin's definition of the performative, it is an attempt to do things with words, to exercise power through words.[48] Accusation is a more routine and lay form of cursing. When someone says: 'So-and-so's book is rubbish, it's worthless', it is a form of curse. There is a kind of will to harm, to destroy, to undermine the author's symbolic capital, to discredit him ('discredit' implying the opposite of 'credit'), therefore to kill him symbolically. The curse differs from the accusation through the logic of the space in which it is pronounced; it relates to a universe where people still believe in magic, where actions of a magical type are socially recognized as legitimate, even almost publicly pronounceable – although magic is always practised rather secretly. Cursing belongs to societies in which actions of symbolic violence against other people can be openly displayed. In more lay societies, we have accusation. I think it is important to constitute the class of cursing/accusation in order to understand accusation better and not pass too quickly over calumny, public opinion and gossip: they are social actions through which agents work to manipulate their identity by manipulating other people's identities, to claim value by devaluing others, sowing suspicion. The Kabyle are voluble on the problem of suspicion: the man of honour is one who is above all suspicion, who kills suspicion even before it can be formulated, who brings suspicion to bear on what makes masculine societies vulnerable, that is, women.

Suspicion, public opinion and gossip are mini-murders. They are the microscopic form of something whose maximal and ostentatious form is the curse. A whole series of studies, particularly those directed by the English anthropologist Mary Douglas focusing on the problem of witchcraft, and edited volumes bringing together specialists on different societies,[49] give us to understand a general law according to which resorting to the curse and techniques of magic and witchcraft are more widespread in societies where insecurity and competition are rife. These societies, with their intense rivalry and poorly objectified stakes, are in other words universes in which competition over morals and values is very strong, and the objective guarantees of success in this competition are unclear; there is no tribunal established to decide who has won and who has lost, there is no objectified classification.

Recognition in weakly objectified fields

You see what I am getting at: this is very similar to the intellectual field as I have described it. The intellectual field is a universe where there is fierce competition surrounding the absolutely vital issues: 'Who am I?', 'What am I?', 'Am I a writer?', 'Have I the right to call myself a writer or am I nothing at all?' These are all-or-nothing universes. Moreover, there is very fierce competition over these very vital issues, more vital than life itself, you might say, because you can die for your works (see the hagiographies). It is one of the objective properties of these universes to set the stakes so high that you can die in trying to attain them. At the same time, the likelihood of success in the struggle to reach these goals is quite uncertain and the social agents are left entirely in the dark as to their chances of success. This is the atmosphere of *The Trial* again, where everything conspires to leave the hero, K., clueless as to whether he is making any progress. These are universes then where vital issues are at stake: K. will be executed in the end, but he never knows what stage he has reached and nobody can tell him. There is a sort of objective uncertainty: we could define this game as pathetic or tragic. It is a particular state of the fields: they are games where vital, fundamental issues are at stake, in a very fierce competition and with almost absolute uncertainty. We can understand why people could have read the concentration camps into Kafka, but the image of the concentration camp has acted as a screen and made us forget that in everyday life there are many highly risky, highly uncertain games, with vital stakes and a very weak institutionalization of the verdicts.

As for the ranking list, I was saying the other day that what is extraordinary is that it is the only one. For instance, when I was working on teachers in higher education, I looked out for an objective classification, one that would be public and where I wouldn't be contradicted, of those who are good and those who aren't in a universe where everyone struggles to find out who is good or not, who exists or doesn't exist.[50] But there is no such thing, and this is a social fact. My first reaction was to substitute myself as a social scientist for the social world: 'I shall create as objective a classification as possible, using reports by the CNRS and citations in international reviews. I shall pronounce the *verdictum*, as a scholar, I shall settle their accounts – not in the economic sense – I shall reveal what is what.' Thank goodness that I then said to myself: 'But what right have I to substitute myself as researcher for the social world?' If it is interesting scientifically, I think we have to draw up a classification, but remembering the important fact that it does not exist in the objective world. In other words, I can establish this classification and treat it as an explanatory principle. In fact, this classification that everyone knows but does not exist – as I repeatedly stated last time – is the principle that explains many practices. It is the true principle justifying people's practices and their degree of assurance – this is a crucial word: assurance for the future, objective assurance, subjective assurance. But it is also important to know that it does not have an objective existence and that it generates some of the most characteristic phenomena of the universe being studied, such as anxiety or an excessive inclination to slander. I remember a businessman telling me that there were no people nastier than intellectuals. That was a very naive judgement, but it follows the logic of what I was saying this morning and has some truth to it: there are universes where our own identity and the identity of others are at stake. It is a game of symbolic life or death. A considerable proportion of the arguments traded under cover of critical reviews (as I was saying this morning) are symbolic murders; we are all surrounded by symbolic criminals.

I think that what we need to note is the fact that these games are highly fraught and highly uncertain. You may say that this is obviously my own projection, and ask me what right I have to project this highly partisan reading of Kafka. I can easily respond thanks to a book by Unseld.[51] I think this book is important because it breaks for the first time with a central aspect of Kafka mythology: Kafka had ordered his friend Max Brod to burn his manuscripts. Unseld shows clearly that he gave this order to someone who had sworn time and again that he would not obey. What I am saying seems polemical: things aren't like that in real life. But it is a very interesting kind of myth, that needs to be understood as such, and not read naively. As devotees of a cult, people who write on literature celebrate this kind of naivety that I denounce when I speak rather wickedly of a 'life or death' game. This naivety of the celebrants prevents them from seeing what the phrase really expresses. It is not insignificant: it is not every author who tells their literary executor to burn their books, and it is even relatively rare. But that does not mean that we should take it literally. Every writer asks himself what he is, and whether he exists as a writer, but this question was particularly acute for Kafka, and the whole of Unseld's book tends to say that questioning his existence as a writer ('Am I a writer? And who can tell me if I am a writer?') was the obsession of Kafka's life. Unseld describes, for example, these shifts in Kafka's existence, as he oscillates between periods of stability, that occur on several occasions between the periods of doubting whether he is a writer – at times when he gets engaged and married, identifies with the objective expectations of his family, of his mother who wants him to settle down – and the contradictory periods of literary excitement and productive writing.

Explaining things through the relation of Kafka to the literary field does not really explain anything, but Kafka's literary existence nonetheless relates directly to the sort of model that he offers. Ultimately, what is at stake is the relation of Kafka to his publisher. In fact, the Supreme Court in the experience of the writer corresponds to the experience with an editor who publishes him, turning his virtual existence into reality,[52] who has the power to consecrate him as a writer, all the more so because he is himself consecrated as editor by the fact that he has published great writers. The publisher grants his *imprimatur*; by placing 'Éditions de Minuit' below the title, he consecrates the author, and in this sense he is Godot, he is the last instance. In fact, Kafka's vacillation does echo his relations with publishers. Kafka lived his relation with the literary milieu as something dramatic, a sort of theological quest for recognition as writer: 'Who can tell me that I am really a writer?' For instance, one very interesting thing is that when his friends told him, 'What you are doing is fantastically good', he always suspected the validity of their judgement. This is the absolute opposite of the mutual admiration society of the *Nouvel Obs*. He said: 'My friend is telling me this because he is being kind to me and not because it is true.' So it needed an authority as distant from him as possible, with objective interests expressed in the concrete form of costs. This point is very important because a publisher who presents you to the public is making a serious financial gamble, as he commits himself, takes sides and runs risks. This is the kind of verdict that Kafka chased after quite pathetically. What is at issue basically is the question of reassurance:

'Who can assure me that I am really a writer?', 'Who can tell me if I am a publishable author?', 'Who can make public the fact that I am publishable?', 'Who has the publicly recognized authority to say in public that Kafka is a writer?'.

This is obviously a problem that is present in the situation of avant-garde writers: it is no accident if avant-gardes always function as mutual admiration societies.[53] Their opponents see this circular aspect clearly, but they must function in this way almost by definition, which does not mean that they don't have a pathetic nostalgia for recognition by those whom they denounce. I have interviewed enough avant-garde artists to know that the *coincidencia oppositorum*, that kind of fantasy of reconciliation that would consist in being at one and the same time in the avant-garde and the Académie française, is sought after. This paradoxical structure is obviously particularly strong when you are predisposed to live out this model of your relation with the social world as a Jew. The structures overlap. I think it is very important, for those who visualize causality as simple and for whom things are always all black or all white, to remember that before we enter the literary field we have a pre-existing dispositional structure that explains how we enter it, which comes to be reinforced by the structure of our relation to the literary field. Ultimately this pathetic, tragic relation to the supreme literary authority, a totally contradictory relation, is the reactivation of a founding relation, the relation to the father – we can't ignore Kafka's *Letter to his Father*[54] – which becomes the relation of a Jew to the dominant society, seeking exclusion or inclusion, and a type of inclusion not requested by those who are obviously included. This leads to a sort of nonconformism that coincides with a conformism and can look like conformism to those who are not troubled by the issue of conforming. This is complicated, but this is how I think it works.

Finally, I would like to say just this: if it is true that the theory of fields has some truth in it, we can understand that someone who describes his experience in a very specific, literary field, can describe something absolutely universal insofar as, starting with the viewpoint that Kafka adopts initially, he finally gives us a vision of something that is at stake to varying degrees in every field at all times. Ultimately, he had no need to see the concentration camps, bureaucracy, Mussolini, and the like, to write his novels: it was enough to describe the intellectual field. It is very interesting to note that Kafka was read almost exclusively by intellectuals and academics, but that nobody before me [*laughter*] and Professor Unseld had seen that it was about intellectuals. This is perhaps the most amusing thing: it makes you think about what it is to be an intellectual.

Lecture of 29 March 1984

First session (lecture): the model of the gambler. – Immanent tendencies to reproduction in the social world. – Comparison between societies and continuity of the social world. – Differentiating between fields and objectification of capital. – Violence and its euphemization.
Second session (seminar): Kafka's The Trial *(2). – The manipulation of the* illusio *and chance. – Power and time.*

First session (lecture): the model of the gambler

I have in front of me a question that is in fact more of a suggested answer. I am told that I could have appealed to etymology in support of my analysis of interest. In fact, I had thought of this, but I didn't do so because I think excessive use of etymological reference – which has no value as proof – can lead to an all-too-common kind of exaggeration. That said, it is true that the notion of interest, as suggested by its etymology, is close to what I was trying to say: being 'interested' is 'being within', 'being part of', 'participating in', and therefore 'holding dear' in the sense of 'wanting to be part of' and 'being held by what you are participating in'.[1] In this sense etymology reinforces my interpretation of the notion: to be interested, in Latin, is to participate in a universe, to adhere to it sufficiently to be held by it; it is this kind of relation of belonging where the person belonging holds dear the relation that binds him. I could have invoked etymology, but that would not have added anything to my analysis. It might even have aroused suspicion in your minds, So many analyses have no foundation other than an often approximate etymology that I avoid resorting to it except when it seems to impose itself; for instance, when I introduce the notion of *illusio*, I invoke etymology[2] – in this case explicitly fictitious and imaginary – because it enables me to give coherence to a conceptual system. Likewise, when I constitute the network of words fashioned around *doxa* (orthodoxy, heterodoxy, paradox, *allodoxia*, etc.), I think I am making a legitimate use of etymology in support of a network of relations between concepts. This reminds us that concepts work in systems and not in isolation: when someone offers you a concept, whether you realize it or not, they are offering you a system of concepts whose coherence lies in the system. Definitions exist only at the level of the system. That is my justification.

Since I succumbed last time to the temptation of replying to questions at too great a length (I spent the whole session on them), I shall move on to the lecture straight away. Otherwise the course of lectures will become completely fragmented in your minds and I shall not be able to offer from one lecture to the next the minimum of continuity that I must count on if my lectures are to follow a coherent sequence.

To remind you briefly where I had got to two weeks ago: I was trying to show that one question raised by social science is that of the continuity of the social world: why is there order rather than disorder? What makes this intelligible order last? Why is there order rather than anarchy? It is a question that is not self-evident, and we credit sometimes Vico and sometimes Hegel[3] with having made this kind of historical discovery of the necessity of the historical world, which, because of the fact that it is not abandoned to chance but has its own internal coherence and duration, bears within itself the source both of its necessity and its durability. I summed this up in two terms from Leibniz: the social world is endowed with a *lex insita*, an immanent law, which is at the same time a *vis insita*, an immanent force. That is what I want to account for, and last time I was recalling the opposition that we might make between a vision of the social world that we could roughly characterize as Cartesian – the social world as the place of a sort of radical discontinuity, where everything happens as if it started anew at every moment, as if we could keep starting from scratch – and the definition that you might call Leibnizian, according to which the social world carries within itself the regular and regulated source of its own continuity.

To illustrate the Cartesian definition, we could describe social games after the model of roulette and conjure up a vision of the gambler. I am thinking of Dostoevsky's book entitled *The Gambler* where we see a kind of down-classed character.[4] I think we are not all equally predisposed to live life as a kind of game – this will be one of the themes I shall develop in a moment, and that our vision of the social world, and in particular our vision of its continuity or discontinuity, of its capacity to last or to change at any moment, depends profoundly on our position in this world. We have a good chance of finding the gambler as I see him among the down-classed aristocrats, who will perhaps also be Bakunin-type revolutionaries, or among the subproletariat living below the threshold where the world might seem to have little meaning. The vision of the gambler that we might call Cartesian is very well incarnated in roulette, the game where there is no link between successive games; at every spin of the wheel you can win or lose everything. Which points to the striking metaphorical power of the novel. Through the description of a relation to a particular game, Dostoevsky describes a relation to the social world whereby you could completely change your position in the social world in a moment; you could win a fortune at the casino instantly and pass from the status of a proletarian or down-classed aristocrat to that of a man integrated in the social world.

This sort of magical, instantaneous and discontinuous vision of the social world strikes me as a good illustration of a possible vision of that world. That being said, roulette is a bad image of the social game: there are very few social games, and even very few social situations, that take the form of roulette. It is revolutionary situations that resemble roulette the most, since, in moments of crisis, the objective potentialities inscribed in the normal world are suspended. This is what is meant by the phrase, 'Every soldier carries a marshal's baton in his knapsack'.[5] At a juncture where all chances are equal, there is no inference or induction possible that leads from the state of the world at the instant t to the state of the world at the instant $t + 1$. This critical state of radical discontinuity, where the future of the world is suspended, where all possibilities become equally probable, is quite exceptional. It is both rare and brief, and to a considerable extent illusory, because the illusion of equal probability is very soon belied by the return in force of the principles that ensure the good continuity of the social order.

It is important to elaborate this discontinuous vision, as I am attempting to do, in order to use it as a sort of imaginary variation enabling us the better to think what a linear order is: it is one of the possible configurations of the social world. Through its possibility, this configuration can perform a formidable seduction of the imagination: I think the myth – to call it by its name – of revolution and of permanent revolution is rooted in the idea that the world could be a game of roulette, where, with every turn of the wheel, things would start from scratch and where the winnings acquired from previous games would be completely suspended and have no influence over the following game. On this sort of vision, which we might call Cartesian or Sartrean, I refer you to *The Logic of Practice*. There, I expounded at some length on what seems to me to be the principle of Sartre's anthropology as presented in *Being and Nothingness* and even more so in the *Critique of Dialectical Reason*.[6] Sartre seems to me to develop in a highly coherent manner, as always, what is, in a very interesting but very false way, the subjective and discontinuous vision in which the social world is at every moment dependent on the decisions of social agents. But this discontinuous vision is only valid for the extreme cases of radical discontinuity that we encounter in certain moments of crisis.

Immanent tendencies of reproduction in the social world

However, the ordinary state of the social fields, and the social field as field of all the fields, is one of a continuity based on the existence of what we might call 'capital' (a somewhat devalued term, but I see no alternative), as the sum of energies accumulated historically and liable to be reinvested at any moment in the social order with determining social effects. In other words, seen from the viewpoint where I place myself – although I do not claim to provide a definition – capital, as a sort of historical memory or historical inertia, is precisely that *vis insita* [innate force of matter], more or less concentrated in the hands of a small number of people, which will become the *lex insita* [immanent law] of the world, given that capital attracts capital, for instance, and tends to become concentrated. If it is necessary to speak of capital, it is because the social world is so constituted that it has a memory. As Leibniz said, 'the present is pregnant with the future',[7] meaning that at every moment in the present people hold the means of fashioning the future; and capital is this kind of bridge between the present and the future – a property mentioned by the most classic definitions given by economists. It is a sort of anticipation of, and right to pre-empt, the future, and often, obviously, the future of others.

Between the discontinuous, 'spontaneist' vision of the Cartesian-Sartrean type and the 'continuist' vision according to which the world obeys immanent tendencies, I myself think the state of the social world is comprised in the notion of capital. The social world has an order, it is continuous, and it obeys immanent tendencies. All sociologists have noted this phenomenon in their different languages. In Durkheim's terminology, they are 'constraints'. Durkheim insisted on the fact that the social world was a place of constraint and even identified the social with constraint:[8] you cannot do whatever you like whenever you like, or imagine whatever future you fancy; some things are not possible, and those who do whatever they like are negatively sanctioned by the social world. In everyday language, we say that they are out of their minds: they act as if the social world had no laws, or as if they were above the laws of economic sanction. There is a very fine page by Max Weber on what happens to those whose habitus is not what I would call suitably adapted: if they are manufacturers, they are driven to ruin; if they are simple workers without capital, they are doomed in advance to unemployment.[8] Since it is home to immanent tendencies, the social world requires social agents to take account of these immanent tendencies (I think the word 'account' is important), which are things that you can count on and that need to be taken into account: the world is predictable, what happens is not entirely random. If you have an academic diploma, you are likely, barring accidents, to obtain the post that the diploma entitles you to, and that is more or less the case for all qualifications: deeds of property, academic diplomas and financial bonds are mortgages on the future, down payments, things that allow you to behave with some assurance, sure in the belief that your subjective assurance will be confirmed by objective reassurance.

Social science, then, is linked to probability: we inhabit the universe of the probable, which is never at the two extremes described by the theory of probabilities. We never have a nil probability ($P = 0$) and never an absolute probability ($P = 1$); we are always in the universe of intermediary chances. In fact, the social order is no more than this immanent tendency to produce stable and regular patterns (I hesitate to speak of 'social order', because it often has political overtones, and often suggests whether you are for or against it. I keep saying this, but it is the sad condition of the sociologist who is obliged, in order to communicate what he is doing, to speak a language normally used to pass judgement on things: the most neutral use of an expression such as 'social order' has to accommodate the fact that listeners will hear it as 'it is good' or 'it is not good'.) This dynamic motive force inscribed in the different fields produces both movement in the field – in the case of the intellectual field, the struggle for the monopoly of legitimate judgement – and, at the same time, the limits within which this struggle may be played out. In so doing, it provides the principles enabling us to anticipate, and to produce behaviour suitably adapted to the objective chances of success.

This is where I had got to. I had raised the question of discontinuity as an introduction to what I intended to discuss next time, that is, a theory of the species of capital, the different forms that capital can take, since I have already given the principle behind this theory. I explained, both this year and last year, that there are as many different kinds of capital as there are fields, that is, places within which resources or properties, in every sense of the term, may function, since they can only function as capital in relation to a space within which they are valid and effective. There will, then, be as many types of capital as there are fields and subfields, which does not prevent us from considering a certain number (two or three) as major species of capital, of which the others are particular forms.

Comparison between societies and continuity of the social world

Before dealing with this, I would like to emphasize this property of the social world and remind you – because it is a problem that we all have in mind, however unclearly – how this vision of the world enables us to understand fairly precisely the differences between various forms of society. The contrasts that people draw between traditional and modern societies, pre-capitalist and capitalist societies are naively simplistic. They enumerate a series of differences and all too often embed them in one of the typically linear or mono-linear philosophies of history, which may take on a more or less secular form: the Marxist or Weberian types of philosophy, with their theory of rationalization, and all the attenuated varieties that today we call 'theories of modernization'.[9] There are debates over these questions. You may quite reasonably not be aware of them, but even if you are not, you surely have your opinions, because when someone says to you, 'We have moved on from the oil lamp and the sailing ship', they are articulating a philosophy of history. Politicians thus go in for philosophy of history every day, for instance when they compare the before with the after. When they make use of the before to name the after, they are doing history of philosophy, they are using effects of prediction, whether prospective or retrospective, whose function is to show the present in a certain light,[10] one of the fundamental stakes of the political struggle being, as I reminded you last time, to impose our principle of vision of the social world. It is for this reason that I think it is important to try, not to resolve this problem of the comparison between societies, but to draw up some of the principles of comparison that I find most important. I must warn you that what I am about to say will not be perfectly clear and coherent because I am still thinking about it, and I am not absolutely sure what I am going to say, but I think it is better than much of what is said about the question, and for this reason I feel authorized to say some things that may be uncertain and even contradictory.

There are, then, immanent tendencies that may derive from two sources: on the one hand, objectivity, that is, things themselves; on the other hand, subjectivity, our minds and bodies. If you remember what I said previously, there are two principles that make the world endure and have consequences: on the one hand, the immanent mechanisms that go to make up the field; on the other hand, the incorporated dispositions of the habitus. In fact, if a field lasts, and its being tends to endure, if it has a *conatus*, a sort of tendency to persist in being, it is because it offers mechanisms tending to perpetuate themselves through agents predisposed to act in conformity with the immanent potential of these mechanisms. Most fields work in this way: there are agents predisposed to act on and anticipate the demands of the structures, largely because their dispositions are produced by the same demands, and the fields tend to persist and remain active. Which does not mean – although people like to protest that it does – that social systems are circular reproductions, which would be meaningless: there is just a tendency to persist in being which is not at all a demand for perfect reproduction (I won't say more about this, it would take too long).

These two principles behind the continuity of the social world may be expressed in terms of capital. We might say that a first principle of continuity is capital in its incorporated state, that is the *habitus*. Here, etymology does, I believe, fulfil its function:[11] the habitus is something having-been-acquired, it is a form of capital that exists in the incorporated state, such as knowledge of a language or what we normally call culture; we can easily see, for instance, that it dies with its owner: cultural capital, unlike economic capital, is so closely linked to its owner that it disappears along with him, at least in its incorporated form – cultural capital can in fact exist in an objective state, for example in agricultural machinery. This incorporated capital, the habitus, is a past that survives in the present, is pregnant with a future and involves a future: saying that we have a habitus means that we are capable of giving birth to something new; the habitus is not something passive at all – which is why I employ this word rather than 'habit' – so many possible actions are not dictated by the stimulus to which the habitus responds, the best example being improvisation. The habitus enables us to engender many possible things, but only within certain limits. As Marx says somewhere, 'the petit bourgeois cannot overcome the limits of his mind'.[12] I think it is the notion of habitus that Marx is intuitively activating. One of the properties of the habitus is, like Kant's categories, to make an organized perception of the world possible, but only within certain limits: I can only conceive a coherent world within the limits of my own organizing principles, and I can only conceive a world-view within the limits of such a viewpoint. As a result we cannot predict exactly what a person with a particular type of habitus will do, but we can be fairly certain of what they won't do, that is, we can assess the limits of their regulated improvisation. Capital, then, can exist in an incorporated state in the form of the habitus. It can also exist in an objectified state, in an apparatus assuming the guise, for example, of the school or the banking system, with these systems able to exist in their own right in two ways: in a non-institutionalized state or in a state institutionalized in the form of rules such as legal statutes or, in different universes, deontological codes. I shall return to this point later.

Differentiating between fields and objectification of capital

That being said, I think that one of the great principles of distinction between the different forms of society lies in the degree of differentiation of their capital, and, by the same token, in the degree of differentiation of the social spaces. Durkheim said quite clearly that archaic societies are fundamentally undifferentiated and that things which we distinguish, such as religion and economics, law and religion, intellectual and artistic life, were completely undifferentiated in archaic societies;[13] he tended to describe the process that we call evolution, that is, history, as a process of progressive differentiation. In my language, one of the dimensions of the process of historical change – I deliberately use the vaguest vocabulary because it is better than a vocabulary implying a specific philosophy that we cannot master – is the constitution of relatively autonomous fields and subfields. One example among many: we can describe the process of autonomization and constitution of the economic field itself. For instance, the economy of ancient Greece introduced a certain number of inventions that enable it to operate as a field – there is a very fine book by Moses Finlay on this topic.[14] This economic field was never completely constituted because, you might say, it never invented a certain number of institutions that would have enabled it to function as a field (we can perceive and understand their absence retrospectively from a more advanced state of the field; as Marx said, 'the anatomy of man is a key to the anatomy of the ape';[15] it is true that we can only understand the state of a field from the perspective of a later state). We could do the same in the case of the artistic field, and rather than ask ourselves whether the artist appears to break with the craftsman in the twelfth, thirteenth, fourteenth, fifteenth, sixteenth or seventeenth century, we can ask ourselves which moment it is when something like a field starts to function, the existence of this field being the truly objective condition for the appearance of something like what we call an artist.

One of the great principles of difference between societies is, I think, the degree of differentiation between their social fields and, concomitantly, the degree of differentiation of their capital. Basically, the more undifferentiated a universe, the more the different types of capital are conflated; the more you can obtain money through honour, the more you can acquire social relations with a beautiful girl and the more you can achieve the conversion of one type of capital into another, and so on. In our societies, the convertibility of one type of capital into another poses many problems, in particular – I shall return to this – because it takes time. Transforming money into academic prestige, entering the Académie française with money: this takes a long time and a labour of euphemization, and sometimes it is just not possible. As long as all types of capital are undifferentiated, these problems of conversion are much less present, which does not mean that life is any simpler. The degree of differentiation of the fields, then, is a first property.

A second difference that I find extremely important is the degree of objectification of the capital, as much in the practical state, in the form of mechanisms or institutions, as in the form of explicit norms or laws. To put it quite simply: the nearer we get to archaic societies, the more the principle or principles of continuity of the social world are based on the habitus of the agents and, consequently, the less a vision of a structuralist type is justified, which is a paradox, because structuralism has been applied by ethnologists particularly to societies in which the principle of continuity lies much more in the dispositions of the agents, in their permanent manner of being, than in the objective structures.

Here I shall refer to a text by Marx, which I call on because it is perhaps one of his least Marxist and because it seems to me to sum up in a remarkable way the process that I want to describe:

The less social power the medium of exchange (and at this stage it is still closely bound to the nature of the direct product of labour and the direct needs of the partners in exchange) the greater must be the power of the community which binds the individuals together, the patriarchal relation, the community of antiquity, feudalism and the guild system . . . Each individual possesses social power in the form of a thing. Rob the thing of this social power and you must give it to persons to exercise over persons. Relations of personal dependence (entirely spontaneous at the outset) are the first social forms, in which human productive capacity develops only to a slight extent and at isolated points. Personal independence founded on *objective* [*sachlicher*] dependence is the second great form, in which a system of general social metabolism, of universal relations, of all-round needs and universal capacities is formed for the first time.[16]

This text is not transparent on a first reading, but I believe that what it states clearly is this: the less objectified the economic patterns and the less they are inscribed in institutions – mechanisms, such as banking mechanisms or market mechanisms, that generate tendencies – the more social relations will depend on personal relations. There are then two statements, that we might sum up in this way: the more relations of personal dependence tend to form the principal basis of the duration of social relations, the less there exist relations of what Marx calls material dependence. In other words, it is what I referred to last time: to put it briefly, the fewer mechanisms of domination there are, the more the domination must be personal, involving individuals.

Violence and its euphemization

Here I think we find a first paradox within the theories of evolution. I have already referred to Norbert Élias's theory that historical evolution progresses in the direction of a tendency towards the monopolization of violence by state institutions, and therefore towards a decline in the direct and physical exercise of violence. This theory has much in its favour, and in fact Élias applies Weber's theory of the state to very different specific domains – sport, citizenship, manners, interpersonal relations and suchlike.[17] In Weber's words, the state is the holder of the monopoly of legitimate violence (which makes the issue of individual self-defence problematic) and, in concentrating violence and claiming the monopoly of its legitimate exercise (whether physical or other), it undermines direct recourse to violence – such as the law of 'an eye for an eye', for instance.[18] This Weberian thesis, linked to a definition of the state that Weber also included in the evolutionist schema that I mentioned just now (he considered the rational state as the culmination of a process of concentration of power and the exercise of violence) seems to me partly true, but it seems to me to be based on ignorance of the complexity of the process of objectification that I am arguing.

In fact we could say that the concentration of violence in the hands of the state is one dimension of the historical process (we see this particularly in the case of the law) by which the state concentrates objectified and institutionalized power, of which the form par excel-

lence is the law. And it concentrates everything that I have mentioned
on previous occasions: the power of nomination . . . In fact, stretching
Weber's definition a little, we could say that the state is the holder of
the monopoly of legitimate symbolic violence. Remember my analysis of the opposition between an official nomination and an insult:[19]
the state has the power to tell someone what they are with relatively
uncontroversial authority. It concentrates its power in the objectified and institutionalized aspect of capital. That being said, another
aspect of objectification is objectification in economic mechanisms, in
the immanent laws of all social games. This power is not necessarily
concentrated or even controlled by the state, and yet it underlies our
regular social patterns. We might say that if direct and physical violence wanes, it is because the state centralizes the institutional violence,
but it is also because the violence operates through the intermediary of
what Sartre called the 'inertia-violence' of mechanisms,[20] a dimension
of the historical process being precisely this tendency to transform
direct violence – the employer who has the right to cut off the hand
of his employee – into a violence that can be exercised through the
medium of the state – the employer can dismiss his employee and be
indemnified – or through the intermediary of objective mechanisms
avoiding the need to resort to this elementary violence, or preventing
this elementary violence from occurring. Consequently, as opposed to
evolutionist schemas, we could say that pre-capitalist societies are at
once much more violent and much gentler: if we wanted at all costs to
draw a graph of their evolution, we would have something more like
a U-shaped curve than the straight rising line that we all have unconsciously in mind when we think of 'progress'.

Since that is all rather unclear, both objectively and subjectively,
I shall explain myself. First, how does this process of objectification
take place? I shall be brief:[21] pre-capitalist economies are distinguished
from more developed economies by the fact that they cannot count on
a set of impersonal mechanisms that function without anyone having
to control them (the most obvious example is the mechanism of the
market: the market for labour, for goods, etc.) and which link a series
of objective regulations together (for example through the mediation
of prices). In the absence of mechanisms of this type, such as a labour
market or a capital market, economic resources function much more
like wealth than like capital.

For instance, the Kabyle say: a rich man is 'rich in order to give
to the poor',[22] which is obviously a very strange use of wealth, from
the perspective of the capitalist mind. That being said, what else can
you do with wealth when there are no institutions to enable you to

invest and draw profit that would procure the benefit you obtain by donating your wealth? Think of the difference between a salary and a gift. In other words, to be 'rich in order to give to the poor' is a sort of imperative that makes a virtue of necessity. The institutions that would give you a hold over others through your economic capital do not exist, and, for this reason, the only way of gaining a hold over others is through the gift, through generosity (which does not mean that the gift is made *with the intention* of gaining a hold). By the same token, this immanent tendency of the economic order tends to produce its own reinforcement: since no other behaviour is thinkable, the economic dispositions that would enable initial accumulation are hardly able to materialize, or, if they did materialize, they would be out of phase; the person who displayed them would appear to be making a break with the immanent laws of the world, which are at the same time explicit, moral laws. As long as wealth does not find the objective conditions to function as capital, it can function according to a different logic: it can function as symbolic capital, transform itself into a capital of obligations, services rendered and generosity bestowed, and by these means it can establish durable relations. You can gain a hold over people then, but on the basis of an obligation that is not legally or economically guaranteed at all, rather an obligation seen as moral and subjective, depending on the good disposition – we must use this word – of the person obliged.

Consequently, these are universes where the absence of objective mechanisms and the absence of inertia-violence and possible recourse to violence condemn them to use subtler forms of violence. Whence the fascination that these societies exert over ethnologists, since the latter come from societies where social relations can be what they are because of the mechanisms of inertia-violence. For the café waiter to bring you what he is supposed to, you don't need to tell him the story of your life, you just need to pay. If you are in a popular bar, you have to say something to neutralize or even deny the relation of servitude, but if you are at the Balzar,[23] you can content yourself with paying, unless you want to pass yourself off as a fashionable writer known to the waiter: [*reacting to laughter from the audience*] that was not a joke, it is important to see that we are not in a linear scenario.

If the institutional violence is missing, there remain only the softer forms of violence. This is all the more true the more absent the objective mechanisms, so that in our societies we will increasingly find the soft forms of violence the more we move towards the fields in which the forms of inertia-violence are less present, as they are in the domestic economy. If, for instance, the feminist movement makes such a bad job of analysing the movements that it claims to analyse, it is largely because of its bias towards economics: ignoring the specificity of the relatively autonomous universe of domestic relations, it finds it difficult to think of these domestic relations in their specificity, that is, as an economy whose laws of functioning are a denial of economics, in other words as an economy that is much closer to pre-capitalist economies, whose functioning is a denial of economics.[24] Even Lukács understood this, saying that the pre-capitalist economies are founded on a denial of the original grounds of their existence.[25] Pre-capitalist economies do in fact function on the basis of a rejection of economics, as if economics were something shameful, censored and repressed – I believe the analogy is quite legitimate – in such a way that, to exercise any economic violence, you had to respect all the formalities.

This theme of 'respecting the formalities' seems important to me. The pre-capitalist societies are universes linked to a very specific mode of domination: you can only dominate at the expense of a high degree of euphemization of the relations of domination, since the violence may not be exercised through the mechanisms of what Marx called the 'blind necessity' of the market. For instance, in everyday life, one can dominate people through the medium of the educational system (or a higher diploma) or through the mediation of the banking system. When such mediations are impossible, the social agents are obliged to act as it were between individuals.

Being humanists (for if they weren't, they would not be ethnologists), ethnologists are fascinated by these societies whose peoples deploy such ingenuity in creating face-to-face interpersonal relations. They return enchanted from these societies where they have seen magical interpersonal relations (the fact that these are highly mystified does not mean that they are not a social ideal . . . I'm not sure of this, I reserve my position). I think that the relations we find remarkable, such as amorous relations, are highly magical or mystified, which do objectively harbour problems of violence, but these are strongly negated, at the cost of a considerable labour of alchemical transformation:[26] basically, it is about transmuting a relation of objective credit in the eyes of the sociologist into an exchange of gifts (people have said that the exchange of gifts is a question of credit; this is rather simplistic, but it is not objectively false), which seems to be the absolute opposite, that is into two successive acts of generosity: A who makes B a gift as if it should absolutely not be returned, and B who will give to A as if he had received nothing. This supposes some considerable effort, a sometimes extraordinary social genius, and notably the art of playing with time:[27] one of the reasons why one should never reciprocate immediately is that the time or interval introduced is precisely a sort of screen between the two successive acts, whereas in our societies, we would say 'it's only fair' that a gift should be immediately repaid (or, if there is a time lapse, this time lapse is considered as a basis for calculating tariffs and rates of interest).

To return to the evolutionist model, pre-capitalist societies are marked at once by extreme violence (in these societies, violence such as murder is all too prevalent) and an extreme euphemization of violence. In other words, contrary to what Marx says in the passage where he describes the passage of pre-capitalist societies to capitalist societies, we don't start from a universe of enchanted personal relations to arrive at the 'icy water of egotistical calculation'.[28] Marx himself bought into this mythology, which more or less makes up the unconscious of all ethnologists. The 'icy water of egotistical calculation' is a very fine phrase if you want to alarm people, but the metaphor describes this kind of mythology of pre-capitalist societies as universes where the humanist genius is fully deployed, where social agents take care not to manipulate one another, or to do it so gently that it does not count as manipulation (metaphors are always the point where sociologists and ethnologists merge with their object . . .).

I have concentrated on the fact that pre-capitalist societies do not possess market mechanisms, but it is the same for the mechanisms of cultural capital. One theory of the educational system in our societies reveals properties of pre-capitalist societies (here is a typical application of the type, 'The anatomy of man is a key to the anatomy of the ape'). One of the major problems of pre-capitalist societies is that the only legitimate forms of accumulation there are those based on the accumulation of symbolic capital, symbolic capital being the most negated form of capital (symbolic capital is the capital that people acknowledge you to have, the capital they grant you). There is nonetheless a mechanism present in all societies, the mechanism of symbolic alchemy. If the rich man is 'rich in order to give to the poor', it means that there is at least a market to transform economic capital into symbolic capital; the institution of the gift exists, whereas it might not exist (we must not forget that everything I am describing is a social invention). The institution of the gift, for instance, comprises a vocabulary, a whole lexicon. In Kabylia, there is an amazing lexicon to describe all forms of the gift: masculine/feminine, small gift/big gift, gift in special/everyday circumstances. It is a formidable institution: each individual starts out in life with a whole apparatus enabling them to pick and choose, and if something has a name, it means you can do it, and even – since it is publicly named and therefore recognized – you must do it; you are sure to be approved in doing it.

Something that exists together with the mechanism of transmutation of economic resources into symbolic capital is the process that I noted in Kafka and that you can find in the educational system or the intellectual field: the process of accumulating symbolic capital, reputation and good fame, that is, the alchemy that transforms monopolized property into socially recognized and approved property, and the owner of this property into its legitimate owner. This means that the accumulation of symbolic capital is one of the forms of accumulation through which domination may be exercised. If, for instance, I have a lot of symbolic capital and there is no institution equivalent to wage labour, I need only say in the marketplace, 'I'm going to harvest my crops next Friday', for all sorts of people, as if by chance, to offer to come and work for me. It's called mutual assistance. Afterwards, I invite them round to dine. But if I said to them, 'I am paying you this much', they would be mortally offended. I would never see them again, and they would say that I am not a man of honour. It is a mechanism that you can safely count on. It helps to establish a stable, functional society, with reliable relations of domination: you can have employees at peak times and not have to feed them in slack periods.

That said, the accumulation of symbolic capital is never guaranteed, although our own societies do have symbolic titles of property. For instance, if you are appointed as a member of the Academy of Moral and Political Sciences, that is an official nomination. You even have a little tricolour card that you can show if you are checked by the police. So you don't have to demonstrate any extraordinary talent to prove your honour at every moment (which is one of the most important forms of capital in a society of honour). Symbolic capital, the capital of nomination, is legally guaranteed, with the educational system playing a capital – dare I say – role in our societies, because it is the institution that guarantees this particular form of capital that we may call cultural capital, and which exists independently of your mental activities, in the shape of a piece of paper giving access to certain privileges. This is evidence of what I was saying just now, extrapolating the logic of Marx: as long as there are no objective mechanisms and institutions, every move that you make takes place between individuals. You can look at Élias's magnificent book on 'court society' to see his opposition between Henri IV and Louis XIV: where Henri IV rules in the pre-capitalist mode (if someone offends him, he reaches straightaway for his sword, and fights in a rather basic and primary fashion), Louis XIV establishes a field with hierarchies, procedural regulations, and the like; to rule, he needs only to rule the field, which is much more economical than ruling in person. Rather than risk bumping into a fencing champion, it is easier to have a *petit lever* and a *grand lever* [private audience and public audience], and so on.[29]

In pre-capitalist societies, the mode of domination is direct and personal, and because of this it can be much more brutal: you have to fight. If, for instance, you need to have six sons, it is so that you are able to fight; having six sons, the Kabyle say, means that a woman can walk around with a golden crown on her head:[30] nobody would even think of attacking her because of the aura of potential force that surrounds her [. . .]. Violence is there, then, and may be resorted to at any moment. Elias says that in societies such as ancient Greece, with the violence of the struggles at Olympus, the potential for violence in all its forms was extremely high.[31] In the film *The Ballad of Narayama*,[32] it is clear that these are societies of unspeakable violence: when they reach the age of seventy, the old women must disappear, but their death is euphemized in an extraordinary way, as a kind of pilgrimage. Everything is institutionalized for the violence to be at once terrible and highly euphemized. I think in fact that if we understand peasant societies so badly, it is because, even fifty years ago, they were much closer to this kind of society than the way they are described in books; novelists so often romanticize the peasant [. . .]. This kind of ambiguity of pre-capitalist societies, which are at once highly violent and yet extremely careful to euphemize violence, is rooted in reality.

To return to the evolutionist schema. To simplify, we could say that the different fields emerge, and become autonomous. Once constituted, the economic field imposes its own necessity ('Business is business', 'There's no place for sentiment in business', etc.). It cuts itself off from the world of the family, for fraternal values are no longer valid in the marketplace. Once constituted, it imposes its own necessity, and it is during this nascent phase that capitalism exercises the highest degree of violence through its mechanisms. The mechanisms operate with all their violence, and there is little anyone can do to counterattack. Antidotes to this violence have not yet been devised. Thus far, the process could indeed be summed up in Marx's words: to start with, we have relations of personal domination between individuals, which are unstable and need permanent maintenance, and, in the end, brutal relations exercised through the inertia-violence of economic mechanisms and – it always helps if we add Weber to Marx – legal mechanisms, institutional violence, and the like. That being said, if the economic field changes and it engenders forces such as contestation and protest, the subtler forms of violence reappear, and then the forces of contestation will develop, and the more the forces of contestation develop, the more the pre-capitalist forms of subtle violence will reappear. Thus we find firms now whose theory of public relations could have been drawn up by the Kabyle, given their attempt to find highly euphemized forms of domination relations in which all forms of social relations will be denied; obviously symbolic forms of domination, will play a leading part in these mechanisms, through the intermediary of culture, and the like.

This linear vision is very simplistic, but I shall add another comment on the role of the formalities. As I have said several times already, the more the violence has to be exercised directly, the less it can count on the anonymous, neutral mediation of the mechanisms [. . .], but, and I shall return to this, the more it has to be euphemized, the more the formalities have to be respected. I said that one of the dimensions of the process of objectification is institutionalization. We might also speak of 'codification', taking the word 'code' both in the sense it has when we speak of a linguistic code and in the sense of a 'code of law'. This process of objectification and codification of social relations is extremely important for understanding the differences between societies. It is one of the dimensions that helps us to start understanding the differences: social relations are more or less codified in different cases, there are not always rules guaranteed by the authorities and backed up by force. If pre-capitalist societies rely so much on the habitus, it is also because the social forms and relations there are relatively undercodified. We get the impression that, to survive and especially to succeed in these societies, you need a kind of genius in what we call 'interpersonal relations'. This is also one of the reasons why ethnologists, who are often not very gifted in the study of their own society, are fascinated by these people, who are past masters in the arts of social skills and games, who have names for all sorts of social manoeuvres: I think we could establish a psychosociological theory of this, more elaborate than the psychosociologists themselves can deliver, by drawing on what primitive societies say should be done in a particular case [. . .].

If to survive in these societies you need competence in the management of interpersonal relations, as we see elsewhere as soon as we meet people who, in our societies, still participate in the universes that are infinitely more sophisticated than any modern etiquette, it is because, since the violence is still there as an underlying threat, the work of formalization is very important. Thus, paradoxically, in a society like that of the Kabyle, it was distant marriage ceremonies that ended in violence. As in many societies, you need to choose between a close marriage and a distant marriage; the latter may bring high symbolic benefits but is risky given its alliance with people who are distant and therefore enemies. Ultimately, the most prestigious marriage is one with your most prestigious enemies. These highly prestigious marriages, which give rise to the most elaborate ceremonials and the greatest exhibitions of symbolic agreement between the groups (with processions and so on), are also the most risky because there is a whole series of bizarre trials: there is target shooting, and if the parents of the bride miss the target they have to don the yoke of an ass, which is a considerable insult.[33] There is a risk, and we note that the greater the risk, the more the observance of form matters, and the more things are governed not by legal statutes but by a sort of deontology of interpersonal relations.

This means that when in the contrary case we say, 'It's a family affair; it's all open and above-board', this signals not only, 'We are all family, there's no need to take precautions, we have nothing to hide', but also, 'At home we can rely on the habitus and its incorporated dispositions, there's no danger'. Problems start when distant people are involved. As there are no police forces, legal system or prisons that might arbitrate, no third party ready to intervene, you need to 'play by the rules', which in this case are politeness, protocol, duty. You can see then that, paradoxically, Elias's mechanism is terribly false – I really appreciate Elias, but in this case I totally disagree with him. The more the violence is present and real – when it might end in a fight, for instance – the more refined must be the civility, codification and respect for the rules. This elaborate observance of rules in societies without writing, by means of hand-me-down proverbs and completely pre-scripted conversations (for instance, to a woman who has just given birth you should say this, she will reply that, and you will respond as follows), this ready-made codification is the elementary form of the objectification that will become one of the great changes, along with the law, since the law allows us to reduce the particular case to a general formula, to find an 'algebraic' equation, as it were, for a particular case.

This process starts with the formalism of refined polite behaviour that enchants ethnologists. The ethnologists are carried away, because they fail to see that this refined politeness is not at all an antinomy to violence: it is the peak of contained violence. We live in universes ruled, I believe, by the general law according to which euphemization increases in proportion with censorship. This general law, which we can apply to understanding the work of Heidegger, for instance,[34] applies to the particular case: the violent impulse, the objective danger of violence and the censorship of violence are all very strong and they engender extremely sophisticated behaviour where violence subsists, but is totally transformed. This is so refined and clever, I must insist, that ethnologists lose track of these hidden traces of violence that are apparent only to the inner circle of initiates [. . .].

Having made this analysis, I shall proceed next time directly to analyse the different species of capital and their conditions of operation.

Second session (seminar): Kafka's *The Trial* (2)

I want to return to my argument on Kafka, which will serve as a transition towards what I want to start to sketch out today, which is a reflection on the links between temporality and power.

My analysis of Kafka's *Trial*, as I have already said, was more of a kind of discourse on Kafka than a genuine reading of his work. Let us say that I was doing openly what everyone does all the time: I was using Kafka as a sort of 'projective test'. I would like simply to admit the limits of what I was doing. I was trying to insist on the fact that Kafka gave us a kind of model of the symbolic struggle, or of the social world as the site of a symbolic struggle for identity. Obviously, if any identity is the object of an anxious relationship, it is the identity of the writer. We should not forget that what is at stake in such a model is an extremely singular profession: a largely unprofessional and yet very prestigious profession. In other words, if the model that I was offering is right, we have to say that it can be most favourably and successfully applied to the case of the field of cultural production, to the intellectual field where what is at stake is this vital identity ('Am I a writer or not?') and where the game is characterized by its acute uncertainty.

Enquiries into writers or artists in general are, moreover, particularly difficult because the attributes of the 'writer' are extremely loosely defined. Even the most naively positivist analysis is obliged to consider this question. Dictionaries or directories of writers are thus very interesting through their rules of compilation. There are some directories where you have to pay to be included. In this case, the criterion is not the degree of legitimacy as writer, but the degree of aspiration to be legitimized as writer. Depending on how much you pay, they may or may not print your photo, or publish your poem. Obviously, the likelihood of seeing 'real' writers decreases the more we move towards this kind of framework, insofar as the most writerly writers know that they would discredit themselves as writers if they appeared in this kind of context. But these directories work as long as the people who pay to be written down as a writer do not know that they would not be there if they were genuine writers [*laughter*]. There are many universes of this type. With what we call the 'decentralization' of the educational universe – that is, the widening of access to secondary education – institutions have been transformed by the fact that they accept people who, in an earlier state of the system, would not have gained access:[35] so there are people who, when they are there, still aren't there, because the place where they are is not the same as soon as they appear in it. It's the same for clubs – remember Groucho Marx's quip: 'What kind of club is it if it would accept me as a member?'[36]

In some cases, an agency or institution is then devalued by the fact that it grants access to people who destroy what was the very foundation of the value of the institution, that is, the fact of excluding them. Although we can see easily enough that the Jockey Club works in this way, we tend not to see that it is the same for many institutions. The status of writer, artist or philosopher, for instance, is not a status like others. They are extremely elastic and diffuse concepts which, by the way, do allow investment [. . .]. For example, the objective futures offered by the different disciplines are more or less varied. Geography is surely one of the most limited disciplines in the space of the arts faculties.[37] Geology too. But philosophy is the most disparate: you can exploit the wilful confusion between the maximalist definition (the philosopher is a philosopher) and the minimalist definition (the philosopher is a schoolteacher at Saint-Flour).[38] This very large spread is one of the specific benefits procured by certain professions, one of whose functions I believe is to entertain confusion over investment and also encourage distinguished disinvestment. For instance, in certain circles, to be a primary school teacher would be a real drop in status; to be a special needs teacher would be better, and a psychosociologist perfect.

There are, then, social identities that are more or less strictly defined and codified within the code of the professions. As a sociologist, you draw up a code and you notice it straight away: faced with professions that are weakly codified objectively, the sociologist has no choice other than to reproduce the objective vagueness or to produce scientific rigour with the risk of forgetting that the rigour is his invention. Very few sociologists know that they codify things that are very unequally codified objectively, and they neglect to include in their act of codification the objective degree of pre-codification of the things that they are codifying, unwittingly granting them legal status, in ignorance of the fact that one of the principal properties of what they are codifying is their varying degree of codification. If you classify 'Provençal potters' among 'craftsmen', you are ignoring the fact that an important property of 'Provençal potters' consists in avoiding classifications, whether scholarly or not.[39] It is important therefore to bear this in mind. We don't reflect deeply enough on the nature of the code. A code translates the professions into figures – it is the ABC of sociology. To devise a code is like drawing up a legal statute, it is putting things in order, it is objectifying, it is creating formal, constant and lasting relations between a set of properties. Some legal statute may be the reproduction or duplication of a pre-existing legal statute, and that is not a problem, you just have to know that this is the case. It may, on the contrary, be the production *ex nihilo* of a legal statute that did not previously exist, and this also needs to be known, because the coding negates one important property of the things encoded, which is the fact that they were difficult to encode.

The profession of writer is a strange and extremely disparate one. It is as disparate as the field of literary production. It ranges from people who are in effect salaried employees writing to order whatever they are asked to write within the constraints of a classic capitalist type (they are paid according to their output at piece-work rates) through to people who write outside the market, with no audience or clientele, except an anticipated posthumous readership. The profession is so disparate that success is very difficult to predict. It is as a result a highly insecure universe. Yet it is at the same time a profession requiring profound investment, for you have to invest your all in it. You could not be a writer before the moment when the artist was constituted as a social role (I am thinking for example that the Florentine painter Ghirlandaio made investments that were closer to those of the craftsmen in the Faubourg Saint-Honoré or the Faubourg Saint-Antoine[40] than those of a modern avant-garde painter . . .). But from the moment when the image of the writer or the artist was constituted, then perpetuated and reproduced by the educational system that characterized the trade of the writer as being 'worth dying for', the profession of writer became something that people were ready to die for. Weber says that one property of religion is that it deals in questions of life and death, and this is very important: there are no stakes higher than life itself. The profession of writer, then, is a highly insecure and highly uncertain profession, on the one hand, and one requiring profound investment, on the other. It is this combination of that generates such acute anxiety. The Kafka effect is this sort of emotive attitude towards the outcome of the game; an emotive structuring of the relation to the future, which gives a very special temporal structure.

The manipulation of the *illusio* and chance

I wanted to remind you of that in order to create a transition towards what I intend to discuss today, which is the relation between temporality and power, and how we can make a sociological study of it – if sociological is the right word – or rather how we can make a theory of temporality that encompasses the social fact. To return very briefly to Kafka. What is interesting in *The Trial* is that, as some critics have seen, the trial is a procedure and a process, that is, a kind of infernal machine: it takes shape gradually, and once you are caught up in the mechanism, there is no escaping it. This is where the notion of interest applies: you are caught up in the game and the more involved you are and the more anxiously you await the results of the game, the more vital they are and the more acute your stress and expectation. This stress and expectation with no guarantee of satisfaction produce an experience of anxiety, given the equal likelihood of all possibilities and, in particular, of the most terrifying possibilities: anything may happen and the worst is the most likely. One important thing about the experience of *The Trial* is that as the trial proceeds like a dramatic scenario or cinematic montage, K. is increasingly caught up in it and finds it more and more difficult to disentangle himself. That said, we are constantly reminded that the game only continues as long as K. cooperates; from the moment he envisages withdrawing and telling the advocate that he no longer needs his services, the game loses its hold on him. This reminds us that fields exercise a force in proportion to our disposition to invest in the game, which is the basis of formulae that I find rather simplistic, such as 'power comes from below'. These modern types of philosophy along the lines that 'the dominated are dominated because they want to be' deserve not much more than a prize for paradox.

The model that I propose to offer is very different. In fact, social games are so designed that they have a hold on you only for as long as you are involved, and in a sense the dominated do collaborate in their domination [. . .]. The possibility of leaving the game often exists only for the detached onlooker. This reminds us of the master–slave syndrome, for example.[41] Obviously, there is always a way out, but the chances of using this possibility are very unevenly distributed [. . .]. When the goal, as for all the subproletariat, is to satisfy elementary needs, then freedom to leave the game – which always exists as a bare possibility – is a purely theoretical possibility. That being said, it is important to remember that in producing the need and appetite for the goals and their attractiveness, the game produces the conditions of its functioning; a game that does not produce players with an urge to win would not work. When you install an institution of a capitalist type in a pre-capitalist society, in order to make an economic field function, you need not only the institutions (banks and so forth), but also the social agents disposed to act [. . .]. This has been noted time and again. It is not just an argument from colonial, neocolonial or postcolonial racist discourse, but also a social fact that in many societies, when the economic agents have obtained the means to satisfy their elementary needs, they can stop working. They can then leave their work when they have obtained what they consider necessary to satisfy their needs; which is the despair of the modern *homines economici*, who want their social agents to be regular, stable and ready to invest even beyond their needs.

When Weber studies capitalism, he studies the constitution of the field, with its objective institutions (the banks, with their mortgages and powers of attorney, and so on, all those devices invented to make up a system and construct an economic field) at the same time as the production of economic dispositions, which he calls the 'spirit of capitalism' [or 'capitalist ethics'].[42] But historically their genesis was contemporaneous: those who invent the bank have the economic disposition to calculate and invest. Colonial situations represent an interesting experimental situation because economic institutions (what Weber calls an 'economic cosmos': a field, with factories, banks, accounts, cheque books and savings, etc.) are imported ready-made and presented to people who have not been produced by this economic field. Which means that we see everything implied by the economic field that we normally forget when we see it functioning with people preconstituted to make it function. We forget, for example, that to work for a whole month when a fortnight's work brings in enough money is not so irrational, although it may cause us to stop and think. We see that economic dispositions are a necessary condition for the functioning of economic institutions.

It is the same in *The Trial*. K. wakes up, he has been accused, he has been denounced and he will gradually enter into the game. At first, he goes away for the weekend and acts as if nothing had happened. Then he starts to worry, he becomes concerned with what is going to happen (see Heidegger on concern[43] as the basis of the theory of temporality: I think that, for once, we can embrace even Heidegger within a rational theory of temporality). At the same time, he takes an advocate, he enters into the game and gets caught up in it. What do the people he has to deal with do? An advocate is normally there to defend you; but the advocate in *The Trial* does nothing of the kind: he manipulates K.'s expectations. I think advocates tend to do this in real life, but we are less aware of it. Kafka's advocate is an advocate redesigned: a fundamental property usually disguised is placed in the foreground. Likewise, in ordinary everyday life a teacher is someone who prepares you for exams and the sociologist discovers that he is someone who manipulates your expectations ('You will pass this test, but you will fail the other one'): if you are too hopeful, he brings you down to earth, if you are not too hopeful, he pushes you on . . . What does the advocate do? When K. relaxes and starts to think that it is in the bag, that he is safe and sound, and that he can save himself with his legal knowledge, the advocate harasses him. He manipulates his aspirations so as to entangle K. in the game. In other words, to become involved in the game you need to aspire after something very strongly, want to get to grips with it and take an interest, rather than say, 'That's nothing to do with me, I'm going on holiday'. In *The Trial*, most of the agents manipulate K.'s aspirations, expectations and hopes. I quote: the advocate, whose function is supposedly above all to defend K., persuades him to invest in his trial by 'deluding him with vague false hopes and tormenting him with equally vague menaces'.[44] I am not making this up. You can think of an analogous situation: the old hands who, in total or totalitarian institutions (the army, asylums, prisons, etc.), as Goffman says, manipulate the newcomer's aspirations, persuade them to lower their expectations, but not too far. Think of the role of the senior personnel in educational institutions that require profound investment, like the preparatory classes for the *grandes écoles*: they need to make you invest, then disinvest, your first marks are catastrophic, which makes you increase your investment, but they must not increase it so far that it discourages you and makes you leave the game. [. . .]

So many social actions are of this type and manipulate the inclination of the incoming agents to invest in the stakes of the institution; what is being manipulated basically is the *illusio*. There are two ways of manipulating the *illusio*: by acting directly on expectations, or by acting directly on the objective chances. These are the two forms of power par excellence – which is why power is so strongly linked to time: power can consist in manipulating subjective probabilities and expectations, or in manipulating objective probabilities. To take an example close to the experience of many of you present here: you are preparing for a competitive entrance exam, and although there were a hundred successful candidates, you are told that there are only ten places available. They manipulate the objective opportunities and everyone calculates the result: what had been a reasonable probability becomes unthinkable madness. This resembles the logic of the writer: to become a great writer is a very risky gamble. What I have just said is a key principle for understanding biographies, individual trajectories, with their series of crossroads. (I didn't want to give you the impression that I am adopting the theory of rational choice that lurks in the unconscious of the economists, but there are crossroads that we perceive more or less as such.) Often, we have started out on the road before even knowing that in real experience there are partings of the ways. There are then many moments of choice, and one of the great principles of difference between the classes, that is, between inherited dispositions, is the choice of the risky branch or the safe branch (philosophy teacher or geography teacher, artist or art teacher?). This sort of choice between careers that objectively offer very unequal futures will be a function of the disposition to take risks, which is itself a product of the internalization of objective opportunity. Those most inclined to make risky choices will be those who in fact risk the least, because they are in universes with the best opportunities [. . .].

There are two very different ways that power is exercised over social agents: one is by acting on the objective chances, the other by acting on the representations of these chances. I think it is important to distinguish between the two. Acting on the objective chances is to really modify the tendencies that are objectively immanent to the fields and their opportunities. The phenomenon of the *numerus clausus* is the extreme form.[45] If you say, as has been said in universities at different times in the past, that 'there shall be no more Jews in the universities',[46] you inaugurate a visible transformation of objective opportunity. It is activated by decree, and if you are a Jew, your chances become null and void. But there are much subtler forms of action, where the social world takes its time to structure opportunity unequally in advance. When he calculates the chances of access to higher education of men and women, for instance, the sociologist describes this social manipulation of the objective opportunities with which the individual agents must come to terms. Very often these objective opportunities are operative and efficacious because the social agents are unconsciously shaped by the universes in which they are at work, and they anticipate and internalize their impact. They say to themselves: 'As a girl, I'm not going to take maths, because the Polytechnique is not for girls . . . .' And people will say: 'Girls like the arts.' These are not the actions of agents, but of mechanisms, for there is a whole social force acting on the objective chances [. . .]. Having power over a society is having power over its objective opportunities. Knowing whether you have that power is important: for instance, does it depend on human action to radically transform the chances of access to higher education? There are cases where the consequences of a *numerus clausus* are clear: for instance, you can say: 'Right, there will be no more than x number of doctors!' – the number of people aspiring to be doctors continues to grow but the number of people becoming doctors stays the same. The aspiring candidates are subjected to forces which diminish their objective opportunities.

Another form of action is the one that can be exerted on the representations of opportunity. This is action of a political type: someone tells you, based on their knowledge of the objective opportunities, or a desire to change them: 'You must hope', 'Every soldier carries a marshal's baton in his knapsack', 'Objective chance does not exist' or 'It doesn't exist for you', 'If you persist, you will succeed', 'If they work hard enough, anyone can get into the Polytechnique'. They act as advocates by subtly manipulating your investment, for it is one of the problems of all social universes to persuade people who can't win to keep on playing the game, without letting them win. How to keep them in the game when they have no chance of winning? The educational system works pretty well, but there are many other social systems of this kind.

This action on representations can assume the guise of conforming to objective opportunity. For instance, Block, the client who informs K. of the hierarchy of advocates, says: 'You know, there are no great advocates, only the Court can decide.'[47] Block represents someone who is entirely alienated. I was saying last week that he is completely juridified – Goffman says that the long-term inhabitants of asylums become asylumized: they have adapted so completely that they can no longer live outside. Block is the ideal client of the legal system, he is so adapted that he anticipates the decisions of the judge. The advocate says to him in exasperation: 'I can't begin a statement without your gazing at me as if your final sentence had come.'[48] Block is the perfect incarnation of the agent implied by a totalitarian type of social game: he expects everything from the institution. This relation of total dependence anchors the absolute power of the institution, and the auxiliaries of the institution, all these secondary characters such as the advocate and the judge, exert their influence over K., making him believe that they are in power, or more precisely that they have a knowledge of the laws of power. They lead him to believe that they know how the system works and they use the authority bestowed on them by their knowledge of its laws in order to make K. reinvest. When K. says: 'I'm going, I give up', they get him to reinvest by telling him: 'All the same, you do have a chance', and when he is too sure of himself, by belittling his chances. Thus K. shows up the link between power and temporality. To some extent, the waiting room is the symbol of power par excellence. Power as described by Kafka is based on a very strong aspiration by those who wait, who could leave but who nonetheless stay, and also on acute uncertainty: they are not even sure how long they will have to wait. If they knew that it would be for five minutes, they could go out and have a coffee, but everything is uncertain, including how long they will have to wait. This kind of absolute uncertainty is the most radical form of power.

Power and time

Now to recapitulate very briefly. We see (with the notion of interest) that for a game to work, and the characteristic forces of a game or mechanism (or their institutional forms) to function, we do in fact need agents to be caught up, and invest strongly, in the game. The other day I gave a number of synonyms of interest. I could also have said 'desire', or 'concern' in the Heideggerian sense (it is because I am concerned with the game and what its outcome will be that I engage with its timescale). Basically, I need only say 'This game doesn't interest me', for the timescale of the game to cease to operate. It is in the relation between my expecting something from the game and the structure of the game, with the objective opportunities it offers to someone like me and endowed with the capital that I possess, in the relation between my aspirations and my subjective appreciation of opportunity, on the one hand, and, on the other, the objective likelihood of success created for me through the power of the game as well by those who control the game. Those who have power over the game have power over the objective probabilities – they can change the rules, they can say, 'Write a shorter thesis'.[49] They can also influence aspirations by making people invest or disinvest.

(Here I hesitate to give examples, but they would be important, if only to show how abstract the philosophy of temporality is. To think that people have been able for generations to give university lectures on time without having thought for a moment that one of the sites of temporal manipulation is the university ... I say this for the benefit of anyone who calls themselves a philosopher, to make them reflect on what philosophy is. In fact, one of the key sites where power takes the form of power over objective opportunities and over the subjective representation of opportunity is the university, which is a universe where people are subject to time and informed by time.)

So people must invest in the game and the game must have a certain stability, but the investment and the temporal experience will be the more emotive, the more uncertain the game, the fewer the number of the elect, and also the more the criterion for electing the elect is undefined, unpredictable and arbitrary. An arbitrary power is an unpredictable power, a power that you cannot depend on whether for better or for worse. Whether it is the number one or the zero that surfaces, you are never sure whether it signals the better or the worse. Anything is possible, which means that the worse is not even sure and the better is not even possible. If people have thought of the concentration camps when reading Kafka, it is because, in extreme cases, the situations that he pictures can be cases where drawing a number at random in a lottery can send you to the crematorium. But these situations are no more than extreme cases of what is ordinary experience in many fields. There are highly unstable fields where the chances of attaining some goal or other are very slight and are allocated on completely random grounds, as if the tyrant were throwing the dice to see what criterion of choice he will select. On one occasion he will say 'I'll take the blue eyes' and the next time 'I'll take the long hair', then, 'I'll take the old' and 'I'll take the young'. Fate is a kind of madman submitting totally vital things to a throw of the dice. In these circumstances the investment too is utterly mad, the uncertainty is extremely acute and the situation is one of absolute anxiety. These situations are an extreme case of ordinary situations where the objective opportunities are distributed according to relatively stable principles that are often unconscious, meaning that you don't recognize their principles. You think you are playing roulette but in fact you are playing poker. In fact, one of the great mistakes made by people who are not in the know, who were not born in the field that they are investing in, is that they are likely to think that they are playing bridge, whereas actually they are playing roulette.

Power then is to a great extent power over aspirations and power through aspirations, so that it would not be wrong to say that the dominated contribute to their own domination insofar as, theoretically, they could always withdraw. For example, the world of writers is a game that is very similar to the extremes case I just referred to. Something very vital is being played for. It is no joke to say that launching into a real career as a writer really is a question of life or death for many. The stakes are so high and they are facing so much uncertainty, and we see clearly in their biographies and memoirs that one of the most recurrent fantasies is the fantasy of withdrawing from the game: 'I'm leaving.' In particular, writers of popular or provincial origins fantasize about returning to their native region. They most often manage it by becoming regionalist novelists and celebrating the common people, if they haven't been able to leave them. All conventional wisdom would plead for them to withdraw from the game and disinvest completely: 'Stop investing and you will be able to release yourself from the grip of time.' It is your relation to a game in which you invest your all without much certainty of success that delivers you into the hands of time, which involves waiting, anxiety concerning the future, the will to succeed and invest, and so on.

Lecture of 19 April 1984

First session (lecture): the field and species of capital. – The relation to time. – Species and forms of capital. – The three forms of cultural capital. – Human capital and cultural capital. – Cultural capital as incorporated capital. – Parenthesis on philosophy and the social world.
Second session (seminar): Waiting for Godot, *by Samuel Beckett. – The timescale of someone waiting for nothing. – The social world as self-evident. – Principles of continuity of the social world in different societies.*

First session (lecture): the field and species of capital

Having shown over the last two weeks how historical developments tended to bring the separate social spaces that I call fields into existence, I now wish to consider the relations between the notion of the field and the notion of species of capital. In order to approach the notion of species of capital that I am going to develop today, I need first to evoke the historical process through which the relatively autonomous social universes, endowed with specific laws irreducible to those of the other spaces, were constituted.

First, I would remind you of the interdependence of the notion of the field and the notion of species of capital. I indicated at the outset that a species of capital is defined in relation to a particular field: capital is always specific. To put it simply, we could say that the specific capital of a field is what works in that field. Even more basically, it is what 'works' in that field, what you need in order to really belong to a field. In fact, although you can always enter a field, charge in uninvited so to speak, like a bull in a china shop, you only really assume existence there if you can produce effects. I have on several occasions mentioned the empirical criterion that we can take to determine the limits of a field: participating in a field means producing effects there.

Most existing research has avoided dealing with the problem that is constantly encountered – or should be encountered – in the course of research: people who study teachers, artists and writers, or any object of sociological study at all, nearly always forget to question the boundaries defining their object; they take them as given, whereas in any field one of the issues is finding out who is a member. For instance, if I wanted to start a new political journal tomorrow, I would just need to find some sponsors, but my journal would only really exist as a political object if it produced effects in the field of the press: I would need not only to be reviewed in the press, but also to oblige other journal editors to refer to me implicitly or explicitly; I would need to restructure the space of the journals, and I would exist fully in this space if I managed, for instance, to force anyone entering this space to situate themselves in relation to me. This is one of the surest indicators of specific domination in a field. In a book on Sartre and his position in *Les Temps Modernes*, an Italian sociologist has shown that one of the surest indicators of Sartre's domination was the fact that, at the height of his influence, he consciously or unconsciously, implicitly or explicitly, compelled all his actual or would-be contributors to situate themselves in relation to him.[1] For instance, a classic strategy of new entrants into the artistic field is to affirm their existence through a polemic against the dominant artists, so that they are acknowledged through the response of the dominant artists to their attack.

Existing in a field supposes a minimum of specific capital necessary to produce effects and, as I have already repeated, the important emphasis in 'specific capital' is on 'specific': you cannot succeed in a field if you import a kind of capital that is not a recognized currency, even if it is current in other fields. An example comes to mind. Since great scientists often have a shorter career than those in the arts (sociologists, who calculate everything, have calculated the average age of the individuals who made great discoveries: for mathematicians it is around twenty, and, as we all know, Kant wrote his great works at the age of fifty)[2], they dispose of extra time earlier than others and often undertake a sort of second intellectual life, reflecting on their research, giving lectures on epistemology and the history of science. This passage from one specific capital to another – for example from the capital of a great mathematician or historian to the specific capital of epistemology – is relatively easy, but not automatic: this transfer or conversion of capital supposes a reconversion of research and time, and a certain number of conditions. *A fortiori*, in the case of a great collector, the transformation of his economic capital into artistic capital can require him to resort to the paid services of artistic advisers or the advice of a spouse steeped in the world of art (there are all sorts of secondary conditions that are extremely important). You can pass easily from one form of capital to another, but there are problems of exchange. This is what I wanted to remind you of, to explain the link between my previous lectures and what I am going to say today.

The relation to time

The process of historical evolution leads to the existence of separate universes, and their games each have their own laws of functioning, which may in some cases be made explicit as established or legal rules of the game. But as I said last time, the schema of evolution that I am proposing is not evolutionist in the ordinary sense of the term: there may be loops, where the conclusion meets the beginning, or the order may be reversed, as I shall show when discussing the problem of symbolic violence. A second point on which I shall want to upset the evolutionist and linear model that we all have at the back of our minds is the problem of the relation to time in the different societies, which is linked to the problem of capital. But I think I shall put this point off until the second session next week, because I am afraid that it might become an enormous parenthesis, which would completely interrupt the flow of the argument that I wish to sustain.

I will simply indicate the theme: one of the reasons why we cannot rely on a simple, linear schema is the fact that capital (which can be defined roughly as time accumulated, either by the actual individual who owns the capital, or by others who have done it for him, on his behalf) has one extremely important property, which is common to every species of capital: when it is linked to an investment of time, it increases the productivity of this time. In other words, one property of capital is to intensify specific profits. This is obvious in the economic domain and I shall not elaborate, but it is true also on the apparently very distant terrain of symbolic capital, which, I remind you, is any species of capital when it is perceived, recognized and acknowledged (which is what we generally call prestige). This form of capital, which obviously takes time to acquire, and in particular through an investment of personal time (as I emphasized amply last week), is much more difficult to acquire by proxy than the others. There are transmissions of symbolic capital, as in the case of the name, but symbolic capital is one of the forms of capital that most require us to pay in person.

It is subject to the law that I have just formulated: when linked to investment in time, it intensifies the productivity of this time. We see this, for example, in the signature effect: other things being equal, a well-known or famous painter will obtain infinitely greater profits, whether material or symbolic, than an unknown painter, for the same temporal investment. Consecration produces illusion effects: the same declaration or the same texts, depending on whether they are signed by X or by Y, will have unequal symbolic value. The history and the sociology of science are full of this kind of anecdote: the same text sent to a learned society that is rejected if signed by an unknown author may be accepted if signed by a famous author. This kind of case shows that the consecration effect and the symbolic value of the author dramatically multiply the profits associated with a measured amount of time invested.

I shall not insist much more, but this has consequences that I find very important in understanding the relations of different societies to time. As all the commentators have noted, the traditional peasant, pre-capitalist or archaic societies studied by ethnologists have a use of time very different from ours:[3] the people take their time, they are less stressed, they are not rushed off their feet. Next week I shall share with you my reactions to an article by Gary Becker on the problem of time and investment in time, where he raises the question of the differential productivity of time. (This American economist hails from a very different tradition from the one where I am situated, but I find him most inspiring because the logic of his formal models, although sometimes rather gratuitous and even slightly mad, does extend the varieties imagined much farther than we do, even when we feel that we are liberated from the prejudices of our tradition.) In particular, I think one great difference between pre-capitalist societies and societies with strongly objectified capital in their relation to time is that time has in a way become more and more profitable.

First of all, as disposable capital – of any species whatever: economic or cultural – increases, the productivity of the time involved in this capital increases. Then, given that the productivity of the time of labour increases, the virtual productivity of the time of non-labour, that we call leisure, tends also to increase in proportion. It is, for example, extremely difficult to interview a senior consultant, because he is in the habit of counting every minute, and attributes such value to his time that he lives in a constant state of tension. As the cost of the time of labour, and by contamination, of the time of non-labour increases, the social agents richest in capital in the societies richest in capital have a relation to time inconceivable to pre-capitalist society, where people take their time to dispose of their time, in particular in social relations. There is an amusing book on the 'leisure class' that asks why we are moving into a society where it is the most privileged who are the most anxious about time.[4]

This is a problem that could be treated by columnists in the Parisian weeklies, but it can also be analysed rigorously: we can ask whether there is not a link between the capital possessed collectively and individually and the relation to time, an element of the profitability of this capital that varies with the importance of the capital. I shall return to this, but I think that much of the debate comparing modern man's art of living to that of pre-capitalist or archaic societies – which I sometimes rather wickedly call *'tristes topiques'* [sad topics][5] – is best elucidated if we refer it to this fundamental difference in the productivity of their actions. I am saying this after some reflection, hoping that you will reflect on it too – for obviously this model is only valid if we accept an implicit definition of the productivity of time that is the definition given by the universe in question itself: the productivity of time is measured in terms of profit that is essentially economic (and secondarily symbolic, but this too may be reconverted into economic profit). This interpretation implies accepting the values objectively engaged in the social order concerned.

Having anticipated my argument here, I now remind you that I wanted to complicate the implicit models of the processes of evolution that we all have at the back of our minds, and try to describe the social genesis of these separate universes, which we accept as self-evident, but which correspond to different games with different rules, and, concomitantly, with different species of capital.

Species and forms of capital

I come now to the description of the properties of the major species of capital. I shall reduce these major species of capital to two (or two and a half, if I include the notion of social capital that I want to mention briefly: it is useful for my explanation, but Ockham's razor[6] would dispense with it and it could be subsumed under cultural capital). I shall first remind you of the properties of the two species of capital, the cultural and the economic, in more or less the same terms that I used to expound this distinction in an article in *Actes de la recherche en sciences sociales* a couple of years ago.[7] I will do this quite briefly because, if you want to, you can refer to this text, which is often more rigorous than what I can say about it. Then I shall go on to develop some more recent thoughts that I have had on these two notions, in particular that of cultural capital: I would like to offer a kind of generalization of the notion, involving a change of vocabulary, and I shall speak rather of 'informational capital' or 'information capital',[8] which will enable me to identify properties that are more general than those that the notion of cultural capital has provided us with. That is roughly the schema that I shall try to follow.

Where economic capital is concerned, it is evident that this is not my topic, nor is it the object of any of my specialist research. It is therefore a window of opportunity: it is yours to open . . . Economic capital will play a very important part insofar as it will be the condition for all the forms of accumulation of all the other possible species of capital, and at the same time, the medium into which any other acquisition can be reconverted; it will be the standard against which any other form of accumulation can be evaluated. Economic capital then has a privileged status compared to the other species of capital as it is the condition of possibility of all other species of acquisition – I shall show this for cultural capital – and also as a real measure (not as a value judgement) of all other forms of acquisition, as a measure socially and objectively constituted to be the measure of all other measures.

I said just now that there were as many species of capital as there are fields and subfields and it is true that juridical capital is a subspecies of cultural capital, and one we can analyse more specifically: there is, for example, the capital of a jurist specializing in Roman law who would find it hard to convert it into the capital of a commercial lawyer. That being said, I think we can reduce the major species of capital to two, or perhaps two and a half, insofar as the subspecies that we can identify in the multiplicity of fields share pretty fundamental common properties.

The three forms of cultural capital

It is cultural capital above all that I want to turn to today. It can exist in three forms. In can exist firstly in an incorporated state, that is in the form of lasting and permanent organic dispositions. At one extreme, it can exist in the form of a cultivated habitus, it is what we call 'culture' in the ordinary, somewhat vague sense: when we say that someone is cultivated we are talking of cultural capital in its incorporated form. Next, cultural capital can exist in an objectified state, in the form of cultural goods: paintings, books, dictionaries, instruments, computers and computer programmes, for instance. When we speak of computer programmes or mathematical formulae,[9] we can see straight away the problems raised by the notion of objectified cultural capital: this objectified state of cultural capital is the record or the result of theories or critiques of these theories and problematics; in other words, it is the objectified product of what was human labour at an earlier stage. Finally, cultural capital can exist in an institutionalized state and this is very important. Although economic capital exists in the raw state, so to speak, in the form of goods, it also exists, and in general simultaneously, as titles to property, that is legally guaranteed goods. It is the same for cultural capital, even if this property nearly always passes unnoticed, in particular by theoreticians of human capital, like Gary Becker, whom I mentioned just now: cultural capital can exist in an institutionalized state, that is both objectified and legally guaranteed in the form of titles, and the concept of the academic title, which we need to think about, is to cultural capital what the title-deed is to economic capital. The result is a series of properties: in particular, objectified cultural capital can exist independently of its bearer and, within certain limits, be transmitted. Those then are the three forms of cultural capital. I shall now elaborate – relatively briefly – on each of these points.

Human capital and cultural capital

I would like first to say a few words on the concept of cultural capital. This will be helpful because, when I first started to use this concept,[10] I was totally unaware of the work by economists who were starting at roughly the same time to talk of human capital.[11] The inventions were simultaneous, but I do not claim any sort of priority. The two concepts were responding to different problems, which means that they have different properties. I shall remind you briefly of this difference, not in order to tip the balance in my favour (although it would obviously suit me to have a concept of cultural capital different from Becker's), but because there are important differences which go beyond my subjective appreciation.

The theoreticians of human capital were trying to respond to the following problem: why is it that people who have studied more also earn more – how do we find the ways in which inequalities of earnings are linked to educational inequalities? They therefore investigated the rate of profit earned through economic investment on the educational terrain, and they tried to measure as precisely as possible the economic investment required for the acquisition of an academic certificate, seeking the equivalent in terms of labour time for the number of years of study, evaluating in monetary terms both the educational investment corresponding to these years of study and the profits from the educational investments ('You studied for fifteen years, and now you are earning such-and-such'). This is the question raised by Gary Becker in his 1964 book, *Human Capital: A Theoretical and Empirical Analysis, with Special Reference to Education*, which insists on the relation between specific investments, considered in their monetary dimension, and the specific profits, also considered in monetary terms.

The problems that I had in mind at the time were very different. Before my research, people had already acknowledged that there was a correlation between the social origins of children and their academic success:[12] as soon as they started to study the *drop-out* rate, that is, fall-out from the educational system, sociologists of education noted a very strong correlation between the parents' professions and the pupils' results. This correlation was often interpreted in economic or economistic terms: to take your studies beyond a certain level, you need money. They realized that economic factors were not alone in determining academic success or failure and that belonging to a privileged milieu went together with social advantages (you have better connections and more information, for instance); some scholars even formulated the existence of a privileging factor, which is the fact that elements of culture are passed down through the family. But there too they were thinking in fairly limited terms of help with study and homework, private lessons, the sort of things that are fairly closely tied to economic capital. The notion of cultural capital was devised to name this objectively (but not intentionally) hidden transmission of cultural capital, which operates inevitably, but without any explicit pedagogical intent, through the social relations within a family: through linguistic communication and routine interpersonal exchange. Ultimately, the most essential things transmitted by the family are perhaps those that are not intentionally transmitted: ranging from language through to what we might call the psychological dimension – such as implicit demands and unconscious warnings, for instance. The notion of cultural capital went further than simply taking into account the inequalities of monetary income associated with different academic qualifications; it intended to account for the unequal chances of success in a very specific market, the education market, which in its turn distributes certificates and titles that are assigned very different values in the economic market.

Arguing in these terms makes us immediately see that the educational investment that has to be taken into account to explain economic inequalities is not limited to a monetary investment, any more than the profit of the initial cultural investment is limited to monetary profit. If you measure the profit obtained from holding an academic qualification in terms of salary, you find some very strange things. For instance, among university teachers, if we move from the science faculties to the faculty of medicine, the indices of economic capital increase, while the indices of educational capital acquired before entering the faculty decrease.[13] Likewise, at the level of the ruling class, the richest in cultural capital tend to be the least rich in economic capital, and vice versa.[14] We will not understand these anomalies if we measure the profitability of cultural capital by its economic profit alone. This is because cultural capital obviously generates profit in a lot of other markets: you need only think of the matrimonial market, for instance, to see straight away that there are profits. This economistic logic may shock, but we need to think of 'profit' in the widest sense, and realize that these profits can be obtained without being sought as such. To account for the existence of a profit, there is no need to postulate an explicit and cynical economic intention: far from it (I feel obliged to repeat these things because, like the Hydra of Lernes, they keep raising their heads in people's arguments),[15] and there are markets where being disinterested is a condition of obtaining profit.

Contrary to what economists like Becker do – his French disciples are even worse – if we want to evaluate the profitability of an educational investment, we must take account of the profits that are irreducible to measurement by monetary standards, which give the salary earned at a certain moment in time. But, something more important, we cannot, as I said just now, measure the importance of an educational investment by its monetary equivalent: a simple equation enabling us to convert a length of study time into a theoretical salary cannot explain the cultural capital that is the object of a transmission system secreted within a domestic system, this earlier, hidden transmission being the condition for the differential success of educational investment in academic studies.

We see the naivety of the economists. (I say naivety, but I respect them greatly.[16] There are opponents whom we may greatly respect, for in the event the opponent obliges us to make explicit things that we would tend to accept as self-evident. Economists, with their sociological naivety, are extremely useful because they formalize things in a precipitate and premature way. By cutting through the complexity of the system of factors, they oblige us to make explicit things that a greater sensitivity to the complexity of the factors might leave floating in the void.) The naivety of the theoreticians of capital leads us to raise the question of the relation of academic ability to investment in study:

if they saw that cultural capital is transmitted as much by the family as by the school, and success at school depends on what is transmitted by the family, they would not focus their questions on this academic ability, which they see as obviously innate (it is the idea of the intellectual gift); they would see that something consecrated as a gift by the educational system is in fact the product of an investment of capital. A more rigorous equation then would take into account, for instance, the mother's spare time (which varies according to the milieu) and her cultural capital, which is itself the product of a heritage (it is inherited cultural capital) and of an explicit acquisition through the educational system. If we take the relation between these two factors into account, we can easily explain differential academic success, which itself provides a good explanation of economic and, better still, overall success measured by the whole set of profits (and not merely the economic ones).

Another effect of this naivety: since they fail to see the link between educational investment and, simply speaking, the social structure, that is, the unequal distribution of cultural capital in society, they consider the very general question (which I call functionalist, in the sense of the sociological tradition thus named), of the contribution of human capital to national productivity:[17] this means – I translate – the social benefit of education as measured by its effects on national productivity; this will raise the question of the social productivity of investments in cultural capital, but in terms of the Whole. They will, for example, compare different countries,[18] and they will ask whether one can establish a correlation between what you might call the national cultural capital (by analogy with economic capital) and technological development, for instance. In a given country, we could try in this way to measure the profitability of economic investment as a function of cultural capital. This kind of reasoning is implicit in so many of the debates that we are constantly hearing all around us these days. I am not saying that the question is absurd, but raising it is tantamount to evacuating the fundamental question of the differential distribution of cultural capital in a given society, and with it the question of the differential profitability of cultural capital; and thereby forgetting that the profit of cultural capital they are claiming to measure – by relating it in fact to ability, in the last analysis – might be due to a great extent to the unequal distribution of cultural capital.

This is a very important point, and one that I shall return to. Let us imagine a society where everyone has a university degree.[19] Interestingly, this would mean that the baccalaureate would lose much of its value. For a marginalist,[20] it is rather extraordinary to think of cultural capital independently of the structure of relations within which it functions. The notion of cultural capital as I conceive cannot be disassociated from the notion of the cultural field, the universe within which each bearer of capital will obtain from their capital a different profit depending on the position (and therefore the scarcity) of their capital in the structure of the distribution of cultural capital characteristic of the universe in which they place their cultural capital. (Perhaps all this may appear abstract to you, but it is a relatively important discussion; it has made much ink flow, there is a copious literature and I am trying to give you the essence of it.)

There is another case where the theorists of human capital are once again naive (these cases of naivety are of course all connected: they are based on a kind of ignorance of the social dimension of economic relations): they act as if the socially guaranteed competence granted by an academic qualification was automatically a technical competence. Thus they entirely ignore the difference between a socially guaranteed ability and a real ability. As for me (and I shall return to this), when I speak of cultural capital in an institutionalized state, I am speaking of a socially guaranteed cultural capital: it is a qualification guaranteed by the state, which ensures, for instance, that any bearer of the title is supposed to know their mathematics (or know how to draft a computer programme), up to a certain point. The theorists of human capital are entirely ignorant of this codification effect – which I shall discuss at greater length in the next few lectures – which is the result of a juridical consecration, and has quite extraordinary effects in the social world. These theorists take social competence at its face value, and pass without hesitation from this nominal value to the real world. I leave the debate there: it may appear to be Byzantine, but it is important because it can enable those who know about human capital to avoid certain misinterpretations.

Cultural capital as incorporated capital

Having offered this critical introduction, I shall now move much more rapidly through the different states of cultural capital. Most of the properties of cultural capital can be deduced from something that marks its peculiar distinction from economic capital: the fact that it is fundamental to the body of its bearer, and that it supposes incorporation. When we speak of culture, *Bildung*, being cultivated, etc., as celebrated in school, we are speaking of something that is in some way coextensive with its bearer. It lives and dies with him. One of the most valued properties in culture is precisely this link with the person, and all theories of culture end up in a kind of 'personalism'.[21] If those who objectify culture, as I have been labouring to do for years now, appear sacrilegious, it is because attacks on culture seem to be personal: there is nothing that we identify with more than our person, and the bearers of cultural capital feel particularly vulnerable, since cultural capital has this property of appearing to be natural. Of all the species of capital, economic capital can always look as if it is dubiously acquired; we are always suspicious of the violence that may lie behind it. Whereas – to repeat something we all know, but which is nonetheless not self-evident – cultural capital seems, by nature and by its own logic, to be natural.

For instance, in the case of culture, the distinction that the Greeks made between *ta patrôa* (the properties inherited from the father – your patrimony) and *ta epiktèta* (things acquired in addition to those left by the father) is not at all obvious, particularly since the transmission of domestic capital, as we have seen in Becker, is largely hidden and unconscious. When, for instance, the individual emerges onto the education market, he is already endowed with an inherited capital that, before any explicit education, can only be interpreted by the institution accepting him as being a gift, because it is there before any education. That is what a gift is: it is what you have without having learnt anything. The education system ignores by definition everything that started beforehand, and, at every moment, this kind of forgetfulness or amnesia of antecedents and genesis is repeated; in a way, each field starts with a blank page and draws a line under everything that was acquired beforehand.

The fact that the acquisition of cultural capital costs time is another property that leads us to naturalize and personalize cultural capital. Whereas economic capital can be transmitted very quickly (within certain limits, laid down by the law) from hand to hand, from person to person, cultural capital can only be transmitted at the cost of a considerable expenditure of time, and one of the implicit criteria of cultural hierarchies is the length of time taken for this acquisition. For instance, the rivalry between the *grandes écoles* tends to be translated into a prolongation of the length of studies, which is not obviously a technical necessity: people tend to say that we need to acquire more and more knowledge today, but if you just think about it for a moment, you will see that there are also many things that become irrelevant and are no longer worth learning, or can be learnt much more quickly. Technical justifications then disguise one of the motives for extending the period of study: the value of a diploma is measured by the time spent acquiring it; an intensive, fast-track diploma is valued less than a diploma needing a longer period of study. Similarly, we find that in matters of artistic culture or, in a completely different domain, peasant culture (how to tell the difference, say, between a field mouse and a sewer rat) some skills are highly valued because they take a very long time to acquire, they are associated with age and wisdom; in the evaluation of cultural abilities, a hidden principle is the length of time of acquisition and this is obviously linked to personal character, because time is something that only you can give yourself. Time cannot be accumulated, it cannot easily be taken from or given to others, and everything that needs time is seen in a 'personalist' logic as a guarantee of culture, because it is precisely what cannot be acquired by proxy or through go-betweens: you need to have acquired it in person and paid for it in person (thus, in cultural matters, you have to have toured the art galleries, and so on).

I could spend whole sessions developing what this supposes: the opposition between the disc and the concert,[22] and a whole lot of other distinctions that are seen as decisive and subjected to trial by journalism[23] or to colloquia at Beaubourg, not to mention doctoral theses, are related to these properties of cultural capital; it is connected with the individual person, it is incorporated, incorporation takes time and the time must be invested in person. To make this clear, I use the analogy between culture and suntan,[24] which is quite telling: people who buy books in the 'J'ai lu' series, for instance, bear the same relation to culture as those who use tanning cream or lamps do to those who have really lain in the sun. All this is intricately bound up with our relation to culture and is linked to very simple properties that can be described objectively.

Another property: since culture in its incorporated state is connected to the body, it inhabits the same space as its bearer; it is tied to its bearer. This is important: its accumulation is not infinite, this culture falls ill and dies along with its bearer, and these are problems that society takes very seriously. I often refer to Kantorowicz's book, *The King's Two Bodies*:[25] all societies have to deal with the problem of the bodily existence of the powerful, who, seen from the perspective of the social conditions of their function, ought to be eternal ('The king is dead, long live the king!'). The king is an imbecile in the etymological sense of the term,[26] and yet he is the king. Now culture raises these questions in an extremely acute form. These analyses are obviously important preliminaries to the understanding of the effects of institutionalization (remembering that I have proposed three states of capital: incorporated, objectified and institutionalized). Institutionalization will be one of the solutions to the problem of the imbecility of the king: a title guaranteed is a title for eternity. Once you have passed the *agrégation*, you are an *agrégé* for life . . .

Parenthesis on philosophy and the social world

I am embarrassed to say all this, because you must have the impression that I am retailing rather banal commonplaces. In fact, given the state of sociology that we find ourselves in, I think we need to import modes of thinking that philosophers tend to consider banal, such as the arts of wonderment, of proceeding at leisure, of rethinking the obvious, that we hardly ever apply to things social because philosophy is so often constituted in opposition to the social world.[27] I am convinced that we philosophize in order not to know what the social world really is, and I am not saying that for the pleasure of shocking those among you who are philosophers. If we do not apply this mode of thinking, it is because the social is the banality that we are fleeing when we take to philosophy – remember the *Theaetetus*[28] – and the social is the sublunary, what is not worth thinking, what we must flee in order to think. This means that the social is what is least conceptualized and you can produce extraordinary effects by the simple fact of transgressing the taboo separating the distinguished from the vulgar – as I have always tried to do – crossing the frontier and considering vulgar things in a distinguished manner. I am giving you the recipe: it is very easy to consider because it has received so little thought. It has received very little thought, and you need to think it through in this slow, Heideggerian manner: what in fact is culture? What does it mean to be cultivated? It is to have a body, to take time, and so on. There is so much to understand in the banalities that we do not think on and yet are worthy of being thought on. The work of acquisition takes time and makes an impact on the bearer. You are working on yourself. When I say: 'I am cultivating myself', I am at once the cultivator and the cultivated in this act of cultural acquisition, in this act of self-cultivation that supposes paying in person, precisely because we need to invest our time (taking that time away from other possible investments) as well as a socially constituted form of *libido*, the *libido sciendi*. This link between culture and asceticism reinforces the personalism, the moralizing vision of culture: someone who is not cultivated will not only be negatively designated a barbarian, but also dishonest, impure, dirty and defiled.

In my rather hostile, but I believe rigorous critique of Kant's *Critique of Judgement* in the postscript of *Distinction*, we see clearly how all the concepts that connote or designate taste, culture and our relation to culture are ethical.[29] They are social judgements. The vulgar are immoral: they like still lifes, that is, pictures representing what we eat; they like nudes; they like everything that we consume at first hand, and pure taste, as Kant says, is defined against sensory taste, against first-hand taste. Being distinguished means breaking with the first hand, and although this break is of course intellectual, it is also ethical. One source of this ethical vision of culture lies in the fact that culture is acquired using time that is subtracted from things that we find more amusing, more first hand as Kant would say: the time that we spend in museums looking at still lives could be spent on consuming the corresponding articles at first hand. If you look at Kant's text, you will see that he can think of nothing else.

Cultural acquisition then supposes some renunciation, and is linked to asceticism. This means that culture is held in esteem. Obviously, one problem is how to measure cultural capital: is it not an unreal notion? Specialists in human capital propose to measure it in terms of its monetary profit and the time taken for its acquisition (the number of years of study). The time of acquisition is surely the best measure of cultural capital, but we should not reduce it to the number of years spent in educational establishments. Family acquisition increases the productivity of the years spent in school. And moreover, as soon as we reintroduce the time of family acquisition into the measurement of cultural capital, we see that there can be negative family acquisitions. Among the social handicaps of those who have not been raised in a universe close to the educational universe, there are not only gaps, but also negative things that it takes time to eliminate, the most typical example being correcting one's accent. The time taken to correct it has to be an extra negative – we could discuss this point at length.

This incorporated capital, for all the reasons that I have advanced, will function as a sort of nature. It is something acquired that presents itself as a living creature. Unlike money or title deeds to property, it cannot be transmitted immediately, it cannot be acquired through purchase or exchange, and one of the great problems that cultural capital faces in an economic usage is the following: how can you buy someone's cultural capital without buying the person? (Sometimes I am tempted to say things rather crudely in order to wake you up, because you might hear what I am saying and think it was self-evident, whereas it is not self-evident at all.) How can we buy the cultural capital of an executive without buying the executive? Since cultural capital is so strongly tied to a person, one problem is finding out how to capture for my service things as personal as cultural capital without buying the person. The problem of state patronage could be considered in this light. What does buying someone's cultural services imply? One problem of the economic use of cultural capital will be the concentration of cultural capital: if you want to set up a big laboratory in the chemical industry, you need to collect cultural capital, but the collection is not self-evident, it can produce undesirable social effects – the workforce may join a union, for instance.[30] These are the specific problems raised by cultural capital. Economic capital does not raise them to the same degree, or at least not in the same terms.

Another property of the social usage of cultural capital is a consequence of its incorporated nature: since the cultural capital appears to be natural, the unequal distribution of cultural capital is itself sufficient to produce what I call effects of distinction. It is important to understand that distinction does not imply the intention to distinguish oneself. Distinction is the fact of being different, which results when someone who sees it as a benefit or as a prestigious difference perceives something different. It works like linguistics. As soon as there is a hat, there is a non-hat. The social system functions like a system of phonemes, and as soon as there are differences and these differences are perceived, they start to function as signs of distinction, there are profits of distinction. Since cultural capital is perceived as incorporated and the social foundation of the unequal distribution of cultural capital and difference is not perceived, the cultural capital will produce a quite special effect: a profit of distinction in the simple sense of the term, that is, a profit endowed with a differential value, a profit of scarcity plus an almost automatic symbolic profit. Of all the species of capital, it is cultural capital that will be most spontaneously recognized as legitimate. This capital does not have to justify its existence: it is automatically justified since it is part of nature. Weber says that the dominant inevitably tend to produce what he calls a 'theodicy' of their own privileges,[31] but ultimately the culturally privileged have no need of a theodicy of their privileges: for all the reasons that I have given, their privilege tends to be spontaneously justified.

I'm afraid I have to stop here.

Second session (seminar): *Waiting for Godot*, by Samuel Beckett

Last week in discussing Kafka I was suggesting that the extreme tension we feel on reading his novels is due to the fact that they reconstruct universes of acute uncertainty and very strong investment. Although this analysis may seem abstract I find that it is an important way of understanding a certain number of social experiences, and in particular extreme experiences, such as the experience of the world that subproletarians may have, or the problems that we come up against every day such as the problem of violence in the young.[32]

In fact, these apparently most abstract analyses seem to me a condition for understanding the most concrete things, for true scientific analysis is opposed to middlebrow discussion. A few lectures ago,[33] I analysed the part that these intellectual-journalists or journalist-intellectuals and essay-writers could play, and I immediately mobilized interests outside my technical competence, which were linked to my particular position in the very field that I was describing, and implied a certain antipathy towards this way of behaving in intellectual life. I can justify this intellectual antipathy on scientific grounds: one of the reasons why the social world is so difficult to conceive is because spontaneous discourse on the social world, apart from being based on the illusion of immediate understanding, nearly always deploys elementary and rudimentary thought systems, and thereby does not give itself the tools to designate the singularity of the individual.

Thinking that I need to mobilize all the resources at my disposal in order to understand juvenile delinquency (suburban kids smashing up a car, stealing a motorbike or taunting the police, for instance) may seem somewhat derisory, particularly to those who are moved by the best intentions. Gide said: 'It is with fine sentiments that bad literature is made';[34] but it is even truer for sociology: it is with fine sentiments that catastrophic sociology is made. The very few sociologists who have the merit of going out into the suburbs for interviews are no doubt the last – for very complicated reasons that should be analysed and which are part of the special conditions of their production – to feel they should invest in reflection on things like time and Kafka in order to understand these apparently trivial matters without lapsing into the kind of neither-fish-nor-fowl discussion that I often dismiss rather cruelly, saying that it is not even false, and is as far from science as the producers of this discourse are far from the space they are trying to describe.

I am not delivering this preamble to sing the praises of my own proposal, but because it is the only opportunity to express it: you cannot say this kind of thing in writing; there are taboos against self-praise, although of course there are ways ... There is even a whole discourse devoted to saying how important it is to observe the conventions of discourse.[35] It is therefore very difficult to communicate and get people to understand what I see as the genuinely rare quality of certain discourses. In the case at issue, what I find interesting in what I have to say is this kind of encounter between completely banal objects and manners of thinking that are usually thought of as distinguished.

I referred to this kind of encounter last week, using Kafka. I can take my argument further by using a well-known example: Beckett's *Godot*.[36] You need to think straight away of teenage gangs, because it is the same world. Once again, one of the (many) virtues of literature is its way of presenting in a dramatic, intense manner things that are sterilized by the school syllabus, which can be thought of by analogy with the priestly: the school system is to creativity as the priesthood is to prophecy, and one of the effects of the school priesthood is routinization, as Weber said – that is, the neutralization of the contents transmitted. We accept as educational something whose truth or falsehood we don't question, something that is destined not to change our lives at all, but to be listened to, noted down, recorded and reproduced when required. This educational process – which I have nothing against – is an obstacle to the adequate reception of sociological discourse, because sociological discourse in its current state can only be produced and assimilated if it neutralizes this neutralization. I emphasize 'in its current state', because 150 years from now sociology will be very different. The accumulated capital will be much greater, many things will have been discovered and formalized, and people much less dramatically invested in what they are doing will be able to work at formulating problems while investing much less of their person. But in the current state of social science, this kind of dramatization of transmission, and therefore of reception, seems to me to be a condition for genuinely capturing people's attention.

The timescale of someone waiting for nothing

I would like to suggest that the social situations in which experiencing a Kafkaesque kind of temporality will be extremely probable are situations where the objective likelihood of obtaining what you aspire to is absolutely uncertain: it is null and void or entirely random, there is no possibility of predicting anything. Such situations are, as it were, modelled in Beckett's *Godot*, which dramatizes people who are waiting for nothing, and, expecting nothing from life, the world or the future, have no expectations. To take an image from real life, it is like an old-people's home for down-and-outs,[37] people on the margins of the social world, who have been withdrawn from the social world. The social world makes no more demands on them, and this means that they have lost that sort of justification for existence that the social world grants people when it asks something of them. The social process functions so as to offer people a *raison d'être*, a purpose, an aim to their existence, *a fortiori* when the function is socially recognized – the message is: 'You deserve to exist because you are still useful for something.' And, as I often say, the social world – and this is why sociology is starting to become a theology – fulfils the function that theologians commonly attribute to God, justifying the existence of its creatures as creatures; it gives them a mission, a *raison d'être*.[38]

People with no future have no aspirations for the future, which is one of the fundamental laws of the social world: expectations tend to be proportionate to opportunity. We can see this as a sort of axiom of sociological thinking: expectations tend to adapt to objective opportunity. To a considerable extent, social agents have aspirations roughly proportionate to their objective chances of fulfilling them (I shall not comment on this, it would take hours, but it is quite fundamental, so I shall return to it) because this adaptation of expectations to opportunity is constituted through a process of incorporation (which I referred to just now in connection with the notion of cultural capital): socialization, apprenticeship and social acquisition are, to a great extent, a process of incorporation of objective structures: social agents tend to make of necessity a virtue, to desire what they are capable of, and then feel that it is right. This is the logic of *ressentiment*, in the Nietzschean sense of the term,[39] which consists in rejecting the impossible and the inaccessible ('sour grapes')[40] or at least to stop thinking about it. There is a saying by Hume that I often quote: 'As soon as we know that it is impossible to satisfy a desire, the desire itself evaporates.'[41]The very idea of aspiring disappears along with any reasonable chance of fulfilling this aspiration. This kind of negative wisdom and symbolic death of the heart, this wisdom through resignation, which leads to rejecting the impossible and not even aspiring to it, or accepting the necessary through a sort of *amor fati*, is one of the fundamental laws of social behaviour. So it is not surprising that, when we ask someone who has no objective future (for example, a youth whom people say has no future) about their future, we find he has no aspiration for the future; then we say: 'He is apathetic, he has no will power.'

The basic law of social behaviour is that those who have nothing to gain do not expect to gain anything. The law of every field is that investment in the game – what I call the *illusio*, the desire to play, the inclination to invest time, effort, good will and aspiration in the game – supposes at least a minimal chance of winning. Below a certain threshold of chance, people switch off and do not invest, and having no more investment in the game, no more *illusio*, they no longer take the time to adapt to the timescale of the game. To take time, to be absorbed by the time of the game, you need some chance of winning, however minimal.

Beckett shows us the end result of a universe where all chances of obtaining anything whatever have been abolished, nothing of any interest can possibly occur, and time has disappeared. There is no longer hope or anxiety, no possible surprise, suspense or expectation, all that is left to do is to kill time. There is still time in the sense of time that passes, but there is no more time in the sense of time to be spent doing something or time saved because you have something better to do. We don't think enough of the meaning of this banal phrase: 'There is nothing better to do.' For people who have all the time in the world – I'll return to this when I come to discuss the comparison between pre-capitalist societies and our own – there is nothing better to do than doing nothing. When there is nothing that needs doing, we can take our time. When, on the other hand, there are hundreds of things to do that can bring in more profit (symbolic, subjective, personal, economic or other), time becomes extremely precious, we don't know which way to turn. Beckett's characters are the absolute opposite of the overworked executive. In *Godot* they invent absolutely anything in order to kill time, they make up conversations, play at repentance, act out accusations, hang themselves and tell stories and insult each other, for instance. In other words, they try to create a substitute of what is routine for the normal man – having 'something to do' – in the ordinary universe as described by phenomenologists.

(It is interesting to note that the phenomenologists nearly always universalize a social experience of the world: they describe as universal the temporal experience of someone living in a normal world where he knows that day will break again tomorrow morning and there will be a certain number of guarantees of what the future will bring. The phenomenological description of lived experience is true, but it is a description only true of an experience lived by individuals inserted in the world and obeying normal laws of continuity – I shall return to this point.)

The universe that Beckett submits to his phenomenology is a universe where there is nothing but crisis. This is why Beckett has been compared to Heidegger: in a universe where time is suspended, the social agents are faced at every moment with an agony of choice. Heidegger says that anxiety emerges from the collapse of everyday routine,[42] which puts an end to the normal law of continuity where I don't have to wonder at every moment why I am doing what I am doing or whether I am going to do what I am going to do, because there are so many things to do. The things to do are objective potentials that exist in the objective world, which are ready and waiting for me, while I am ready and waiting for them. When we say of someone that he did what had to be done, it means he saw that something needed to be done, he did the right thing at the right time, he did what he had to do. In the eyes of those who want to avoid anguish, the ideal situation is one where the sequence of events unfurls unaided: the world is the world, I know that today I have to go to my lectures, then I shall come back knowing what I have to do at home; one thing leads to another, I am not going to find myself suddenly discovering that I might have no idea at all what to do, that my business and busy-ness might seem absurd and meaningless or simply disappear because no one wanted me to do anything any more.

To move from Beckett to reality: this kind of experience of the possible as merely possible, that is, able at every moment not to occur, is linked to a certain type of social experience: there are in the social world, in our everyday environment, people who are spontaneous Heideggerians: for example, the subproletariat. This was one of my first pieces of research:[43] I tried to describe the world-view of those who do not know whether they are going to find work tomorrow: they set out in the morning looking for work, they don't know if they are going to find anything, they stop off at the café at lunch time because they don't know if they will find anyone at home. These people, whose time is like a series of disconnected instants that can be interrupted at any moment, have no kind of project, except for completely unrealistic ones, detached from the present. This is one of the observations that struck me most in my interviews with these subproletarians: the link between present and future experience was completely cut; the same people could say: 'My daughter will pass her baccalaureate and go on to be a doctor', and a moment later 'I took her out of school two years ago'. These people live in universes marked by objective incoherence: there is no objective structure of ongoing expectation, no law promising a reliable future: the future is unpredictable, indefinable and arbitrary. This means that the structure of their perception of the future is of the same type: they dream up fantastical projects.

I shall not prolong this analysis, but this approach should help us understand the link between the subproletariat and the millenarian movements that historians have always noted. I refer you, for instance, to Norman Cohn's well-known book *The Pursuit of the Millennium*,[44] but others after him have developed this theme: the subproletariat, that is people with no future and no roots in a socially guaranteed universe, doomed to insecure employment and housing, are particularly vulnerable to the seduction of millenarian prophecies that announce and promise everything and all at once: the end of the world, happiness on earth and other miracles, for when nothing is possible, all things are possible. The essence of this relation to the future is the kind of absolute uncertainty that forbids rational calculation. At one and the same time you have nothing to expect and you can expect anything: anything may happen, for better or for worse . . .

(This structure of temporal experience is linked to an objective structure of the world and I notice that very often social psychology, and especially the spontaneous psychology of teachers and social workers, and the like, records properties as psychological when they are actually properties of the world producing the embodied social subjects observed. The child who is labelled 'unstable' has perhaps simply incorporated the objective instability of the condition of its parents, the fact that its father, for instance, has changed his job and place of residence five times. This is an important practical consequence of what I have to say: if an important part of the psychological properties of social agents derives from the incorporation of objective structures, we should not make a fetish of these properties, we should admit that the true principle of what we are describing lies not in the person but in the social conditions producing that person – this elementary rule seems to me important in understanding relations between teachers and pupils, patients and doctors, and so on).

The subproletarian then incarnates extreme situations where there is nothing to be expected. All things are possible, there is no future and, as in *Godot*, the only thing left is to kill time, to do something rather than nothing. Instead of twiddling their thumbs and waiting, they must smash something up, make something happen. In a way, this notorious violence is the way in which the desperate create a timescale for themselves when there is nothing to expect and nothing to hope for; they can create an event or an incident, even an accident – discussing motorbikes and fatal accidents, the English sociologist Willis makes a very fine analysis of the motorbike *society*[45] where people play with death in order to give some direction to their temporal experience. It is very Heideggerian: it is all that is left to introduce an authentic relation: these people speak of being-towards-death[46] in an absolutely Heideggerian way, the true gang member is the one who can risk his life, the man who dies on his bike is a hero.

Here I hesitate. It is very difficult to say things like this in the sort of situation in which I find myself. This experience of the social world as extreme test case encapsulates a negative analysis of the everyday experience of the world; it is an inverse mirror image. Here we can use Heidegger again: when he describes inauthentic temporality, that is the temporality of 'they',[47] he describes another temporality, that is a time frame within which there are things to do, where there is a future, a time frame where we have a future and where our universe obeys laws of successful continuity. Once started, things have a good chance of coming to an end. It is very unlikely, for instance, that a teacher will suddenly stop talking and pack his bags and walk away; it is very unlikely that something that has been announced will fail to materialize – if that happens, it will be reported by the press.

In a famous analysis, the phenomenologist Alfred Schütz – one of Husserl's disciples who developed an aspect that the latter had left rather open-ended (in *Ideas* II and *Ideas* III) – undertakes a sort of phenomenology of our ordinary experience of the social world. He tries to analyse the lived experience of the social world by developing a certain number of Husserl's indications on natural and doxic attitudes, doxic relations to the natural world, and so on. In particular he analyses someone posting a letter:[48] someone putting a letter in a letterbox has a typical, generic attitude; he acts as 'we' or 'they', and his attitude has a meaning because it is part of a whole bureaucratic system. The bureaucratic system is a sort of algebra in which everything is made up of formulae and formalities, in which the x can be replaced by anyone, by 'us' or 'them': I post my letter, but anyone could do the same; my letter will be collected by someone who could be replaced by anyone who is defined by the fact that he has to sort the letters; unless he goes on strike, I know that my letter will be delivered, and so on. The everyday universe is a universe in which collective and individual futures are assured: it is a regulated universe where what is anticipated has a good chance of materializing. Remember the Heideggerian and Husserlian analyses on the fulfilment of expectations: the social world will not spring surprises, traps or snares on us; if I put a letter in the mailbox, it will not jump out and slap me in the face, and that is important to know.

This is obviously quite different from the subproletarian universe. For instance, the life stories of subproletarians are extremely surprising because they lack rhyme or reason. The reason is very simple: the ability to structure and organize a narrative, in particular the story of your own life, varies according to your social position,[49] and one of the properties of people living in an unpredictable universe is that they themselves become in some ways unpredictable. They mix everything up – times, dates, past and future . . . They don't have the temporal coordinates that are most usually connected with work: 'I'm expected at x o'clock', 'I have an appointment', 'I have an agenda' – 'agenda'[50] is an extraordinary word that encapsulates a whole philosophy; if you have an agenda, you will know what I mean. I'm putting it like that because I need to speed up a bit [*laughter*] . . .

The experience of the world as an orderly place implies a reliable sequence of well-fulfilled anticipations, but these well-organized universes can be disrupted in situations of crisis, which are moments when all things once more become genuinely possible. For instance, with the crisis of the university system in May 1968, all things became possible, and to understand what people were saying in lecture halls and meetings then, you have to bear in mind that when all things are possible you can say anything and everything to anyone, however you like, and you can dream, as the subproletarian does, while knowing that it is a dream, which is the difference between a subproletarian and a student [*laughter*] . . . At the same time, there is nonetheless an analogy between the subproletarian and the student: I am thinking of Weber who speaks of a 'proletaroid' or 'proletarian' intelligentsia, an acute if slightly polemical formula used to designate people who are often highly successful in millenarian movements.[51] Similarly, Cohn, whom I mentioned just now, shows that, very often, the couple that combines to make a historical movement in the great millennialist movements of the Middle Ages is the raving subproletarian with an insecure future and the unfrocked priest, the proletaroid intellectual. Between the two, there is a structural analogy, in particular in their relation to time, and I think that a profound analogy between the insecure worlds of the subproletarian and the student is formed by the problem of an insecure future, especially in a critical period where the objective chances of finding a market for a diploma are very tenuous. But this analogy only works within certain limits: which is what I intended to show just now by way of a joke.

The social world as self-evident

I would like to move on more rapidly now. Phenomenologists always speak of imaginary variations. I have been doing something like that, but trying to use real situations. Sociologists try to 'live all lives', as Flaubert said,[52] but use means different from those that phenomenologists call self-projection onto other people: they prefer to use the analysis of objective conditions, observation, and the like. They try to construct not the lived experience of existence, but the logic of the experience and existence of people very different from themselves. I took the extreme case of the subproletarian, which test case shows something we don't see in the world as described by Schütz, because his was a self-evident world. Schütz is the person who has most developed the notion of the 'self-evident' or the *doxa*, taken from Husserl, and he insists on the fact that our experience of the everyday world is experience of the world as self-evident. Simply, he refuses to draw conclusions and say what it is that makes the everyday world self-evident. What are the social conditions that make experiencing the everyday world as self-evident possible? You have to feel remarkably at ease in this world to feel that it is self-evident. Schütz has omitted to apply *épochè*[53] [suspension of judgement] to his own social position in the social world, and this is what I reproach the phenomenologists with rather obsessively: they apply *épochè* to everything, except the social conditions making the *épochè* possible, that is, their *épochè* as social subjects. Imaginary variations of this type have the virtue of making us see by its absence that the *doxa*, the doxic experience of the world, the everyday relation to the everyday world as an orderly world fulfilling my expectations, presupposes a number of certainties.

Among our solid certainties, there is for instance the notion of a career. Usually, when we say that philosophers of the state are professionals, it is to underline the fact that they are submissive to the state and that the Prussian state makes them do terrible things. This is stupid, because if the philosophers were not bright enough to avoid such gross perils, they would be a lost cause . . . It is not the state that affects their thought or even that tells them what to think. Besides, if philosophers issue so many warnings about the state, it is precisely because they know that it is a source of danger. The real danger comes from simple things: they have a career, they have a status, they know that they will have a pension, etc. We should not think of that in economic terms, but as a small part of the social conditions of the options that ground our everyday experience of the world: the fact that you know when the next bus is due, that it should be on time and get you to your next appointment, helps compose an orderly world which presupposes people who assume that the world is orderly, that working is worth the trouble and is better than staying in bed . . . (I shall not take this any further, and yet I really ought to: I shall stop, leaving suspension marks. I am not sure that you will be able to fill in all the gaps in what I have left unspoken, but I invite you to try . . .)

How do the different social universes ensure this continuity, or rather (since phrasing it this way commits the very sin that I constantly denounce, by taking society as a subject . . .), how does it come about that things are self-evident? (or that the 'it' is self-evident, if I may speak like Lacan . . . and why not? [*laughter*]). How does it come about that things run on all by themselves, and just keep going, with people finding them self-evident and thinking that it's fine like that (in fact, 'it's fine like that' is already orthodoxy, although in this case we are looking at the *doxa* which precedes orthodoxy: I don't even need to say that it's fine, I don't even start to think that things could be different).

Principles of continuity of the social world in different societies

Obviously, one of the principles of difference between societies lies in the means they use to make things work smoothly so that they seem acceptable as they are, to make the fulfilment of expectations successful, so that their discourse meets the conditions of what linguists call a happy or felicitous utterance – a lovely term for the conditions that make for the successful reception of a discourse: I give an order and it is obeyed.[54] The *doxa* is absolute happiness: you feel no anxiety, see no problem. You would really have to be a Heideggerian philosopher to say that it is wrong, that it is not authentic, that it is not right, that it is 'they' (because they are thoughtlessly renouncing their freedom whereas they should be thinking thoughts of 'Being towards death', and the like, at every moment). There is a whole psychologico-Heideggerian literature, epitomized for me by Fromm's *Fear of Freedom*,[55] whose theme is 'men fear freedom, beware the Grand Inquisitor', but this is not at all the philosophy of the social world. All societies wish that their social order were organized in such a way as to avoid all anxiety. They are not making a value judgement here. The social world, if it could, would make everything smooth-running and self-evident, with none of those crises where people wonder what is going to happen next, and not even any of those minor crises you face when you turn thirty, or forty, for instance. The crisis is that moment when everything tumbles and falls, when we say: 'I have to stop and think', 'I must judge', when – as Leibniz says[56] – we do not know what the present is big with . . .

There are several solutions for making the world stable: in pre-capitalist societies, it is socialization; everything is based on the habitus. People are socialized in such a way that they are very responsible, which means that they will respond as predicted, they will be responsible and predictable from the outset, they will do what is expected of them, what has to be done: the man of honour is he who acts as a man of honour, he does what has to be done at the right moment, he knows what he is doing ('That is what people do') and people will say of him: 'He is really a man of excellence' (as in Aristotle, for instance). In addition to the habitus, there is a whole collective effort to master any crisis. Ritual, for instance, is a kind of formalization of the world destined to avoid accidents: in all circumstances, we know what we should say, which person should respond and what their response should be. There is then a sort of timetabling, as detailed as possible, of potentially critical situations. One illustration is what we call the agricultural calendar,[57] which is not a calendar in the sense that we understand it but which can be described as a calendar: it is a sort of very rigorous structuring of the sequence of events which means that everyone knows at every moment what he has to do and even knows that the time between midday and 2 pm is when the men have their siesta and the women do whatever they have to do; everyone is in the right place at the right time. In Hesiod there are some very fine remarks on this subject.[58] The social order is a chronological order, and it is no accident if the first stage in framing society is framing time.

In our societies there is a whole series of things in place to limit the risk of individual or collective crises erupting. Among the means of this sort of advance management of hazards, there are the law and the habitus . . . here I shall go straight for the essential since my time is limited. The goal is to produce a social space endowed with as great as possible an objective predictability. It must be predictable, therefore calculable, either theoretically – you can make trigonometrical calculations – or practically – with a feel for the game – which in the case of collective actions implies a maximum of synchronization and orchestration of practices.

I have just suggested the metaphor of an orchestra, which we could reflect on at length. There is a very fine text by Schütz, 'Making Music Together'.[59] This text observes a very different phenomenological logic from the one that I am adopting here, but it can be transposed. Basically, it considers the issue of orchestration, seen as what ensures that all the members of the group do what they are supposed to do at the moment when they should. In a pipers' band, everyone has to do the same thing at the same time. In a modern orchestra, whose solidarity is organic (rather than mechanical, for those of you who know the distinction),[60] with a more sophisticated division of labour, they have to do different things at different moments in order to make music. The dream of social universes would be to provide everyone with a score of their own. Most often, and unwittingly, sociology has at the back of its mind the metaphor of the musical score or, and it comes to the same thing, the metaphor of the theatre (they talk of 'social roles', for instance, and the term has passed into ordinary usage, but you can look for sessions and you will find that I have never used this term in my writings, because it implies quite a wrong philosophy of the social world).[61] We imagine, then, that if things function and work out well in due order, it is because there is a kind of great composer or conductor, with the agents being the players, each with their own score. But in the social world things do not happen like that at all: there is a place for the score, where things are subject to the rule of laws – which, according to Weber, are charged with ensuring calculability and predictability, which is one of the principal functions of rational law[62]– and a place left open to orchestration improvised by each person's habitus. Produced by different circumstances and adapting to different circumstances, people act in ways that suit their circumstances and are orchestrally arranged among themselves, because they reproduce in their behaviour the differences that have produced them. I am going too fast, but it seems to me that the social world is the product of two modes of regulation: on the one hand, the legal type and, on the other, that based on the habitus, which may have a negative correlation.

I'll stay with that for a moment to finish up and make the link with what I said at the start of the lecture: the most tragic situations that have often been evoked when talking of Kafka, that is the concentration camps, have this property: they create – but at the absolutely extreme limit, well beyond Godot and the subproletariat – universes where absolutely anything becomes possible, where there is nothing that is impossible. They correspond to universes where anything can happen. In the article 'Des mots qui tuent' ['Words that kill'] which appeared in *Actes de la recherche* in 1982,[63] Michael Pollak refers to the period around 1935 when the status of the Jews was codified juridically, translating arbitrariness and discrimination into law, and, amazingly, it appears that the arbitrary and the violence were already so objectively present that the German jurists found in this codification of the arbitrary a modicum of security. It is therefore in these extreme and paradoxical test cases that we really see the function of the law: an unjust law is better than pure arbitrariness and, against this law codifying discrimination, the most hard-line Nazis – who, to tell the truth, are pure Heideggerians – defended the Führer's absolute right to decide arbitrarily at any moment and in total freedom whatever he wanted (this is on page 36 of the article). In other words, the codification of the arbitrary sets a limit to the limitless arbitrary that abandoned Jews to individual terrorism and violence. Rendered official, and licensed by law, injustice in a way becomes a limitation.

Which brings us to the concentration camps – I refer you to the interview with a survivor analysed by Michael Pollak in the same issue.[64] Those who make the connection between Kafka and the concentration camp are not as absurd as they seem, they have noticed something: the concentration camp is the ultimate avatar of a universe where all things are possible and there is no limit at all, no possible prediction or anticipation. Which means that it is surely the most authentic experience of the nature of time.

Lecture of 26 April 1984

First session (lecture): educational space and forms. – Distribution of capital and profits of distinction. – Cultural capital objectified and appropriated. – Means of production and cultural capital. – The legitimate appropriation of cultural works.
Second session (seminar): time and power. Acting on structures and acting on representations. – Symbolic action. -The reassuring role of the rule. – Time and the exercise of power.

First session (lecture): educational space and forms

I would like to make some preliminary remarks on the form that I have given to these lectures, which may surprise some of you. It seems to me that, as with any social relationship, the pedagogical relationship is confronted with more or less objectified forms that exist either in the objective world in the guise of more or less elaborate codes, or in people's minds in the guise of patterns of thinking that guide our practices and perceptions. When you listen to someone placed in my position, your expectations are structured by these patterns of perception and association. The model of the guest lecture, for instance, implies eloquence, and you look forward to a certain kind of intellectual delight. The model of the lecture course invites a different attitude: you sit there with your sheet of paper taking notes, you have come to learn and retain things that have been prepared in advance for you to retain. We can't take this kind of argument too far (it always seems a little too surgical or even sadistic), but it is important to clarify these things, because they manipulate both the speaker and the audience. Making them explicit can help clear up a number of misunderstandings. I am sure that I do not fit into either of the two logics that I have briefly sketched: neither the logic of the guest lecture nor the logic of the lecture course. Since this double negative is likely to provoke some frustration, I would like to justify it: when the point is to convey something of the nature that I want to convey, we often have to break with existing forms, and particularly those of the established models. Very often when we are asked to 'play by the rules', as people say, observing the formalities of politeness, respect and expression in general – we exercise a form of censorship. Although it is evident that no discourse can be totally free of all censorship, I believe that it is often important to break with the most obvious structures in order to convey something new. To take an example from my own experience: when we wanted to set up a review called *Actes de la recherche en sciences sociales*,[1] we very soon realized that the simple fact of looking for a style of expression enabling us to express what we wanted to express led us to break with the social constraints that the majority of reviews obey without even realizing it. For instance, hardly any social science journals, except some in anthropology, use photographs as a means of communication. There is one exception, but it is an American journal that was devised from the outset to be less highbrow. In fact, I had often cited the tendency of sociologists to situate their discourse at a semi-concrete semi-abstract level: you have to know what they are thinking of in order to understand what they are saying, you need a concrete reference, but this concrete foundation is never named. Sociological discourse wanders somewhere between the abstract construction of the self-contained concept and the pure and simple demonstration of the concrete, but its *metaxu*[2] status, neither fish, flesh nor fowl, which is not apparent, is revealed as soon as a different language juxtaposes the constructed and the concrete and thereby communicates a completely different relation to the object.

I don't wish to prolong this analysis unduly, but it has considerable social implications. Institutions, in particular those of legitimate language, are organized in such a way as to attract certain types of form. A social space like this one [*the lecture hall*] – with its rostrum and micros, its audience, tradition and mental structures – makes an implicit appeal to a certain language, a rather rhetorical oratory. I think that one of the simplest ways to inhabit a rhetorical space is to slip into that space, to embrace the forms invoked by the social form of the space insofar as this commands the social form of the relationship and the social content of the discourse. This is relatively important and I shall return to this during the formal part of my discourse because, even if I am not enamoured of facile formulae, forms are, as Aesop says, the best and the worst of things.[3] In a sense, as I hinted last time, forms are guarantees against violence and barbarity: respecting formalities is to apply the brakes in advance to the brutal irruption of nature and the uncontrolled violence that it can invoke. At the same time, forms, when they become formalism, for example logical or mathematical, also have the extraordinary virtue of being self-regulating: one can to a certain extent allow oneself to be borne by the automatism of form that gives a certain guarantee of logical safety.

I can sum up this kind of ambiguity in a word: forms nearly always fulfil two functions, one logical and the other social, and one of the forms par excellence of the symbolic violence that I have been trying to analyse for some time now consists in passing social forms off as logical forms, for example taking a refined accent as a sign of intelligence. If you stop to think about it, this remark has considerable implications. You can pass off an exercise in rhetoric as an act of scientific communication. At one extreme, then, there is the purely social form (the languages of rhetoric or manners or etiquette, for instance) and at the other extreme the logical form. One of the most perverse cases of symbolic violence is the case where the logical forms serve as social forms: thus, in the social sciences there are purely rhetorical uses of mathematics (or more generally the superficial symbols of logic) and here we see the full extent of the ambiguity of form. One thing then that I attempt to introduce (as always, we are never either totally unconscious or totally free . . .) is a sort of distance from forms that is a conscious and deliberate social distance from these two social phenomena: the society guest speaker – if indeed that still exists – and the college lecturer.

I continue for a moment, because it might be useful for some of you to see where your reception fits in with the different forms of social reception. In fact, if we were to analyse the space of the places of legitimate expression, we would find, even on an initial assessment, a schema where the space of the strictly academic (for example the *grandes écoles*, and some other academic institutions) is party to forms of communication that we might call authoritarian. The academic is characterized by a love of definition: scholars give definitions, they classify and label, they designate classes and instil order, they transmit order above all and they want to introduce order into the mind, replying to an unconscious request for security that is contained within the definition of the lecture that I gave you just now. What we call a 'good lecture' is a lecture that presents a guarantee of security, a lecture that starts and finishes its sentences, whose definitions are coherent; we could even call it Socratic, although that may be going too far. We have to admit (and this is not a value judgement) that there are places where such schooling functions well. There are times and a situation of crisis where its function is as useful as is military discipline in wartime.

That having been said, one property of the institution where we are lucky enough to find ourselves at the moment [the Collège de France] is that it enables us to take liberties with these academic definitions [. . .], even if there are obvious limits to the leeway allowed, which never extends to absolute freedom. I would simply like to say that the academic institution is committed to explicit definitions: it transmits predigested, preconstructed knowledge, it is in league with the diction-aries, which are instruments of power and assign a certain meaning to words (although words are always more or less important objects of dispute); it says: 'there is one definition, and only one', ' "ideology"?: I'll tell you what it is'. Obviously, the academic reaches into domains where we didn't expect to find it. You need to open your eyes: people who define things are often people with intellectual power, who want to impose a legitimate vision. By definition, research is not at ease in these spaces because it often breaks with forms, upsets definitions by limiting or generalizing them, and always treats them as provisional.

These remarks are obviously an apology and you may rightly see in them a biased justification of the limits of my teaching, but I do nonetheless believe in what I am saying.

Distribution of capital and profits of distinction

I shall now return to what I was saying last time. I distinguished between three states of cultural capital: the incorporated state – which I described briefly – the objective state and the institutionalized or codified state. To remind you briefly what was pertinent from the point of view of what I am going to say now: incorporated capital has a distinctive functional value insofar as it is unequally distributed. To explain it most simply, you only need to think of the particular status of the literate in largely illiterate societies. The literate person – who is not the intellectual – is basically the person who knows how to write in a society where most people don't. This is a facile definition, but if we develop it and make it more explicit, we find a lot of properties: the lit-erate person, for instance, will be the person who writes spells (or often pretends to write them), who writes signs looking like Arabic or a verse of the Koran, and the distinctive value of his acknowledged ability to write is manifest in the fact that he is accorded a power he can use to draw profit: he will be respected, he will be treated deferentially, he will receive gifts for the Eid al-Adha sacrifice, and so on. There will then be profits from this difference that distinguishes his practice.

In our own societies, the break is obviously differently placed. Moreover, there is not one principal break, but a series of breaks, starting with the different levels of education and leading up to the breaks between intellectual and non-intellectual, scholarly and profane. These breaks are not necessarily all clear-cut. An educational qualification has the particularity of creating clean breaks, whereas beyond educational qualifications we have continuums. Each break represents a separation, a distinction between those who have it and those who don't, the former benefiting from the profits of distinction. We might argue like those sociologists who, in order to measure 'social mobility' – a notion that is scientifically highly dubious[4] – in a given population, refer to the hypothesis of absolute noncorrelation between the profession of the father and the profession of the son. In these cases, they often resort to statistics: they compare a known frequency to a theoretical frequency in the hypothesis of the absence of relation between the two variables considered. This theoretical hypothesis is in fact the hypothesis of the equality of chances. This is an interesting theoretical hypothesis – it does not imply an egalitarian philosophy at all – for measuring the effects of the inequality of a distribution. Every time there is an unequal distribution, the effect of comparing it to an equal distribution enables us to see the effect of an unequal distribution: in the case of educational qualifications, for instance, the inequality of distribution of the knowledge of Mozart or Joyce has in itself an effect of distinction and brings with it profits of distinction. Thus, seeing the utopia of a society in which everyone has read Joyce enables us to see what happens in a society where nobody has read him This is a simple argument, but it is important for understanding one of the most important effects of the distribution of cultural capital.

Imagine that neither you nor I had writing at our disposal, and that we never had had it: everything that we do now would be practically impossible.[5] In a society without writing, where the accumulation of cultural capital in objectified form is not possible and where capital exists only in the incorporated state, there are inequalities in the distribution of cultural capital because there are always poets, or those who speak more eloquently than others in assemblies. But the inequalities of capital are much less marked than in our society. Their culture (knowledge of rites, traditions, the agricultural calendar, proverbs, sayings, and the like) is much more evenly spread and distributed, and ultimately does not function so powerfully as capital.[6] What I was saying in the abstract (capital exists only in relation to a field or a market, etc.) can be seen very clearly in this case: a cultural competence only functions as capital on the basis of unequal distribution. This means that we can see that the symbolic, polemical and practical value of a competence will depend on the structure of distribution of that competence: once a capacity is universally shared (for instance, the ability to ride a bicycle), it loses its faculty of distinction ('distinction' does not need to imply 'an intention to be distinguished' – I may have no intention of being distinguished and yet may be perceived as distinguished through the simple fact of displaying an uncommon competence).

I would like to draw your attention in passing to the universe of adjectives: if you want to amuse yourself by looking up 'unique' or 'common' in a dictionary, you will discover, between one and the other, your social unconscious: as in the interpretation of dreams. These two entries are no doubt the best key to understanding the implicit social philosophy that we breathe: the unique and the common (or the vulgar, etc.), is always the opposition between the one and the many, the rare and the distinguished. It finds its source in the objective structures that I have just been describing, in the fact that a certain number of properties are unequally distributed and derive their value from the inequality of their distribution: these oppositions function in the objective world, but they become the structures of our minds through which we perceive other people's behaviour and by virtue of which we spontaneously attribute value to things that are rare.

All this may seem to be verbal play; as always, the principle, when discovered, appears trivial. But putting it into practice would be enough to engender the whole of rhetoric, through a kind of proactive definition that passes the fundamental test: rhetoric can be constructed on the basis of what I have just said about the common and the rare, since the work of rhetoric always consists in creating a distance from what is most current. There is no more a substantive definition of rhetoric than there is of the beautiful: it always remains grounded in structural relations, insofar as the generating principle of all social classifications, of which the aesthetic is one dimension, is this opposition between the rare and the common, the unique and the current. Cultural capital, like all the other kinds of capital, takes its value from its relation to other kinds of capital; each fund of capital takes its value from its relation to the other funds.

It is wrong to describe the relations of cultural appropriation in terms of cultural communism: the spectator in a museum looking at a painting, the concert-goer listening to a piece of music, the reader reading a book ... although so much of the discourse on works of art does in fact make us think of what Spinoza wrote about the *amor intellectualis Dei*. There is no monopoly of God, everyone can partake of him without anyone being deprived of him.[7] Many of the things that are written about culture are of this type. If there is a domain where the spontaneous communist illusion is widespread, it is that of cultural matters and in particular language, where all the Saussurian definitions are of this type: 'language, that common treasure'.[8] In fact, this 'common treasure' is not as universal as all that, insofar as the structures that enable us to appropriate language, as objectified for example in dictionaries or the classics, are very unequally distributed; all our relations with the 'common treasure', in other words between an individual agent and the resources historically accumulated by man (libraries, for instance) are mediated by our competitive relation with the other holders of the means of appropriation.

Here again, these remarks may appear facile, but if we develop them we can see that they have multiple consequences. For instance, topics that are happily discussed in school ('What do we do when we read?', 'What is reading?', for instance)[9] are born, it seems to me, of a mythified, or (if 'mythified' seems too pejorative) erroneous representation of the real relation of the subject endowed with cultural competence to the cultural object that he applies this to. In a way, the relation to the cultural object is never one-to-one: this relation, which is experienced as something that constitutes the 'personal' par excellence, is always an impersonal relation insofar as, on the one hand, the cultural competence needed for deciphering is socially acquired and, on the other hand – as we now realize, although it was not obvious fifteen years ago[10] – the relation to the object hides a relation to other people, whether co-readers or non-readers. It is clear that in the case of 'readings' (as in 'Reading *Capital*',[11] 'reading the *Iliad*', 'reading Mallarmé'), that the reading is always a re-reading, a counter-reading, that is, a social reading. Nothing could better illustrate the notion of the profit of distinction that I have referred to than this notion of 'reading': in a sense, 'reading Marx' is a way of securing profit from capital, and it is important to know this, because the pursuit of profit from capital can lead us to *Reading Capital* . . . Knowing that there is no pure, solitary reading, that reading always takes place in a space of readers, is very important from an epistemological point of view (this is one of my theme tunes; you have heard it often, but I think it is worth repeating for every case, on every occasion): knowing that when I read a text, I co-read it with others, against others, and so on, is an epistemological tool that helps keep a check on my reading and my probable misreadings. Perhaps if every time I read something I asked myself whether

what I find when I read might not be the product of my covert relation
with the co-readers that I want to refute, confound, overcome, answer
or impress, the reading would be more scientifically guaranteed. Often,
I don't have time to explore all the implications of my propositions,
and it is not always easy to find the right example at the right moment,
but these facile propositions soon become corrosive and embarrassing
when applied to the right site, that is, our own work.

To put this argument more formally – holding my written text
before my eyes to create an academic impression: the structure of the
field, that is the unequal distribution of capital, is the source of the
specific effects of capital, which are the appropriation of the profits and
the power to lay down the laws that make the field function in ways
most favourable to capital and its reproduction. I'm afraid you won't
have understood what I've just been saying, but that doesn't matter,
because I have already explained it in different terms! I haven't done
this on purpose, but it shows you the effect of an academic discourse,
which does not necessarily suppose that you understand, and moreover
doesn't try to be understood. This is not a joke; it is a scientifically verified truth. A long time ago, using an empirical experiment to measure
the reception of a professorial discourse – in one of our first ventures
onto pedagogical ground – we invented in particular a sort of test
designed to measure the different levels and forms of understanding.[12]
There was, for example, a fictitious but plausible text delivered by a
professor in which a certain number of words were wrongly used. The
idea had been suggested by Éric Weil, a well-known professor of philosophy and reader of Sheridan, who told me that 'There is in Sheridan
a character called Mrs. Malaprop who always uses words wrongly'.[13] I
jumped for joy, I said 'That's fantastic!' So we devised a text that gave
a context and a dozen lines in which some words were wrongly used,
but we did not say which, and we said: 'Identify the words wrongly
used.' There were two traps to avoid: they might designate as being
wrongly used words that were perfectly apt, and vice versa. A further
test asked them for definitions.[14]

The conclusion arising conformed very closely to the professorial
ideology on communication, according to which 'they don't understand a word we say, we are not getting through to them'. This first-
degree conclusion would be of no interest, largely because it is too
full of professorial prejudice. But there is a second conclusion to be
drawn: if the professors are so sure of this, lamenting so solemnly and
yet continuing to lecture in the same way, there is something afoot,
they are making some profit out of it. If we push this questioning to
the limit, we might ask how it is that so many systems of communica-

tion can continue to function in cases where nothing is actually being communicated (at Mass, for instance). People often say that language is an instrument of communication, but what is this extraordinary instrument that, although it no longer fulfils its function, continues to be accepted by everyone, and what are the social conditions required for this situation to subsist? The notion of pedagogical authority[15] (for any teacher this consists in unconsciously saying: 'I am worthy of being listened to' – where 'listened to' does not mean 'understood') is born of the realization, for example, that when a message is sent, 80 per cent of it is lost through noise and interference. That being said, as in the natural sciences, the empirical facts do not explain anything. It is not enough to draw up an inventory of interference and loss. You need to know why and under what conditions things still continue to function. How is it that nobody says, 'But we don't understand a word of this'? (You should never say what I am saying here in a teaching situation, because you would be laying yourself open.) So that is what underlies all the things that I have been saying this morning. If you are interested, it is in a book published in 1965 by Mouton, *Rapport pédagogique et communication*, that you can find the report on this test as well as analyses of dissertations and other things concerning the communication between teacher and pupil in a pedagogical situation.

Language, capital or any other kind of cultural competence (it might be possessing a refined accent, a musical culture or knowledge of matrix calculus) starts to function as capital if the structure of distribution in the field is suitable; if everyone possessed this competence it would lose all its value, as in the case of writing. That was a first point that I argued. I also pointed out that one of the factors that helps to facilitate the symbolic effects of the possession of capital is the fact that the transmission of this capital tends to pass largely unnoticed. Without wishing to linger over this point, I would like to be more specific about one small property: I mentioned, among the number of hidden inequalities, the inequality of the time spent exposed to legitimate culture and the fact that, for children whose family culture is closest to the educational environment, the time of exposure to culture imposed by the school is more or less increased by all the years preceding entry into school. This kind of hidden acquisition procures, in addition to a real advantage, an ideological advantage insofar as this hidden acquisition is perceived as given by nature.

I shall not return to this point, I merely wanted to point out that one of the important forces mediating between economic capital and cultural capital is time: if we had to find a sort of universally equivalent standard to measure exchange rates – how do we transform economic capital into cultural capital or cultural capital into economic capital? – one of the possible standards would be time. In this particular case, the link between economic capital and cultural capital is established through the time that it takes to operate the exchange. Specialists in human capital have seen this quite clearly – and it is to the credit of Gary Becker to have pointed this out – but it seems to me that they have lost the theoretical profit that they acquired, by basically turning this equivalence into a simple tool for evaluating cultural capital in monetary terms. If it is true that cultural capital will depend on the number of years of study, we will measure the value of cultural capital by the number of school years that it takes to acquire it, based on the idea that the time during which an individual can prolong the exercise of acquisition depends on the time during which their family can provide them with free time; which means that we can calculate in terms of lost salary, so to speak, the equivalent number of extra years. I won't return to this point, it is just a reminder or a footnote.

Cultural capital objectified and appropriated

I had started to speak a little of the objectified state of cultural capital, and I would simply like to add some new points. As I said just now, its objectified state is to be found in things like libraries, computers or a city like Florence. We can draft an economics of cultural capital: we can measure it against objective indicators – how many paintings, books and maps, for instance? – but we can also evaluate profit by counting, say, the numbers of visitors. Thus we could say that Lourdes represents an objectified religious capital measurable in terms of numbers of pilgrims and altars, and the like. Here again, I am stating the obvious, but if I developed the argument (which would take me too far from the logical track of my discourse, which I don't want to lose completely), we would discover very important things on the question of the initial accumulation of capital or on pilgrimage as a primitive form of the accumulation of capital in many societies. There is a whole world of research and study to be undertaken or revised on the basis of that idea, but I shall not develop it here.

One thing to note: although, unlike objectified capital, incorporated capital is transmissible as juridical property or material reality (you can transmit paintings or libraries, for instance) it is not self-sufficient. In fact, you can transmit a painting without handing down the culture that normally goes with it, which we would consider to be the true condition of appropriating it. Here, when we say 'normally' we are introducing a value judgement: it will correspond to the break between the bourgeois who are rich in economic capital and those who are rich in cultural capital. This absolutely fundamental break is at the heart of permanent social struggles; so many cartoons or comments by people returning from holiday refer to the fact that there are people who possess things without possessing the legitimate manner of appropriating these things.

To give one example among thousands, a very interesting document is Daninos's discourse on the *petit bourgeois* who carry a camera round their neck and, instead of looking at things, photograph them because they can't appropriate them in an authentic way.[16] Like most of the things that we say about other people, this is obviously a racist discourse, about class. At the same time, it contains its part of sociological truth: one of the functions of photography is probably to give to those who want to appropriate things and who have a confused feeling that they don't have the legitimate instruments of appropriation – we know that photography is statistically *petit bourgeois* – a roundabout way of appropriating things despite everything, which is what we might call a mechanized cultural appropriation.[17] The camera is in fact a great example of objectified cultural capital. We might recall everything that Bachelard said about scientific instruments as reified science.[18] The camera is reified science, and used to photograph monuments for instance, it is a way of procuring a substitute for legitimate appropriation, which consists in knowing how to study and decipher the frieze of the Parthenon and establish its typology.

Objectified cultural capital then raises the question of the legitimate mode of appropriation: you can possess a painting, hang it on your wall as your own legal property, without possessing it as legitimate symbolic property. There is a sort of dissociation of the two modes of appropriation.[19] For instance, within the dominant class, there are those who visit galleries but cannot afford to buy and those who do not visit, but who can buy. This is a division that gives rise to the most diverse discourses. In many cultural places there are books where people can record their reactions and you can find extraordinary, completely Flaubertian texts there, expressing quite innocently the ideological production of the culture that I have just described rapidly and discreetly, because it would be unbearable if I took it further.

This opposition between artists and bourgeois, between those who possess cultural capital and, therefore, the legitimate means of appropriation of cultural works, and the holders of the economic means unaccompanied by cultural capital, has its roots in this property of objectified cultural capital: cultural possession is not necessarily accompanied by economic possession. From this starting point, one could delve much more deeply into aspects of the social history of art and literature: any cultural object, whether a Dogon statue or a computer, bears a kind of implicit expectation of its legitimate reception.[20] In other words, the cultural object calls for an appropriate habitus, that is, someone who is disposed to recognize that object for what it is. At Beaubourg, if you see a pile of sand [which happens to be the work of a contemporary artist] and a kid comes to play in it – which has happened – there has been a misunderstanding. The cultural object was not recognized, in both senses of the term: it was recognized neither as a cultural object, nor, by the same token, as a cultural object calling for an appropriate response, that is, respect. The cultural object should not be touched, which is one definition of the sacred: you badly want to touch, but you don't. If you fail to recognize the dignity inherent in the cultural object as cultural object, you commit a solecism and you deprive the object of its meaning.

Modern painters, who are very sophisticated, make much play with this – they set traps, they invite us to 'Touch!'. I think the most advanced cultural objects, like conceptual art, are tending to assimilate into their work a metadiscourse on the cultural object that resembles the kind that I am considering. The painters do not necessarily think this metadiscourse through, but in practice they have a practical mastery of a theory of painting as something sacred, that you should not touch (they paint a moustache on the Mona Lisa [as Marcel Duchamp did], for instance); in practice they play on our various visions of the cultural object. This supposes a highly autonomous field, which leads us back to one of the properties of a field: the more autonomous a field becomes, the more play there is with the game itself, the more a work becomes a metadiscourse on metadiscourse . . . I am not depreciating this game, which raises the question of the relation between scientific metadiscourse and practical metadiscourse: there are moments when certain fields, through the laws of their own beliefs and functioning, produce a discourse on themselves close to one that science might pronounce, with the difference that science speaks from the outside whereas the indigenous producers speak from the inside, with the benefits that this entails. In philosophy we have our own contemporary examples,[21] and when you speak as an insider with the benefits entailed, you never say everything, otherwise you would find yourself outside: you stay on the margins, the margin of a field being the place where you can enjoy the profits both of being inside and of being outside. I think that if you are up to date with these matters, you will have understood what I am saying . . .

(I shall say no more about his, because it is so difficult to analyse one's contemporaries, which leads into one of sociology's permanent problems: the historian can tell all, and is fêted for saying things that would hang a sociologist. There was a magnificent article in *Annales*, 'Le lobby Colbert', that offered a formidable description of the half-friends, half-family network of relations that underpinned the power of the 'Colbert lobby'.[22] But if we wrote the same things about the X, Y or Z lobbies today, naming their names, with an analysis of genealogies, relations and liaisons, it would be monstrous. If you stop to think about it, this says a lot about the natures of history and sociology, and what people often say about sociology – that it is not scientific – but I won't go on.)

Means of production and cultural capital

From the gap between legal ownership and legitimate, symbolic ownership, a host of conclusions may be drawn. I have indicated some of them in the area of cultural appropriation of cultural works, such as works of art, but there is a domain where you would no doubt be more surprised to see this notion developed, which is the evolution of the machine and therefore of what the Marxist tradition calls 'constant capital'.[23] One of the problems raised by my present analysis is that the machine itself is susceptible to the same type of analysis as the painting: as history advances and machines and technical objects incorporate energy (they incorporate energy, they also produce and transform it) – this is what differentiates the machine from a computer, for instance – but also incorporate what we might call informational energy and cultural capital, machines join the category of the work of art, in the sense that their legitimate social but also technical appropriation supposes an appropriate incorporated capital on the part of the person who wants to make use of them.

We could go on in this way to develop a whole materialist theory, in the widest sense,[24] of the executive – a category incomprehensible to traditional Marxists, whose definition of capital leaves no place for cultural capital, or introduces it only marginally and superficially because they don't know what to do with it. Executives have an ambiguous status, due either to the fact that they are not the owners, in the strictly economic sense, of the instruments of production that they use and serve, or to the fact that they draw profit from their cultural capital by selling the services that they command given their ability to make the economic capital objectified in the machines function successfully.

Although their ambiguous status derives from this relation, I think the ambiguous strategies of the titular legal and economic owners of the machinery and the means of production are explained also by the ambiguity of purely economic ownership, once we progress beyond the generation of the proprietary inventor: in firms where the owner must draw on the services of the holders of an appropriate specific capital, especially in group enterprises – such as collective research organizations, for instance – there are clearly contradictions, tensions and conflicts of quite a special order between the holders of economic capital and the holders of the cultural capital that enables the functioning of economic capital with an objectified cultural component. The problems raised by the concentration of cultural capital needed to enable the space – of an R & D department, for instance – to function can be analysed on the basis of this kind of dual ownership of the economic instruments.

Here I might venture to formulate a tendentious little law, even if I am usually reluctant to do so: we might think that, as the cultural capital incorporated within the organization and its economic structures increases, so what Arrow calls 'information investment'[25] (I shall look at this terminology next time) – that is, the collective power of the holders of cultural capital needed for the objective economic capital to function successfully – tends also to increase. This tendency would doubtless be much stronger if the holder of economic capital did not have the means to set the holders of cultural capital to compete with one other and if the latter, given the conditions in which they have been trained – in the logic of competitive examinations, and so on – were not already predisposed to compete with one other, and thereby neutralize themselves through their rivalry.

The legitimate appropriation of cultural works

I shall leave it at that, but I opened a perspective just now that I have not yet fully followed through: when referring to the Dogon mask, I said that any cultural work encloses a sort of implicit definition of the legitimate means of appropriating it. A cultural work says: 'I am what I am and I demand to be approached in a certain way, so as to be acknowledged as a work of culture', with consequences for the attitude of the viewer – 'I shall not move, I shall not make a noise, I shall lower my voice to adopt the right tone', and also 'I must have the right code'. The producer of the work has in fact invested his work with an implicit code, without this being deliberate or explicit – I shall return to this –

and this code is tacitly solicited by the work.[26] This raises the question of the legitimate key to decipher the code.

To put it simply: the cultural work demands a form of belief, acceptance and acknowledgement, but also a specific form of knowledge. Misunderstandings in the historical perception of cultural works arise from the fact that they very often outlive the habitus for which they were produced without so much as ceasing to be revered and acknowledged, even if for the wrong reasons.[27] This is a commonplace, but here too you would surely have some surprises if I completed this development. In any case I think a whole part of literary history would be widely called into question: cultural works, from the Bible to Mallarmé, not to mention the tables of Hammurabi,[28] have the property of outliving not only their producers, but also their implicitly legitimate consumers and addressees. This means that their survival as cultural works depends on their being reappropriated, perceived and understood in a state of permanent misunderstanding. This is what Weber says of the Bible: the first Protestants read the Bible 'through the spectacles of their whole attitude', their whole habitus,[29] which means that they brought an awful lot to it. Everyone knows this, but they fail to draw all the conclusions, if only by questioning on the one hand the original, historically validated reading, as solicited by the work, and, on the other, the historical conditions of this sort of rereading.

The pre-Socratics, for instance, are an enormous historical misunderstanding and we might wonder whether the history of philosophy is not a history of enormous layers of sediment of misunderstandings, which doesn't mean that it isn't interesting. But it does perhaps mean that making a doxography of readings is a precondition of any reading. 'Reading Marx' would be first of all reading the readers of Marx, not to supersede them, but to consider what their readings would have constituted in terms of the categories of perception that orientate my reading and its attempts to supersede. I assure you that this is no trivial ambition: a whole form of literary or philosophical celebration would be deprived of its foundations.

Second session (seminar): time and power

What I was saying at the start applies very well to these sorts of provisional attempts and reflections on risky subjects that I am offering during this second session. My research topics are often highly risky, but they may be profitable, or they may sometimes lead into error or failure. So you should not treat what I say as gospel truth, but rather as suggestions inviting reflection, triggering further thought, and so on. This is especially true of this second session.

Last time I insisted on the way that the most powerless people might experience time, because of their position in the social world and their deprivation. What I said could be resumed in two words: time and impotence. What experience of time can people with no power over the social world have? I analysed a certain number of extreme test cases, in particular the situation of the subproletarian[30] and the situation of people who find themselves placed in totalitarian institutions such as concentration camps, which are an extreme example of a range of institutions – like the barracks or the convent – where anything may happen.

I need to correct something that I have just said. I mentioned one of the great works of sociology, *Asylums*, where Goffman attempts to isolate the invariants of the institutions (such as asylums, convents, boarding schools, concentration camps, and others)[31] that he calls total or totalitarian. These institutions are characterized by the fact that those who enter must in a way abandon their previous personality, and joining these institutions is often symbolized by kinds of rites of passage, of deculturization and anonymization – for example the zero-degree military crew cut – designed to provoke a sort of *metanoia*, to borrow a word from the mystics.[32] *Metanoia* is a change in body and soul, since one of the surest ways of causing a change of soul is to change the body, with its appearance, techniques, rhythms, and the like. This sort of total manipulation of the social person aims to produce what turns out to be the 'confinement effect' of the asylum. These institutions, which may appear awful to varying degrees, paradoxically manage to produce in their inmates a sort of habituation or even attachment to the institution, which Goffman calls 'asylumization': in a lunatic asylum – which is Goffman's main example – the inmates are so moulded, so to speak, to the asylum that they realize they would find it hard to leave.

This process of asylumization is in fact common to these institutions, but while I spoke of features common to these institutions, I was thinking that there was a difference.[33] The convent and the prison have some rules in common, and you would find *The Rule of St Benedict* a most interesting document to read: total institutions control the tiniest details of practice so as to institute a perfect synchronization of everyone's individual behaviour. One of the properties of socialization is that it synchronizes. I insisted last time on Schütz's description of our temporal experience in the normal world, the kind of universe subject to the laws of good continuity and perfect predictability: the condition of this predictability is the synchronization of practices, which is not necessarily submission to a perfectly homogenous time, for the division of labour modifies these things. Synchronization is one of the means used by groups to create this kind of uniformity and anonymity.

Bearing this in mind, I was thinking that the concentration camps are an exception among Goffman's examples: although they share a number of the properties of the total institution (confinement and deprivation pushed to the limit) and retain a certain number of properties of the conventional world (regularity and ritual, for instance), they introduce a radical difference, which is the absolute unpredictability of the most essential things, the questions of life or death. Pollack, for example, writes that, in the camps, the objective strategies inscribed in the institution seemed to be orientated towards two ends: on the one hand, to crush all hope, that is, forbid any structure of expectation for the future by destroying the laws of good continuity inscribed both in our habitus and in ordinary objectivity; and, on the other hand, to forbid any rational expectation by making a sort of institution of the unpredictable.[34] In other words, the most radical way of destructuring, of destroying the structures of, expectation, as a phenomenologist would say, is to constantly disappoint them. I don't want to take too long over this, but we can easily see this in the case of the barracks and their function as a total and totalitarian institution (it is difficult to use a language free of pejorative values and connotations when we speak of this).[35] There are procedures within barracks that remind us of what I have just been saying. They create permanent unpredictability: the time spent by the new recruit is always open and empty – in this, very similar to that of the subproletarian – yet, at the same time, always occupied, because at any moment anything may happen. This institutionalized arbitrariness has the effect of producing a kind of destruction of expectation that keeps the recruit on the alert for any instructions. The 'barrackized' men (using 'barrackization' as the equivalent of 'asylumization') are ready for anything, at any time, with the same disenchantment and the same submissiveness, for even revolt is partly a form of submission to a universe where all things are possible.

These extreme situations where the arbitrary is instituted as the absolute power to decree absolutely anything at any time, enable us to analyse everything that is implicit in normal situations where it is tacitly understood that a whole lot of things cannot possibly happen, without even having to be mentioned as excluded or impossible. The Nazis had formulated the theory of absolute and absolutely arbitrary power – I pointed this out with reference to Pollak's article – by defining the Führer as the charismatic producer of legitimate law who is not answerable to any external constraint of a juridical or contractual nature. This sort of theorization of the purely arbitrary, which Weber would have called a charismatic juridical creation, and which answers to nobody but the producer himself, this sort of law of the lawless, of delegitimation or refusal of any juridical constraint, makes us see the kind of lived experience of time involved in a space of this type, but also the social conditions of the possibility of our ordinary experience of lived time. That is more or less what I wanted to say. In fact, I have analysed the experience of time in situations of total powerlessness and, thereby, the relations between a form of power and a certain type of temporal experience.

Acting on structures and acting on representations

I would now like to analyse the two forms of power that seem to me to emerge from an analysis of the relations between time and power. The power that we observe in extreme cases like the concentration camps is directed at the objective opportunities and possibilities, the chances that this or that will happen or not happen. In other words, it is directed at the game itself. Absolute power is the power to change the rules at any moment: 'Heads I win, tails you lose' – it is the arbitrary power that, being able to change the rules at any moment, will always win the game. 'Might will always be right': absolute power can at any moment dictate the rules that are most favourable to its expectations and desires. Obviously, the extreme form is very rarely attained: it is in fiction and magic that absolute power, which is a magic power, the power to have everything immediately, is sought. The most ordinary magic, the black magic that consists in sticking a pin in the heart of a doll that is the effigy of your enemy, is, as we all know, a long-distance action, but it is above all an action that negates time: magic is instantaneous, it does not wait; the search for absolute power is the search for the power to have everything, and to have it straight away.

We could connect this with well-known research into child psychology or psychoanalysis: for desire to be granted instantaneously, it needs an absolutely arbitrary power. In our everyday social existence, we are quite unlikely to see situations of this type – thank God, I am tempted to say – but they are only an extreme case of the ordinary situations in which social agents can manipulate the objective chances. A minister can thus decree that there will not be thirty *agrégés* but sixty, or the contrary. This is a very simple and quite familiar example from our own experience, but there are many other actions by those in power that consist in transforming what Cournot calls the objective probabilities, the objective chances, inherent in the objective world, that something will happen or not.

The second form of power consists in acting, not on the objective probabilities, but on what Cournot calls the subjective probabilities,[36] that we might also call epistemic probabilities, that is, our lived expectations. This is the power to transform our aspirations. To give you a brief and provisional definition, there is, on the one hand, the real, effective political power that transforms structures objectively, and, on the other, the type of symbolic power exercised by the cultural powers (clerical or intellectual authorities, for instance) who, since they cannot transform the objective opportunities, can transform our relations to them. Examples of typical symbolic actions that directly manipulate our subjective representations are the 'Be realistic, demand the impossible!' that we heard in May 1968, or, on the contrary, exhortations of realism. It is the classic problem that the trade unions face in raising expectations ('Now is the time to act!') while restraining them: one of the problems for union leaders is how to manoeuvre in this very narrow margin between these two possibilities, the sociological and the utopian; they want to incite the dominated, whose subjective expectations tend to be objectively adapted to the objective opportunities, to raise their aspirations, but this may reach a point where these become crazy, dangerous, utopian, millennialist or suicidal. A leader exerting symbolic power will need to devise strategies capable of manipulating this relation between hopes and opportunities.

The power of the first type, which affects the objective structure of aspirations, can really disturb expectations, as we see with certain political measures. Lowering the age of retirement,[37] for instance, is an action that profoundly changes the structures of expectation in depth, as well as the way the gap between youth and age is perceived.[38] There are then manipulations of objective opportunity with knock-on social effects that go considerably further than their superficial primary effect, if, for example, they manipulate the age limits: such as setting the age of majority and the right to vote at eighteen.[39] Let us suppose that we pass a law to change the legal age of marriage: this could transform all of a young maiden's dreams.

I have been saying implicitly that whoever has the power to act on the objective structures also acts on the incorporated, subjective structures, insofar as the incorporated structures tend to adapt themselves sooner or later to the objective opportunities. In other words, whoever acts on the objective structures acts on the incorporated structures as well, and transforms representations by transforming the structures in relation to which these representations are composed. The converse is less true and we see straightaway that the symbolic power which acts on representations is a subordinate power, in the sense that it can say to people, as the Stoics did: 'Adapt your aspirations to your opportunities' – *amor fati. Fatum* is the objective chance that defines us socially. It is a series of chances connected with our birth; defined in social terms, our birthplace could be described as a series of probabilities. Political measures can change that ('Every soldier carries a marshal's baton in his knapsack'),[40] and in quite real ways if, for example, they impose quotas as they did in Eastern Europe requiring every contingent to include x per cent of working-class children. By transforming the structures of the objective opportunities, you can then affect representations indirectly, whereas, conversely – and this is what makes symbolic power remain a subordinate power – transforming aspirations can only lead to transforming structures in reality insofar as the representation of chances transformed leads to an action transformed in relation to the structures. Symbolic power can only really transform structures through the mobilization that it produces if it can render thinkable actions that were tacitly excluded before as not just impossible, but unthinkable. Here we see an important difference between the two forms of power.

That said, the first type of power, which acts on the objective structures, shows its superiority and its particular strength in that it can create conditions favourable to the success of the second type of power. The most perverse thing in situations like the concentration camp is that the total disorganization of the objective structures on which expectations may be based engenders a kind of demoralization, in every sense of the term, that creates the most favourable terrain for all the manipulations exercised by the second type of power. Last time, when I was discussing the subject of the particular link between the subproletariat and the millenarian type movements that are movements of a magical type, I was saying implicitly that when nothing is possible, all things are possible, and the destructuration of all expectations, of all the objective structures of time, provides a basis for almost unlimited manipulations.

For instance, we are puzzled by certain past or present movements that disturb the political rationalism that we are accustomed to, because we were born amid social movements of a very special kind, and I am thinking of an excellent book by the Tillys on the 1830–1930 period called *The Rebellious Century*.[41] They show that an important historical phenomenon that often passes unnoticed is the codification and rationalization of a movement of rebellion. Following Hobsbawm and Thompson,[42] the book contrasts the pre-capitalist types of revolt, usually emerging brutally from an immediately tangible economic effect, such as an increase in the price of bread (an increase in the price of bread is announced, and a riot follows) or the arrival of the tax collectors, with the forms of demonstration and revolt that gradually took shape in the nineteenth century with the invention of national corporate agencies capable of organizing movements on a national scale and disposing of rational techniques of mobilization. The banner, the placard and the slogan constitute a series of historical inventions that contribute to the organization of the demonstration and the control of its limits. The trade union strategy that I mentioned just now, aiming to raise aspirations but not to the point of making them so unreasonable that they would destroy their own intentions, is incarnated in the stewards of the CGT [Confédération générale du travail], something that was not invented overnight. These historic inventions show the ambiguity of the modern type of demonstration. The spontaneous or magical vision that developed in the leftist movement of May 1968 forgot that the Stoic kind of control of these modern types of movement – 'Do not demand the impossible' – are the product of a historical genealogy.

Returning to my argument, we see that the so-to-speak rational politics developed by organized movements has become natural – we are no longer surprised, for instance, by the fact that a demonstration is announced for a particular date, but imagine a hunger riot announced for 14 July: even the disorder is predictable; it is, as they say, 'channelled', managed, to avoid uncontrolled excess. This supposes social universes of the type that I have described, with relatively constant objective expectations, chances and probabilities. We can evaluate in advance the number of demonstrators, and check the statistics before and after. The role of statistics is very important; they become a political weapon, never to be ignored. When we see demonstrations in Iran,[43] for instance, it is true that we don't understand, and I think that some things, including radical differences between different contemporary demonstrations, illustrate what I was saying just now: universes where, for economic or political reasons, the objective structures of expectation are upset, where all things become possible, are terrains very favourable to a form of manipulation by the second type of power, which can be exercised almost without limit. These are things that common sense knows: the strategies of despair are the strategies of people who have nothing left to lose, who are beyond winning or losing. And at this point all things become possible; life itself can cease to be what matters the most.

I find these things an important key to the understanding of certain historical facts. The symbolic type of power manipulates the representation of chance and tells people: 'You have more opportunities than you think.' 'Be reasonable, do not demand the impossible.' 'If you demand that, you won't get it', or 'If you stay on strike too long . . .'. These strategies of manipulation are also at work in the educational system: 'You would do better to go to an IUT [Institute of Technology, or Technical College]; a [University] science faculty would be aiming too high.' Obviously these strategies of manipulation of the representation of opportunity contribute to the objective logic of opportunity: as I always remind people, structures never determine behaviour mechanically, they act through the mediation of the representation that agents have of them, so that, in this particular case, the representation of opportunity allows some small chance of escaping the structures. If there is a measure of freedom in relation to the effect of the structures, it is insofar as the representation of the structures is within certain limits manipulable, with corresponding effects (what has been called 'awakening consciousness',[44] a terrible term that has made the scientific sociology of social representations waste a hundred years of time) because a margin of freedom is left to those who hold symbolic power.

Symbolic action

This symbolic power is exercised through discourse, but also through actions of a certain type. For instance, so-called 'acts of provocation' show that certain limits, which we cannot imagine being transgressed, are transgressible, by the fact that someone has transgressed them. One of the most typical actions of May 1968 was the transgression of unsuspected limits, as in the case of the student addressing his professor in the familiar 'tu' form; some of the strongest barriers, those whose transgression is so unthinkable that they are not even thought of as barriers, were shown to be such through the fact of symbolic transgression. The symbolic crossing of a frontier is the sacrilegious act par excellence. It is reserved in general for the priesthood, who in Durkheimian terms[45] hold the monopoly of crossing the frontier separating the sacred from the profane. Provocative sacrilege has a liberating function because it makes us see the frontier and then the practical possibility of transgressing it: 'He called the professor "tu", but he isn't dead, they didn't kill him, they didn't shoot him.' But although we need to insist on this symbolic power and on the freedom provided by this sort of analysis effect – which has nothing to do with awakening consciousness – we should also note its limitations.

A symbolic action, for instance transgressing a barrier, is only thinkable for the person accomplishing it and exemplary for those observing it if certain objective conditions are fulfilled, since the same transgression can lead to the Pantheon or the lunatic asylum. For behaviour that upsets objective probabilities to have an objectified chance of being recognized as legitimate, reasonable and praiseworthy, the objective structures must be in a state of objective uncertainty, encouraging the possibility of subjective uncertainty over these structures. Max Weber insists on the fact that the prophet is the person who speaks when the others have nothing left to say, when everyone has fallen silent in the face of the world and its uncertainty and inconsistency, its cataclysms and famines, and so on. The prophet, or the charismatic hero, does still have something to say: 'We have crossed the wilderness, we will find a solution.' This logo-therapeutic capacity of the prophet has been attested by the research of ethnologists, but it is only at the moment when the priesthood has more or less collapsed that the man dressed in rags and bearing a staff arrives and speaks.

We saw it in May 1968: it is amusing to see the statistics of people who made official statements in *Le Monde*. Throughout the critical period, we see names of unknown people, but, as order is gradually restored, the well-known names reappear, to tell us that nothing has happened.[46] It is the role of the priesthood to re-establish the symbolic order and so say: 'Look, there was a moment of collective folly, a psychodrama,[47] but the objective structures have been restored and everything is back in order, take my word for it.' If, as I said last time, we still have the impression that the symbolic forces are useless, it is because the conditions of success of the second type of power are so inscribed within the first type of power that people can say: 'But what are they up to? They are teaching their grandmother to suck eggs' – an observation as applicable to the discourse of disorder as to the discourse of order. In the period of objective disorder where the objective structures are under attack, we no longer hear the speakers of order. First, they can no longer speak, they are crushed by contempt. And second, even if they cried out loud, nobody would listen. And vice versa.

And yet, it is not true that putting into words what can be heard, and what is spoken differently in the objective world, is to do nothing. The assumption of discursive form that characterizes the second type of power is in a way the complete realization and social accomplishment of what happens objectively in the social world. A situation of crisis – think of the metaphor of the baton in the knapsack – can be described as a transformation of the structures of objective opportunity: for a moment, all things become possible, or at any rate the impossible ceases to be as impossible as usual. In situations of a 'revolutionary' type, as long as the transformations of the structures of objective opportunity are not accomplished in a discourse saying, 'Citizens, people, and so on', these possibilities are less possible than when they are declared to be possible. Conversely, the restoration of order goes without saying: in the normal social order described by Schütz, when I put my letter in the letterbox, I am supposing that one postman will sort it and another will deliver it to its addressee.[48]

These are hypotheses that I do not even formulate as hypotheses. It is only as a scholar that I formulate them, because one of the properties of these hypotheses, of the *doxa*, is that they do not even need to be formulated: I am certain of a certainty which is beyond certainty because it doesn't even have to be stated. But as soon as a crisis has occurred and the possibility that a letter might not be delivered tomorrow has arisen, it is important for someone to announce that the postal service has been resumed. This is not redundant: as Mallarmé said, 'it is not pleonastic with the world'.[49] The symbolic is the kind of false tautology that helps to make things happen.

The reassuring role of the rule

To take this further, I wanted to return to Kafka for a moment, because he is central to these questions. To put it in a nutshell: what is bizarre – as has been noted by one of his commentators, Doležel[50] – is that Kafka produces a kind of upside-down world. If you remember what I was saying about the Nazis and what Weber says about the law as being what ensures predictability, we should expect the tribunal to be the place of maximum predictability, the place where the objective structures of expectation are solidly established. Yet in Kafka the tribunal is completely unpredictable. It sits at any time, does anything at all, whereas the bank, on the other hand, is a place of rationality, predictability and good organization.[51] The same commentator remarks that all the names associated with the tribunal are taboo, as if the whole thing were unnameable: the judges have no names, and the fact that someone is painting a portrait of a judge but does not know who he is adds to this impression of unpredictability.[52]

Here we see the reassuring role of predictability. The social world functions not only in accordance with objective reality but also with the rules, even when the rules merely state what would happen in the absence of rules. There are dozens of rules that are, I think, only *flatus vocis*, empty words[53] that emphasize a regular pattern that would prevail in any case. I think ethnologists are making a serious mistake in believing that rules are active. According to a splendid phrase by Weber (I remember quoting it in a lecture at Princeton[54] and as I hadn't said that it came from Weber, my colleagues thought it betrayed an advanced state of materialism), we only obey the rules when our interest in obeying them is stronger than our interest in disobeying them.[55] This proposition is not entirely true, but it is important to bear it in mind in order to think about the question. Too often, in fact, ethnologists think they have found an 'explanation': 'The rules say that . . .', 'For a Kabyle, you do not marry on a Tuesday', and so on. In fact, the principle may not lie in the rules at all, or in any case, the effect of the rule is of the kind that I have mentioned where the rule echoes a regularity. I remind you of the distinction I made between regularity ('The train regularly arrives late') and rule ('As a rule, the train arrives late').[56] If the rule has operated insofar as there is a regularity that forms the basis of its efficacy, it is better to know it, so as not to stop the analysis when we have found the rule, for example when it is a case of rules of kinship. Second, when we have found what we believe to be the objective principle of the regularity, there again we must not stop and say, 'Rules are an ideology' – sociology is not so simple, especially in this day and age when we live with dualisms such as materialism versus idealism.

The rule then may have the effect of contributing to the efficacy of the regular by stating the irregular; whence the behaviour that I mentioned last time: behaviour that consists in following the rules is the typical illustration of the distinction between rule and regularity. We all know this in practice, and sociologists take years to discover things that they have known in practice since their childhood (which does not mean that they are useless, because even if we know something in practice, it may be very difficult to enunciate it). When we say, 'Follow the rules, it costs nothing', or 'Drop a line to your cousin', we are setting in motion something of this kind, 'You have to do it anyway, it costs nothing', but this tiny little something that costs nothing changes the sense of the action entirely. It is not the motive of the action but the truth of the action. In the social world, everyday life is full of such things.

This is where the problem of the law arises: if we obey the rules as long as it is in our interest to do so, does that mean that the law is of no use? Not at all. First, it is absurd to take the law as an explicative principle of practices. When I started out as a sociologist, I called this tendency to take the law with its written rules as an explicative principle of practices 'juridicism' (where English-language ethnologists spoke of 'legalism', I believe).[57] But although we should avoid seeing explicit rules as the motive for action, we should not fall into the symmetrical and converse error of saying that the law is of no use, that it is a pure ideology or superstructure – with all the stupidities that we are used to hearing. In fact, this superstructure works precisely through the fact that it transforms the nature of reality, transforms experience and blocks representations: if I think it is the rule, I will listen less to the person who comes to tell me, 'You know, your sister, if you really fancy her, etc.' [*laughter*]. This is very important: one capital function of the rule is to assign limits to the manipulation of the representation of objective chance, and when we are confronted with a properly constituted law, we are faced with a stronger case than when we are confronted by someone armed only with their moral sentiments. It is easier to discuss with Sancho Panza, with *Kadi*-justice as Weber calls it, because you can always place the two senses of equity in contradiction: 'You say that you should cut the object disputed by two people in half, but if it is a child, what do you do?'[58] Whereas the law, as Weber says, is rationalization – that is, two millennia of accumulated legal precedents. Every case is foreseen, and this means that charismatic, disruptive, prophetic or negative action is met with very strong resistance, especially when the law has become an incorporated structure and has entered our lives as a given, legalistic cast of mind.

Time and the exercise of power

I shall finish with one last topic, which I shall merely outline: the problem of the relation between time and power. I have noted two forms of power, but I have left hanging the fundamental question of the time that the exercise of power takes. It is, I think, a question that is vital for our theory. The point of departure of the reflection that I am about to offer you is provided by a remark by Max Weber – I think it was on the subject of the problems of political power – according to which the problem of the initial accumulation of political power would be a question of time: notables emerge only when there is a small amount of surplus and people have time to turn away from their personal affairs, and Weber draws a comparison with the situation of the university head who ceases to engage in research.[59] This kind of comparison, which is uncommon in sociological literature (because many sociologists are university heads or could be), is very important because it makes us aware that a problem for anyone in power is that wielding power takes time.

We can, for example, put the question in the case of the two kinds of power that I have distinguished: which kind of power takes longer to manage – type one or type two? Rapidly, because you can extrapolate from what I have already told you: the less the power is institutional-ized, the more you have to exercise it personally, the more you need to pay with your person.[60] I contrasted the personal, pre-capitalist type of power with delegated power, and one of the solutions to the problem of managing the timescale of power is the delegation that gives the gift of ubiquity: I exercise the power by proxy, and I can be both here and elsewhere if I have a plenipotentiary who grants me omnitemporality. I said that absolute power is magical power, it is God. In fact, I built up a whole commentary around a classic saying by Lagneau: 'Time is the mark of my impotence.'[61] I doubt that he wanted to say all that (I point this out, not to boast, but to say that he was certainly not thinking of this kind of thing).

Power gives the vicarious, the proxy and the substitute, and therefore ubiquity, which is the age-old dream that, according to Feuerbach, we have projected on to God.[62] It grants omnitemporality because I can be here and elsewhere. That said, not all kinds of power lend themselves to that in equal measure, and we see that the 'cultural capital' type of power is difficult to delegate, for the simple reason that cultural capital is incorporated: the prophet can hardly delegate his power, or else someone betrays it, like Peter.[63] When he is not betrayed, the prophet, despite being the author of the legitimate message, sees something worse (when someone else says: 'But why not me?'), that is, his message being 'routinized' – this is what Weber calls 'the routinization of cha-risma'.[64] The bureaucratic type of power is much easier to delegate.

One last point: managing power takes unequal time, depending on the type of power and the type of objectification of power: how firmly it is written into the objective structures, how far it is delegated, and so on. For instance, if Weber thought of the antinomy of the university head, it is because the academic world is based to a great extent on cultural capital, which is an incorporated capital that keeps a personal dimension, even when it is strongly bureaucratized and written into syllabuses, dictionaries and educational projects.[65] The antinomies of time are particularly noticeable in this universe.

One final remark. I don't know if I can put it into a couple of sentences . . . I hesitate because it will seem so simplistic that it will almost seem false . . . Let us say that one of the antinomies of power is that, since exercising it takes time, more powerful people tend none-

theless to have less time than others. Afterwards, we can nuance this
... Because one obvious property that has never been expressed is
that time is not cumulative. I should have said that at the outset; it is
axiomatic.

Lecture of 3 May 1984

First session (lecture): Sartre and 'canned thought'. – Thinking the trivial. – Reappropriating cultural capital. – Generic alienation and specific alienation. – The institutionalized state of cultural capital.
Second session (seminar): delegation and representation (1). – The delegation relation. – The representation relation. – The fable of the Société des agrégés.

First session (lecture): Sartre and 'canned thought'

In my last lecture I stopped at the point where I was describing a certain number of properties of cultural capital in its objective state and signalling a certain number of problems posed by the individual or collective use of this objectified cultural capital. And I pointed out that one property of capital in this state is that objectified cultural capital can function only if the holders of an incorporated cultural capital reactivate it, so to speak. This subordination, as we may call it, of objectified cultural capital to reappropriation has been criticized, or even exploited. The aphorism 'the letter killeth, but the spirit giveth life'[1] may resume this theme, but this kind of discourse has occulted the important properties of objectified cultural capital that I was elaborating. As so often happens, there are social obstacles that hinder attempts to render the properties of something social explicit, as does the particular interest that the producers of discourse on the social world – in this case, on cultural capital – have in developing some vision or other of the social world and cultural capital.

In *The Family Idiot*,[2] for instance, Sartre develops at length this idea that 'the letter killeth, but the spirit giveth life', in terms of the intellectual stereotypes of the effects of the objectification of cultural capital. In this text, which is not one of his most original, Sartre insists on the virtually lifeless aspect of the very vague ensemble that he calls, after Hegel, the 'objective Spirit'. For instance, he describes this objective Spirit becoming a thing, or an objective reality, as a 'mineralized thought':[3] it is in a way the relapse of the for-itself, that transcendental self irreducible to its objectifications, back into the linear discourse of materiality. Another typically Sartrean and typically false formula is 'canned thought'.[4] Sartre here puts his finger on something important: objectified capital is conserved and, in a manner of speaking, it is not wrong to say that writing, for instance, is canned thought, but it is something quite different to say it as I say it rather than as Sartre does, denouncing instead of enunciating – and it is so often this procedure, denouncing instead of enunciating, that prevents us from seeing what it is that we are denouncing. Once again, one of the difficulties in sociology is that so many things that have been said, even when true, have been said in tones of denunciation rather than enunciation, which is a manner of saying them without saying them, without knowing that we are saying them and without knowing what we are saying. The expression 'canned thought' stigmatizes; the analogy with 'canned food' functions immediately on the level of unconscious connotations: 'canned thought' evokes *'mass media'*, *'mediatization'*, *'mass mediatization'*, in fact a whole discourse that was current in the intellectual world in the 1950s and which consisted in saying that the massification of thought was processed through this kind of 'canned thought', that very artificial thought, sealed in an air-tight container served up by modern means of communication.[5]

This denunciation of 'canned thought' hides something very important that I hope to elaborate later: writing, which is the elementary form of objectification, is historically the condition of all intellectual capital accumulation. As long as you can't objectify, that is, preserve and conserve, there are so many things that you cannot do with thought. So you just need to change the wording to make this 'canned thought' appear in a favourable light: it is thought conserved, reserved and hoarded, a treasure that can only be amassed if you dispose of the basic techniques of conservation. It would then not be scandalous to say that writing is to thought what modern refrigeration is to consumer goods. It is true that we can conserve almost forever goods that previously were perishable and non-transmissible, or transmissible only with the distortion caused when the reporter of a discourse is the same as the person who spoke it (this would lead to a critique of bearing witness, which we could develop in another context).

I am anticipating rather what I shall be saying later on: Plato's critique of poetry has been systematically misread.[6] It is unfortunately one particular case of a general misunderstanding of ancient thought: reading the word 'poetry' as if it concerned Mallarmé (or in the case of Plato's readers, François Coppée), we always tend to think of condemnation of poetry as a condemnation of poetic discourse. According to Havelock, an American historian of ideas who has written a very important book on Plato,[7] his denunciation of poetry is not directed at the kind of poetry that we know, but at the poetry of the archaic poet, who was basically improvising his recital, and, since he virtually embodied what he spoke, could not know what he was saying. He had no canned thought, he had no written text to hand that we could criticize and study, that we could read over and again with the possibility of finding contradictions, or comparing things that were said on different occasions. If we manage so easily to get away with contradictions in everyday life, it is because we do not do contradictory things at the same time. Writing places the Socratic exercise, which consists in holding in our mind everything that has been said in order to note contradictions in the successive phases of the speech, within anyone's grasp, since it allows us to look back and say: 'He said that, and now he is saying this: he is contradicting himself.' What Plato was denouncing under the name of poetry is not simply the kind of moralizing reading that he has in fact often inspired, which is the fact that the poet says whatever he fancies, and is amoral. According to Havelock's research, which I find convincing, what Plato was condemning historically was the fact that, in the tradition of oral poetry, the poet is a mime.

The notion of *mimesis* [in Plato and Aristotle] should likewise be rethought, as should the notion of *poiesis*; we should understand *mimesis* as signifying not 'imitation' but mimicry or the act of miming, we should think of a mime, rather than the seventeenth-century problematic of someone imitating. If we think of *mimesis* as an almost bodily manner of acting out what we are in the process of saying, we can readily see that Plato is saying: 'Long live canned thought!' Canned thought, or thought conserved, is the beginnings of logic, because we can submit fleeting speech to the scrutiny of a third party, but also to the speaker himself. The poet himself is caught up in this process by the Platonic topos of enthusiasm,[8] which has also been the subject of fanciful comment, whereas it is simply a characteristic of mime.

Aristotle, if we translate him literally, has expressed the idea that man is 'the most mimic of all the animals':[9] using his body he can act something that is absent; with his body he can create something that is not there (we see that what is at issue here is the body) – for example, the story of Achilles, the story of Patrocles – but insofar as the instrument of his expression is his body (his mouth is part of his body), he is not separate from his speech and therefore he has no distance from what he says, and he knows not what he says: he is in a way more *possessed* – a crucial term – than possessing. What he says, he does not truly produce in the etymological sense of the word 'produce'.[10] He does not bring it out into the daylight in front of him to look at it, stop, and go back over it. In societies without writing, the poet enlists the help of musical instruments, he chants what he is going to say before he begins, he creates a kind of quasi magical evocative ritual in order to capture inspiration – another nineteenth-century word that we project back onto archaic societies – in the sense of memory, but also in the sense of bodily presence both to the subject related and to the audience before him. To revive all that, he performs a bodily process very different from the exercise of the logician, the commentator or the housebound reader who analyse effects, comparisons, metaphors, enjambments, and the like.

This analysis enables us to see to what extent, when we fail to pay attention to what we are saying, words have their own way, and speak in our place. Through them, the education system vehicles a kind of semi-scholarly *doxa* (inspiration, and so on). To manage to say a little of what really happens in the social world, we need to demolish this association of scholarly ideas. To return to Sartre, he speaks of 'mineralized thought', 'canned thought' or the 'opacity to transcend', which is the Sartrean retranslation of a commonplace, the 'capacity to transcend', which refers to the opaque *en-soi* and the transcendental *pour-soi*. We see how one can always give philosophical clothing to a commonplace, or worse, philosophically inhabit it. Another formidable formula: 'The written, that is, the thing-a-fied, idea.'[11] 'Thing-a-fied' is an excellent expression, but you can also hear 'reified' or 'objectified', which is not the same thing. That does not mean – I shall discuss the problem – that the danger, the probability or the possibility of reification is not implicit in any objectification. It is nonetheless important to think in a more complex and dialectical manner and to ask what is implied in objectification, what objectification makes possible. But we live in a society of objectification, as we are born among books (especially Sartre – who is honest enough to admit it, to his greater merit),[12] objectification is second nature. The *épochè* of the book, the idea of what a world without books might be, a world where memory is strictly oral, is surely most difficult for someone like Sartre who is born surrounded by books. This means that the properties of objectification are disguised for the benefit of the properties of thingafication or reification, that is, the alienation of the speaking subject in the thing said – this is what is meant by 'the letter killeth'.[13]

Finally, the theme of 'the letter killeth, but the spirit giveth life' is an old essay title, because Sartre, like everyone else, was raised on school essay topics. 'The letter killeth, but the spirit giveth life' may be an old exam question that he wrote on as a teenager. He looked like a thinker, and people noticed that he spoke in quotations. It can happen to anyone – even to the speaking subject you are listening to at the moment – but I think it is important to try to bring these temptations of would-be liberated thought out into the open.

Thinking the trivial

There is a precautionary rule, particularly suited to things epistemological, which can be enunciated humorously: just as only fools try to look smart, it is always when thinking feels most free that it is most vulnerable to escaping its own attention. It is, for example, when we strike out for radical doubt that we fall into the most typical philosophical prejudice, which consists in equating radical doubt with the philosophical act. We then gasp in admiration when Wittgenstein, in the twentieth century, three centuries after the Cartesian assault, dares to say: 'But what is this coup? Should we not cast doubt on doubt?' (Leibniz had done it before, but it went unnoticed, like many of Leibniz's coups).[14] Wittgenstein has provided an excellent commentary on this radical doubt identified with the philosophical act,[15] which is so consubstantial with the philosophical act that, when you are immersed in the scholarly tradition of philosophical liberty, you cannot feel yourself more free than when you reproduce this liberating coup. But the trap lies precisely in a disciplinary tradition whose status as tradition, like all traditions, gets forgotten and imposes itself with the illusion of liberty.

I wanted to say that because, so often in the social sciences, a scientific discovery that has taken so much work to attain seems obvious, when it is presented without being dramatized and without any explanation of what it replaces. Thus, when I said in earlier lectures that to reappropriate the capital objectified in a book, you need an agent whose incorporated capital is capable of reappropriating the objectified capital, you must have agreed, or at least said to yourselves: 'Is it worth the trouble making such a fuss about it? Isn't he just telling us that you need readers for books to function as books and be digested appropriately?' It is not quite so simple, because this immediately strings together all the pearls of the ideology of reading that an important part of literary teaching relies on, all those things likely to pass through the mind of the listening reader or the mind of someone who was thinking absent-mindedly. This is why it is necessary to return to these trivial certainties.

Despite having been so rude to the philosophers, we could in fact say that two of the greatest philosophers of modern times have said the same thing: Husserl said that thinking correctly often means rehearsing trivia,[16] and Wittgenstein spent his life saying that, to think of simple things, you needed simply to rethink things that were falsely complex. In sociology you have to keep doing this all the time, and if there is a universe where you mustn't be afraid of being trivial, it is sociology. If genuine sociology is so rare, it is because to truly think about social matters implies something very trivial in sociology.

Reappropriating cultural capital

Having made this parenthesis, I shall return to objectified capital: it is in a way a dead letter, it can only be 'reactivated' – in Husserl's words[17] – if it is reappropriated actively by a social agent endowed with the specific instruments of reappropriation: to reappropriate a culture you need to have the specific suitable capital. 'Reactivate' and 'reappropriate' are two different words and they lead down two different paths: 'reactivate' leads to Sartre – 'The letter killeth, but the spirit giveth life' – whereas 'reappropriate' represents progress by reminding us that reading, for instance, is an act of appropriation that supposes the possession of a specific property. This simple word denies the myth that I referred to last week of a linguistic and cultural communism where culture belongs to everyone: in fact, objectified cultural capital belongs to those who have the means to appropriate it and the distribution of the appropriate culture will be proportional to and homologous with the distribution of the instruments of appropriation.

If we take this a little further, onto one of the terrains where the illusion of communism is strongest, that of language, we see whole edifices of commonsensical ideas crumble and fall, such as Saussure's notion of language as a 'treasure trove' that I mentioned last time. One property of cultural capital in its objectified state, which Popper, for example, saw quite clearly,[18] is that it presents itself as a world, a sort of autonomous and coherent universe that tends to exist in its own right. Although it is the product of historical activity, it is a world with its own laws, transcending the individual will. This is obvious in the case of the sciences: you cannot do what you like with this world; there is an objective force that can be experienced as a sort of intrinsic force of true ideas, to use Spinoza's terms.[19] An objective force of this objectified cultural capital imposes itself on each and every agent caught up in this culture, but also on the collectivity. In fact, the existence of an objectified cultural capital engenders quite naturally an ideology of self-production or self-reproduction of culture. Phrases like 'science is making progress' or 'scientific progress' thus suggest a world with its own laws, a cosmos analogous to the economic cosmos that Weber describes (the economic cosmos has its own laws, and, as Weber says, he who tries to transgress the laws of economics finds himself unemployed if he is a workman or bankrupt if he is a businessman).[20] Objectified cultural capital is a world of this kind: it is a sort of economics of cultural production which goes *motu proprio*, it is self-generating, automatic and self-developing – there are in fact all the organicist metaphors: it 'develops', 'grows', 'makes progress', and the like. The spontaneous philosophy of the history of cultural matters is a kind of soft Hegelianism.

In a lecture published as a little book,[21] Gombrich tries to describe this sub-Hegelianism that impregnates the social sciences, and in particular the historical science of works (especially artistic) which reduces Hegelianism to two dimensions. There is first of all the theme of the *Zeitgeist* (the common spirit of the age), that is, the unity of the cultural works of a given society. On the original cover of the book published by Oxford University Press in 1969, there is a circle divided into quarters each of which represents a dimension of this culture (science, art, etc.), to objectify the confused representation that we have of them: everything belongs to the same period. Gombrich shows how this idea (which is already a major error) haunts one type of art history in particular. He shows that even Panofsky, who is one of the art historians least prone to intellectual confusion, seeks out correspondences between the arts, between the arts and sciences, between philosophy and history, and so on. This is the first dimension of the spontaneous philosophy of history that I associate with the existence of objectified cultural capital.

The second dimension would be the idea of an autotelic history, that is, one establishing its own ends and steering under its own power towards those ends. This illusion, whereby the cultural world proceeds on its own behalf, can be found in very different writers: in Popper, for example, as in Althusser. They suppose a scientific order secreting its own development, taking the word 'development' in the sense of 'developing a mathematical formula', or thinking in terms of an enlargement, in the sense of 'growth' or 'transcendence', etc. But these two illusions are very strongly linked to the existence of objectified cultural capital and they both share in a sort of realism or reification of the intelligible. We could say that this illusion relates to cultural capital as market fetishism relates to economic capital, if we wanted to make the analogy – but I need to cancel this comparison immediately after formulating it. It is an illusion: a history of ideas without agents, a history of literature or art without artists, without philosophers, agents or spaces.

In my opinion, this autonomous and self-propelled history of ideas is rooted in the existence of libraries, and we arrive at a kind of parthenogenetic vision of ideas expressed in formulae such as 'art imitates art' or 'understanding a philosophy means understanding the philosophy it attacks', which is obviously not false, but we cannot understand the movement of ideas, especially since the time when the field became autonomous, without supposing that the producers of ideas are referring to the ideas of the other producers of ideas. Ideas are obviously very important in the history of ideas, but the self-propelling vision of the history of ideas contains a dangerous error because it forgets what I said just now on the subject of triviality: there is no life, there is nothing objectified – in this sense it is not untrue to say that 'the letter killeth, but the spirit giveth life' – unless someone brings the ideas back to life, reactivating them, but who, if not the social agents, can reactivate them? The ideas are not going to start fighting among themselves, they are not going to do anything on their own: they are reactivated by social agents, and thus, while still remaining ideas, they become once again strategies in historical struggles; they will still function on the twin levels of the relation between ideas ('X's idea contradicts Y's idea') and social struggles and strategies ('X wants to be stronger than Y', 'X would like to take Y's place' or 'X wants to disprove and therefore annihilate Y'). The flat, trivial formula that I pronounced just now ('In order to function, objectified cultural capital must be subject to a reappropriation') did in fact hide something very important that leads us in a way to call into question one manner of practising the history of philosophy, art and science, this illusion being particularly probable in the case of the history of the sciences.

However, I believe that, as always, we need to see how complicated things are and admit that in this case the illusion of theoretical parthenogenesis is well grounded. (In the social sciences, every time we discover an illusion – Hegel said that 'illusion is not illusory'[22] – we need to ask why this illusion, which is a very real illusion, does not appear to be an illusion, and why its illusory currency fulfils a real function.) We all know there are moments when a problem is blowing in the wind and that the three or four mathematicians who are able to find the solution can only do so because, for them, a problem is purely and simply a problem, and because the solution is in a way contained within the problem. This is a banality repeated by academics: once understood, the problem is half solved; in science, identifying a problem already supplies some very important information.

The hagiography or mythology of the scholar or the artist creating *ex nihilo* exploits these objective facts in the wrong way, but we do need to go over them in order to explain why this ideological exploitation is possible; they are part of the real properties of the space in which ideas are produced. If a history of ideas with no agents and no space of production is a fantasy, a history of ideas being reduced to the history of a space of production without introducing the space of ideas as a space structuring the possibilities of all the agents in the space of production would be just as stupid. (There is a social law at work here: if dualist thinking is so frequent in all societies – not only in Bororo society,[23] but also in our own research – it is because we think in binary oppositions. Thus the 'individual/society' pairing is one of the most fruitful sources of platitudes, which means that any sociology worthy of the name must break it apart from the start.)

Faced with this extremely complex reality, we need to question the idea of a space, of an objective Spirit possessing its own inner dynamic and logic, and at the same time see that the existence of an objectified cultural space, with its libraries, founds the appearance of an objective space of this type and even the reality of what is the practice of the agents, whom we must reintroduce in order to understand that the world of objective ideas changes. The social agents do not come face to face with libraries, but with other social agents who are libraries. (This analysis reveals the difficulty: we keep having to brush up against trivia, keep them at bay and not be satisfied when we have sidelined something trivial, because it may contain, for example, the source of the explanation of the error that we want to fight.)

Developing what is implied in the idea that cultural capital can exist in an objectified state, that is, in a manner independent of social agents, and transcending them, is to discover in a way the potential for cultural alienation, which is not simply the alienation of those who, being deprived of the instruments of appropriation, are deprived of the possibility of appropriating the objectified culture and are even deprived of their deprivation. (One spectacular property of cultural capital is that deprivation does not confer awareness of that deprivation; this proposition could almost be widened to include economic capital, even if absolute deprivation cannot help being perceived to some extent – although the problem of the subproletariat that I touched on[24] shows that things are not so simple.) The paradox, in the case of cultural capital, is that deprivation is not accompanied by awareness of that deprivation.

Once again, this is something that cultivated people have always said, but to the tune of 'how stupid . . .', that is, developing a theme of stupidity. (It would take too long to show this at work in *Bouvard and Pécuchet*, but one could make a close analysis of how universal suffrage or democracy relate to Flaubert's praise of mandarins,[25] using the correspondence between Flaubert and Taine while Flaubert was writing *Bouvard and Pécuchet* and Taine his essay on contemporary history, which was a kind of denunciation of all the flaws of democracy.)[26] The denunciation of lack of culture or deprivation of culture as stupidity, with everything implied in the connotations of *'bêtise'* (bestiality, venality and all their attendant vices), is a self-cancelling observation: it is a way for cultivated people to voice the fundamental fact of cultural appropriation, without admitting it. If we draw on the appropriate language that I believe allows us to use the neutral, formless, cold concept of 'cultural capital in an objectified state', we would say: 'Bodies of knowledge, methods, systems, styles of thinking, mathematical formulae and codes of etiquette do exist in objectified form in books, etc., but can only be appropriated by those who possess the instruments of appropriation.' And it is in the family, at school, and so on, that one can acquire these instruments of appropriation – but I shall not develop this point.

Generic alienation and specific alienation

Now, since the instruments of appropriation are unequally distributed, access to this objectified cultural capital is bound to be unequal. Which means that we cannot speak of generic alienation as Sartre does. When Sartre says 'The letter killeth, but the spirit giveth life', and that objectified thought is a mineralized, canned thought, he is denouncing a generic alienation, an invariant for humanity. In sociology, phrases that apply to all men, factoring in a sort of universal quantifier, such as those that start with 'Man', are very difficult to write. Philosophy, on the other hand, very often uses essential analyses; and analyses in the phenomenological tradition where Sartre is situated lay claim to universal validation, since, when subjected to the *épochè*, they are not answerable to historical relativization, or inserted within history. Sartre claims to offer a description of the universal anthropological effect, an anthropology of objectification, whereas a sociology of objectification dissolves this invariant. The anthropology of objectification is not without interest. No doubt these essential analyses are themselves extremely dangerous, for all the reasons that I have given. But when we put them in their place – however unfair that may seem – they do allow us to see that there is a problem. Here we might not realize that there is a problem, and the essential analysis makes us see that when thought objectifies itself, it escapes its own speaker to a certain extent. There is then something transhistoric here: any objectification encloses a universal potential for alienation; this is what we can call generic alienation.

(The tendency to substitute generic alienations for specific alienations is a great mistake, both political and scientific. A brief parenthesis here. When we contrast the alienations of a sexual type discussed by psychoanalysts with the alienations described by sociology, we are leaving the domain of specific alienation and moving into the domain of generic alienation. It is an old strategy, that of Malherbes's famous verses: 'Death also knocks on doors of kings', 'We are all mortal'.[27] This is the most generic alienation – and the very definition of the syllogism 'Socrates is a man', etc.'[28] – which is typical of anthropology and the universal. The sociologist will immediately say that 'we are all mortal, but not all in the same way', we don't die at the same age, from the same causes, or on the same occasions, etc. This is why sociology is so irritating: basically, anthropology is much better, much more reassuring and universal – everyone loves the universal: I think this is one anthropological proposition that we may formulate.)

Is it possible to enunciate a universal proposition, given the fact that when we say something, it is *verba volant*, it flies away, whereas when things are written, they remain? In fact, it depends on who is speaking, and who is writing – there are people whose words seem cast in bronze. That does not mean that we don't have to question these inherent tendencies, but we should question them with the suspicion that I have introduced: there is in objectification a universal anthropological potential for reification (if I may give a name to these kinds of anthropological law . . .), in the sense that objectification and reification are two faces of the same phenomenon, and any profits of objectification are always liable to be paid for at the cost of reification – to coin a phrase.

That said, we should ask what the social conditions that govern the process of objectification are. What conditions enable reappropriation? What is their social distribution? What are the economic and social conditions behind their acquisition? Then we shall see how a kind of universal potential for alienation that is written into all objectification is transformed into a differential structure of the chances of alienation.

We could apply this argument to the subject of language, since language has been the ideal-typical cultural object attracting the most advanced theories of a self-justifying, self-motivating and self-dynamizing development: you can read a form of Hegelianism into Saussure. It would take too long to explain the whole of the *Course in General Linguistics*, although it would not be a waste of time because it contains another structure, which passes unnoticed: there is an order of reasons in Saussure as there is an order of reasons in Descartes, and if we interrupt the sequence of the order of reasons in Saussure's discourse, it would be like taking on Descartes's God without passing through the phases of doubt, yet this is what people did frequently in the 1960s with automatic and mechanical transliterations of Saussure (in semiology for instance).

Saussure raises the question of the construction of language as an autonomous object. He wants to constitute it in its own right against all the other forms of construction. The relation between language and geography is one of the questions that he raises: are the limits of languages given in geography?[29] He could have also asked whether they might not exist in the history of the state, for instance. Then he defines an extraordinary philosophy of the history of language – which you can check in the text: putting it metaphorically, language in his eyes is like a sort of glacier that keeps moving until it runs out of energy. In a way, language defines its own limits: it is not geography that limits language, but language that defines its geography and its territory. There is a philosophy of history here: language is autonomous, it functions unaided, it reproduces itself, and it exists independently of its speakers who are in a way only its performers. They are there because, for speech to be an issue, the language has to be spoken. Here we get to the heart of the matter: you can only speak a language if you know it. But if you read Saussure you don't see clearly how it is that people come to know it. He doesn't ask the question. If Saussure is so popular, it is because his thinking is absolutely nongenetic; in fact this philosophical type of thinking finds genetic thinking profoundly unattractive. For Saussure, language exists for itself, it makes its own laws and limits, and its laws, which transcend the individual will, are at once laws of operation and laws of development. This means that language is described as a universe existing above and beyond the social agents, and consideration of the conditions of subsistence and persistence of this universe are not raised. (The problem of change does however appear here and there: does change come from language or speech? I am discussing Saussure in a way that may seem alien and arbitrary, or even authoritarian, because he is not indispensable to my argument, so I beg your indulgence; but I could show you texts that would provide a detailed illustration of what I am saying rather crudely.)

If we put the question of language in such terms, we reinforce the image of a self-sufficient and self-generating universe. We are excluding the question of the conditions of operation of language and ignoring the fact that linguistic resources in their objectified state – in dictionaries, grammars, literature and suchlike – only exist and survive as a materially and symbolically active, efficient and 'living' capital insofar as they are appropriated by agents, according to their capacity for appropriation, that is, their incorporated linguistic capital, which means that linguistic resources are used as weapons and stakes in the struggles that take place in cultural production, or even merely in everyday symbolic exchanges. It also means that the cultural alienation associated with objectification is not a kind of generic alienation. To link the two phases, we could say that the generic possibility of alienation that is inherent in any process of objectification can only exist historically and socially, in the form of specific possibilities of alienation realized and differentiated according to the possession of incorporated economic capital. Which possession is itself linked to things like the possession of economic capital, free time, and so on. This then is the analysis that I intended to undertake to show that starting from a trivial, banal proposition, through a series of amendments, we can arrive at results that are less banal – and which would merit further exploration.

The institutionalized state of cultural capital

I now approach the third state of cultural capital, which I shall call institutionalized. We could say that the institutionalized state is a form of the objectified state, but I think it is better to distinguish it and see in it a specified case of the objectified state. The school diploma is the perfect example of the institutional objectification of cultural capital. It represents an objectified form of cultural capital that is not of the same order as a book; it is an objectification, but in a different sense. Institutionalized cultural capital is incorporated capital guaranteed; it is an objective guarantee of the ownership of an incorporated cultural capital. That said, it is important to see that this socially validated guarantee does not imply a technically valid guarantee. However, we must say that they are not entirely independent, otherwise the social magic would not work. This is the sense of what I want to say: the school diploma is social magic, it is an act of institution that acts through the force of collective opinion: 'I say that he is cultivated and I sign to guarantee this, and if I am authorized to say that he is cultivated and to sign to guarantee him, that means people have faith in my signature.' The signature is an act of social magic – it is like an amulet – it inspires faith. We are in the realm of faith and belief, and diplomas are *credentials*[30] – a word that does not exist in French – a socially guaranteed credit or credo. The school diploma is a guarantee of incorporated cultural capital. It is the objectified form of incorporated cultural capital, but it does not necessarily imply incorporated cultural capital, and that is why things are difficult.

What is its social interest? Here again, we need to give a more specific analysis than the general, anthropological type. The diploma exploits a property of writing that Sartre described: writing eternalizes, it remains and does not change. Once you have pinned your diploma up on the wall, you are a graduate forever, unless there is an earthquake or the house burns down. A statue is a sort of bronze diploma: with a statue you are forever the person who invented organic chemistry, you are socially guaranteed for eternity, *aere perennius*[31] ('more durable than bronze'). Statufying is a form of objectification that is of the order of social magic: you are statufied as cultivated.

This operation of institutionalization is a 'skilful' exploitation of this property of objectification (I say 'skilful' – difficult not to become purposive when we talk of the social world – while repeating that these are acts with no subject), which is to grant eternal duration – in writing, in bronze, and the like. Moreover, objectification makes public. If nobody gets up to say that you are an idiot, it becomes an official, publicly and collectively acknowledged fact that you are cultivated. Next week I shall look into the properties that are entailed by objectification. The diploma in a way 'exploits' – once more my purposive vocabulary – this anthropological property of objectification, which is to eternalize and make public – there are other properties that I shall go on to explore later – and it applies it to the particular case of that very vulnerable thing, incorporated cultural capital.

In previous lectures I have said that incorporated cultural capital lacks the fluidity of economic capital. It is bound to the body of its bearer. This is the problem of the *imbecilitas* of the prince, that I often refer to by quoting Kantorowicz: when the prince is sick, you still need to make him king; likewise, when the bearer of cultural capital is tired and sick, his cultural capital is tired and sick, and the cultural capital dies along with its bearer. The school diploma, on the other hand, survives down the ages. It can of course, like financial currency and titles, be devalued, but it is different, however, and it leads to a specific form of alienation: if my cultural salvation is linked to a diploma that becomes devalued, I have a problem, but I do not find myself in the situation of the diploma-less person, who is perpetually called into question, and always vulnerable to cultural challenge, as in the extreme case of the autodidact, who is obliged to prove his worth anew at any given moment.

The analysis of the autodidact in *Nausea* provides yet another fine example of partial analysis – poor old Sartre, it starts to add up. It is one of the best examples of the ethnocentrism of a cultivated man, who is very generous except where his specific capital is directly concerned: the autodidact in *Nausea* is someone who has learned everything in alphabetical order:[32] if he has only got as far as C and he comes across an F, he stumbles and falls, whereas the graduate benefits from the effects of the educational guarantee, since the man with guaranteed culture is precisely someone who will not be subjected to questions, or who can brush them aside as trivial or simplistic. The autodidact, whose only cultural capital is the incorporated kind, is constantly in the line of fire. This means that he is exposed even when he is not being deliberately targeted, and that is how we recognize him. He feels bound to answer in cases where any really 'cool customer' will know how to flash a knowing and slightly superior smile [*subdued laughter in the audience*] . . . In short, we could deduce from this contrast between the socially guaranteed state and the nonguaranteed state of culture a series of what we might call psychological properties.

This leads on to something very important. I shall stop here, but I just want to return for a moment to the criticism that I made of the economists of the Chicago School, and Gary Becker in particular. They don't know that what they call human capital is academically guaranteed: they measure it in numbers of years of study, which does not necessarily imply taking account of the guarantee. They forget that educational capital is not merely 'human' capital, with all the vagueness that this word suggests (the word designates the areas of knowledge, know-how and skills transmitted by the school, which is a very optimistic vision of the educational system); educational capital is essentially the guarantee that all this has been distributed and acquired. Consequently, the correlation that we can establish between diplomas and academic performance or a salary, for instance, does not depend on a sort of technical capacity existing in an incorporated state in the bearer of the diploma, but on a title, which may be a magical social title. The correlation is similar to that relating the wearer of a lucky charm to his actual properties. I think this is a very important aid to understanding those economic mechanisms that are affected by this so-called 'human' capital. I shall stop here, but I shall return to this.

Second session (seminar): delegation and representation (1)

What I wanted to offer you in this second session is a reflection on the problems of delegation. Normally, we phrase these problems in the language of delegation, whereas we should perhaps couch them in the language of representation. So I shall substitute for the language of delegation the question of representative democracy, which is a form of regime where citizens delegate their power to representatives or delegates who act on their behalf. This process of delegation and representation emerged from an extremely obscure process, which I shall consider for a moment in an attempt to tease out a certain number of trivial questions. I shall proceed as always by starting out from the trivial in order to arrive at something quite amazing, at any rate I hope so. If I hesitate as I draw up my schema (below), it is because, as you will see, there are so many obscure points.

Normally, in this process of delegation, we see individual agents who, through their vote for instance, delegate their power to other agents, whether ministers or any other kind of proxy, who then go on to exercise their authority over the agents who have delegated them. My work will consist in bringing to light, from beyond the visible part of reality, a series of hidden processes that seem extremely important to me.

I shall first of all attempt to reconstitute the political type of common

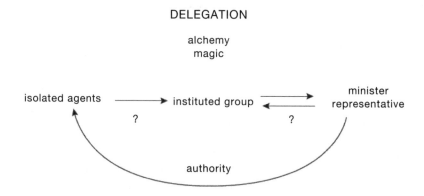

DELEGATION

representation that I have mentioned. This spontaneous vision of the democratic system would be worth an empirical analysis which, especially through interviews, would show up its variations according to social milieu, gender, and so on. Since I have not done this empirical research, I propose a spontaneous sociology of the spontaneous sociology of representation – what I shall say then is not very assured – but I think we can accept a kind of freestyle Bachelardian psychoanalysis of the primary representation of the political mechanism. We should reflect on another situation where there is delegation: by reviewing the law of proxy through the legal texts, we could study all the situations in which a social agent grants power, as we say, to another agent, transferring to him the power to act in his stead. This is the logic of proxy.

To help throw up some unexpected links, I shall signal an important problem in Heidegger's thought[33] – at once in his philosophical thought and in his political thought, which is disguised beneath the cloak of a purely political thought – which is the problem of delegation or proxy, or, if you like, 'great concern', 'concern for' or 'concern on behalf of'. In Heidegger's argument, this problem was strongly emphasized in parallel with an attack on the question of democracy, which anticipated the denunciation of the welfare state that is so fashionable today.[34] I believe that what underpins Heidegger's discourse on 'concern for / on behalf of', and the inauthenticity of the proxy, is the 'observation' that the welfare state, social security and paid holidays – which were being mooted in the 1930s – enabled the agents, in Heidegger's language, to dispense with looking after themselves in the first instance: some anonymous '*they*' took care of them, and went to great pains on their behalf, so they were no longer concerned for themselves; posing as an authentic *I*, the agent was freed from concern. The problem of the proxy was posed in what we might call conservative-revolutionary or pre-Nazi thought, and took the form of a kind of horror of the plebs who invade the beaches with hardly a care or concern in the world, dressed only in their hopelessly unfashionable underwear. (As I so often say, I think it is worth visualizing these images because, behind the theories, there are social fantasies.)

Calling delegation and representation into question, as I intend to, may appear to suggest a context of the kind that I have just mentioned, whereas it is very different, which is why I need to issue this kind of warning in order to avoid creating confusion with my argument. (If it is so difficult to say some things in the social sciences, it is very often because people who had very dubious reasons for doing so have already said them. For instance, if it is so difficult to make a successful sociological study of intellectuals – implicitly identified as left-wing intellectuals – it is because right-wing intellectuals, who were well placed to see, and willing to say what there was to say, have already got there first; and what often protects intellectuals against scientific objectification is the fact that what it reveals has been said by people whom they can accuse of lying, with a good chance of being believed.)[35]

These problems of delegation and procuration have been raised by everyone in the authoritarian tradition, like the sons of Taine whom I referred to earlier. This results in a sort of delayed reflection that almost inevitably involves a critical distance, as our reflection encounters the obstacle of what I call screen analyses that tell half the truth, or raise the problem only to immediately demolish it, so that, among the defence mechanisms countering the kind of analysis that I have to offer, one is the possibility of cross-infection from these polemics.

The delegation relation

Having said that, I think I can make a start. The problem of delegation is important because we need to know under what conditions a social agent can speak on behalf of another. Being a proxy means being concerned 'on behalf of': someone is concerned for my interests on my behalf and in my place. This 'someone' can be a delegate to whom I have granted plenary powers to buy a house on my behalf. It can be a man of straw, a politician, a bishop, a parish priest or his proxy, for example a stand-in who acts on behalf of the parish priest as the parish priest does for me – there are procurations at several removes. They are people who do for me things that I hold dear and who (implicitly) manage my interests better than I would myself – otherwise I would not delegate these to somebody else . . .

The problem of delegation leads us to consider the social fact that I mentioned just now, which sociology must acknowledge: social agents are embodied. Sociology always forgets that social agents have a body: these noncollective, socialized beings that I call a habitus experience the principle of individuation through the body, and the biological body presents many problems in the social universe. There are so many things that social agents would like to do, but, having a body, are unable to do. For instance, you cannot be everywhere at once, shopping and cooking, sitting in parliament and visiting your constituency, lecturing and writing a book . . . There are some things that you cannot delegate, and among those that you can, some are easier to delegate than others. Being incorporated, cultural capital is difficult to delegate, whereas economic capital can be delegated under certain legal provisions. These problems then are an anthropological issue, for procuration is a major historical invention. Research by economic historians, for instance, emphasizes the fact that procuration as a legal procedure is a very new mechanism. There will always be some historian wanting to show that it is older, but we could say that it is an invention of the Renaissance, which spread to become a general social phenomenon in the sixteenth century, I think. We don't realize how many things were impossible as long as you couldn't delegate to grant representative power.

If you look in a dictionary, you will read that to 'delegate' is to grant power to someone. I have a power and I give that power away. I can do it in the form of a blank cheque (I grant the power to speak and act on my behalf), but I can also grant more restricted powers (for example, I can authorize my lawyer to act for me in a specific case). You may then question the extent of the powers that I grant and my awareness of the delegation that I am granting (for instance, when I delegate to a member of parliament, what is it that I am granting?), and – to put it briefly – we can compare the extent and degree of objectification of the powers granted to a bishop or a *préfet*, for instance. The procuration is granted to someone who is going to represent me. The word 'represent' is important because we could say that the person who represents me is going to take my place. In a way, he or she is going to lend me their body: I cannot be out there myself in person, but it is just as if I were; through them I gain the gift of ubiquity and omni-temporality, and thus fulfil a sort of divine dream ('God exists in all places, he is eternal').[36]

Someone very powerful politically would have everyone else as his delegates, he would be everywhere. These imaginary fantasies are useful instruments in the analysis of the limitations of those who have only themselves to speak for, and who can say, for instance, 'I can only speak for myself'. In a recent work, Pinto uses these terms to analyse the rhetoric of 'the people', which consists in saying 'because I say so'.[37] He insists on the fact that this is the rhetoric of the poor, of those who, having no guarantor other than themselves and, at the limit, their own body ('I was there', 'I said it there', 'I did it there'), must put their own body on the line, so to speak, to guarantee what they say, through the exclamation, indignation and rage, for example, of what we might call popular exhibitionism (there is a whole literature on the subject). In fact, this is the last resort of the person who is condemned to authenticity: if he narrates something tragic, he must weep. He can be authentic only by paying with the currency that is the supreme guarantee of his authenticity: showing emotion, conviction

and passion. Whereas the more incorporated or objectified the guarantees you possess (titles and diplomas, for instance), the less you have to
put your own self on the line: the titles say it for you, and it is sufficient
for you to say: 'It seems to me . . .'; you can be a relativist, or, on the
other hand, if you have enough so-called 'natural', that is, objectified,
authority in objective matters, you can offer yourself the luxury in a
debate of keeping your distance and evaluating the pros and cons, for
instance. These remarks are a key that helps us to understand political
rhetoric and confrontation. We can then retranslate this into what we
might call a psychosociological logic: social agents who bear a greater
or lesser objectified capital will have a different approach to whatever
it is that they may have to guarantee.

The act of delegation in the case of an elementary, legal procuration
leads me to nominate my son or my wife or my uncle as my proxy: I
sign a form and it will act in my name. The procuration starts to get
more complicated, and – to return to the type of schema that I was
using just now – the potential for alienation, which is inscribed within
any delegation objectifying someone else who has their own specific
interests, will increase when I no longer delegate to someone I know,
or at least to someone known and whose competence – and limits,
of course – or remit are known and recognized (thus the remit of the
lawyer is defined: he is not to get involved with my personal business,
he must take on my case but not my affairs). The delegation may be
circumscribed in time, within a social space and group, but as soon as
we approach, say, delegation by several people to one person (or from
one to several), the problem becomes more complicated.

If, for instance, I join with a lot of other people to delegate my
power to someone who will combine all our powers, this produces
a kind of transcendence effect: the delegate can rise up before me in
the name of the power that my small contribution has helped grant
him, and can remind me for, example, that his power transcends me
because my contribution to his power is only one in a thousand. Thus
the delegation can lead to a process where the famous transcendence
of the social, a kind of social constraint that Durkheim discusses,[38]
comes to be concentrated in one person. (This is very interesting:
Durkheimians give us all the instruments to understand politics and
yet this is truly what they gave the least thought to, which means that
we can come up with some very interesting theoretical arguments by
translating onto the political terrain what they thought of without
thinking of politics, and since what they did think through (religion,
for instance) was very well theorized, they give us useful tools for
thinking about politics. Weber for instance, despite leaving us his

'Profession and Vocation of Politics', is not necessarily the best aid to political thinking.)

Durkheim introduces the important observation that society is experienced as something transcendental. What is interesting is that in the case of politics this transcendence comes to be incarnated in a single individual and takes on the unrecognizable form of a naturalized social transcendence. This is charisma, and we can use Weber to help us here: *charisma*, in Greek, means 'grace' and, ultimately, the 'gift'. Weber, in a text that like quite a lot of his work has not been much read, says that when he speaks of 'charisma' he is talking about what others call *mana*.[39] This happens when contemporaries want to mark their distance from each other: I think that Weber had read Durkheim (all the scientists in Europe spoke of nothing else) and it is very useful to know that his concept of charisma is a synonym for *mana*, because two things that we thought of separately start to communicate with each other, and it is very beneficial to consider the two together. I think, then, that what Weber says with the word 'charisma' is what Durkheim understood by *mana*, that is a sort of ineffable and intangible power of the type of *baraka*, *mana*, *wakanda*, all those ineffable things, much discussed by ethnologists, that leave us speechless when we are faced with them – I refer you to Lévi-Strauss's analysis in his 'Introduction to the Work of Marcel Mauss'[40] – forcing us to cry out and gasp in wonder. Fundamentally, these are things that solicit exclamation, they have the luminosity of *hau*, which is both terrifying and fascinating and which, in the normal order of things, remains in a floating state: they are mysterious and extraordinary, they have something intangible, fantastical and formidable about them, and sometimes, under certain conditions, they may be incarnated in a man who becomes charismatic and appears to be someone who concentrates that luminosity, who is able to stop the clouds moving, bring victory and save the country from ruin. Charisma is the incorporation, and therefore the naturalization, of that luminosity.

We need to combine Weber and Durkheim because Weber's 'charisma' is always slightly suspect, since his sources were bizarre (Mosca, etc.). I have nothing against this, it was very useful for social science, but knowing where people got their inspiration from sheds light on the limitations of their concepts: in Weber, the concept of charisma remains very naturalist, it is not very sociologized, although Weber insisted as much as Durkheim on the need to historicize social concepts (he says, for instance, that *auri sacra fames*[41]explains nothing and even that it is 'greed for gold' itself that needs to be explained sociologically.[42] We need then to sociologize the charm, or charisma – it is the same word – of the leader or *Führer*,[43] through the type of analysis that I am now doing. Charismatic leaders appear to be gifted by nature with the capacity to perform miracles, exploits and extraordinary, unheard of, unthinkable things, which are not within the grasp of the ordinary mortal.

Of course, they perform these extraordinary feats in extraordinary circumstances, at the most difficult moments (on 10 June 1940, it was a voice crying in the wilderness).[44] In terms of my argument, the charismatic leader is someone who captures, as it were, the potential of magic, who concentrates in his person the ability to work miracles. He can say: 'I offer up my body to France.' Charisma is personal and individualistic. In every act of delegation, the representative of a group is established as the person who imposes himself as extraordinary.

I analyse this as a process of fetishization.[45] In fact I intend to make a typically Marxist analysis of charisma – you see how it is possible to conjugate two supposedly incompatible modes of thinking: I shall try to show that the charismatic leader is a fetish, a 'product of the human mind', as Marx says,[46] that men adore as something objective. In the context of a delegation by several people to one person, this sort of self-generating transcendence of the social into one person, this naturalization of power that is conferred through unanimous collective recognition and the collective applause that is the public display of passionate approval, this practical plebiscite, this sort of consecration in the magical sense of the terms, endow the person consecrated with a transcendental power that has an impact on every one of those who find within him the consecration that they have granted him. That is the first phase.

The representation relation

I would like to expose the main outline of my schema straight away and then I may come back to fill in the details. In the first phase, in fact, we remain within a logic of the relation of delegation: singular individuals, one by one – destined for what Sartre calls seriality:[47] their actions will be purely cumulative – will in a way recognize themselves as a consummate Whole, personified in a charismatic leader capable of exerting symbolic or even political pressure on them. This first phase, with its relation of delegation, illustrates the movement which goes from the isolated agents to the minister [*Bourdieu refers to the schema that he has drawn on the board*]. The minister is the person who acts 'on behalf of'. But does this relation not hide another one, more subtle and

difficult to detect – as is often the case? It seems to me that the delegation relation of a group of men to one man hides what we might call
the representation relation, which gives us to believe that it is the group
that creates the spokesman. We can analyse and demystify the relation
of delegation to some extent, as I have just done ('You are worshipping
your own creation, you bow down before a fetish, a human product'),
but are not things rather more complicated in reality? Is the demys-
tification itself still somewhat mystified? Saying that it is the group
that creates the man speaking in its place, or that the group creates
the spokesman, may be forgetting that the spokesman also creates the
group. We are faced with a kind of mystery of spontaneous generation:
although it is true that the men who create their spokesman are in
fact created as a group by the spokesman, the spokesman can live his
experience and be experienced as *causa sua*, as the generative principle
of the authority that he exercises over the group, since the group would
not exercise it if he were not there to exercise it. Now I shall repeat this
in simpler terms.

(This is always a problem with exposition: if I proceed in a slow,
analytic fashion, you will not see what I am getting at and all my preliminaries will be lost on you, but if I give you the key straight away,
it will look arbitrary. I often quote a novel by Faulkner, *A Rose for
Emily*,[48] which is a paradigm of the pedagogical model as I experience
it. This novel tells the story of a very respectable aristocratic lady in the
American South who lives in a beautiful old house, and who does not
act like everyone else: she doesn't want to pay her taxes, she doesn't
want to adapt to change, and so on, although the South is changing
and the town council wants her to accept the rules of the game. There
are minor anomalies that we attribute to the follies of what we see as
aristocratic eccentricity, but in the end we learn that she has killed her
lover and kept his body at home, which means that all the oddities that
seemed inexplicable are gradually explained. Then you need to reread
the whole novel to understand everything that you did not understand
while reading it. Teaching is comparable: you ought to say straight
away what it is that you are going to say in the end, but if you do that
you spoil the suspense [*laughter*], and, at the same time, you only really
understand if you go back to the beginning. Which explains the real
difficulty of teaching – except obviously, if you say 'firstly / secondly /
thirdly . . .', which would be easier, but I just can't do that.)

We need to take this word 'representative' seriously: for changing
the word has consequences. The representative is not simply a delegate,
someone mandated, that is, someone who has been granted a mandate,
whether limited or open-ended, precise or unspecific. By avoiding the

word 'mandate', we can acknowledge the fact that the person mandated is a representative, that is, someone who offers a representation of what he is supposed to represent. When the representative says, 'I am the working class', 'I am the Christian people' or 'I take the plane and the whole of Christendom is flying with me' – which we see happening every day[49] – he is not simply someone who has been granted the power to do what he is doing, he does something much more important: he gives us to believe that the group in whose name he is acting does exist, and that he is really accomplishing the act that he is performing. He is thereby accomplishing an extraordinary philosophical feat, the ontological argument. In the press, the phrase 'The CGT was invited to the Élysée' means that, depending on the year, M. Séguy or M. Krasucki,[50] that is, a person, was invited to meet the president. If the papers say, 'The CGT was invited to the Élysee, and condemned the demonstrations', they are doing several things: they are affirming the assimilation made by canon law that I have already explained[51] ('the Pope is the Church' or 'the Church is the Pope'), which is the identical nature of the spokesman and the group in whose name and place he speaks, but they affirm at the same time something much more important: the people represented exist because their representative exists.

From the moment that you utter a phrase where God is given as the subject, you commit yourself to a theory of existence. A sort of predication of existence is implicit: 'I am the representative of the people, I provide the representation of the people, I am the people, I manifest the people, therefore the people exist.' Insofar as I manage to have this manifestation recognized in practice, I can have a power that allows me to demonstrate up to a certain point what I manifest: I can organize demonstrations, cry 'All to the Bastille!'. Here we are dealing with social alchemy, and what happens is very complicated: individual agents are voiced, someone speaks on their behalf, someone speaks of them and for them, and so long as the agents do not speak up to say that it is not what they would say if they themselves were speaking, they are spoken for. Someone says: 'I am whom I speak, I am his voice, and he whom I speak would say what I am saying if he could speak, I am his proxy, but – something much more important but is not at all self-evident – is that he whom I speak exists (and exists, as I say, he exists through my representation).' My representation is always dual: it is a purely material representation – I exist, I am whom I speak, in body and in speech: but also a sign, a speaking sign that can say what it has to say as a sign, who can make you believe that what it says is said by a sign. The essence of what it does not say is how it functions as a sign. That is what is profoundly disguised, and constitutes, I believe, the essence of political alchemy.

Since I am not sure that I am expressing myself very clearly, I shall read you a written statement that sums up the whole schema: 'It is because the representative exists, because he *represents*, that the group represented exists, and, in turn, makes its representative exist as the representative of a group.'[52] Obviously, this is circular, but the vicious circle is central to social mechanisms (alchemy and fetishism are vicious circles – remember what I was saying just now about charisma) and this schema [*the one drawn by Bourdieu on the board*] is totally false [*laughter*], because it creates a kind of linear relation. It's like the theories of the social contract: you have to understand them as an effort to rethink genetically, like a kind of theoretical genesis – but if you rethink them as a real genesis, they become absurd: in reality, there are not individuals who grant their power to someone, it doesn't happen like that at all.

The fable of the Société des agrégés

An example will help you to understand what I mean. At the same time, like all examples, it will largely demolish everything that I have been saying – no [*reacting to some laughter in the audience*], it is true, examples are like schemas. This is an experience that I had during May 1968, as did others, I am sure. As I was saying last time, this period of crisis allowed an upsurge of unauthorized voices, voices with no mandate. For instance, if a newspaper like *Le Monde* agrees to publish a paper that you have submitted, they ask you straight away for your title, and they add an asterisk indicating 'professor *agrégé*': this authenticates the value of your argument – which illustrates what I was saying this morning; it is not as a person that you are accepted (and even then you are accepted into the sector of relative liberty entitled 'Free Opinions'). Someone who stands up outside the Sorbonne to say something very striking, like Ferdinand Lop – perhaps he is no longer with us[53] – creates a social event: in every age there is somebody who speaks in his own personal name and tells the truth about the social world and what needs to be done, and he is treated as a madman, idiotic, an *idios*, a singular character who speaks for nobody but himself. He ought to have authority, he ought to have a microphone and be backed up by a committee, as symbols of authority. He ought to be driven in a car, holding his microphone and reading out slogans that are a collective and collectively agreed discourse, choosing specific targets. There is a whole organizational 'apparatus' in the Marxist sense and spectacular 'apparel' in Pascalian terms (the two senses often overlap).[54] This double meaning is a key issue for me: the problem of representation implies both apparatus and apparel, with their strategy of objectifying representation. The principal function of a committee is to produce the bureaucratic apparatus, or to reproduce itself as an apparatus that can produce the apparel in the Pascalian sense.

To return to May 1968. We hear that everyone spoke, that everyone had the right to be heard, but this is never true: even in situations of maximum openness, the chances of getting to speak are unequally distributed. For example, one of the conditions of access to speech-making during May 1968 was possession of incorporated political capital, the strategic skills that small factions had acquired in their far-left leagues and miniscule splinter groups. You needed that apprenticeship in order to be able to intervene. That said, compared with ordinary situations, the hierarchy of access to speech was radically disrupted. If you look at *Le Monde* and make a scientific study of it – as I have done – you will note that, as in pre-capitalist societies, the prophet has more chance of getting to speak in a situation of crisis than the priest – I mentioned this last time. This is a general law: extraordinary times enhance the chances of people lacking the competence required to speak in ordinary situations; this gives the prophet his revenge over the priest. In May 1968, free speech seemed to be dispersed and distributed completely at random, but the conditions of access remained unequal, and were governed in particular first by cultural capital with its political content incorporated – as was implied in what I was saying in the first part of this lecture – and, second, by cultural capital with its political dimension objectified in slogans and committees. If you rang the editors of *Le Monde* saying: 'I am the Secretary General of the *Snesup* [*Syndicat national de l'enseignement supérieur* – the university teachers' union]', you were treated to the honours of a ritual press conference in virtue of your name and function: legitimate speech then was speech legitimized by the agencies empowered to legitimize.

One interesting case that struck me at this time was an appeal that emerged from time to time in the press, voiced by the committee that was supposed to represent the *Société des agrégés*. As you will see, there is a moral to the story, it sounds like an apologia or a fable. The representative of the *Société* spoke out regularly to say 'It's terrible', 'It's scandalous', 'We can't do this, we can't do that', 'We must do this, we must do that', etc.[55] Yet even without any empirical evidence, people know the *Société des agrégés* to be a movement with hardly any members. And, if you check the figures, it is indeed shown to have hardly any members – which needs analysing. It is a virtually nonexistent group, which exists only as a title. It is, so to speak, a group in name alone. When I referred just now to the ontological argument – 'I say that the people exist and therefore the people exist' – there is a semblance of truth. But if I say 'I am speaking on behalf of the *agrégés* therefore the group of *agrégés* exists', we can see that something is wrong. The potential for usurpation is thus unequally distributed according to the conditions under which the spokesman is appointed and recognized. This spokesman for the *agrégés* was speaking for *agrégés* in general, who, for understandable sociological reasons, did not share the position attributed to them, and the spokesman triggered a revolt by a certain number of *agrégés* who wanted their own opinions to be heard. What could they do? They found themselves reduced to the state of isolated and serial individuals faced with a spokesman claiming to speak on their behalf. They faced the spokesman as they had faced the social world before the emergence of the spokesman: they reverted to a pre-contractual, pre-delegational state. So what happened? A certain number of these people, deprived of their speech by someone who spoke in their place, were tired of being spoken for and founded a new group, a different *Société des agrégés* under another name.

Remember, for example, the period preceding the 1981 presidential election: there was a series of petitions by people who, as members of different parties, denounced their own party.[56] This is a situation of the same type: people are reduced to a serial state by the agency designed to release them from seriality. In other words, there are situations where the magical logic of delegation resurfaces, where the spokesman supposedly producing the group and representing it, in every sense of the term, ceases to be an instrument expressing the group and becomes an obstacle to the expression of what, if not the group, at least a part of the group, wanted to be heard saying. But what is interesting is that these are not universal and general oppositions – in this day and age we should always be wary of equations like 'x = the gulag' – it is an objective possibility that can exist at very different degrees depending on the nature of the group and its delegates, according to the way in which the delegates are organized. It seems to me that every time a situation of this type occurs, we cannot avoid the logic of the petition, which remains a prisoner of the logic of seriality (we collect a thousand signatures to say 'Replace X or Y', 'Throw Z out'). For instance, the petition by Christians who said they could not recognize themselves in what the Pope was saying could only escape serial logic by founding the Reformed Church – that is, a new Church that would have a committee, a title, an apparatus and a signature, in short, all the properties that I have mentioned, and would reproduce a certain number of the properties of the delegates, such as their structural hypocrisy and the duplicity of their game, for instance.

Lecture of 10 May 1984

First session (lecture): educational qualifications, discontinuities and bureaucracy. – 'Information capital'. – Codification and logical control. – The officialization effect of formalization. – Vis formae, the force of form.
Second session (answers to questions and seminar): towards a history of the technologies of thought. – Delegation and representation (2). – The structural hypocrisy of the delegate. – Homology and the coup double. *– Constituents and representative bodies.*

First session (lecture): educational qualifications, discontinuities and bureaucracy

In my last lecture I had started to analyse the institutionalized state of cultural capital. I would remind you simply of what I briefly concluded from a reflection on the autodidact and on the opposition between cultural capital with no guarantee, like that of the autodidact, and cultural capital guaranteed by educational qualifications.

One property of institutionalized capital, whose most obvious form is the educational qualification, is its capacity to transcend individual, biographical and biological accidents. It is a sort of licence of knowledge and cultural competence, and fulfils an institutional function. I would like just to indicate some guidelines for this notion by referring to a formula by Merleau-Ponty,[1] who says that collective magic has a sort of creative power that we can understand by observing how the living use rites of mourning to institutionalize their dead. Taken in this sense, the word 'institution' is, I believe, extremely important. Along with the educational qualification, it partakes of the order of magic in the veritable sense of the term. Institutionalization is a kind of collective action that bears all the outward signs of rationality: it is collectively recognized and accredited, since there is a sort of consensus over its meaning. That said, it is nonetheless magic, because it produces permanent states and permanent differences. Here the best example would be the analysis of the competitive examination effect and more generally the boundary effect, which is the most typical form of this operation of social magic.

Durkheimian sociologists always insisted on the break between the sacred and the profane and on the fact that social magic works by tracing limits,[2] boundaries, *templa* (the *templum* is what you obtain by the demarcation that produces an inside and an outside: if you draw a rectangle on the ground, a *templum* or temple, this produces a sacred interior and a profane exterior). If this fundamental social operation of demarcation, which is the juridical operation par excellence – the law belongs to the domain of social magic – is constantly exercised in the educational universe (with its hierarchy of sections and titles, for instance), the most conspicuous case is that of the competitive examination that establishes absolute, permanent, lifelong differences between people who are in fact part of the same continuum. This kind of 'discontinuity' is typical of the magical operation: between the lowest pass and the highest fail there may be a difference of one decimal point, but the social break creates an absolute difference, lasting a lifetime: the first are appointed *polytechniciens*, the others, nothing.[3] These brutal breaks and discontinuities established by the social operation of institutionalization, are the source of those enduring realities that are educational qualifications.

The universalizing process of social magic is plain to see in the social effects of the existence of the educational qualification. Max Weber underlines the importance of the link between educational qualifications and the emergence of modern examination systems, which are not as old as all that. The major competitive examinations emerged in most European societies in the nineteenth century in connection with the development of a 'rational bureaucracy', as Weber calls it.[4] This is because educational qualifications have the function of producing interchangeable agents, and one capital property of bureaucracy is precisely – as I shall discuss in a moment – to treat individuals as 'they' or, we might say, as 'Xs', that is as people having no existence outside a very general formula, and therefore being substitutable one for another.[5]

In his theory of the different types of authority,[6] Weber underlines in particular the fact that all these types of authority are put to the test in the problem of succession: each type of authority reveals its ultimate truth at the moment when the problem of succession has to be settled.[7] In fact, it is under the traditional type of authority that succession causes the least trouble: the patrimonial type of succession, from father to son, is relatively simple. In the case of charismatic succession, on the contrary, the problem is posed in dramatic terms: who can succeed de Gaulle? Or Chanel? Who can succeed some particularly dominant intellectual? Bureaucracy solves the problem of succeeding the charismatic persona largely by means of the educational qualification, which ensures a supply of individuals socially defined as interchangeable in terms of criteria relevant to the aims of the bureaucracy.[8] The educational qualification claims to guarantee that holders of the same diploma are identical, not in all respects, but in respect of the set of legally guaranteed technical and social competences required by the bureaucracy. Here we see the link between the state, the state's guarantee, the phenomenon of nomination that I have previously discussed, and the educational qualification.

It would therefore be interesting to study the notion of a national educational qualification as opposed to regional ones: debates on the subject of national or regional qualifications engage extremely important issues, since they are linked to the objective imperatives of the bureaucratic mechanism.

'Information capital'

Having examined the three states of cultural capital (incorporated, objectified and institutionalized) during the previous lectures, I now propose, starting from the reflection that I have just shared with you, to move on to a generalization of the concept, which I believe will show its full power.

As I have often said,[9] changing the name or the sense of a concept frequently produces important theoretical effects and enables us to construct social reality differently. One part of what I intend to do consists in a game of retranslation: substituting the notion of information capital for the notion of cultural capital enables us to see how the incorporated, objectified information that defines cultural capital is information that is both structured and structuring. I shall speak therefore of 'information capital' rather than 'cultural capital' in designating dispositions that compose a habitus; on the one hand they are informed and structured by experience of the social world, on the other hand they are formative; we might also call them structured structures and structuring structures. This capital of structured and structuring information is, as it were, stored somewhere in the brain, the memory or the more general bodily dispositions, but it is also stored in the objective world, as things or institutions. This stored and structured information will have the property of structuring any new information as it is received, and because of this the information capital will function as a 'code' – in both the legal and the linguistic senses – that can be incorporated or objectified. What I would like to analyse briefly today is the notion of codification or formalization.

When I started my research as a social scientist, I was struck by the fact that specialists in the social sciences, like a certain number of anthropologists, were often content to explain social facts by attributing them to rules. Indeed, English anthropologists often attacked their 'legalism'[10] – which I termed 'juridicism' in French – that is, their inclination to explain agents' behaviour by explicit rules that the agents would be formulating as principles underlying their behaviour. To contradict this vision, I have elaborated the notion of the habitus, whose specific function is to show how social agents can generate practices that are structured and regulated, without necessarily having any explicit rule for the production of these practices. The notion of habitus means that there is a sort of information capital that structures and is structured, which functions as a principle of structured practices without these structures that can be found in the practices having existed before the production of practices in the form of rules. Hence the opposition between the notion of the pattern, which I constantly use to explain the conditions underlying the principles of practices, and the notions of code, schema, model or rule, which, unlike a pattern – which remains incorporated in a practical state and is embodied in the person who uses it – are explicit and objective.

But I may have gone too far in my efforts to react against legalism or juridicism and question the specific efficacy of the rule. The question that I would like to ask today addresses the following point: although it is true that we tend too often to explain practice by rules and Weber is right to say that social agents obey the rules only when their interest in obeying them is stronger than their interest in disobeying them – quite a remarkable formula[11] – rules are nonetheless a social fact, and we need to investigate the specific efficacy that they may have. In this debate on the specific efficacy of rules we may encounter some very strange people, like Wittgenstein, who spent his life asking these questions: what does it mean to obey a rule? What is a rule? What is a juridical, or a formal, or an algebraic rule? My task today is to emphasize how strategies that consist in 'playing by the rules' (which I believe to be very important – as I explained in my last two lectures), show that the very fact of appearing to conform to the rules procures a specific supplementary profit.

I would now like to show the significance of the opposition between practices based on incorporated patterns of behaviour and practices that may be based on objectified patterns; and I would like at the same time to investigate this process of objectification. This reflection on the process of objectification is important: it is part of the reality that the sociologist studies, but it is also part of the very procedure undertaken by the sociologist. Reflecting on these processes of codification, then, implies reflecting on the difference between behaviour that derives from these patterns and behaviour that derives from rules, while also reflecting on the effect produced by the sociologist who is codifying practices. The most elementary exercise in codification, such as producing a statistical code, even the mere fact of writing and transcribing a schema or some objectified representation, generates a social effect that the sociologist must take as an object of study. Otherwise, he is in danger of subjecting the object of his analysis to an effect that he has himself added to reality. In other words, he runs the risk of unwittingly becoming a jurist. (Here we find the problem of legalism once more.) We may, then, codify the effects involved in the act of codifying a practice. The most basic example is the codification of a language: language is a set of linguistic patterns, but we may legitimately speak of a code when we are dealing with a language that really has been codified by the objectifying activities of grammarians. Language objectified as grammar displays the same properties as do logic, law or methodology, and thus I would like to identify the general properties of all the objectified forms of the principles that generate practices.

Codification and logical control

The first property: all codification supposes an attempt to objectify. That may sound banal to you, but it is not self-evident. To explain it, I propose to refer to research undertaken by ethnologists into the passage from an oral to a written society. I am thinking of the book by Jack Goody, *The Domestication of the Savage Mind*, which has been translated into French under the title *La Raison graphique*.[12] We can place Goody in a tradition that attempts to reflect on the social effects of the emergence of writing; he considers that some of the properties that we attribute, often rather automatically, to 'the primitive mind'

or 'archaic societies' may be explained by the fact that these societies
lacked the techniques of conservation of thought that writing provides.

In a book on Plato in which he pays particular attention to Plato's
criticism of poetry,[13] Havelock insists on the fact that Plato's criticism
of *mimesis* – translated as 'imitation' – has in fact been misunderstood:
what Plato had in mind was the poetic practice whereby poets were
obliged to mime (not to imitate) with their bodies what they had to say,
in order to memorize it, recall it, and reappropriate it. Obviously, we
should point out that, like all breaks, this break between 'society with
writing' and 'society without writing' is not an absolute break: there
are still in our societies a host of things, sometimes among the most
important, that are transmitted outside writing, in the mimetic mode.
This happens, for instance, within the family. This analysis of mimetic
transmission therefore is valid not only for pre-scriptural societies, but
also for a considerable part of the knowledge that is transmitted within
our societies.

This mimetic appropriation of knowledge could be described as a
dispossession. Plato says that the poet is possessed by the gods, that he
is mastered by a knowledge that he does not master. The Romantics
took over the themes of inspiration and the muse, but this is a kind of
retrospective illusion that leads us to project very modern representations onto the past, and prevents us from seeing that this pre-Socratic
mimesis is in fact a kind of dance where the poet can reproduce his
discourse only by engaging his body. The absence of techniques of
objectification means that the mimetic production of knowledge fails
to produce the distancing, so to speak, that objectification provides.
Plato says that in fact the poets do not know what it is they are saying:
it is a knowledge that speaks through them and that they discover as
we do, but as soon as they discover it they lose it, because they are
engaging with something else. Writing, on the other hand, enables us
to make a logical check, to compare different moments of the discourse
(what was said at the moment t and at the moment $t + 1$): logic starts
with objectification.

Here I would like to quote a phrase by Cavaillès (I am connecting
up two very distant theoretical spaces, but I believe that there is good
reason): he writes in *Méthode axiomatique et formalisme* [Axiomatic
method and formalism]: 'A written argument cannot deceive you, for
its design would indicate the figures excluded.'[14] Cavaillès identifies
written objectification with logical verification, which is basically what
Plato wanted to do. The archaic forms of knowledge witnessed by
ethnologists, in particular everything concerning systems of myth, are
useful from this point of view. I remember an extraordinary text by

[*name inaudible*][15] who analyses the particular manner of speaking of people reciting the myths, for example a special tone of voice, which shows that, to get into the state where they can produce the knowledge that the ethnologist will transcribe, social agents must adopt a corporal and vocal posture, a *mimè*, a whole relation to what they are evoking: it is only on this condition that they can retrieve the knowledge. This means it is different from the objectified knowledge that we can read whenever we want, since it is enough just to open the book – this knowledge may come or fail to come, and when it does come, it is in a form that they are not sure they are in possession of.

The officialization effect of formalization

A first property of objectification that we can detect in the passage from oral to written, then, is the fact that the objectivity is explicit. It is universally communicable, you can put your finger on it, you can say: 'You said that', you can agree – this is the word *homologein*, to homologize[16] that I shall return to – you can say the same thing, you can be sure, you can transform the tacit linguistic contract (linguists sometimes use this expression)[17] into a legal contract that can be mutually agreed. But the ambiguity of the notion of objectification lies in the fact that in passing from the implicit to the explicit, from the tacit or practical to the written and communicable, we render things objective and, at the same time, official: the process of objectification is inevitably a process of officialization. There is then no technical effect of officialization that is not at the same time a social effect. Writing, for example, allows logical control, but inseparably and simultaneously it allows all the effects of publication, officialization, public proclamation, and so forth. This kind of ambiguity of objectification seems to me to be central to a reflection on notions which are themselves central, at least to sociological problematics, such as the notion of rationalization and its procedures. We could say that objectification is a condition of rationalization, which is always at one and the same time both a technical operation and a social operation of publication.

To go into some more detail: what does 'to officialize' mean? To officialize is to put something into what we call 'the public domain', and a certain number of social procedures, especially those involving 'social magic', consist purely and simply of publication. A typical example is the publication of the banns of marriage: we could say that marriage is a liaison made public, a liaison that may show its face and speak its name, that is underlined by permanent signs such as a wedding ring;[18]

this publication effect is an effect of officialization that saves what is published from secrecy, from the unofficial and the shameful, by rendering it known and acknowledged. Recognizing a child is typically a procedure of the same type: it consists merely in declaring publicly and solemnly, in official circumstances, something that existed already as a fact. This kind of genuinely magical transfiguration performed by officialization is always tied in with the properly logical transfiguration that I was discussing just now: to publish is always at one and the same time to motivate, render logical, homologize and universalize.

This is where I may perhaps link the two meanings by saying that any codification tends to produce both a universalization and an officialization: what is published and made explicit, established according to the rules instead of existing only as a pattern of practice, becomes something universal that can be reproduced by absolutely anybody. You could take the example of the traditions of a craft: as long as they are not codified, apprenticeship depends on direct contact between the generations. This mode of transmission, handed down directly by one individual to another and remaining in an implicit state, creates an effect of inertia, which is that, since the transmission of knowledge does not pass through objectification, knowledge escapes criticism to a certain extent: it is communicated only from body to body (the notion of *mimesis* would be the most suitable to describe these types of transmission of craftsmanship: 'Do as I do', 'Stand beside me and watch what I do'), where verbalization is reduced to a minimum. Because of this sort of postural transmission, what is transmitted remains as it were unconscious, or in any case implicit.

Building patterns of thought into sets of rules can give rise to the phenomenon of academicism, which consists in producing according to explicit rules of production, which are those of the previous generation.[19] But if making explicit generates academicism, it also occasions a break, because explicit rules can be attacked, whereas implicit rules have a kind of clandestine force of persuasion. (I think we could say the same of the implicit instructions internalized by a family. A certain number of contemporary reflections on the injunction effects at work in the world of the family do in fact tend to show that the essence of what is communicated between parents and children is of the mimetic type; it does not emerge into language, it occurs as a kind of dance, or bodily entente. This means that the power of these things over you is much greater, and the bodies of knowledge thus acquired are much more difficult to counter.)

Vis formae, the force of form

Objectification officializes, it renders public and official, it universalizes, but I would now like to show how the technical effect of formalization contributes to the effect of officialization and to the social effect of symbolic imposition. In fact, I would like to exploit an old Latin expression, according to which something or other acts *vis formae*, 'by force of form'. What is this *vis formae*? What specific force does an injunction or a precept acquire when they are formalized and made explicit in the form of general formulae? The two most typical forms of formalization, the logical and mathematical on the one hand and the legal on the other, are the two extremes, but what I want to say is that social formalizations combine the two. In fact, what I call symbolic violence is the effect produced when formalization combines the effects of logical formalism, that is the generalization effect ('this applies to all x, to all citizens') with the symbolic magic effect of officialization.

Just as an algebraic formula is valid for any number whatever, so a juridical formula is universal[20] – if we follow Weber in the chapters that he devotes to law in *Economy and Society*: what he calls rational law is opposed to customary law, which he calls *Kadi*-justice. *Kadi* is the *cadi* of Arab society; the justice of the *cadi* is basically the law of Sancho Panza in his island,[21] it is the justice of common sense, of guesswork and instinct, of the practical systems that everywhere pass for reason. This justice says that if two women argue over an object, you divide it between them, but if it is a child that they are arguing over,[22] the *cadi* is caught wrong-footed. The law commands us to act in such a way that the rules apply to all cases, including that of a child. The kind of generalization that is inherent in the work of codification consists in establishing correspondences that are logical and universal, so that all you have to do is apply the universal formulae to particular cases, whereas traditional law, for example customary law, as Weber says, always relates the particular to the particular.[23]

The best example to illustrate all that would be the contrast between a customary law and a rational law, even if that would require a long analysis. Customary law, as everyone has noted, is characterized by the fact that it does not pronounce any universal principle. We find a whole analysis of customary law in Durkheim (for example on 'repressive law' in contrast to 'restitutive law').[24] Weber too has his analysis. Customary law says: 'If a man strikes another man with a stick, he will pay for it with three blows; if he strikes a child, it shall be six.' There is a series of particular sanctions that match particular transgressions, but it is never stated that 'a man should never carry a stick', that 'all men are equal before the law' or that 'a man is worth three times more than a woman', etc.; yet we see that striking a man does cost three times more than striking a woman. There are therefore particular applications of universal rules, without these universal rules ever being formulated. As Weber says, we always move from particular case to particular case without passing through any universal mediation. Rational law, on the other hand, makes its grounds explicit, and draws on a kind of axiomatics.

We could say of the law what we have said of axiomatic formalization: rational law, according to Weber, formulates its fundamental conventions explicitly, just as an axiomatic leaves nothing in an implicit state, but claims to subsume all the postulates into a positive discourse. Likewise, a rational law must leave nothing to chance ... Here is a quotation from Blanché that concerns axiomatics but which could apply to the law:

> The situation we are in, when faced with an axiomatic system is like that of two players between whom there is disagreement about the rules of the game: if they fail to take the precaution of seeing that these are explicitly formulated and agreed upon, they will not be playing one and the same game, or indeed any game. If, on the other hand, their disagreement is made explicit at the start and they decide, for example, to use alternatively two sets of rules, they can play successive games without being impelled to accuse each other of cheating.[25]

You can play draughts; if one player rules that 'you can huff' and the other argues that 'a huff is not a move', you can take it in turns ... These explicit conventions are the beginnings of axiomatics, whereas in everyday practical logic these fundamental things are left in an implicit state and resolved each time, at the cost of a ceaseless labour of inspired casuistry.

I should say straight away that one property of objectification is to make life simpler. As long as fundamentals are not made explicit, they are left up to people's appreciation and social instincts, that is, to the habitus. When we analyse the series of acts of customary jurisprudence transcribed in some village or other, as I have done for Kabyle customary law,[26] we see that they clearly follow a logic. There are principles, as I said just now: an act committed at night is more serious than an act committed in daylight; an act committed in a house is more serious than one committed outside; an act against a man is more serious than one against a woman; and so forth. But since these principles are not explicit, but left to social instinct, there is always room for haggling and mutual accusations of cheating. One property of formalization is to enable us to homologize: to check that we are saying the same thing at the same time. Saussure's definition of language (as enabling us to attribute the same meaning to the same sound and the same sound to the same meaning)[27] only becomes completely true when the language is codified: in ordinary communication, you are never sure of connecting the same sounds with the same meanings, there is a considerable amount of misunderstanding. To be sure to associate the same sound with the same meaning and the same meaning with the same sound, you need to objectify and codify the rules of codification themselves, axiomatics being the space of the metadiscourse on the principles of codification of discourse that allows us to be sure that we are really speaking of the same thing.

Strangely, no one has ever made this connection, but this work of axiomatization is common to algebra and to rational law. In fact, since the rational law that suits a rational bureaucracy must make universal rules for agents interchangeable, it is a sort of algebra for social behaviour: a law valid 'for all Xs'. I quote Weber on the subject of formal law: 'It takes into account exclusively the general and unequivocal characteristics of the case under consideration.' That seems to me to be a very fine formula. Law suits are necessarily polysemic, they can be defined in dozens of different ways, and juridical procedure selects a finite number of aspects based on certain forms of relevance, and once these aspects are decided and characterized unequivocally, the law can pronounce rules valid for all cases. Insofar as the law must take into account unequivocal general characteristics, it automatically generalizes. Whereas *Kadi*-justice moved from the particular to the particular, rational law generalizes, even when it handles a particular case. Here we might return to Saussure and the problem posed by the notion of the legal case: I think that when, in the *Course in General Linguistics*, Saussure characterizes the passage from language to speech as an execution – the word keeps recurring, you can check in the text – he treats the linguistic code as a juridical code comprising explicit rational principles, and the work of the judge, or the speaker, consists in applying the general rules to the particular case. Language, then, which is a system of patterns, is treated as an objectified code, of which any speech act is an application.

To explain the kind of universalization operated by formalization, we could refer to the famous analysis by Schütz of the person posting a letter:[28] this character knows that they can count on an objectified and formalized social order, on people who have been trained to obey the rules, who know that they must frank the stamp, sort the mail and deliver it, that there will be sanctions if the stamp is not properly franked, and so forth. The social agent who puts their letter in the mailbox is an interchangeable X, made possible by the universe of rules that will produce the interchangeable acts implied by the interchangeable act that triggered the process. This is what Heidegger described in pejorative terms as the universe of 'they' and their inauthentic acts,[29] but we make clear progress when we say 'X' where Heidegger says 'they', for a formalized system transforms social agents into Xs, with a whole series of ensuing effects.

I have pointed out one of those effects: we can easily see that rational law, compared to *Kadi*-justice, economizes on genius – you have to be Solomon to solve the riddle of the child needing to be cut in half[30] – and it is one of Weber's most powerful insights to have seen that the process of rationalization brings within the grasp of everyone acts that, as long as they are transmitted only as patterns, are accessible only to the few. This is basically the problem of excellence posed by Plato in the *Meno*:[31] can excellence be taught? As long as excellence remains something that you acquire as Themistocles does horse-riding, by watching your father, there are risks of failure in transmission.[32] As soon as knowledge is objectified, formalized and transmitted in a formal and rational way, we may hope that acts requiring the improvisation of genius will become accessible to everyman.

This is exactly what Leibniz said about Descartes's overestimation of intuition: 'Descartes asks us to be too intelligent; for him, we have to be intelligent all the time'; we would do better to trust in the *vis formae*, which Leibniz himself called *evidentia ex terminis*, the evidence derived from the formulae themselves.[33] As Leibniz would have said,[34] algebra is a kind of *spiritual* automaton that thinks for us, and checks for mistakes: contradictions show up straight away, we are as it were trapped in logic. To a certain extent – I think this is one of the extraordinary properties of objectification – objectified cultural capital, once formalized, places operations that used to be the work of genius within the grasp of a twelve-year old child. This is something that we often say, but without explaining it in the light of this logic. Objectification economises the need for genius, but at the same time it creates an effect of disenchantment: Weber consistently develops both aspects.[35]

That said, to return to what I was saying just now about the ambiguity of objectification: objectification is an act that proceeds towards rationalization, but at the same time, insofar as this rationality is given publication, the *vis formae*, the force of algebraic or logical form, exerts an effect of symbolic violence. Insofar as the rational effects of objectification are inseparable from and concurrent with the symbolic effects of objectification, we might say that rationalization in Weber's sense is accompanied by a rather Freudian rationalization. Here again, we see this clearly in the case of the law. Legal bodies have their own practices. Lawyers are relatively autonomous people who have a specific interest in coherence and logical control. They have to assimilate all the previous acts of jurisprudence, and eliminate all the contradictions. Their specific professional capital is therefore a capital of rationality and they are committed to rationality.

That said, the juridical effect of rationality that the law can create by having an answer to everything will mask the assumptions and the implicit axiomatics of a law that is obviously not the product of a purely rational construction: the basic axioms of a legal system are provided for the jurist by the political universe, they are the assumptions of the political universe. The formal work that the jurist will accomplish will garb in rational clothing what might have been an axiomatics, a system founded on an arbitrary axiomatic, and this mixture of the arbitrary and the rational will produce the effect specific to rational symbolic systems. That is what I meant by *vis formae*: formalization in the algebraic and juridical sense exercises an effect of reason through which the effects of violence are transformed and transfigured. We could demonstrate this for cultural, educational or many other forms of capital that I have mentioned, but I must end the first part of my lecture at this point.

Second session (answers to questions and seminar): towards a history of the technologies of thought

Many of you have asked me whether modern forms of conservation of thought, in particular the tape recorder or similar instruments – think of the computer, for instance – are really able to play a part comparable to that of writing. What I think is that in general we are too conscious of the infrastructure of intellectual work, whereas we ought to write a sort of materialist history of intellectual work that would try to relate the form of intellectual labour to the state of the instruments that produce, conserve and transmit knowledge. We forget for example that education, or the school, are not self-evident, but are historical inventions. It was the Sophists, for example, who invented the school system, and part of the debate between Plato and the Sophists can be read as a discussion of what are the adequate and reasonable social technologies, and therefore what are the suitable manners of thinking, of reflecting. There is a debate on writing and on the poet [referred to above], but also the debate on mercenary knowledge; should you be paid for teaching?[36] These debates are linked to technological changes.

There are some guidelines for such a social history of the technologies of intellectual labour: Havelock's *Preface to Plato*, which I have mentioned, for instance. Another book that would definitely help us to understand literary form, and even what can or cannot be thought, is *The Art of Memory* by Frances A. Yates.[37] I think this extraordinary book summarizes what I have been saying. It traces the history of a technology of memory that emerged in Greece, and that then was elaborated and codified by the Roman orators Cicero and, above all, Quintilian. It was a genuine technology in the sense that we speak of technology in industry. The problem that faced the orators was to make a sort of plan to memorize their speeches. They learnt to associate each part of their speech with a part of the house ('In the atrium, I place the introduction, in the bedroom, I place . . .') and the speech became a visual pathway that they could follow in their memory. During the Renaissance, this technology was put to different, more esoteric uses, but initially it was nonetheless something that existed in societies with writing.

Here I must draw your attention to another false idea: we always imagine that as soon as writing appears, the oral disappears, but in Greece, for example, the written and the oral have coexisted for centuries, with poets coming together to form something like guilds to transmit their knowledge in an entirely oral fashion: they had to learn by heart mile after mile of verse and reproduce it with mnemotechnical tools. There is some fine research by Lord and Parry[38] studying the techniques of semi-improvisation of archaic poets, and in particular by Yugoslavian bards who had techniques that seem similar to those used by the Homeric poets both for memorizing and for improvising, with systems of patterns and formulae, and the like. These techniques of invention and memorizing are very important because they generate quite different forms of thinking.

In a way, attacking the poet is already a field. For we may suppose that in the fifth century BC something like an intellectual field existed, with professional teachers, Sophists who wanted to rationalize the transmission of knowledge, arguing that everything can be taught (think of the ENA),[39] that you can transmit the arts of engaging in politics, exercising power and acquiring eloquence. You can teach not only how to speak well, but also how to speak relevantly: it is not enough to know the forms, you also need to master the form that detects the relevant opportunities to apply the forms, which is the major problem for all formalized teaching and knowledge: you have mathematical formulae, but you still have to find the object to apply them to, which is not at all simple. Whereas the Sophists wanted to teach by formalizing, you have at the other extreme people who still used very traditional methods to teach total knowledge, transmitting it in mimetic fashion, with hardly anything made explicit or codified, challenging their rivals. And, somewhere between the two, acting like prophets, were the famous pre-Socratics, whose argument was: 'Because I say so.' We could then draw up a sort of sociology of cultural production, relating the forms of the cultural products to the modes of cultural production.

I think that in these modes of production we make very great use of the techniques available. Today, for instance, I see the tape recorder as one technique of production. However, as so often, there are effects of hysteresis. For example, I think that, for a long time after writing had been invented, people didn't know what to do with it – we could see this in Plato – they continued to use writing as a tool for transcribing the products of other modes of production, and the Socratic type of work that consists in saying 'I criticize you, I check up on you by memorizing everything that you have said as if it were written' took time to develop. In a way, a new logic had to be invented in order to best benefit from the possibilities offered by writing. Similarly, today, there are very many instruments that we don't use yet because the dispositions of the agents who have these tools to hand lead them to use, for example, the tape recorder[40] as if they were taking dictation. We don't know yet how best to exploit it, but there will be interesting ways to make use of photography in the social sciences,[41] for this extraordinary technique, photography, has hardly yet been used as a specific tool.

All of which leads me to say that I think a social history of instruments would be very important, since the instruments also cover forms of organization. The seminar was a historical invention. The formal lecture was a transposition of the priestly sermon. The seminar was an invention of the nineteenth-century German philologists: the participants are seated around the same table, they have read a certain number of texts in advance; this is an invention liable to profoundly transform production and production relations (to use an analogy with economics), the content produced, even what is thinkable or unthinkable. For those of you who work on these subjects, the project of a social history of thought in its relation to the instruments available seems to me a very promising line of enquiry.

We might think of all those debates on the contrast between

individual and collective labour: is collective labour not destructive of the very idea of intellectual labour? It was no accident that this type of debate emerged in May 1968, in connection with problems of hierarchy: and more profoundly than that, there exists on an unconscious level a whole representation of intellectual labour. To understand artistic or intellectual vocations, we should analyse those more or less fantasmatic images that newcomers to the craft have of the profession, for example the tradition of interviewing artists: 'How do you work?' 'I work at night, drinking coffee.' Many of those who launch into intellectual work are inspired by these fantasies. But this is in fact a factor encouraging inertia: if you think that being a writer is holding a pen or developing a style, this excludes a host of possible uses of instruments. In the debates over the individual and the collective, there is the contrast between the literary, which is individual, and the scientific, which is collective: can you collectivize (with all its political connotations . . .) intellectual production without destroying it?

Antoine Compagnon's recent book on the Third Republic[42] gives a very good description of the debates over Lansonism[43] and the struggle over the reform of the university, which set the modernists, including the social scientists (such as Seignobos, Lanson, Durkheim) against the traditionalists, who tended to be historians of literature or teachers of French, for instance. This struggle, which so strangely resembles our present struggles,[44] often focuses on the social techniques that imply a self-image, a sort of personal mythology of the intellectual.

Another example would be the *salons*, which are an astonishing historical invention; they are a social form where men and women, artists and bourgeois, mingle. Similarly, the galleries and museums that we know so well are historical inventions. I think Kant's theory of the beautiful cannot be understood if we do not know that, at about the same moment, there emerged in Dresden,[45] as well as in a certain number of other cities, galleries where paintings were hung in order to be viewed independently of their context or function: you no longer saw that an altar piece was a work that fulfilled a religious function.[46] The specifically aesthetic culture that consists in observing the work in itself and for itself was, if not the product, at least reinforced by the existence of galleries and museums. In fact, the invention of the aesthetic approach is simultaneous with the objectification of the aesthetic approach, when they started hanging works in museums. This did not happen overnight: there were galleries in the fifteenth century; but the modern type of museum as objectification of the pure, aesthetic gaze is another of these technical-aesthetic inventions.

It would be the same for books. The French hardly ever use an index: what does that mean? The index is a technical invention that creates a very special relationship with the book. Similarly, the table of contents is not self-evident, it too is an invention. There are connections between many of these things, which appear to be inseparable from the art of thinking. The three-point plan is an invention (see Panofsky's book, *Gothic Architecture and Scholastic Thought*, which is one of the world's great books . . .). It is what St Thomas called the 'clarification principle', 'the postulate of clarification for clarification's sake':[47] the idea that things should be said in such a way that they are as far as possible self-explanatory, and signal their own organization. You can see this in the French edition of Panofsky: there are facing facsimiles of twelfth- and fourteenth-century manuscripts;[48] in the manuscript pre-dating clarification, everything is rolled up together, there are neither headings nor chapters, whereas the clarified manuscript has been organized into three points, like a gothic cathedral. You could find numerous other examples.

Knowing that these are historical inventions liberates us from those things that the educational system so often transmits as if they were eternal requirements of the mind, prolonging them eternally beyond their social utility [. . .]. The debate over the essay plan in three points or two parts is very important [. . .], for there are things that cannot be conceptualized in two points. The historical perspective is what is most often ignored. I am not saying this out of spite, but intellectuals hate being given historicist analyses of things intellectual. They think of themselves as universal thinkers, whereas, to have the faintest chance of being universal, you have to know how to historicize: the more I know that the tools I am using are historical – manners of speaking and patterns of thinking are the incorporation of a whole sequence of historical inventions that have been codified, transmitted and institutionalized – the more I am able to de-historicize myself, or at least to hold in abeyance the most arbitrary parts of my historical heritage. A history of the technologies of thought would also have a crucial epistemological function. You can find a lot of the elements of this subject in Bachelard, who was very alert to the problem: he constantly shows up the unexpected, surprising and historical character of things that have become commonplace in scientific thinking.[49]

Delegation and representation (2)

To return rapidly to what I was saying rather clumsily about delegation last time, I shall now try to underline some of the consequences of the propositions that I was putting forward. I was trying to show that the sort of process of delegation that is imposed on us – I think since Rousseau – whereby an individual mandates another individual to speak in his place, conceals another, more powerful and dangerous process: that of representation, whereby a certain number of people recognize themselves in someone who, by representing them in the theatrical sense, leads them to exist as a group.

Strangely, I shall start with this effect of theatrical representation, which has always been seen and yet unseen, I think, because of our attachment, so to speak, to this model of delegation. I shall read you a passage from Hobbes's *Leviathan*, which I find helpful in explaining this:

> A multitude of men are made one person, when they are by one man, or one person, represented; so that it be done with the consent of every one of that multitude in particular. For it is the unity of the represented, not the unity of the represented, that maketh the person one.[50]

This text is most interesting because it mixes the two forms, both delegation and representation: '*A multitude of men are made one person, when they are . . . represented* [represented in the symbolic sense]; *so that it be done with the consent of every one* [here we have the aspect of delegation: I delegate with an act that is deliberate and free, etc.]. *For it is the unity of the represented, not the unity of the represented, that maketh the person one* [it is because the represented is unique that the represented is unique: it is the unity of the person representing and not that of those represented that renders the person one].'

In other words, we have here the most succinct summary of what I was saying last time: does the fundamental political effect not lie in the capacity to unify that is given to the representative insofar as he is unique? If I am the sole representative of a collective, my unicity is a sort of manifestation and exhibition of the unity of the group. For Hobbes, this symbolic effect of representation that unifies, this power of representation to unify, so to speak, achieves its maximum effect when those represented do not exist before the representation. There is a sort of absolute beginning: it is when the representative affirms himself as representative that in this very act he makes the group represented exist. I think this effect of unification through representation is most powerful when the group that their spokesman makes exist by manifesting it is least vocal. Hobbes's paradox is most effective, then, when dealing with the representatives of dominated groups: the Hobbesian theory of creative and unifying representation is never more valid than when it deals with people who, for social and economic reasons, through the effect of mechanisms linked to cultural capital, have least access to speech and, because of this, place themselves entirely at the disposal of the spokesman who makes them exist by representing them. Hobbes's analysis, which has often been seen as anticipating modern forms of the theory of contract and delegation, is in fact more medieval than modern.

I give you two references: Gaines Post, *Studies in Medieval Thought, Public Law and the State, 1100–1322*, Princeton: Princeton University Press, 1964; and Pierre Michaud-Quantin, *Universitas: Expressions du mouvement communautaire dans le Moyen Âge*, Paris: Vrin, 1970. The latter book discusses the notion of *universitas*, that is, a group that exists as one, precisely through its unitary representation. The *universitas* is the group par excellence, the corporation that is constituted by the fact that it has legitimate spokesmen, endowed with the legitimate attributes of representation. One of the most important attributes is what Post calls the *sigillum authenticum*; ultimately the *universitas* is a seal, the seal of the dean who is responsible for the corps and who in a way incarnates the collective body; the dean is a biological body who incarnates the social body and who, in incarnating it, makes it exist. He is endowed with the symbolic attributes of his representativity, in the form of the *sigillum*, the seal that will legitimate his signature and certify its authenticity.

This makes us think of the *skeptron*, the baton that Benveniste says was given to the orator to show the fact that he had the right to speak,[51] that he was the legitimate speaker because it was he who held the sceptre. It is one of those symbolic objects that are the incarnation, materialization and objectification of the group in its unity. Post and his branch of scholarship have also reflected on the notion of the crown: we talk of 'the possessions of the crown', the crown is an object that displays the fact that the person who wears it is king[52] . . . And if it is possible to say 'the king is dead, long live the king', it is because the possessions of the crown, like the sceptre, outlive the king; there will be kings as long as there are crowns, as long as it is possible to pass the crown from one king to another, within the rules. These problems of representation were elaborated in the medieval tradition on the basis of a concern to define a legitimate group. A group that really exists, a *universitas*, is a set of people who recognize themselves in the same spokesman. Obviously, we enter the realm of pure magic here, as we see with the crown.

A first-degree reading of these symbolic attributes would show them to be rather as Pascal shows them: Pascal's 'apparel',[53] like the ceremonial of the church, would be a symbolic exhibition whose aim is to impress and overawe people. But things are more complicated. These symbolic attributes are the incarnation of the group. A seal is nothing extraordinary, and yet the seal is quite simply the group. The person who bears the seal or the sceptre is the group. So it is not simply the case that the sceptre impresses with its ornate decorations . . . I think we might find an analogy in the ritual of the microphone in a modern assembly: passing the microphone to the speaker is a transposed form of the technology of the sceptre (and of the *skeptron*), a way of saying: 'You are credited with legitimate speech.' Mechanisms of the same type are at work in our own societies, because speech can only be assumed without violence by people who are mandated to assume it and whose mandate is visible in the form of the seal or the sceptre. To put it simply: the seal is the mandate reified, the mandate made thing, it is what attests and authenticates the delegate as legitimate delegate.

The structural hypocrisy of the delegate

While analysing the social genesis of a group and the mechanisms of symbolic production of groups, I would like to investigate the properties of the delegate. Too often we use the language of psychology and morals (and often moral deviation), to describe properties of social agents that could, in a way, be deduced from their position in the structure, but I think the particular talent of sociology is often to show that the things we would describe as individual character traits are in fact inscribed in their social position, as in the case of the cleric. I intend to proceed by using very different texts, some by Nietzsche against certain priests, which you certainly know, and some by Kant. These texts denounce a certain number of properties of the cleric as representative, as X who speaks in the name of the group. But these properties are in no way personal properties that we could describe in terms of hypocrisy (Nietzsche says that the clergy are hypocrites).

What I want to show is that the holder of a *sigillum* is destined for structural hypocrisy, and one property of the representatives is that, being the group, they must say that they are only the group and that they exist only through the group. In other words, the statements of the trade union or political leader or the delegate in general imply a sort of forced modesty: I can only be the whole, that is, the group, on condition that I say that I am nothing but the group. Because of this, the analyses of the bad faith of the representatives, which have in general been applied to the priesthood (as representatives par excellence) seem to me to be applicable in a much more general way. The bad faith is inherent in the position, and has nothing to do with the ethical or psychological dispositions of the representatives.

The problem of the representative who is consecrated, who holds the sceptre, is how to consecrate himself as sacred. And he will self-consecrate, saying that he is neither more nor less than the sacred that makes him exist. Here I wish to quote a text by Kant.[54] Kant says, more or less, that 'a Church founded upon this last principle [unconditional faith and not rational faith] does not have true *servants* (*ministri*), [. . .] but commanding high *officials* (*officiales*)'. So often, when these problems are discussed, we return via Latin to this very elaborate medieval tradition, the Church being no doubt the first historical invention of a grand bureaucracy: an enormous amount of research has been devoted to this sort of unconscious genesis of a grand bureaucracy, with the phenomenon of delegation, the invention of the minister as someone who does not exist in his own right, who is only the representative or vicar of the group or corps.

[These *officiales*], although (as in a Protestant Church [*which is a euphemized kind of church*]), they do not display themselves in hierarchical splendour as spiritual officials clothed with external power but even protest in words against any such thing [*Kant means that it is a second-degree hypocrisy*], in fact wish to be regarded as the exclusive chosen interpreters of a holy Scripture. [. . .] Thus they transform *service* of the Church (*ministerium*) into a *domination* of its members (*imperium*) – even though, to hide this presumptuousness, they make use of the modest title of the former.

I believe that this text says it all. It is a complicated passage, but it can be construed quite simply: there is play on words between *ministri* ('minister', which means, etymologically, someone mandated as delegate merely to act 'for' and 'in the place of')[55] and *officialis* (that is, someone mandated who ceases to be a delegate and becomes autonomous and self-motivated). How is a delegated power transformed into a power that makes us forget that it was delegated? How is the minister transformed into an *officialis*, the *ministerium* into *imperium*? How is the secretary general transformed into the general chief of staff? Kant says that there is a sort of usurpation: the service of the group becomes a service of self through the group, and the usurpation is smuggled in with the slippage: 'they make use of the modest title of servants'. In other words, the strategy of modesty is structural: I can only become imperious by a kind of self-abnegation, by eclipsing myself before the law. This kind of self-effacing habitus, which is typically priestly, is a fair description of the clerical habitus in general.

The ministers, says Kant, attempt to obtain the monopoly of the Holy Scripture: the Scripture that they consecrate consecrates them. They will say: 'You need to re-read Marx – the early Marx as well as the mature Marx',[56] 'You need to re-read the Old Testament as well as the New Testament', 'You need to make distinctions', 'There is good text and bad text', 'You need to read Marx better than Marx did', and so forth. In order to establish their holy status, they must establish themselves as holders of the monopoly of the definition that consecrates them. Therefore, when the consecrating principle is a book – which is often the case for traditions grounded in an objectified cultural capital – they must hold the monopoly of textual exegesis. Nietzsche says it most clearly in *The Anti-Christ* (a truly striking text, that would merit quotation from page after page): 'One cannot read these Gospels too warily; there are difficulties behind every word.'[57]

A question that is obviously of great interest from an analytical point of view is: how is it that we can use philosophical texts of this nature in a sociological analysis? What do we do to them when we study them? In fact, these texts are nearly always written in a spirit of indignation or condemnation, and although indignation is a source of lucidity (we see clearly what we detest), it prevents us at the same time from seeing the principles underlying the thing that we detest. A sociologist may be attracted to something that makes him indignant, but he is a sociologist only if he overcomes his indignation so as to discover the principles underlying the existence of the thing; which does not prevent him from feeling indignant, but enables him to establish its basis. In Nietzsche, the tone of prophetic indignation is obviously constant, but he touches on real mechanisms that are very important and very general: 'One cannot read these gospels too warily, there are difficulties behind every word.' In saying that the gospels are difficult, the interpreter claims the monopoly of exegesis. To some extent, many texts are rendered difficult by interpreters who attempt to claim the monopoly of exegesis. We could easily illustrate this proposition with a host of examples: the hermeneut is hermetic in order to justify his hermeneutics [*laughter*].

Another example from Nietzsche: he says that the delegate must . perform the transformation of himself into something sacred.[58] To perform this self-sanctification, he must consecrate himself as the only person able to assume holiness. Among the strategies the delegate uses to consecrate himself, there is the strategy of personal devotion:

'Nothing works more profound ruin than any "impersonal" duty, any sacrifice to the Moloch of abstraction.'[59] This is another property of the delegate: he says 'the People', 'the masses', he speaks in abstractions, he generalizes, and this is a strategy. Another quotation, the delegate always assigns himself sacred tasks:

> the philosopher is, in virtually all nations, [*for Nietzsche, the philosopher and the priest are the same thing*] only the development of the priestly type [*which is true*], one is no longer surprised to discover this heirloom of the priest, self-deceptive fraudulence. If one has sacred tasks, for example that of improving, saving, redeeming mankind [. . .] – one is already sanctified by such a task.[60]

This very fine aphorism reveals the very formula of fetishism: I save, I am a saviour, therefore I must be considered as saved. This kind of transfiguration, this inversion of cause and effect that the alchemy of consecration performs, is what Nietzsche calls 'this self-pretence of "holiness"', 'the art of holy lying' whereby the priest sanctifies himself.[61] The priest is someone who calls his own will 'God'.[62] It is easy to prove that the delegate is someone who calls his own will 'the Nation' or 'the People'.

I quote again:

> The 'Law', the 'will of God', the 'sacred book', 'inspiration' – all merely words for the conditions under which the priest comes to power, by which he maintains his power, these concepts are to be found at the basis of all priestly organizations, all priestly or priestly-philosophical power-structures.[63]

Nietzsche continues: the delegates lay claim to the universal values, they 'have placed a distraint on morality'.[64] This is sublimely said; they take charge of God, Truth, Wisdom, the People, the Message, Liberty, in order to be able to say, 'I am the Truth', 'I am the People', and in this way, Nietzsche argues, they become 'the measure . . . of all the rest'.[65] This strategy is not self-evident, it is a difficult performance: they constantly have to act small, unsuccessful, meek and humble in order to triumph and dominate.

The form par excellence of this 'self-pretence of holiness' is what we might call the *oracle effect* – which Nietzsche enunciated in one of his quotations: the priest is he who calls his own will God, the oracle effect consists in the spokesman saying that what speaks through him is the People. There are many ethnological and ethnographical works on the great oracles of Antiquity and on the strategies that were used by the priests. We see oracle effects in everyday politics; the spokesman composes answers and formulates discourse in the name of the people he speaks for, legitimizing himself to speak in the name of the speech that he produces, rather than what legitimizes him to speak. He gives voice to what he speaks on behalf of, to those in whose name he has the right to speak, and they are made to say things that authorize the speaker to speak. This 'naming' effect is capital: the spokesmen are people who speak 'in the name of' something, they speak in the name of the Lord . . . They are as vicars, they are there *for* something and *in the name of* someone.

This is very important: the Durkheim school always wondered how to move from a science of morals, that is, a science recording what happens in the social world, to an ethics.[66] How can we pass from the positive to the normative (which no science has ever done)? They claimed for sociology the right to state explicitly what is implicit in the social world, with its constraints and collective imperatives. There are some extraordinary texts in Durkheim. It is a temptation to which the sociologist is bound to be exposed. As I often (rather wickedly) say, sociology for many sociologists is a way of pursuing politics by other means: they become the exponents of the immanent truth of the social world, and in the name of this immanent truth or its tendentiously interpreted laws (for example, the opposition between the normal and the pathological in Durkheim),[67] they enunciate norms and state not only what exists, which is difficult enough already, but also what should be. This sleight of hand is central. It allows them to pass from the constative to the performative . . . In fact, the Durkheimians had perfectly well understood that, since transcendence is the group, managing to speak in the name of the group is the way to acquire the monopoly of the expression of transcendence, and thereby exercise over all the members of the group the constraint that collective action involves. But although it is true that, to a considerable extent, it is the expression of the collective that makes the collective exist, this constraint is itself produced by the very act that constitutes the collective.

Thus the oracle effect that I mentioned just now consists in exploiting the transcendence of the group over the individual. This transcendence, which is enacted as a form of constraint, permits an individual who wants to pass himself off as the group to exploit this transcendence of the group over the individual. It is therefore a way of monopolizing the collective truth by grounding one's authority in the group in order to exercise authority over the group. If I am a spokesman, as soon as I ground my authority in the group that grants me authority, I can exercise authority over the group. I think this is the fundamental sleight of hand of the social world. It can happen that the group becomes aware of this constraint, liberty is never total. It is an old rule ('You only preach to the converted'): the spokesman is the more likely to have the constraint that he exercises over the group recognized, the more he expresses the confused, latent expectations of the group, and the more explicit he is in expressing these latent expectations. That said, the sleight of hand remains, because there is a margin of liberty written into the fact of delegation.

To conclude this first point, I would say that modesty and hypocrisy are seemingly psychological, but are in fact structural and social, properties of the delegate. You could re-read Robespierre and Saint-Just in this light: their terrifying identification with what justifies them to terrorize.

Homology and the *coup double*

Now, in a word: am I not reverting to a cynical vision of the delegate, to the old eighteenth-century vision of the deceptive priest exploiting people's credulity, that we find in Helvetius or Holbach? I think one of the advances of social science (with Marx, and the sociologists) is to have understood so well the limitations of a naively material vision of the kind: 'The priests manipulate the people to satisfy their own interests.' In fact, the spokesman or manipulator manipulates only because he is himself manipulated; he induces belief only because he believes, and one of the mechanisms that make manipulators and spokesmen believe their own arguments – which reinforces people's belief in what they say – is the effect of homology between the space of the delegates and the space of those mandating them. To express this in abstract terms (I will try to explain later): if the delegate is not a cynic, it is because most often each delegate (each cleric or religious agent) entertains with the other, rival delegates (the other clerics and religious agents) a relationship homologous to his relationship with his audience and the other audiences.

For instance, in a relatively autonomous political field, someone holding a left-wing position, a, relates to someone holding a right-wing position, b, just as someone holding a left-wing position, A, in the social space relates to someone holding a position, B, in the social space: the spokesman for the dominated relates to the spokesman for the dominant in a way homologous to that relating the dominated themselves to the dominant. Which means that we are subject to a logic of duplication, which is one of the most complicated things to understand in the social world. It signifies that each act carried out by agents within a relatively autonomous field (every move of the prophet against the priest, of the avant-garde poet against the rearguard poet, the Academician against the Symbolist poet, and the like) will be over-determined, because of the homology between the relatively autono-mous field and the wider spaces (the space of the bourgeois readership in literature, the electoral space in politics). They can kill two birds with one stone. If I am the spokesman for the Proletarian Left and I put one over on the Trotskyites,[68] I also speak for the homologous sect in the wider field . . .

I don't know if you are following me.[69] The specific interests of the delegates following their own special interests are, moreover, in far more cases than you might think, also in line with the interests of those mandating them, which leads us to forget that the delegates are serving their own interests. They seem so convincingly to be *really* speaking for their mandators that we forget that the roots of their standpoint lie in their relation to the other delegates. This homology means that in most cases 'it comes to the same thing'. We only notice the specific interests of the delegates in cases of a manifest discrepancy between the interests of the delegates and the interests of their mandators (for example, in cases of disputed leadership). Then the delegates start to criticize their *petit bourgeois* a-politicism or anti-parliamentarianism. We cannot denounce the specific interests of the delegates without calling into question what Nietzsche called their 'generosity' and being suspected of anti-parliamentarianism or some variety of Poujadism or fascism.

That said, there are all those situations where the delegates are pri-marily serving the specific logic of the relatively autonomous field they are involved in, since the effects of homology ensure that they fulfil their declared function more often than we might think, which means that they serve so well simply because they serve themselves as they fulfil their service; most of the time, in serving their specific interests, they also serve the interests of those in whose name they speak.

Constituents and representative bodies

To make one last point: having analysed the effect of the group being established by their representatives, we should analyse the relations between the representatives and the corps, when the representatives exist as a body which, like the priesthood, has its own concerns. Max Weber says that any investigation of religion should analyse 'the tendencies of the priestly body as such',[70] that is, the specific interests dependent on the fact of belonging to a church. Likewise, any sociological investigation of the political should analyse the specific tendencies of political organizations to reproduce themselves. Like any group, all political organizations are concerned with their own reproduction and may sacrifice their nominal function to ensure that end.

I simply want to show that, although we gain the impression that the mandating body elects the delegate, the existence of relatively autonomous bodies of delegates means that, in reality, this delegation becomes a delegation made by the body of the delegates themselves on behalf of the mandating body. According to Weber, the Church, as the body holding the monopoly of the legitimate manipulation of the goods of salvation, by the same token holds the monopoly of the consecration of priests: the priests possess the sacred essence of the ecclesiastical body. This is the difference between the priest and the prophet: the prophet consecrates himself, he is the source of his own charisma, whereas the priest (like the professor) receives his charisma from the institution that consecrates him and gives him the instruments of consecration, and thereby lays down limits for him to observe ('Take care, you must perform a miracle every morning, but not a real miracle, and above all avoid being charismatic'). It is the same for political organizations: the political apparatus has its own logic with its concern for its own reproduction and its laws of consecration, whereby everyone fulfils his mandate from the mandating body with the same functions and limits (the man in charge does not perform miracles, he speaks the language of bureaucracy, he must voice the opinions of the apparatus, he must not be prophetic).

One last question: how does the body of delegates choose the mandating body? What does it ask of them? If it is true that the body of delegates is motivated by its own self-preservation, it will tend to choose the mandators best placed to reproduce the body of delegates. This is basically the golden law of any organization: the body of delegates gives all to those who give it all, to those who are nothing outside the apparatus. Here we can find the structural form of priestly modesty: the perfect, typical priest derives his whole sacred nature from the Church; he is not sacred in himself. Likewise, the delegate of the organization draws all his charisma from the organization, and we could use this structural analysis as the basis for a social psychology of the delegate.

I would have liked to quote some passages from Zinoviev: the basis of Stalin's success lies in the fact that he was someone 'extraordinarily mediocre'.[71] Another formula: he says of an apparatchik that he has 'an extraordinarily insignificant and therefore invincible force'.[72] Like Nietzsche, Zinoviev felt very strongly and indignantly that one of the properties of the legitimate delegate is a certain mediocrity or nullity. Why? Because he who is nothing outside the corps gives his all to the corps. Churches adore 'oblates'[73] those that their families consign to the Church in their childhood, those who give all to the Church because they owe everything to it. Today, among the French bishops, there is a strong proportion of oblates who are totally dedicated to the Church because they are nothing outside of the Church.[74] The more I am something outside the Church, the more I am tempted to try to be clever, to be prophetic and protest. If I owe everything to the Church, I am devoted and I further my career in the Church . . .

Lecture of 17 May 1984

First session (lecture): the effect of forms. – An analysis of discipline. – The ambiguity of discipline. – An ethnocentrism of the universal.
Second session (answers to questions and seminar): the problem of historical parallels. – The coherence of the lectures. – Historical parallels ('that reminds me of . . .'). – The false eternity of academic debates.

First session (lecture): the effect of forms

I would like to return to the problem that I was discussing last time, concerning formal structures and the part they may play in the social world. This is an extremely difficult issue, and I am not entirely clear myself what I want to say, but I don't think that this obscurity is due only to the obscurity of my thinking, I think that it is one of the most difficult issues facing scientific analysis. In fact, from the outset, and more especially since Max Weber, sociology has raised the question of the rationalization of the social world, as its processes have evolved from time immemorial, seemingly orientating the social world towards ever more rationality, coherence and logic . . . This problem is often resolved through a logic of the philosophy of history that draws on a sort of Hegelianism, sometimes mature and self-conscious, sometimes less so. What I have been trying to do in these last sessions is look at some concrete social operations to try to see where this experience of rationalization is grounded. I tried last time to show that all the social activities rooted in an academic discipline, like Law, are infused with a sort of formal character that gives them an intrinsic generality, and even a 'generalizability' that confers on them all the appearances by which we ordinarily recognize rational practices. It is such kinds of practice that I would like to analyse now, to try to see how they are constituted in the social world and how they work.

To get an idea of how difficult the problem is, we need to reflect on the notion of competence. As you know, the notion of competence was the subject of some extremely violent criticism around 1968: those criticizing the notion saw it as one of the typical ideological weapons used in any defence of hierarchies. *Grosso modo*, the critical analysis of this notion tended to reduce technical competence to the level of social competence, and say: 'The competence that you claim, whether scientific, technical, technocratic or political, and that you describe as intrinsically founded ['intrinsically founded' implying 'rational'], as capable of being judged on the merits of its coherence alone, has only social foundations; it is grounded in external authority, delegated by the social order.' Opposing the inclination of social competences to ground themselves in reason, rationalize themselves and claim that their foundation is not arbitrary but necessary, that is, logical and therefore rational, sociological analysis bases its questioning on relativism, which tends to reduce all cultural power and any affirmation of cultural universals to a 'cultural arbitrary'. Thus, in the analyses I made of the educational system,[1] I introduced the idea of the cultural arbitrary, which, although banal enough in anthropology or ethnology, presents a way of questioning the very foundations of the cultural universe when it is applied to a universe with claims to rational self-sufficiency. In fact, the question I am asking is whether kinds of expertise and authority with rationalist pretensions are founded in reason, as they claim to be, or whether, instead, they are strictly social.

It seems to me that a scientific analysis should be prepared to question the semblance of rationality, that is self-sufficiency, produced by these competences, which play at least some part in their social effect. To speak of symbolic violence, as I often do, is at least to recognize the existence of forms of (symbolic) power that cannot be exercised without the consent of those who are subjected to them. Among these powers, powers of the rational type are in the front line: the universality of their authority depends on the fact that they are valid for any possible subject and that there is nothing that can oppose them since they are declared (or declaimed, if you like) in the name of rational reasoning . . . This is the essential sense of what I was trying to say last time: I wanted to formulate these questions not in such general terms that there can only be dogmatic or ideological answers, but in concrete terms, dealing with particular practices, trying to show for instance what might connect modes of thinking as far apart as the juridical and the mathematical. Today, I would like to take this argument a little further and try to see how this notion of the rule, the formal rule that to some extent constitutes the social, contains the ambiguity that I have just mentioned.

An analysis of discipline

I shall begin by looking at the notion of discipline, which, strangely, has been very little discussed by sociologists. The only study of the question that I know is to be found in volume 2 of Weber's *Economy and Society*.[2] Weber insists on a certain number of points: discipline, he says, designates both the collective rule destined to ensure the order of an institution and the disposition inculcated by the training that leads people to obey this collective rule. If you look it up in the *Robert* dictionary, you will see that the French word implies both senses. On the one hand, we speak of the 'discipline of a religious order', the 'discipline of a military institution' or the 'discipline of a college': the objective sense of 'discipline' here is that of an explicit collective rule, most often codified, written or printed, which is designed to ensure the order that characterizes what Goffman calls a 'total institution'.[3] On the other hand, we say of someone that 'they have discipline' or we remind someone to be disciplined: in which case, the word refers to the disposition inculcated by the exercise. When we say 'discipline is the strength of an army', we are applying both senses; we are thinking both of the military order and of the order incorporated in the disciplined habitus of the good soldier, which is the product of the discipline imposed upon him. Discipline then is both the external rule and the disposition inculcated by being trained to obey this rule.

One point that I find important: discipline is the disposition to obey by executing the order immediately and exactly, without critical discussion, that is, absolutely instantaneously . . . It is the immediate obedience that gives discipline its mechanical, automatic and immediately orchestrated character. It is a means of obtaining the uniform and mechanical characteristics of the automaton from human behaviour. In fact, where Durkheim said that 'we should consider social facts as things',[4] we could say that total institutions treat social agents as things. They manage to make them behave like things, to make them function like machines that don't have to think or reflect (reflection takes time); they must obey before they reflect. If someone tells you to 'throw yourself down onto the ground', you mustn't look to see whether the ground is wet or not, you must throw yourself down onto the ground. In the light of this logic, we can understand the absurdity that characterizes those exercises designed to obtain discipline in the subjective sense. Spontaneous critics of the military machine tend always to attack the absurd and arbitrary aspect of the exercises through which the army aims to produce the spirit of discipline, but this absurdity is one of the very conditions of the production of discipline as a Kantian kind of obedience.[5] We never think of this, but there is nothing more Kantian than the army: military imperatives are categorical imperatives[6] that exclude any reasoning of the type, 'but, if it is raining, should I still throw myself down onto the ground?' To produce this universal disposition to immediate obedience you have to demand obedience, following the logic of the hypothetical imperative, in situations that are as hostile as possible to obedience. If you only obeyed when it was easy, there would be no need for obedience. This analysis enables us to see that discipline aims to make social agents act like automata, but spiritual automata objectively orchestrated by the effect of discipline. In a way, discipline is like a musical score for everyone's practices: everyone plays the same note at the same moment without having to reflect.

Here we find an issue that I raised earlier in these lectures,[7] the orchestration of social practices: how do we get a group of men to do the same thing at the same time, that is to get the group to act as a single man (I think that is the best way to put it)? If dance plays such an important part in so many societies – especially in archaic societies where it enables the group to affirm its structures, its unity and differences, its division of labour between the sexes, in short, to make a spectacle of its unity in diversity – it is precisely because it is a manifestation of the sort of orchestration that organizes the group. Military or monastic types of discipline then have as their first function to make people act as a single man, which is not self-evident and is always a sort of victory over the spontaneous dispersion or entropy of the group . . .

We should pay more attention to a second function: in making a group of people act like a single man, discipline is a way of preventing them from thinking of their actions as collective and rational. There again, Weber's analysis of discipline is very Kantian (it sounds like a commentary on Kant): discipline tends to replace enthusiasm and dedication. Against spontaneous morality and morality based on sympathy, against any ethic that expects agents to bring personal feeling to their moral action, Kant put forward the following argument: when spontaneity is not driven by sympathy, there is a danger of immoral action.[8] So you should not rely on the spontaneous feelings of the agent. If I have to be in a state of sympathy with the person to whom I owe charity before I offer him charity, I will only need to be unsympathetic for my charity to disappear. If we want actions to be moral, morality must have as its principle a morality of pure obedience, that is, a pure, universal principle, irreducible to contingency, to what Proust called the 'intermittences of the heart',[9] the fluctuations of human caprice.

What Weber says is that discipline tends to replace enthusiasm and dedication to a cause or a person (without excluding them – where there are heroes, discipline can make use of them . . .). In this way, rational discipline is opposed to dedication of a charismatic type, which follows a logic of the morality of sympathy, where I plunge into the fire to save someone only if I feel like it – if my mood happened to change, I might be insensible to any appeal (charisma is vulnerable because its effects are notoriously intermittent). As opposed to the charismatic dedication and enthusiasm inspired by the leader, discipline constitutes for Weber a form of rationalization, because it is protected from the fluctuations of sentiment that affect all human practices as long as they are subject to an authority of the charismatic type. In other words, Weber sees the structures of a formal type that I described last time as historical inventions that guaranteed the social world a constancy and permanence that no other principle can ensure. He shows, for example, that inventions of a disciplinary type are as important in the history of warfare as the technical inventions and progress in weaponry that are so often mentioned:[10] the evolution of armament is in fact secondary compared to transformations of organizational structures, and the greatest military advances are in fact social inventions (the phalanx, the revolutionary army, conscription) rather than purely technical advances. In fact, we could take Weber's analysis further, contrasting it with an analysis often forgotten because it is to be found only in a footnote to Durkheim's *Suicide*.[11] To explain why soldiers tend to commit suicide more often than others, Durkheim speaks of a 'fatalist suicide' that is provoked by an excess of regulations. This contrast between Weber and Durkheim has the merit of reminding us of the ambiguities of the formal type of structures that I am describing. We could contrast the optimistic vision offered by Weber of discipline as a form of rationalization with a pessimistic vision where an excess of discipline and regulation, what Durkheim calls 'oppressive discipline', is liable to provoke 'excessive physical or moral despotism'. Durkheim notes that, although discipline may be a rational force, it also lends itself to what Kant calls a 'pathological' usage;[12] the despotism of the users of discipline can lead to excesses liable to provoke what he calls 'fatalist suicide', which is particularly prevalent among soldiers and

– this will remind you of what I was saying earlier about our relationship to time[13] – 'persons with futures pitilessly blocked' who suffer 'the ineluctable and inflexible nature of a rule against which there is no appeal'. Durkheim means that discipline, wielded in a totalitarian way, can have anomic effects, and drive those who are subject to it to suicide, insofar as its effect negates any vision of the future. In other words, if discipline has the immediate efficacy that Weber mentions, it is precisely because it negates any anticipation of a space of possibilities. If every single agent acts as a single man, it is because they have no alternative. They are faced with a non-choice, and this means that their future is 'pitilessly blocked'; there is only one thing to be done. This experience of discipline summoned by Durkheim is not at all contradictory to Weber's proposition.

This is the analysis that I wanted to make at the outset, to show one of the effects of this kind of formalization of practices. If we think of social action as I did last time, concentrating on these strategies directing social practices where the social agents are subjected to universal forms, discipline appears as an extreme case of the formal regulation of practices where the individual and subjective aspect of the social practice is completely abolished. By comparing Weber's analysis to Kant's analysis of moral action, I wanted to point out how the rule of discipline tends to transform social agents into total anonymities: when they obey a formal rule, they are liberated from everything that Kant calls the 'pathological self',[14] that is, their personal singularity, passion, self-interest and impulses.

In a sense, the mode of organization of human actions that discipline achieves, the military universe at the limit of the Kantian universe, is the absolute opposite of a social organization of a Fourierist[15] type in which, as you know, each agent would be guided by the good use of their passions and impulses. The rigorous universe that discipline imposes is opposed to a spontaneous universe where everyone, doing whatever they fancy, would do what is best for the group. I think social universes oscillate between the utopia of the barracks and the utopia of the Abbey of Thélème,[16] where the anarchy of the passions leads to a harmony of practices. Between the two there is another myth – in discussing the social world, we go from one myth to another – that of the invisible hand,[17] which haunts economists and which has nothing to do with Fourier or Kant: it is a universe where everyone, in obeying their passions and interests, which always have a rational or at least a potentially rational dimension, lives in concord with one another through the mediation of the mechanisms of the market.

The ambiguity of discipline

Structures of a formal type, and practices obeying formal rules, tend to produce completely orchestrated behaviour, leaving minimal scope either for random chance or for individual improvisation. In fact, the form of capital that I called 'information capital', and included in a wider definition of cultural capital, gives certain agents control over the rules of action of everything in the social world that tends to regulate the practices of agents in conformity with disciplinary rules. In other words, this information capital underpins all types of expertise. By showing the very ambiguity of this competence,[18] I shall try to establish the existence of a very general form of power that is not reducible to purely economic power and is based on the mastery of the information structures that organize real practices. The two most typical forms of this power are the competences of the legal and political kinds, insofar as they aim to shape the practices of social agents by configuring their representations of practice.

How is this specific effect of rationalization achieved? Here, I shall repeat what I said last time, if perhaps in simpler terms. Following Hegel[19] – in a moment I shall read you some little-known arguments from Durkheim, which are very reminiscent of Hegel, although we don't know if he was consciously influenced by him – analyses of bureaucracy have very often tended to think of the holders of bureaucratic authority as the holders of a sort of rational power, and to think of bureaucratic structures as rational structures, as the site of rationality in the social world, the bureaucrat being in a way the agent who is the repository of the universal; he it is who arbitrates, decides and chooses between antagonistic interests. But if bureaucracy finds itself spontaneously invested with this power, it is not only, as Hegel says, because the bureaucrat holds power over formal or universal resources, it is not only because he controls the instruments of communal, public administration and management, but also perhaps because the objects and the means of his manipulation have the property of being the product of a process of publication and objectification. By combining legal terminology with a mathematical formula, I hope to show that the characteristic of a certain number of the principles of formal action is to produce a form of universalization of the principles of practice. This universalization may be more apparent than real, more formal than substantive, as Weber would say;[20] there exists what I referred to as a *vis formae*, an intrinsic force of coherence, and it is perhaps because bureaucrats are the repositories of forms that act through their own motive force that they exercise this universal force, at least in appearance.[21]

Here I would like to remind you of a text that I quoted last time. It concerns axiomatic logic but applies very much, I find, to the social world at large:

> The situation we are in, when faced with an axiomatic system, is like that of two players between whom there is a disagreement about the rules of the game: if they fail to take the precaution of seeing that these are explicitly formulated and agreed upon at the start, they will not be playing one and the same game, or indeed any game. If, on the other hand, their disagreement is made explicit at the start and they decide, for example, to use alternatively two sets of rules, they can play successive games without being impelled to accuse each other of cheating.[22]

This text shows us that, at the very heart of the rule, there is explicit assent to the rule. There is no explicit, publicly proclaimed and published rule without explicit assent to the rule itself among those who obey the rule. Rules of grammar, law or algebra are a product of an agreement that produces the agreement. For a rule to exist, for there to be a *homologein*, a compatible discourse, for the two participants to accept to associate the same sounds with the same meaning and give the same sound to the same sign (to return to the example of language),[23] they must in so doing also reaffirm the agreement that has produced their agreement. In other words, the rule is in a way the perfect example of the social: it produces a consensus on the basis of a given consensus. I think that this kind of fundamental agreement is inherent in the very fact of objectification. Objectification, as I was saying last time, in making things public, official and explicit, assumes and makes manifest the agreement of the subjects and a kind of transcendence of the social. Objectification is a way of achieving objectivity as an agreement between subjects. To objectify in the form of a rule a principle that governed practices in an implicit state, as do players who agree to say 'henceforth, we shall no longer "huff"',[24] is to make a rule exist independently of the subjects and in a way definitively, independently of the occasion, the subjects and their states of mind or moods – a rule that will be the universal rule of the practices.

It is clearly in the realm of the state that this kind of norm is practised: the official is that interchangeable agent whose practices are guaranteed by universal rules and who is himself the guarantor of these universal rules. We could then deduce from this definition of the rule the dual reality of the official as expressed, for example, by Durkheim or Weber. The official, like the Kantian subject, is a dual being: he is the rule insofar as he is a product of the rule and guarantor of the rule, and, in a different perspective, he is an individual who can at any time exploit the rule in order to transgress the rule. I quote Durkheim:[25]

> Every official has a dual personality. He is an agent of public authority to some degree or other; but at the same time he is a private man, a citizen like any other. His function does not fill his life; he has the right and the duty to be interested not only in his service, but also in the affairs of his country and in human affairs, and to take part in them. If he could live these two personalities successively in such a way than neither interfered with the other, there would be no problem. In his service, he is answerable to special rules that govern his service and he simply has to conform to them. In his life as a man, he should be answerable only to his conscience and public morality. Unfortunately, this radical dissociation is impossible. It is sometimes difficult for the official in the exercise of his function to forget his conscience as a man and it is often impossible for the man, even outside his function, to divest himself entirely of his nature as an official. It follows him even into his private life. That is what causes the problem; this is the cause of so many cases of conscience difficult to resolve . . . The personality and authority that the official obtains from his function should serve that function alone.

It is sufficient to compare this text with the one I quoted on the subject of suicide[26] to see that the ambiguity of discipline that I noted depends not on discipline itself, but on the fact that those who are supposed to serve this discipline can make use of it to reintroduce the pathological self in place of the formal self required by obedience to discipline. What Weber's discipline produces and demands is a Kantian self that acts as a transcendental subject and prostrates itself in the mud because it has been constituted in such a way as to obey categorical imperatives categorically. That said, the pathological self uses all sorts of ruses in order to reappear. We could, for example, analyse the strategies used by agents negotiating with an official, trying to awaken the noncategorical self in him: 'But I was running late, you see, I had to jump the lights . . .'. Saying that, we appeal to the policeman's non-formal side, who replies: 'Rules are rules' – meaning, 'I am an X and, whatever you do, I have no passion or feeling, I execute the rule that I incarnate.' The same social agent who can identify with the rule can also smuggle himself surreptitiously into the rule, in his uniform, to make use of it to serve and exercise his pathological impulses. This ambiguity of social practices founded on rules is inherent in the very status of the official and the very status of all practices of a formal nature.

What Durkheim says of the ambiguity of the official, Weber says too, but in more optimistic fashion, insisting on the fact that the bureaucratic type of rationalization tends to produce a separation of the person from their function. This separation is particularly evident in the separation of the place of residence from the place of work, which Weber sees as an important characteristic of the capitalist process of rationalization.[27] A traditional small shopkeeper may mix the family funds with the business takings in the same till (during my interviews, I came across an Algerian shopkeeper who said to his son: 'Here, take 100 francs and go and buy something for yourself'), confusing the domestic economy with the business economy, whereas the modern type of business separates the place of residence completely from the place of work, the domestic self from the rational self. Durkheim rightly reminds us that this dissociation, evidence of which Weber sees in the very structure of the living space, is never completely realized; social agents are never the X that rationalization requires.

An ethnocentrism of the universal

We see this most clearly when the competence of experts that I am trying to analyse today is at work. I would like to draw your attention to an analysis by Aaron Cicourel of the practical usage of one form of competence – medical competence.[28] In a series of studies, Cicourel has analysed conversations between patients, doctors, interns and consultants, to try to understand how the medical version of competence functions. He shows, for example, that when he questions a patient, an intern mobilizes a codified body knowledge[29] of the type that I described last time: we see a confrontation between the practical competence of the patient, which is constructed from practical models, and a specialist competence constructed around explicit, rationally composed, published models that obey a rational coherence of a scientific nature. The confrontation of these two forms of competence generates some major misunderstandings, which escape the holder of the dominant, rational competence, because he does not have the key to people's practical experience of his own code. (We find the same kind of analysis in Goffman's *Asylums*: one of the strengths of psychiatrists in the mental asylum is to have a powerful language on their side, the psychiatric, scientific discourse, which is a form of institutional power; the institution is not merely the straitjacket, the bars, the walls, the guards and their physical force, it is also the invisible force of the language of the expert.)

In the case of the relation between the patient and the doctor, two languages confront each other – I hope that I can manage to explain this notion of the force of the form. Behind the appearance of a face-to-face conversation between two people, there is a face-to-face confrontation of two forms of competence. The patient has a competence of the kind that people have in oral societies. It is at once linguistic, social and medical. It is composed of strategies that have been rough-hewn to be appreciated by the doctor, make a good impression and provide the right answers to his questions. The doctor asks where it hurts, and the patient does his best to reply, pointing at the spot ('Here'); the doctor asks: 'Does it hurt more in the morning or the evening?' The patient feels the spot and says: 'It's more when I wake up.' 'Then it's an inflammation.' The patient translates: 'Yes, it swells up, it goes red.' The patient has two languages to offer. He offers his body, which has a voice of its own – this is lucky, since the body can be examined – he offers his body as a language that can more or less express his disease. He also responds to the expert's questions with complementary verbal expressions, things that can't be seen (expressing his pain, for instance; 'Does it hurt in the joints?' . . . 'Mainly'). The doctor for his part has elaborated a competence that draws on published texts: in the case of arthritis, for instance, there is a list of visible symptoms of differing frequency, established by statistical studies. His is an expert competence. You might think of a barrister, an insurance broker or a jurist who must use a series of questions to obtain all the information indispensable for the application of their competence; the value of their competence is dependent on their ability to ask the questions that adequately elucidate the points relevant to the application of that competence.

The expert is empowered by his competence and is not aware of it. The competence of the expert, then, exercises a form of ethnocentrism, which is an ethnocentrism of the universal. In a way, the competence of the expert is limited only by the fact that it does not recognize its own limits: any expert competence imagines itself to be universal and tends to universalize itself unconsciously, which does then bring it up against its limits. As Cicourel shows, the patient often finds answers rooted in his own competence, which the expert is not competent to judge. The expert has his own rational, scientific competence, often established at the expense of people's naive, native confidence, but in universalizing this competence he uses his own code to interpret messages produced by another code, and without realizing it he engages in a process of retranslation: he translates as 'inflammation' what has been expressed as 'goes red', whereas 'goes red' might have indicated something else. One of the objects of Cicourel's research is to provide some assistance to doctors to help them make more accurate diagnoses, and he shows that in many cases mistakes in diagnosis are due to the fact that the experts don't share the framework within which the proposition has been formulated, and they interpret it with a different code; they don't even realize that there is this gap between the codes.

Because they are formal and rational, the expert competences of a rational, bureaucratic type that underpin our societies are supported by solidarity with the arguments of everyone else's rational competences. This is something important that I haven't yet mentioned: all experts are objectively mutually complicit. A rational law will, I venture to say, immediately find an echo in rational mathematics. All these little islands of rationalization will support each other objectively, and we can pass easily from one to the other. Rational music as defined by Weber,[30] the mathematized music that has been rampant since the twelfth century, has become complicit with rational law, formal bureaucracy and form-filling. The forms to be completed for an administrative service become complicit with the doctor's rational questionnaire. This kind of ethnocentrism of the dominant rationalism encourages blindness to local rationalities of other types, which means that we need a kind of ethnology of the patient, along the lines practised by Cicourel, a sort of ethnology of the client for legal aid, of the good citizen who fills in his social security forms. We need an ethnology of the simple agent engaged in his basic practice, in order to discover the gap between a strong and a weak discourse, between the *vis formae* and the weakness of the mere agents whose actions follow their passions, interests and dispositions, using all the means at their disposal, drawing on medical notions inherited from their grandmother, popular wisdom and a more or less fantastical symptomatology.

Thus I believe that analysing these formal languages helps us better to understand where the strength of modern organizations might lie. Following the logic of the questions that I raised at the outset, people often launch into apocalyptic diatribes on bureaucracy as the modern Leviathan, but without grasping the true practical root of this ordinary violence. What I have been trying to do in these analyses is locate the principle of this seemingly insubstantial violence in something specific: filling in a form. You can of course remark that there are people who can neither read nor write, but these are extreme cases: you have all seen an immigrant at the post-office counter wanting to send a money order to their family. But I think that what is important is that form of violence of the universal that I would see as the worst kind of violence because there is no way of opposing it. A universal violence is by definition noncoercive because it appeals to the universalist inclinations of the person suffering it, and bureaucratic formalities, in common with mathematical formulae, claim to be valid for all and require every agent to behave as a universal subject. You cannot ask more of a subject, this is what all universal moral systems have always required, and it is the height of humanism. This is why, to really account for the very special phenomenon that we call the process of rationalization, we must try to get to grips with this kind of paradox of the cultural arbitrary that operates under the name of rationality. I think the characteristic of the modern cultural arbitrary, of rationalized societies, is for its form of arbitrary violence to operate behind the mask of rational universality.

Second session (answers to questions and seminar): the problem of historical parallels

I would like to use the start of my second session to reply to a number of questions. One of you asks about the problem of the law in extreme cases, because I said, perhaps rather rashly, when speaking of Nazism, that the existence of a discriminatory law seemed retrospectively to be a lesser evil compared to a situation of total arbitrariness.[31]

On the other hand, I am embarrassed by some of the questions that you have put to me [*Bourdieu reads out two of them, but so rapidly that we are unable to reconstitute them*]. It is not because they seem any less relevant to me, but my work attempts to exclude them, or at least to transform them and create a situation where they cannot be raised, or at any rate formulated in their usual terms. As I have often said during the course of the year, one of the difficulties of what I am saying in my lectures is that these questions are often similar to what people have been saying for many years. They are worth raising, but the way in which I am expressing things renews these problems so completely that we ought not to be able to think of them in the terms of the questions put to me by the public. I think, for instance, that what I said this morning can be related to a number of questions of a school essay type. Our reflection should address very obvious things ('What is a bureaucratic formality? 'What is a rational action?', etc.), but in such a way as to avoid writing exam essays on them ... Sometimes we succeed, sometimes we don't. Sometimes, after speaking, we feel that we have not really succeeded, that we have only managed to make things a little more complicated without properly managing to change the way we think about things.

To return to the example of this notion of competence that we use without a second thought (I am not entirely satisfied with what I have told you about it) – the 'competence of a judge', the 'competence of a tribunal', the 'competence of an expert': 'Is this psychologist competent to declare that my child is an idiot?', 'Is this teacher competent?', 'Are the examiners who refused to award this eminent doctoral thesis a grade of distinction competent?' Although these are questions that we ask every day, they are extremely difficult because the question itself always implies the suspicion that a competence of any kind whatever is rooted in some source of power, authority or violence, or some trial of strength, etc. This is true even of the relation between doctor and patient. One of the things noted by Cicourel that I forgot to mention is that one source of misunderstanding in their relation is time. The doctor has very little time, and one of the conditions for applying the scientific grid to formulate a diagnosis in full knowledge of the facts is to be able to take one's time. Since the intern is very often in quite a hurry, he uses questions that contain their answer, which means that the patient, with his lesser competence, has no defence against the interrogation: 'Are you in pain?' 'Yes, yes.' 'Is it mostly in the morning?' In this way the diagnosis is implied by the way the questions are put. In other words, the most ordinary exercise of an expert's competence – like all power based on information capital – exerts a form of violence that is not always and not only that of reason. That said – and my own interrogation was leading to the same conclusion – this violence is itself not without its own effects of reason . . . If medical power were only an arbitrary power, it would not operate as a medical power. Its specificity, like that of legal power, lies in the kind of ambiguity that defines the specific form of its violence. If you bear this kind of difficulty in mind . . . what I hope in fact is at least to have sown in your minds the idea that this difficulty is a real difficulty, and not simply a difficulty in my mind.

The coherence of the lectures

I have however received a different question, on the notion of the field. Rather than reply, I shall tell you briefly about one of the difficulties that I have encountered in this course of lectures. As you can see, my audience is disparate and discontinuous, and hardly formal in the sense that I am using the word today: you are never the same people, and never in the same place . . . It is nothing like the universe of discipline that I have been describing. Given my intention to give my teaching continuity over time and create a cumulative effect, this poses considerable problems and is a source of some personal pain for me [. . .]

I shall now very quickly recapitulate the logic of my argument. The lecture that I delivered just now was the last in a series of lectures that has been spread over three years. During the first year,[32] I focused on the notion of habitus, with the intention of rejecting the ordinary representation of the social subject as an individual, conscious and organized subject, the self-motivating source, as it were, of his own behaviour. I tried to show that the subject of the majority of our actions is a system of dispositions that may or may not be explicit. This first series of lectures was then complemented by an analysis of the notion of field and the general principles of this mode of existence of the social.[33] I tried to describe the fundamental laws of the functioning of fields, to explain why we need to think in terms of fields. What social relations are involved in making society function in terms of fields? What is the advantage of using the notion of the field? I started by illustrating the logic of fields through the example of the artistic field in the nineteenth century. I showed the existence of a link between field and capital, and showed that each social space of the 'field' type corresponds to a different form of capital. Literary capital, for instance, corresponds to what you need in order to play and win at the very special game of literature.

Having defined the notion of field through its relation to the notion of capital, I have tried this year to describe the relations between the two fundamental forms of capital which I then define in more specific terms: economic capital and cultural capital, which I renamed 'information capital'. Today I have been trying to synthesize the most general properties of the cultural or information types of capital in their most rationalized and objectified form, hoping through this description of the notion of information capital to understand and identify a certain number of the general properties of some autonomous fields: the literary, intellectual, political and scientific fields, for instance. What I have attempted to identify are the properties common to all these specialized fields as places where bodies of experts endowed with an appropriate specific competence vie for the monopoly of the imposition of a definition of legitimate competence. I have tried to describe the general properties of the expertise that fields as different as the scientific, the legal or the literary, for instance, have in common with each other, it being understood that this formal and formalized competence, invested in more or less codified rules, becomes specific and takes on very diverse forms in each case: the mathematician, whom I have compared to the jurist for his possession of a formal expertise, will become totally distinct as soon as I spell out the specific laws of functioning of his particular competence.

I am embarrassed to return to the notion of field; I would rather refer you to the previous lectures. That said, I would like to repeat something that I said at the start, since someone has asked me what would be the closest synonym to field: I would willingly answer with the word milieu,[34] in Newton's sense of the term, but we can't do that, because the word has been used so much that its original sense has been lost. But the word milieu, as I explained with reference to an article by Canguilhem,[35] when it passed from Newton's theories of physics to the social sciences, did for a time keep its original sense of a field of gravitation, etc. It only gradually weakened and took on its vaguer, looser meaning.

To conclude, I would like to take the opportunity of placing what I have been saying in a wider context. Having spent this year describing the main types of capital and emphasizing the process of institutionalization that exerts its general effects in every field, I shall return in the coming years to deal with the relations between field and habitus (which in fact I never fully elaborated). I would first like to describe what belonging to a field entails, and what is the founding relation of social agents to the field that they are immersed in. What does it mean to be in a social space, to inhabit it and be immersed in it? What do involvement and investment in a game, which I call the *illusio*, mean? What is a social investment? And then, having in the first instance described fields as fields of forces within which agents obey forces of attraction and repulsion, which would ultimately reduce them to the status of physical, mechanical beings, I would like to show how social fields are distinguished from astronomical and physical fields, insofar as agents are not simply bodies: even when they obey *perinde ac cadaver* [in the manner of a corpse], as a single man, in mechanical fashion, they remain social agents who can rebel, who can think on what they are doing . . . (Let us say that they can't help thinking: even soldiers who leap into the water can't help thinking.) To give an adequate account of the social world, we must think of agents as thinking, even when they are placed in situations inimical to thinking.

Otherwise, the discipline would not have to be so strict, violent and extreme, so anomic. (This is why it was so useful to compare Durkheim and Weber – as I did during the first session . . . Nobody had done this before, there was something truly original there, but I was tired and didn't manage to illustrate it properly. If you can face up to re-reading the two texts that I gave you, you will see that the argument speaks for itself.) This absolute discipline that reigns over social agents, reducing them to mechanisms, does not prevent them from thinking about the machinery involved, except in the last extremities . . . I am very interested in extreme cases because they have the merit of challenging the imagination and showing up *a contrario* what is implicit in ordinary situations. The soldier who obeys like a robot reminds us that, in everyday life, things do not always work out like that and also reminds us at what cost we manage to get people to obey like robots. Even the coercive violence that has to be applied in order to get people to obey like robots reminds us that normally they do not respond as robots but as a habitus that improvises and invents. In fact, we could see the two poles as the tennis player who improvises a drop shot and the soldier who leaps into the water simply because he is told to leap into the water. The test case of a single, extreme, definitive act is simply one particular case of the universe of possible situations.

That being understood, I would like to show – in my next series of lectures – that social fields are not fields of forces where the agents are manipulated like iron filings in a magnetic field, but are also fields of struggles to transform the balance of power: within a field the nature of the field itself is always called into question, and agents do not think of the field in some haphazard fashion, they think of it in ways dependent on the position that they hold in the field. Thinking of the field then is shaped and limited by the field. That is what I wanted to show in approaching what I see as one of the most difficult problems in sociology, which is power – the field of power and struggles for power, that is, struggles within each field of expertise to define the monopoly of legitimate competence, and struggles between the fields, to define so to speak the competence of competences, that is, to decide who is authorized to wield power. One paradox of the social world (which I mentioned when discussing Kafka)[36] is that power is constantly at issue in the social world, as is, more precisely, what authorizes the exercise of power and what constitutes power, that is, what you need in order to be able to exercise power legitimately. This is what I am working towards . . .

(What you have been listening to worries me somewhat, because although I try to give a kind of unity to each session, the coherence of each lecture depends on its relation to the whole series . . . [. . .])

Historical parallels ('that reminds me of . . .')

Since I have little time left, I would like to set a problem rather in the
logic of a card game than set out a genuine reflection. It is the problem
of historical parallels. It is a very real problem. Journalists in particular
often use the logic of the precedent, 'X's visit there is a new Yalta'. An
event is considered by analogy with a previous event. This is most often
a manner of explaining *obscurum per obscurius*. This style of argument
is also very frequent in our perception of works of art. For instance,
Proust repeats a joke that must have done the rounds of the fin-de-
siècle salons, calling Monet a 'Watteau à vapeur . . .'[37] These analogies
amused lots of people. They are relatively amusing in everyday life. This
is how literary or artistic judgement proceeds: you deliver a confused,
syncretic judgement on a work (by Proust or Mondrian, for example),
referring it to another equally obscure, syncretically perceived reality.
In this way an artistic judgement places in relation with each other two
terms that are themselves equally ill-defined. Our everyday judgement
of other people proceeds in the same fashion: 'He reminds me of . . .',
'He is just like Françoise.'[38] In other words, we try to articulate the
characteristics of a singular reality, which is defined for instance by a
singular abundance of meaning, polysemy, inexhaustability . . . Just
like the singular event, individual people in everyday life are characterized by all these properties: they are inexhaustible, they can be articulated in dozens of different ways, we don't know how to describe them.
If we want to describe someone to a person who has not seen him, we
can say, 'He reminds me of Delon, but . . .'. This would leave us with
nothing but a kind of recitation evoking still more individuals, and I
could give you a whole series of analogies.

Faced with a painting, a person or a historical event, then, we tend
to think along the lines of this logic of precedent and incantation. 'May
1968' for instance was an event that caused much discussion. How can
we say something intelligent about it? Intellectuals facing up to May
1968 were all put to the test: the event concerned them above all, and
it was crucial to have an argument, an intelligent argument that was
unique and singular, but with at least some foundation in objectivity.
To have something to say when faced with this kind of situation, there
are all kinds of strategy, and in particular the strategy of the precedent:
we can liken May 1968 to the 1848 Revolution or – as has often been
done – to the Dreyfus case. These analogies between phenomena are
in fact not without foundation, they have an objective basis. But what
are they worth? What does this comparison of one event with another
amount to? I think that the question is worth asking. Once again, I

am trying to debanalize a question that you have heard many times on 'the difference between historical fact and sociological fact', the historical fact that is never repeated twice – Seignobos, Durkheim, etc.[39] How can we account for the singularity of a historical event without betraying science, since 'there is no science that is not general', in Aristotle's words?[40] Can a historical juncture be the object of a scientific argument, or can it only be the object of a sort of designation in the way that singular individuals are? The problem that I am putting here is that of the science of the individual: is it possible to formulate a scientific argument concerning an individual event? Is there a science of historical junctures and conjunctural events? In other words, can I make a general scientific analysis of the crisis of May 1968, and, if I can, will this general science of the crisis of May 1968 not encompass a general theory of crises and make the singularity of May 1968 disappear? And then, if I manage to make a general theory of May 1968, can I subsume other crises under this theory?

Having put the question in this way, we may now undertake an analysis. Where May 1968 is concerned, for instance,[41] let us accept the analogy between '68 and the Dreyfus case: one thing that immediately provides a basis for the comparison is the fact that, in both cases, the movement started in the intellectual and academic field and then spread outwards from there. All the commentators have noted this. If you read Proust (*The Guermantes Way*), where the Dreyfus case is constantly mentioned, you will see that the quarrel over Dreyfus goes from the salon to the kitchen: one day, the narrator comes home to discover the Guermantes's manservant in discussion with his own, and finds that each has espoused the cause of his masters.[42] This is an insight of Proust's, but Charle's research into the Dreyfus case[43] shows quite clearly how the cleavages created by the Dreyfus case went on to have an impact outside: the political field at the moment the Dreyfus case broke was relatively amorphous and undifferentiated, the oppositions were weak and it was the intellectual cleavages of the Dreyfus case that affected it as they spread. This is a characteristic common to both situations.

Another characteristic is the fact that the division into camps within the intellectual and academic field was organized more or less in the same way. Charle shows that, during the Dreyfus case, there were on one side the avant-garde, with the Symbolists, and, on the other side, people like the Academicians, just as, in the literary field there were, on one side, the sociologists, the historians and some philosophers, and, on the other side, defenders of the most traditional kind of literary history. So the cleavage opposed modernists to traditionalists. Then in 1968 we find something of the same order. The great dispute between Barthes and Picard,[44] which we all remember, was a sort of dress rehearsal for May 1968. It allows us to study *in vitro* what came to pass in '68. We have, on one side, the social sciences, ethnology, sociology and the like; on the other, the literary tradition. There are many analogies.

Another important common characteristic: this general property of critical situations, which lies in the fact that a specifically political principle of division, relatively arbitrary from the point of view of everyday life, becomes the source of every division. There again, if you read Proust, it is amazing: you see that there is no escape from the division between Dreyfusards and anti-Dreyfusards, revisionists and anti-revisionists ... For instance, at one moment we learn that in his barracks (in barracks, the issue is particularly acute because the army is under fire), Saint-Loup refused to discuss the affair, because at his table everyone was an anti-Dreyfusard and he was the only Dreyfusard.[45] In these situations, everyone is situated (and summoned to situate themselves) in relation to an issue. There is no possible alternative: everything turns on a central issue, and any other opposition derives from this; from your attitude to May '68 we can deduce your standpoint on sexual relations, seminars, formal lectures, guest speakers, and so on. All the principles of division can be deduced from the one principle of division established as principle. It is an interesting property common to the two situations.

Here we can see the outline of a theory of the invariants of a crisis. In both cases, a certain number of characteristics would be candidates for recruitment into what we might call the 'civil war effect': on the basis of one principle of division among various possibilities (Dreyfus is innocent or not; the May movement is good or bad ...), we can construct all the possible divisions among men. In normal times, an infinity of principles of division is available. If an ordinary social life is possible, it is because we do not align all our principles of division one with another and we are not subject to a demand for total coherence: what we think about the formal lecture does not have to be compatible with what we think about sexual freedom, and what we think about Afghanistan does not have to perfectly match what we think about relations with our family. One property of certain situations of crisis is the demand for total coherence. Knowing that X is revisionist [in the Dreyfus case], you can deduce what he thinks of the Jews, the army, the lay question, the Republic, *et al.*

We see the general properties, then, but is this sufficient reason to superimpose the two crises? Can we say that Barthes is to Picard as Proust is to Brunetière,[46] for example? If we take things further, it gets more complicated. In our everyday polemics, we might call someone a 'new Brunetière, or 'a new Émile Faguet'[47] . . . Essay questions work like this too, and this is significant. If you are asked to write an essay on a passage from Proust that deals with the 'case', you are going to follow the logic of precedent. But you are not very sure who Brunetière is. If you are highly cultivated, you know that he was against Lanson: it was left (Lanson) against right (Brunetière). You can tell that Lanson was scientific and Brunetière in favour of creativity, for instance. But if you have to decide for or against, what would you base your opinion on? On the basis of the position you inhabit in a homologous space, because in your current space you will be to Brunetière what Lanson was to Brunetière. This means that you will experience the passage through a misreading, a misreading grounded in homology, which is identity in difference.

There is no harm in saying that Barthes is to Picard what Lanson was to Brunetière . . . But what is more disturbing is that it is Picard who is Lanson's heir. What happened is that the two homologous fields became separated by a whole historical process that has made Picard the heir to Lanson. So we could say that 'Picard is Lanson plus Agathon',[48] that is, a scientific, progressive Third Republicanism that has finally internalized the criticism it faced from the people represented by Agathon. But are things so simple? We can see two different states of the same field whose effects of homology will lead us to understand what is most singular in the conflict, but our understanding will be based on some formidable misunderstandings. I shall not elaborate, because it would take much too long, but it is our historical culture that gives this kind of immediate understanding, our 'historical culture' considered in the ordinary sense of the term, which is: 'I know Lanson existed, I know that he was the only Dreyfusard among the literary academics, I know that Lanson opposed the Sorbonne, I know that Lanson wrote about literature, that he founded the "L'Homme et l'oeuvre" ["The Man and his Works"] series, I can even write essays on Lanson, who invented the modern dissertation.' This historical culture can at once permit a semi-historical understanding and yet prevent a true historical understanding of what Lanson was and what the difference is between 'being Lanson' and 'being Barthes'.

The false eternity of academic debates

I have taken a risk in launching into this topic, but if you want to look deeper into what I have been sketching out today (to confuse your minds one last time), you can read the book by Compagnon that I mentioned last time.[49] There you will find all the elements needed to raise the question that I have raised, and at the same time find a perfect illustration of the ambiguity that I am in the process of explaining. Compagnon's book is very interesting for the sociologist. I think that it typifies the sort of interplay between history and historical culture that is so common today. The social history of the social sciences has made progress and it is becoming difficult to write social history and social science without having at least a modicum of historical culture and without introducing into our relation with our own science a minimal acquaintance with science. At the same time, I think that we use social history not to objectify the social history of our own science, but to create a historical effect, that is, the appearance of being cultivated.

Compagnon's book is typical in that he touches on what should be done, while remaining infinitely distant: he is certainly the person who comes closest to what should be said, and at the same time remains the farthest away. The problem is that if you fully accomplish what should be done, you risk falling into outer darkness, that is, leaving the literary field, becoming unfashionable and losing the benefits of being in the literary universe. You take the risk of objectifying literature and objectifying yourself as having a subjective benefit in being objectively literary, and so on.

What is most interesting is that the book starts with a sort of text that displays literary pretensions, with verbless, postmodern phrases on the status of Barthes, and the style is crucial. This kind of literary game, playing on precedent, amounts to saying: 'You think that Barthes is a meteorite fallen to Earth from some obscure disaster[50] but there are historical precedents: look at Lanson. It is both new and not new . . . on new verse, and so on.' Thus there is a sort of literary overture. Then in the first part of the book we move on to history: 'There have been these debates over literature, what were the issues? Why the reform, why this role of literature? Why the German model? Why were some people internationalists and others nationalists? Why were the modernists internationalists, as they are today?' This is another homology: the opposition of national to international is superimposed on the opposition between formal lecture and seminar. There are invariant oppositions. Then, in the second part of the book, we return to two eminently literary readings of Taine and Proust. Having apparently historicized, he de-historicizes once more, and in particular with the re-reading of Proust, where he reconstructs in terms of a transhistorical literary opposition the opposition between Proust and Taine or Proust and Lanson, and Barthes returns.

If while reading this book you bear in mind the network of problems that I have tried to weave around it, you will see that one of the basic questions is: what is reading?[51] What is re-reading? What is reading historically? What is the role of historical culture in reading? Today everyone knows that reading is reading through grids that are themselves a product of history. Everyone knows that you need to trace the history of these grids, which are a product of history, and seek out their source not in history in general but in the history closest to home, that of the literary field itself. All very well, but in that case how can I read writers like the critics, who claim to read and provide grids for reading without fully historicizing the grids for reading that they produce and reproduce. The effect of recurrence is very interesting: if people write dissertations on topics such as 'individual and society' that are eternally the same and eternally different, it is because homologies exist. Although we may never tread twice in the same historical stream,[52] if the Dreyfus case and May '68 had nothing in common, it would not work. For it to work, there has to be history, and this history has to have invariants.

This form of semi-historicized, a-historical reading has the effect of producing the kind of false eternity of academic life. In fact, what I wanted to reveal today is that sort of false eternity of the dialogues in the academic afterlife: how is it that we can still stage dialogues between Taine and Barthes, Renan and Foucault, Bourdieu and Durkheim? If through some feat of jiggery-pokery we are able to stage this kind of dialogue, it is because we do not ask too many formal questions. Here I am pleading in favour of the competence of the expert: I think that one way of making real progress in the scientific and intellectual debate would be to axiomatize the intellectual game as much as possible, that is, to objectify as fully as possible whatever remains in an implicit state and precisely what is linked to nonanalysed historical elements. Intellectual life, especially in areas like literary history, doggedly inhabits that space of the universe where everyone obeys the illusion of the *déjà-vu* and the *jamais-vu*: people are constantly claiming to have made an original discovery when what they have dug up is in fact a museum piece. But even discovering that these are museum pieces is still a way of not thinking deeply enough about them, by historicizing too much, or not enough.

This should give the sense of what I am often trying to do when I revive old debates: I think one of the most powerful functions of historical culture, if it were really used, would be precisely to destroy this kind of complicity in the half-baked analysis that constitutes the debates claiming to be 'eternal': no true debates are not historical.

Which does not mean that there are not invariants transcending the historical debates, with laws transhistorical to even the most historical events in their absolute singularity, such as that of the crisis.

Situating the Third and Later Volumes of General Sociology in the work of Pierre Bourdieu

Julien Duval

This third volume continues the publication of the Course in General Sociology that Pierre Bourdieu delivered during his first five years of teaching at the Collège de France from 1982, at the rate of eight to ten two-hour sessions each year. It contains the lectures given during the academic year 1983–84. Two further volumes will cover the years 1984–85 and 1985–86.

In the words that he used during his very first lecture, the Course in General Sociology presents the 'fundamental lineaments' of his work.[1] The first year of lectures following his inaugural lecture of April 1982 was relatively short. It concentrates on the question of the constitution and classification of groups and 'social classes'. It functions as a kind of prologue to the whole course. During the second year, Bourdieu explained how he envisaged the object of sociological study and developed his thinking on knowledge and practice, then he started to present the major concepts of his sociological approach, expounding their underlying theoretical assumptions as well as the function that he assigned them in the general economy of his theory. He devoted a whole series of lectures to the concept of the habitus, taking account of the fact that the subject in sociology, unlike in philosophy, is a social-ized subject, that is, one invested by social forces, and he showed how that concept enabled us to think about social action without falling into the alternative of mechanism and purposiveness. He then made a first, 'physicalist' approach to the concept of the field, presenting it as a field of forces, and leaving to a later stage in the lectures the analysis of the dynamics of the field seen as a field of struggles aiming to modify the field of forces.

The third year, which forms the present volume, focuses on the concept of capital. Bourdieu reminds us of the link between this concept and the concept of the field, and then goes on to elaborate the different forms of capital (which are linked to the variety of the fields), as well as the different states of cultural capital. He pays particular attention to the codification and objectification of capital: this is designated as one of the sources of the coherence of the social world and an important source of the divergence between pre-capitalist societies and our differentiated societies. The fourth year (to be published in due course) tackles the concept of field in terms of a field of struggles, insofar as it is the object of perceptions by the social agents, these perceptions being generated by the relation between the habitus and capital. In this fourth year, Bourdieu develops the project of a sociology of social perception, conceived as an inseparably cognitive and political act in the struggle between social agents to define the *nomos*, the legitimate vision of the social world. The fifth year (also due to be published later) continues to develop these analyses, but, as he prepares to conclude the course of lectures, Bourdieu also seeks to link the two aspects of the concept of the field (the field as field of forces and as field of struggles) through the simultaneous mobilization of three major concepts. The symbolic struggles aim to transform the field of forces. To understand them, we need to introduce the notion of symbolic power and symbolic capital, or the symbolic effect of capital, which is constituted in the relation between habitus and field, a relation of *illusio*. The fifth year finishes with questions arising from the position of the social sciences in the symbolic struggles that aim to impose a certain representation of the social world, and with the idea that the social sciences should combine both structuralist and constructivist perspectives in order to study the social world, which is both a field of forces and a field of struggles that aim to transform it but are also conditioned by it.

Coherence over five years

This five-year-long course of lectures enabled Bourdieu to look back over the theoretical system that he had been progressively constructing. Shortly before the start of this course, and before his election to the Collège de France, he had published two sizable volumes of synthesis, *Distinction* (1979), comprising all his research on culture and social class in France, and *The Logic of Practice* (1980), comprising his investigations in Algeria and the theory of action that he derived from them. The Course in General Sociology covers both research enterprises at once, and aims to elaborate a social theory as valid for pre-capitalist as for highly differentiated societies. Rejecting the usual division between anthropology and sociology, it not only displays the coherence of these various research projects, but also promotes the unity of the social sciences. In 1984–85 and 1985–86, in particular, Bourdieu is a sociologist enquiring into the process that leads from pre-capitalist to differentiated societies, while drawing attention to their continuity. More than once, he points out how pre-capitalist societies act as analysts of our societies: they 'zoom in' on relations between the sexes, they show 'close up' the symbolic struggles that are less perceptible but still at work in differentiated societies (25 April 1985); and he emphasizes, for example, what his analyses on social class owe to his work on kinship relations in Algeria (2 May 1985).

The work of synthesis is also applied to the concepts. One of the objectives of his teaching, in fact, is to 'show the articulation between the fundamental concepts and the structure of the relations that link those concepts'.[2] For the sake of clarity, part of the course during the second and third years consists in presenting the three key concepts in succession, with some lessons using the first drafts of the generally rather short theoretical summaries that Bourdieu published in his review *Actes de la recherche en sciences sociales* at the end of the 1970s and the beginning of the 1980s, on the species and states of capital, on the properties of fields, on the effects of the corps, etc. But even in this stage of the course, the concepts remained linked to each other. The concept of capital, for instance, is first introduced in relation to the concept of field and the habitus reappears when the notion of 'information capital'[3] is introduced. The question of codification and institutionalization, tackled during the third and fifth years respectively, as was the question of the field of power, returns to the relations between capital and the field; and the problem of perception, central to the fourth year, involves the relation between the habitus and the field directly. Countering the temptation of selective borrowing from Bourdieu's sociology, this Course in General Sociology reminds us how far the concepts of habitus, capital and field have been thought through as ' "systemic" concepts because their use presupposes permanent reference to the complete system of their interrelationships'.[4]

If Bourdieu takes pains to recapitulate his arguments (more and more often as his teaching progresses), it is because he fears that his concern to 'produce a discourse whose coherence would emerge over a period of years' might escape his audience (1 March 1984). In addition to the spacing out of the lectures over a period of years, there is the fact that Bourdieu is addressing an 'intermittent public' (*ibid.*) that changes over the years. His style of teaching, moreover, leaves room, within a pre-established canvas, for potential and sometimes quite substantial improvisations and 'digressions'. Finally, the exposition cannot follow a perfectly linear course: its nature is to circulate in a sort of theoretical space that authorizes different pathways. When he starts the fourth year of his teaching, for instance, Bourdieu says that he hesitated between several possible 'pathways' (7 Match 1985).

The lectures were not intended to be published, at least not in their given form,[5] but their 'overall coherence' will perhaps be more apparent to the readers of the transcriptions than it would have been to the audience at the time. The time spent in reading the published lectures is not the same as that devoted to their preparation or that of their oral delivery. Reading acts as a kind of accelerator of the process of thinking that informs the lectures. The juxtaposition of the five volumes, for instance, will show up the loop operated very discretely in one of the last lectures of the Course in General Sociology as Bourdieu returns to the 'notorious problem of the social classes, which is absolutely central for the social sciences' (5 June 1986), that was at the heart of the first year of his teaching (1982–83). This return to the point of departure, as it might seem on first analysis, demonstrates the coherence of the whole of the course. It allows the reader to measure the distance travelled and become aware of the questions that have been investigated or that have taken on another dimension through the developments proposed in the meantime.

It may also suggest an approach to reading the lectures. The first year, in the spring of 1982, was presented as a reflection on classification and the social classes. The arguments that Bourdieu deployed there drew on insights gained from *Distinction*, but were also based just as much on the research that he was finishing at the time: in particular, his book on language, and his analyses of the process of naming or the performative power invested in words under certain social conditions; Bourdieu thus added considerable depth to his theory of the social classes.[6] The movement of the Course in General Sociology could then be understood as a manner of expanding, exploring and generalizing the thoughts on the subject of the social classes that he expounded during the first year. For the second and third years, Bourdieu explored his theoretical system, to return in the last two years to the question of the symbolic struggle over the principles of perception of the social world, whose division into classes is a sort of special case. Competition within the 'field of expertise' and the very particular power of the state in matters of nomination are generally two major aspects of the symbolic struggle in our differentiated societies, which the problem of social classes forces us to face.

Read in this way, the lectures do not come full circle. Far from returning to the point of departure in an attempt at closure, the final return to the social classes represents an opening out and a progression that are linked to a form of generalization. It is less of a loop and more of a 'spiralling'[7] movement that he achieved over five years. The image of the 'spiral', like that of the 'constant reworking' of research[8] that Bourdieu also used to describe his manner of working, is relevant not only to the structure of the course; it also applies to the numerous echoes that reverberate from one lecture to another. Because he is afraid of seeming to repeat himself, Bourdieu sometimes specifically emphasizes the fact that these are not identical 'repetitions'; 'I sometimes pass through the same point on a different trajectory' (17 April 1986); 'I have said it in a previous lecture, I am reworking this theme today in a different context' (18 April 1985); 'I have already developed the objective aspect of this argument in a lecture two years ago: I am pointing this out in case you want to make the connection' (15 May 1986). There are themes that recur (for instance, the discussion of purposiveness and mechanism and the critique of decision theory, both broached in 1982, recur in 1986), and the same examples may be used to illustrate different analyses: thus the careers of nineteenth-century regionalist authors are referred to within the literary field in which they fall (25 January 1983), but are related later to the space where they originate and terminate in order to show the contribution of these writers to a certain educational mythology (12 June 1986).

The 'improvisations' of the second sessions

The year that this volume covers corresponds to the moment when Bourdieu's teaching at the Collège de France settled into a stable pattern. From the start of his appointment in 1982, Bourdieu had been obliged to abandon the standard format of this institution, which was to deliver a one-session lecture and, at a different time and in a smaller hall, a seminar of the same duration. Researchers who worked alongside him remember how the first seminar session broke down in an atmosphere of great disorder, since the room could not hold the numbers of the public who flooded in.[9] After this experience, Bourdieu decided in 1982–83 to deliver his teaching in the form of two successive hour-long sessions with no distinction between a 'lecture' part and a 'seminar' part.

He proceeds somewhat differently in the years published in this and the following volumes. As he notes regularly in the course of the lectures, the formula of the open lecture to an anonymous and heterogeneous audience reduced to the role of listener is an ongoing problem for him: he finds this framework ill-suited to what he is trying to transmit (a 'method' rather than a body of knowledge in the literal sense),[10] and he refuses to conform to it entirely. He cannot resist the temptation to launch into partly improvised digressions, which lead him very often at the end of a lecture to regret[11] not having said everything that he had intended, and having to postpone certain developments until the following session. At regular intervals, he also continues, as he did already during the first two years, to reply to written questions submitted to him during the interval or at the end of the lecture, and which enable him to have at least some contact with his listeners.[12] But at the start of the 1983–84 year he reintroduced a distinction between the two hours of his Thursday morning sessions:[13] while the first hour, from 10.00 to 11.00 a.m., was spent on 'theoretical analysis' (1 March 1984), the second, from 11.00 a.m. to 12 noon, showed a change of subject and tone.[14]

Since he did not feel able at the Collège de France to organize a real seminar, he tries in the second hour to give an idea of what a seminar would be, showing how an object of study might be constructed and how a problem might be elaborated, and above all how his theoretical formulae and formulations could be deployed in concrete operations, which is the essence of the craft of the scientist – the art of detecting the theoretical issues to be found in the most singular or banal details of everyday life (1 March 1984). With only a few exceptions, the second sessions of the lectures published in this volume are devoted to 'work in progress' (19 May 1984), 'tentative essays, reflections on risky topics' (26 April 1984), or 'improvisations' (17 April 1986). Bourdieu 'allows himself more freedom' than in the first hour (15 May 1986), in particular to depart from a 'linear itinerary' (12 June 1986) and a 'sustained discourse, with long-term coherence' which would run the risk of being 'slightly enclosed and totalising (some would say slightly totalitarian)' (17 April 1986). As far as possible, he looks for some degree of correspondence between 'the applied studies of the second session and the theoretical analyses of the first session' (1 March 1984). Thus, in the fourth year the 'theoretical analyses' concern the perception of the social world and the second hour focuses on a social category, the painters who, with Manet, accomplish a revolution in vision and perception (23 May 1985): the lectures develop in particular the notion of the *nomos*, while the second hour draws attention to the 'institutionalization of anomie' operated by modern art.

The second hour is generally devoted to research that Bourdieu is presenting for the first time. In 1984–85 it is his research into the field of painting carried out with Marie-Claire Bourdieu. In the years immediately after these lectures, he published the first articles arising from this.[15] At the end of the 1990s he devoted two whole years of his teaching to it.[16] The lectures given in 1985 enable us to judge that this research, probably started at the beginning of the 1980s,[17] was already well under way, even if it still lacked, for instance, the analysis of Manet's works that he was to offer in the 1990s. In 1985, Bourdieu was working in parallel on *The Rules of Art*, which appeared in 1992, and the object of this research seems to lie above all in 'a series of analyses of the relations between the literary field and the artistic field' (7 March 1985): the study of the relations between the painters and the writers takes a central place in the exposition, and some developments refer quite directly to the analyses of the 'invention of the life of the artist' undertaken in the framework of the research on Flaubert and the literary field.[18] At this time Bourdieu was very concerned to show that the process of autonomization affects the whole range of the artistic field and cannot therefore be entirely grasped in research focusing on a single sector (such as painting, literature, or music).

In 1983–84 and 1985–86, the second hour concentrates on more limited research projects, which usually last for no more than two or three successive sessions. The first piece of research presented, which Bourdieu says he has 'found while rummaging through [his] notes' (1 March 1984), is his analysis of a 'hit parade' published by the magazine *Lire* in April 1981. He may well have used the lecture to draft the text that appeared as an article a few months later as an appendix to *Homo Academicus* in November 1984.[19] Four years later, he would link it up with the analysis of a sort of 'Chinese game' that he had given a few years earlier.[20] He speaks of a sort of ' "masterpiece", such as those made by a medieval craftsman' and presents his approach in these terms:[21] 'I'd say: There's the material, in front of you; it's available to everyone. Why is it badly constructed? What does this questionnaire mean? What would you do with it? . . . You have to question the sample: who are the judges whose judgements led to this list of best authors? How were they chosen? Isn't the set of authors implied in the list of judges chosen and in their categories of perception? . . . And so an idiotic survey, of no scientific interest, can yield an exciting object of scientific study if, instead of reading the results at face value, we read the unconscious categories of thought projected into the results obtained . . . you're dealing with already published results that needed to be re-constructed.'[22] At all events, this research into the ranking list is more than just an exercise in method or style. Bourdieu also uses it as an opportunity to reflect on the properties of the intellectual field, its weak institutionalization and its vulnerability in the face of a journalistically procured 'social action'. The choice of a limited and easily accessible but also very well chosen and intensively exploited object of study may have something to do with the fact that Bourdieu must certainly have reflected during these years on how he could best continue to engage in empirical research. For his election to the Collège de France brought with it new obligations and necessarily reduced his presence in his research centre,[23] as well as at the École des hautes études en sciences sociales – an institution that, unlike the Collège de France, allows its teachers to direct doctoral theses.[24] His availability for the kind of research that he had been practising since the 1960s was no doubt restricted, even if the enquiry into private housing that he had started during the first half of the 1980s (2 May 1985), like *The Weight of the World*, show that he managed to launch important new collective research projects based on first-hand material.

Among other research projects presented in the 'second sessions', several are distinguished by the fact that they are based on literary texts, an approach that Bourdieu had previously practised only in his analysis of *Sentimental Education*.[25] He studies Franz Kafka's *The Trial* (22 and 29 March 1984), Virginia Woolf's *To the Lighthouse* (15 and 22 May 1986) and, rather more briefly, Samuel Beckett's *Waiting for Godot* (19 April 1984) and Kafka's *Metamorphosis* (22 May 1986).[26] He appears to show more interest in literary material and analysis than previously. The analysis of *The Trial* led to a paper read after the end of the academic year 1983–84 in a multidisciplinary colloquium organized at the Centre Pompidou on the occasion of the sixtieth anniversary of Kafka's death.[27] It is possible that this interest for literature is linked to the writing of *The Rules of Art*. Bourdieu does more than find a kind of allegory in *The Trial*; he also in a way practices the 'science of works' whose principles are developed in this book in 1992, in the way that he links the 'Kafkaesque' vision of the world to the insecurity that characterizes the literary field that produced it (and Kafka's position in that field). A few years later, he notes a slight change in his attitude to literature: he gradually frees himself from the temptation, felt strongly at the beginning, in a context where the scientific nature of sociology was insecure, to distance himself from his own literary education and tastes.[28] In the lectures, he retains his concern to circumscribe the place allocated to literary analysis ('I shall not develop this further – since I have already done my little literary turn, you would find that I was going too far' – 15 May 1986), but his sociologist audience are invited to reflect on their relation to literature.

Explaining his reflections on the 'biographical illusion' exploited by William Faulkner and Alain Robbe-Grillet, in particular, Bourdieu draws attention to the 'intellectual double life' led by sociologists, who can make a personal reading of the *Nouveau Roman* without drawing conclusions for their professional practice (24 April 1986), and he emphasizes how much the repression of the 'literary' by sociologists owes to their position in the space of disciplines; the particular form taken by the opposition between the arts and the sciences in the nineteenth century masks the advantage that writers have over researchers on questions such as the theory of temporality.

Announcing later research

As it intersperses Bourdieu's presentation of projects in progress with reminders of his previous research, his lecture course is driven by a dynamic in which the contemporary reader can see the bones of some of the studies that he was to undertake in the second half of the 1980s, and even during the 1990s.

Above all, the present volumes announce the whole range of the lectures that Bourdieu was to give at the Collège de France from 1987 to 1992. It is no accident if the lecture that opens this volume remarks in passing on the failings of the French edition of Max Weber: this author will often be referred to during the year 1983–84.[29] A little earlier, moreover, Bourdieu had published in the daily newspaper *Libération* a text entitled 'N'ayez pas peur de Max Weber!' [Who's afraid of Max Weber!']'[30] which seems to have been triggered by his preoccupations at the time. In his lectures Bourdieu comments on extracts from *Economy and Society*,[31] discussing codification, the notion of the 'discipline' or the sociology of law, which he knows only from the German or English editions. Weber's observations on *Kadi*-justice and the justice of Sancho Panza or Solomon are frequently referred to in the lectures. It is probably during the years that he was giving these lectures that Bourdieu's interest in Weber and the sociology of law were so strongly developed. The theme of the *vis formae*, which was never mentioned during the two previous years, is referred to on several occasions during the year 1983–84. His article on the 'force of law' would be published in 1986,[32] that is, during the year of teaching that closes the present set of volumes and which contains references to research in the sociology of law (15 May 1986, 5 June 1986), as well as reflections on the juridical field, which would be at the heart of his teaching for 1987–88.

It is not only the law but also more generally the state that becomes the central object of his reflection. The formula that Bourdieu uses to widen Weber's definition of the state ('an enterprise [. . .] that claims the monopoly of legitimate physical coercion') recurs frequently in his lectures in the early 1980s. His critique in 1983–84 of linear interpretations of the process of rationalization (29 March 1984) prefigures the reflections to be developed a few years later in his lectures on the genesis of the state. References to the state are very numerous in the last sessions of the fourth year. Indeed, the main theme of social perception leads into a study of the state's monopoly of authorized perception. The analysis of certification also implicates the state, defined in this case as a 'field of expertise, or [. . .] field of the agents competing for the power of social certification' (9 May 1985), and the last lecture of the year finishes by acknowledging that a sociology of symbolic struggles should question this 'last analysis' that the state represents. Bourdieu notes that the state has become a major concern for his arguments even before starting his lectures in 1989–1990 on the state:[33] already in 1987–88 he called his course 'Concerning the state'.

The article (1990) and then the book (1998) that he devoted to 'masculine domination'[34] may also be seen being sketched out in the lectures. During the year 1985–86, several developments relate to the political dimension of masculine domination or the 'androcentric unconscious' of Mediterranean societies. It is in 1985–86 too that he comments on *To the Lighthouse* (which became an important reference in his later writings on the relations between the sexes); he is particularly attracted to its feminine vision of masculine investment in social games.

While it is more difficult to detect in the lectures the signs prefiguring the work that Bourdieu would publish in the 1990s, today's reader, seeing Bourdieu's methodological reflections on the difficulty of retrieving and explaining the experience of social agents (12 June 1986), cannot help thinking of the organization of the collective enquiry that culminated in 1993 in *The Weight of the World*. Likewise, it is tempting to connect the study of the 'hit parade' with the analyses that Bourdieu would apply ten years later to the 'grip of journalism';[35] although he does not use this expression in 1984, he sees in the ranking list the sign of a transformation of the balance of power between the intellectual field and the journalistic field in favour of the latter. However, the media and Bourdieu's relations with them were significantly transformed in the ten years or so that that separate the analysis of the 'hit parade' (that Bourdieu published only in his review, and in an appendix to an academic work) from the brief polemical work that he was to publish at the end of 1996 for a wider readership, *On Television*, which is partly a book about 'media-friendly intellectuals'.[36] Essentially, we could say that the lectures published here do slightly predate the turning point represented by the privatization in 1986 of the most popular channel, TF1. At the beginning of the 1980s, the spirit of public service inherited from the beginnings of television remained fairly strong.[37] Bourdieu was still liable to participate in television broadcasts from time to time or to take part in a debate with leading journalists. In 1985 for instance he intervened in a forum organized by the Comité d'information pour la presse dans l'enseignement,[38] and, encouraged by his Collège de France colleague Georges Duby, he started to participate in the 'educational television' project that would lead to the creation of 'la Sept' (Channel 7), which gave birth to Arte.[39]

The framework of the Collège de France

To understand the space where Pierre Bourdieu was situated in the years from 1983 to 1986, we have to think of the Collège de France. Georges Duby was one of his closest colleagues. Their relationship went back a long way: Duby was one of the founders of the review *Études rurales* in which Bourdieu had published a substantial article (more than a hundred pages long) at the beginning of the 1960s, when he was almost unknown.[40] In the lectures for 1986 where he elaborates the notion of the 'field of power', Bourdieu often quotes his medievalist colleague's book, *Les Trois Ordres, ou l'imaginaire du féodalisme* (1978). He also refers to the analyses of Indo-European triads developed by Georges Dumézil, who had retired in 1968 after nearly twenty years teaching at the Collège de France (he died in 1986). Bourdieu discusses Claude Lévi-Strauss's arguments even more often (although Bourdieu referred to his anthropological studies continuously throughout his career, even when he no longer attended his seminar). Lévi-Strauss retired from the Collège de France in 1982, but a lecture he gave in 1983 marks a moment of tension between the two men, as reflected in one of Bourdieu's lectures in 1986 (5 June 1986). Bourdieu's lectures also contain glancing allusions to, or passing discussions of, research by younger professors at the Collège de France: Emmanuel Le Roy Ladurie (18 April 1985), Jacques Thuillier (2 May 1985) whom Bourdieu had known from the École normale supérieure, and Gérard Fussman (28 March 1985).

Bourdieu played his part in the life of the institution. He refers twice to seminars or colloquia which united participants from the different historical and literary disciplines represented at the Collège de France (22 May and 19 June 1986). He participated until his retirement in various events of this nature. In 1984–85, he urged his audience to go to the lectures that Francis Haskell had come to deliver at the Collège de France (18 April 1985, 2 May 1985). Bourdieu's lectures do not refer to any of the works of the 'Collège scientists', but when the right returned to power in 1986,[41] Bourdieu joined several of them (the biologist Jean-Pierre Changeux, the physicist Claude Cohen-Tannoudji, the pharmacologist Jacques Glowinski and the chemist Jean-Marie Lehn) in signing a 'solemn appeal' to the government that intended to reduce the public funds allocated to research. In addition, the lectures are contemporary with the preparation of the 'Propositions for the education of the future' that the President of the Republic [François Mitterrand] had asked the professors of the Collège de France to prepare in 1984 and which was remitted in March 1985.[42] Bourdieu was the editor-in-chief, and even, to some considerable extent, the initiator of the project.[43]

During these years, one of the members of the Collège de France whose lectures were most popular was Michel Foucault. Bourdieu was to explain much later what attracted him to and what distanced him from Michel Foucault,[44] whose seminar at the École normale supérieure he had attended. In the 1980s, Foucault and Bourdieu joined forces in appealing to the French government to support Polish trade unionists, but the lectures published here bear witness to a mixture of esteem and distance. Although Bourdieu makes explicit reference to Foucault's work, such as his notion of *épistémè*, his fourth and fifth year lectures are marked by an ongoing critique of the analyses of power elaborated by the philosopher: in particular, the formula 'power springs from below' is seen as showing naive thinking, inspired above all by a spirit of contradiction (17 April 1986). Bourdieu's lecture course had already finished just over a month before Foucault's death at the end of June 1984. Bourdieu joined André Miquel and other professors from the Collège de France to attend the ceremony in Paris that preceded his funeral.[45] He published two notices in homage to 'a friend and colleague', one in *Le Monde* and the second in *L'Indice*.[46]

The intellectual field in the first half of the 1980s

The lectures also show the influence of the contemporary intellectual field outside the Collège de France.[47] They contain allusions to major figures from previous decades, such as Jean-Paul Sartre and Jacques Lacan, who had died in 1980 and 1981 respectively, and Louis Althusser, who was interned in November 1980 after murdering his wife. In one of his lectures, Bourdieu alludes to the contemporary journalistic debate over finding a 'successor' to Sartre.[48] The dominant figures of the moment who combine intellectual recognition with public notoriety are a group of fifty-year-olds that include Bourdieu, with, principally, Michel Foucault, Jacques Derrida, Gilles Deleuze (and Félix Guattari).[49] They became known during the years preceding May 1968 and shared what Bourdieu calls an 'anti-institutional attitude' (2 May 1985). These 'consecrated heretics', according to another of Bourdieu's formulae,[50] distanced themselves from traditional philosophy and the traditional university. In the first half of the 1980s, they often found themselves signing the same appeals or petitions. However, a younger generation emerged and started to relegate them to the past: in autumn 1985, an essay much hyped by the media took as its target the 'anti-humanist '68 thinking' that they allegedly represented.[51] Bourdieu alludes to this work in one of his lectures (5 June 1986) and on several occasions mentions the thematics of the 'return to Kant' and the 'return to the subject' that its authors stand for.

If he mentions only in passing the development of the 'postmodernism' that dates from the second half of the 1970s (in discussing research into the sociology of science, whose relativism he criticizes), he does make several references to the appearance, at roughly the same time, of the 'nouveaux philosophes': 'As soon as someone new, even a "new philosopher", emerges in the space, his existence becomes a problem, makes people stop and think, and risks making them think askew – not to mention the fact that this threatens to consume energy that could be fruitfully applied elsewhere' (18 April 1985). The attitude to adopt in the face of this new type of rival, and more generally in the face of the threats that seem to confront 'philosophy' at this time, then provoke debate; several allusions in the lectures reveal Bourdieu's reservations, as he takes his distance from Deleuze's declarations on the 'nouveaux philosophes' (which he finds counterproductive) or from the Estates General of philosophy organized by Jacques Derrida.[52] His analysis of the 'hit parade', however, shows his awareness of the accelerating structural transformations at work at this time,[53] and of the danger that they represent for the perpetuation of the intellectual model that he incarnates.

At the beginning of the 1980s, his own status in the intellectual field changed, but according to a logic that is not easy to characterize unequivocally. His election to the Collège de France, for example, or the success of *Distinction*, which made its mark as an important book with an impact well beyond the circle of specialists, increased the recognition of his work, but at the same time make him the incarnation of a discipline and a body of thought that many intellectual schools of thought attacked for being a 'determinist' or even 'totalitarian' 'sociologism'. Among these various criticisms and attacks (which on occasion find an echo in the lectures published here), we could mention, even if they are only a few examples among others, those emanating from collaborators or intellectuals connected with the review *Esprit* or the book that appeared in 1984, *L'Empire du sociologue*.[54]

The subspace of sociology

We find this ambiguity in the subspace of sociology. Since his work was already at a stage that authorized a retrospective viewpoint, Bourdieu sometimes ventures in his lectures to grasp and formulate the general sense of his enterprise; he can insist on the efforts that he has made, in opposition to 'economic and economistic analysis', to highlight 'the decisive role of the symbolic in social exchanges', 'all these struggles that history is full of and whose stakes are never reducible to their material dimension' (22 March 1984 and 30 May 1985); he may also point out that his 'historical contribution' will have been to 'take his work as a sociologist to its conclusion, that is the objectification of the professionals of objectification' (19 June 1986),[55] or to 'encourage a very respectful attitude towards everything that could help a better analysis of the social world' (14 March 1985). Moreover, he starts working on a synthesis (which includes these lectures) and popularization. In parallel with his research, Bourdieu started to publish books designed to give accessible insight into his work: in 1980, for the first time he collected in one volume oral presentations given in diverse circumstances.[56] In 1983, one of his early students, Alain Accardo, published the first book that undertook to lay the major concepts of his sociology before a readership of scholars and militants.[57] His international reputation also grew. Thus, just before starting the fifth year of his lectures, he spent a month travelling round the United States, where he gave fifteen seminars and lectures in American universities (San Diego, Berkeley, Chicago, Princeton, Philadelphia, Baltimore, New York University). In the years that followed, he made similar tours in other countries.

This growing consecration does not mean that he enjoyed magisterial authority. In sociology, as in the whole of the intellectual field, the growing recognition that Bourdieu attracted seemed to generate even fiercer forms of rejection. In the first half of the 1980s, there were several attempts to describe his sociology as 'out of date', with some talk of an 'actor's last farewell'. The attacks were mounted, in particular, in the name of a 'methodological individualism' that claims to explain social phenomena on the basis of a desocialized *homo sociologicus*. Their leader was Raymond Boudon who, having been in the 1960s one of the principal importers into France of the 'methodology' of Paul Lazarsfeld (which Bourdieu attacked on epistemological grounds),[58] developed in the 1970s an analysis of educational inequalities challenging the views imposed by *The Inheritors* and *Reproduction*. If Bourdieu in these lectures repeats his criticism of 'methodological individualism' on several occasions, or points out his divergence from the view of his work that it propagates, it is because this current of thought, which was making inroads in the United States at the same time, had entered a particularly aggressive phase. In 1982 Presses Universitaires de France published a *Dictionnaire critique de la sociologie*, edited by Raymond Boudon and François Bourricaud, whose project 'to scrutinize the imperfections, uncertainties and flaws of sociological theories, but also the reasons for their success', is an attack on Marxist- or structuralist-inspired sociology.

Bourdieu's remarks on the 'ultra-subjectivism' and 'facile radicalism' that are emerging in the sociology of science, are a response to the appearance in 1979 of the book *Laboratory Life*.[59] Based on the ethnographical study of a laboratory of neuroendocrinology, this book claims to found an approach explicitly different from the analyses that Bourdieu had been offering since the mid-1970s on 'the scientific field and the social conditions of the progress of reason'.[60] Bourdieu rejects this approach, which radicalizes to the point of relativism the thesis according to which scientific facts are socially constructed. The authors' insistence on the scientists' search for credibility and their reliance on rhetorical apparatus leads them to ignore the fact that not all strategies are possible in the scientific field (28 March 1985 and 19 June 1986). Some fifteen years later, by which time this 'new sociology of science' had developed considerably, Bourdieu would return to this criticism.[60]

In these lectures Bourdieu also discusses the imports into sociology that took place in the 1980s. These years saw a wave of translations in France of a German contemporary of Durkheim, Georg Simmel, and the 'discovery' of interactionism and ethnomethodology, 'heterodox' currents of American sociology dating from the 1950s and 1960s. At the intersection of sociology and philosophy, the work of the Frankfurt School, largely unknown in France before the 1970s, was also published copiously at the start of the 1980s, particularly by Payot at the instigation of Miguel Abensour. In one lecture Bourdieu offers in passing an analysis of these imports of the 1980s (5 June

1986). Although he mocks the provincialism that leads the French to translate research when it has gone out of fashion in its native land, he cannot help being irritated by these imports when they are introduced by more or less declared rivals in the sociological space and presented as innovations that require immediate attention. In fact, they are sometimes explicitly opposed to his own sociology, despite being authors that he had read long before and whom he had helped to make known in France (most of Goffman's work had been translated in the 1970s and 1980s by Éditions de Minuit), and above all whom he had already integrated into his approach.

The political context

The concern to offer teaching that was theoretical but not divorced from the most concrete reality inspires frequent allusions to the political context of the times, to the questions and problems constituted as such in the media and in the political world. Bourdieu finds an almost perfect example of his reflections on the 'science of the state' in the unemployment figures published by INSEE. This statistical indicator in fact became a central stake in contemporary political debate: the unemployment rate was very low until 1973 but then rose continually until the mid-1980s. Among other things, the arrival in France of mass unemployment helped to foreground the question of immigration – the electoral scores of the Front national after 1982 are only the most spectacular manifestation of this. In this way 'current affairs' are a direct illustration of one of the ideas developed by Bourdieu: it is the principles underlying the vision of the social world (and in the event, the question of whether the division between immigrants and non-immigrants can replace the division between rich and poor) that are at stake in the struggle. In the first half of the 1980s, the growing stigmatization of immigrants inspired a mobilization of opposition opinion that Bourdieu associated himself with. Thus, he signed a text in support of the march for equality and against racism that took place in autumn 1983,[61] and he played a part in the activities of SOS Racisme, close to the Socialist Party, launched in 1984. In November 1985, for example, he took part in a meeting with the association during which he warned them of the danger of an 'ethico-magical movement' and denounced those who analyse immigration in terms of cultural difference, because this provides a smoke screen hiding the economic and social inequality between Frenchmen and immigrants.

The lectures also include echoes of the rise of neoliberalism, whose acceleration at the start of the 1980s was symbolized by the accession to power of Margaret Thatcher in Great Britain and Ronald Reagan in the United States. The economists of the 'Chicago School', mentioned on several occasions by Bourdieu, are said to have encouraged economic policies that, contrary to the interventionist policies employed in the postwar decades, consider, in a now-famous formula, that the state (or at least its 'left hand') is 'the problem, not the solution'. When at one moment he discusses the difference between private charity and public welfare (9 and 23 May 1985), Bourdieu mentions the attacks that the welfare state was subjected to at the time. In the first lecture published in this volume, the connection that he establishes between the tragedy that had just occurred at the Heysel stadium and the politics of the 'Iron Lady' announces the theme of the 'law of conservation of violence' that he will use to confront the neoliberal politicians in the 1990s.[62] Moreover the lectures often echo events and situations that were being discussed in the 'foreign affairs' columns of the French media at the time. Thus Bourdieu alludes to the Iranian revolution or the Irish troubles and offers elements of reflection on them based on his theoretical analyses.

At a national level, the period corresponds to François Mitterrand's first seven-year mandate. The lectures make few allusions to internal political events, apart from some critical comments on the restoration of the school of the Third Republic sought and proposed by the socialist minister of education, Jean-Pierre Chevènement (12 June 1986).[63] The last lecture of the series makes a few (anecdotal) references to the return of a right-wing government as a result of the legislative elections of March 1986. We can, however, note that without alluding to this in his lectures, Bourdieu did take public stands on some aspects of the policies implemented by successive governments: he signed several petitions condemning the position of the socialist government towards events in Poland,[64] but also an appeal relating to conditions in prisons and, after the return of the right to power in 1986, appeals against cuts in the budget for research and against the proposal to halt the construction of the new opera house at the Bastille.

The lecture of 19 June 1986 that closes the final volume brings Bourdieu's five-year 'Course in General Sociology' to a close. It was the first general introduction to sociology ever given at the Collège de France. The following year, Bourdieu took advantage of the opportunity that members of the Collège have to suspend their teaching temporarily. He started his lectures again in 1988 with a new title, 'A Propos de l'État' ('On the State'). This marks the start of a five-year cycle devoted to the analysis and deconstruction of this institution and, more generally, the start of a period when Bourdieu's lectures at the Collège focus on specific themes: after the sociology of the state[65] came the sociology of the economic field, the sociology of domination, the sociology of a symbolic revolution in painting;[66] then, in a sort of conclusion to his teaching, he analysed research into the sociology of science in general and the sociology of sociology in particular.[67] as if to remind his audience, in opposition to a certain kind of radical relativism, that it is possible, given the right social circumstances – precisely those that constitute the scientific field – to produce truths that are not reducible to the social world that produces them.

Summary of the Lectures
of 1983–84

As a space of relatively long-lasting objective relations between the agents or institutions defined by their position in its space, the field is a site of specific investments (In the case of watchmaking as studied by Mr Eymard-Duvernay, for instance, these are: methods of production, manufacturing procedures, modes of workforce management and ways of enhancing the value of the product), which suppose possession of a specific capital and ensure material and symbolic profits (notably a firm's 'reputation', principally dependent, both in the economic field and in the field of cultural production, on its history and tradition). The strategies of the agents (businesses, authors, etc.) depend on their positions in the field, that is, on their positions in the distribution of the specific capital that is in play there, and therefore on their relative competitive strength.

The question of the boundaries of the field is always an issue in the field: for instance, enterprises of economic or cultural production may work at differentiating themselves from their nearest neighbours in order to limit competition and ensure themselves a monopoly over a subfield. Only research can determine the boundaries of the different fields: these rarely take the form of juridical boundaries (such as a numerus *clausus*), although they are marked by more or less institutionalized 'entrance hurdles'. The boundaries of the fields are to be found where the effects of the fields cease to work, and the passage from a subfield to the field that encompasses it – for example, from a literary genre like poetry to the literary field taken as a whole – is marked by a qualitative change.

The source of the dynamics of the field lies in its structural form, and in particular in the distance between the different specific forces present. The dominated have powers that are by definition never entirely lacking, at least in potential, since being part of a field means being capable of producing effects there (for example, to provoke reactions of exclusion or excommunication in the holders of the dominant positions). The properties that are active in the field – and therefore noted by the analyst as pertinent because they produce the most decisive differences – are those that define the specific capital underlying the specific investments. Capital exists and functions only in relation to the field in which it operates: like trumps in a card game, it exerts power over this field, in particular over the materialized or incorporated instruments of production and reproduction whose distribution composes the very structure of the field, and over the regular patterns (or mechanisms) and the rules (or institutions) that define the ordinary functioning of the field; and thereby over the profits engendered in the field (for example, the cultural capital and the laws of transmission of cultural capital, as mediated by the educational system).

Here we now take time to define the social system as a site of immanent tendencies, of a *vis insita* and a *lex insita*. Games of chance, like roulette, give an idea of a universe of perfectly equal chances, without accumulated bias, where anyone at all may win or lose all at any moment. Capital, with its capacity to generate profits and reproduce itself in identical or augmented form, harbours a tendency to prolong its existence, which means that all is not equally possible or impossible for all people at all times. We can distinguish between societies, particularly between the pre-capitalist and the capitalist, according to the degree to which they harbour spontaneous or institutionalized mechanisms liable to produce regular patterns, especially in social relations among agents: in pre-capitalist societies, because of the low degree of objectification of capital in their economic or cultural mechanisms, social relations – even among kith and kin – can only endure through a perpetual labour of reinvention; in capitalist societies, reproduction of social relations of domination is entrusted to mechanisms, allowing agents (at least in an initial phase) to dispense with having to work at maintaining these relations. Whence the fact, contradicting the evolutionist vision of Weber or Elias, that we find not only increasing instances of brute physical or economic violence, but also more gentle, euphemized violence ('enchanted' relations) in pre-capitalist societies than in capitalist ones, where the 'inert violence' of the economic and cultural mechanisms dispense the dominant from working at euphemizing violence (cf. the passage from the domestic servant to the working man). This condition pertains at least until the dominated develop their own strength enough to force the dominant to fall back on their reserves of symbolic violence, which, in both pre-capitalist and more developed societies, operate through a process of formalization.

Thus we come to analyse the species and states of capital. Although there are as many species of capital as there are fields (as many different trumps as there are games), we may distinguish two fundamental species, economic capital and cultural capital, which are effective to different degrees and in different forms in all the social fields. Leaving economic capital to one side, we concentrate on characterizing the three states of cultural capital – which we first distinguish from what economists call 'human capital' – the incorporated state, the objectified state and the institutionalized state. Widening the notion of capital to include 'information capital', a structured and structuring stock of information and dispositions that enables information received to be given form and structure, we finally examine the process of objectification and codification of information, and in particular the specific effect of formalization, common to science and the law, with their mathematical formulae and juridical formalism. We also try to explain the *vis formae* that is the basis of specifically bureaucratic competence and to understand the particular logic of its so-called 'rationalization' processes.

In the second sessions, we use documents or our research to examine a series of more limited problems: the links between the intellectual field and the journalistic field – looking at a 'hit parade' of intellectuals; the links between time and power – looking at Kafka's *Trial*; and the notion of crisis – as it concerned May 1968.

Notes

Editorial Note

1 *Science of Science and Reflexivity*, trans. Richard Nice (Cambridge: Polity, 2004).
2 *On the State*, trans. David Fernbach (Cambridge: Polity, 2015).
3 *General Sociology*, vol. 1, *Classification Struggles*, trans. Peter Collier (Cambridge: Polity, 2018); vol. 2, *Habitus and Field*, trans. Peter Collier (Cambridge: Polity, 2020).
4 See the editors' note in *On the State*, pp. xi–xii.

Lecture of 1 March 1984

1 Here, Bourdieu is applying to the teaching relationship the analysis of linguistic exchanges that he had developed in *Ce que parler veut dire* (Paris: Farad, 1982); new, augmented edition, *Langage et pouvoir symbolique* (Paris: Seuil 'Points Essais', 2001) / *Language and Symbolic Power*, trans. Gino Raymond and Matthew Adamson (Cambridge: Polity, 1991).
2 A reference to Max Weber's *Economy and Society*, ed. Guenther Roth and Claus Wittich (Berkeley: University of California Press, 2nd edition, 1978 [1921]), vol. 1, pp. 246–254, vol. 2, pp. 1121–1123, 'The Routinization of Charisma'. Bourdieu had proposed a re-reading of Weber's sociology of religion, which gave pride of place to the opposition between the priest and the prophet, in Pierre Bourdieu, 'Genèse et structure du champ religieux', *Revue française de sociologie*, vol. 12, no. 3, 1971, pp. 295–334; 'Une interprétation de la théorie de la religion selon Max Weber', *Archives européennes de sociologie*, vol. 12, no. 1, 1971, pp. 3–21.
3 These lectures were delivered some time after the first wave of French translations of Max Weber between 1959 and 1971 (the translations were to start again in the middle of the 1980s; they were to become more numerous by the end of the 1990s and in the 2000s). At the time of the lectures, for example, there was only a very partial translation of Max Weber's great work, *Economy and Society* (which corresponds only very roughly to the first part of the German edition of 1956). [For the standard 2-volume

complete English translation of *Economy and Society*, see previous note.]

4 An allusion by Bourdieu to certain readings of *The Craft of Sociology*, which, contrary to the positivist vision then predominant in the social sciences, recalled the need to make a theoretical construction of the object of research, which appeal was understood, especially by young Althusserian philosophers, as an injunction to undertake 'work in theory' and to 'refine their theoretical concepts' before even starting out on any 'empirical work'. See Pierre Bourdieu, Jean-Claude Chamboredon and Jean-Claude Passeron, *The Craft of Sociology: Epistemological Preliminaries*, trans. Richard Nice (Berlin: de Gruyter, 1991 [1968]).

5 See the last three lectures of the previous year, in *Habitus and Field*, pp. 260–343.

6 The phenomenological method, as conceived by Husserl, expands examples taken from life by 'imaginary variations', as a geometer would: 'The geometer when he thinks geometrically operates with imagery vastly more than he does with percepts of figures or models; [. . .] In fancy he has perfect freedom in the arbitrary recasting of the figures he has imagined, in running over continuous series of possible shapes, in the production therefore of an infinite number of new creations; a freedom which opens up to him for the first time an entry into the spacious realms of essential possibility with their infinite horizons of essential knowledge': *Ideas. A General Introduction to Pure Phenomenology*, trans. F. Kersten (London: Routledge 2012 [1913]), pp. 199–200.

7 Émile Durkheim, *The Rules of Sociological Method*, trans. W. D. Halls (London: The Free Press, 1982 [1895]), p. 147: 'Moreover since social phenomena clearly rule out any control by the experimenter, the comparative method is the sole one suitable for sociology.'

8 A reference to the 'method of concomitant variations' that Émile Durkheim sees as 'the supreme instrument for sociological research' (*The Rules of Sociological Method*, p. 153), and which he demonstrates in an exemplary case in *Suicide*, trans. John A. Spaulding and George Simpson (New York: The Free Press, 1979) [1897]).

9 Bourdieu is no doubt referring to Ludwig von Bertalanffy, author of *General System Theory* (New York: George Braziller, 1968).

10 See the lecture of 30 November 1982, in *Classification Struggles*.

11 The simplest meaning of the Greek word *historia* is 'research, information, exploration' (and, by extension, the result of the research and the account or report of what has been learnt from the research).

12 Bourdieu develops this notion of *loci incerti* further in *Manet: A Symbolic Revolution*, trans. Peter Collier and Margaret Rigaud-Drayton (Cambridge: Polity, 2017 [2013]), p. 147.

13 Enrico Castelnuovo and Carlo Ginzburg, 'Domination symbolique et géographique artistique dans l'histoire de l'art italien', *Actes de la recherche en sciences sociales*, no. 40, 1981, pp. 51–72.

14 On the *numerus clausus*, see the lectures of 2 June and 30 November 1982, in *Classification Struggles*.

15 Bourdieu is no doubt thinking of the references that he makes a little later in this lecture to Weber's analysis of the notion of 'rationalization', in particular in the cases of law and economics.

16 Émile Durkheim, *The Division of Labour in Society*, trans. W. D. Halls (New York: Free Press, 1997 [1893]).

17 Gaston Bachelard, *The Formation of the Scientific Mind. A Contribution to a Psychoanalysis of Objective Knowledge*, trans. Mary McAllester Jones (Manchester: Clinamen 2002 [1938]).

18 Durkheim, *The Rules of Sociological Method*, ch. 2, 'Rules for the Observation of Social Facts', pp. 60–84.

19 Bourdieu may be referring to the mobiles that the American sculptor Alexander Calder (1898–1976) started constructing in the 1930s and which were composed of geometric forms set in motion by the air or electric motors. In 1992, Bourdieu explained that, against a common tendency to imagine the social world in the shape of a pyramid, he saw 'the social world more and more like one of Calder's mobiles, where there are as it were little universes drifting around each other in a multi-dimensional space': 'Questions à Pierre Bourdieu', in Gérard Mauger and Louis Pinto (eds), *Lire les sciences sociales*, vol. 1, *1989–1992* (Paris: Belin, 1994), p. 323.

20 An allusion to the Marxist approach that systematically sees the mode of economic production as the cause of events and behaviour 'in the last analysis'.

21 It is probably a legend, but this phrase is reputed to have been engraved over the entrance of the Academy, the school founded by Plato.

22 An allusion to Schwarz's theorem on the derivation of functions, which takes its name from the German mathematician Hermann Amandus Schwarz (1843–1921).

23 An allusion to the enquiry into the professors of the University of Paris: Pierre Bourdieu, *Homo Academicus*, trans. Peter Collier (Cambridge: Polity, 1988 [1984]).

24 An allusion to the enquiry into the episcopate: Pierre Bourdieu and Monique de Saint-Martin, 'La sainte famille. L'épiscopat français dans le champ du pouvoir', *Actes de la recherche en sciences sociales*, nos. 44–45, 1982, pp. 2–53.

25 On this metaphor of the card game, see Pierre Bourdieu, 'Some Properties of Fields', in *Sociology in Question*, trans. Richard Nice (London: Sage, 1993 [1980]), pp. 72–77.

26 Bourdieu analysed the problem of the riposte in his writings on the sense of honour in *Outline of a Theory of Practice*, trans Richard Nice (Cambridge: Cambridge University Press, 1977 [1972]), pp. 10–15. It is very possible that he is thinking here of the situation created at the end of the 1970s by the newcomers known as the '*nouveaux philosophes*', to whom a 'major holder of capital' like Gilles Deleuze replied in 1977: 'À propos des nouveaux philosophes et d'un problème plus général', *Minuit*, no. 24; reprinted in *Deux régimes de fous. Textes et entretiens (1975–1995)* (Paris: Minuit, 2003), pp. 126–134 /*Two Regimes of Madness. Texts and Interviews, 1975–1995*, trans. Ames Hodges and Mike Taormina (New York: Semiotext(e), 2007 [2003]), 'On the New Philosophers (Plus a More General Problem)', pp. 139–147. [The *nouveaux philosophes* were a group of repentant ex-Marxist thinkers, led by Bernard-Henri Lévy and André Glucksmann, attacking the communist revolutionary ideas promulgated by certain left-wing philosophers in France. (Translator)] Bourdieu referred to this text afterwards: 'Some time ago, Deleuze wrote a short pamphlet on the nouveaux philosophes. I told him: "You are making a mistake." This is something that everyone knows in practice but which is not theorized: when you are important and you attack someone unimportant,

you grant them some symbolic capital – it functions like a preface. In short, I thought that it was a strategic cock-up': 'À contre-pente. Entretien avec Pierre Bourdieu', *Vacarme*, no. 14, 2000.

27 A reference to the critique made of structuralism, in particular by existentialism and Marxism, for analysing language or myth as if they were synchronic phenomena, without taking their genesis into account. Bourdieu for his part claimed allegiance to a 'genetic structuralism': 'If I liked playing games with labels [. . .] I would say that I am trying to develop a genetic structuralism: the analysis of objective structures – those of different fields – is inseparable from the analysis of the genesis, within biological individuals, of the mental structures which are to some extent the product of the incorporation of social structures inseparable too from the analysis of the genesis of these social structures themselves': *In Other Words*, trans. Matthew Adamson (Cambridge: Polity, 1990 [1987]), p. 14.

28 Weber, *Economy and Society*. Bourdieu, who had read the book in German, tends to have in mind the whole of the section 'Economy and Law (Sociology of Law)', only a small part of which figures in the French edition. In the Roth and Wittich edition, this section is chapter VIII of Volume 2, pp. 641–900.

29 *Lire* is a monthly magazine devoted to literature that was founded in 1975 by Jean-Jacques Servan-Schreiber (best known as the founder of *L'Express*) and the literary journalist Bernard Pivot, who in the same year started to present the television broadcast 'Apostrophes'.

30 At more or less the same time, Bourdieu published his commentary under the title 'Le hit-parade des intellectuels français ou qui sera juge de la légitimité des juges?', in *Actes de la recherche en sciences sociales*, no. 52–53, 1984, p. 95–100 / 'The Hit Parade of French Intellectuals, or Who is to Judge the Legitimacy of the Judges?', in Bourdieu, *Homo Academicus*, pp. 256–270.

31 Bourdieu gives it at the beginning of the next lecture: 'Who are the three living French-language intellectuals whose writings seem to you to exercise the most powerful influence over the evolution of ideas, literature and the arts and sciences, etc?'

32 *La Quinzaine littéraire* is another literary periodical, rather older than *Lire* (it was founded in 1966) and with fewer readers.

33 Born in 1939, Catherine Clément was an academic philosopher who resigned from the university in 1976. Founded in 1977, *Le Matin de Paris* was a daily newspaper with links to the Socialist Party. It disappeared in 1988. Clément edited the cultural section, and wrote the book reviews herself.

34 The term *'nouveaux philosophes'* ('new philosophers') seems to have been launched in 1976 by a newcomer (Bernard-Henri Lévy). During the second half of the 1970s it came to designate a group of writers who attracted the attention of the press and the media (in addition to Bernard-Henri Lévy, there were André Glucksmann, Jean-Marie Benoist, etc. [see note 25]). These 'nouveaux philosophes' were inclined to announce the end of 'structuralism' or 'Marxism', which they accused of dominating the prevailing intellectual climate. *Marx est Mort* ('Marx is dead') is, moreover, the title of a book published by Jean-Marie Benoist (Paris: Gallimard, 1970). As with the allusion to 'new economics', it refers no doubt to a group of French liberal economists that took shape in 1977, who called themselves *'nouveaux économistes'*; among them, in particular, were Jean-Jacques Rosa and Pascal Salin, who were very influential in the press.

35 On 'constative' and 'performative' utterances, see J. L. Austin, *How to Do Things with Words* (Oxford: Oxford University Press, 1980 [1962]), pp. 1–11. (Translator)

36 'But indeed, that was quite a clever remark that Cato made many years ago: "I wonder", said he, "that a soothsayer doesn't laugh when he sees another soothsayer."' Cicero, *On Divination*, II, 51, trans. W. A. Falconer (Boston: Harvard University Press, Loeb Classical Library, 1923), p. 430. The Roman soothsayers, the 'augurs', read the future in the entrails of animals.

37 Sartre died in April 1980.

38 The singer and cinema actor Yves Montand was one of the celebrities from the world of 'culture and the performing arts' solicited by *Lire*. We should perhaps relate his presence in the panel to his political commitments, and the reply that Bourdieu reports, if it is true, reflects his social trajectory (he was of working-class origins and had trained as a hairdresser). In December 1981, Yves Montand had been one of the first signatories of the text published by Bourdieu and Foucault protesting at the reaction of the French government to events happening in Poland (see Pierre Bourdieu, *Interventions 1961–2001. Science sociale et action politique*, ed. Franck Poupeau and Thierry Discepolo (Marseille: Agone, 2002), pp. 164ff.

39 As indicated a little later, Max Gallo is in fact classified as a 'writer'.

40 The taxonomy includes a category of 'writer-teachers'.

41 *Metaxu* is a Greek preposition and adverb. The word is used in particular by Plato in a passage in the *Banquet* (202–204), as well as in *The Republic*, where he notes the intermediate state of the soul as being at rest as opposed to in pain or pleasure; there follows a series of reflections on this state, which is 'midway between the two' and which is 'neither of those things' but may 'come to be both of them'. There is no 'truth', there is only 'illusion' in this state of 'what seems pleasant beside what is painful, and painful beside what is pleasant': Plato, *The Republic*, trans. Tom Griffith (Cambridge: Cambridge University Press, 2000), pp. 301–302.

42 Bourdieu refers successively to the three types of legitimacy distinguished by Max Weber (rational, traditional and charismatic legitimacy). See *Economy and Society*, vol. 1, *The Types of Legitimate Domination*, esp. pp. 215–216.

43 Jules Huret, *L'Enquête sur l'évolution littéraire*, with preface by Daniel Grojnowski (Vanves: Thot, 1981 [1891]). Bourdieu had referred several times to Huret's enquiry in his lectures of the previous year, 1982–1983.

44 Bourdieu is referring to the writer Régis Debray, who was appointed counsellor to the President of the Republic [François Mitterrand] in 1981, and in 1982 publicly accused Bernard Pivot and his literary broadcast of 'exercising a veritable dictatorship over the market of the book'. Bourdieu had already evoked this attack on Bernard Pivot the previous year, in his lecture of 14 December 1982.

45 Bourdieu had already raised this question the previous year in his lecture of 23 November 1982 (see *Habitus and Field*, p. 159).

46 The idea, if not the exact formula, is to be found in passages such as: 'For each new class which puts itself in the place of one ruling before it, is compelled, merely in order to carry through its aim, to represent its interest as the common interest of all the members of society, that is, expressed in ideal form: it has to give its ideas the form of universality, and represent them as the only rational, universally valid ones': Karl Marx and Friedrich Engels, *The German*

Ideology, trans. Tim Delaney and Bob Schwarz (Progress Publishers, 1968 [1845-46/1932]; Marx/Engels Internet Archive, 2000).

47 Pascal, *Pensées*, ed. Louis Lafuma, trans. John Warrington (London: Dent 'Everyman': 1960), §217, p. 58. Bourdieu returns to this theme in the conclusion to his last lectures at the Collège de France published under the title *Science of Science and Reflexivity*, pp. 115–116.

48 In 'Espace social et genèse des classes', *Actes de la recherche en sciences sociales*, no. 52, 1984, pp. 3–14 – reprinted in 'Social Space and the Genesis of Classes', in *Language and Symbolic Power*, pp. 229–251 – Bourdieu cites Charles C. Gillespie, *Science and Polity in France at the End of the Old Régime* (Princeton: Princeton University Press, 1980) pp. 290–330. He also refers to Robert Darnton's analyses in 'The High Enlightenment and the Low-Life of Literature in pre-Revolutionary France', *Past and Present*, no. 51, 1971, pp. 81–115.

49 On Thersites' point of view, see Pierre Bourdieu, *The Rules of Art*, trans. Susan Emanuel (Cambridge: Polity, 1996), pp. 191–193. Bourdieu also refers to Shakespeare, who used this character from the *Iliad* in *Troilus and Cressida*.

50 Pierre Bourdieu, 'Public Opinion Does Not Exist', in *Sociology in Question*, pp. 149–157.

51 This technique, which was developed in the United States after the war, is sometimes called 'snowball sampling'.

52 See in particular the lectures for 8 and 15 March 1984. See also Pierre Bourdieu, 'La dernière instance', *in Le Siècle de Kafka* (Paris: Centre Georges Pompidou, 1984), pp. 268–270.

53 Bourdieu discusses Kafka at greater length in the lectures that follow.

54 The Science Citation Index is one of the leading bibliometric tools. It was devised in the 1960s by Eugene Garfield.

55 See Pierre Bourdieu, 'Habitus, code et codification', *Actes de la recherche en sciences sociales*, no. 64, 1986, pp. 40–44.

56 See the lectures that follow, and the article: 'The Force of Law. Toward a Sociology of the Juridical Field', *Hastings Law Journal*, vol. 38, no. 5/3, 1987.

57 The monthly review *Lire* specifies that they had approached 600 people but only 448 replied.

58 See note 40 above.

59 Socrates uses the term *allodoxia* to designate a false judgement. Plato, *Theaetetus*, 189b–c (London: Penguin, 1987), p. 95.

60 Georges Dumézil, a comparative philologist and mythologist (1898–1986). Bourdieu is no doubt taking him as an example of a scientist who ought not to be treated as a mere 'journalist-writer'. (Translator)

61 Claude Lévi-Strauss, *Tristes tropiques*, trans. John and Doreen Weightman (London: Penguin, 2009 [1955]). (Translator)

Lecture of 8 March 1984

1 See Bourdieu's analyses of the 'first person to fail': 'Social magic always manages to produce discontinuity out of continuity. The paradigmatic example of this, and my starting point, is the competitive academic examination (concours): between the last person to pass and the first person to fail, the competitive examination creates differences of all or nothing that can last a lifetime.

The former will graduate from an elite institution like the École polytechnique and enjoy all the associated advantages and perks, while the latter will become a nobody': 'Rites of Institution', in *Language and Symbolic Power*, pp. 120.

2 'The Purloined Letter' (1844) is a story by Edgar Allen Poe: a minister steals a letter from the queen, the police makes the most thorough investigations to find the place where it has been hidden, but, instead of hiding it, he has left it out in the open for anyone to see, counting on the principle that 'the intellect suffers to pass unnoticed those considerations which are too obtrusively and too palpably self-evident': in *Selected Tales* (Oxford: Oxford University Press, 2008), p. 262. The story, translated by Baudelaire, became fashionable in France again when, in April 1955, Lacan gave his 'Seminar on "The Purloined Letter"', published in *Écrits*, trans. Bruce Fink (London: W. W. Norton, 2007 [1966]), pp. 6–48.

3 See Weber, *Economy and Society*, vol. 1, esp. pp. 246–249.

4 See Bourdieu, 'Public Opinion Does Not Exist', in *Sociology in Question*, pp. 149-157.

5 See the postscript 'Towards a "Vulgar" Critique of Pure Critiques', in Pierre Bourdieu, *Distinction*, trans. Richard Nice (London: Routledge, 1984 [1979]), pp. 485–500.

6 It is possible that there is an allusion here to the book by Raymond Bourdon on this topic that was published a few years earlier, *La Logique du social* (Paris: Hachette, 1979), which in a way raised the same question of the 'mystery of social facts' (and gave the answer as 'methodological individualism' founded on the notion of 'emerging effects').

7 Another allusion to the sociological current called 'methodological individualism', one of whose major theoreticians is Raymond Boudon.

8 This is the enquiry into professors at the University of Paris published in *Homo Academicus*, which appeared in 1984. The question that Bourdieu refers to here is treated in the section of the introduction to the book devoted to the distinction between 'Empirical Individuals and Epistemic Individuals', pp. 21–35.

9 See Bertrand Russell, 'On Denoting', *Mind*, vol. 14, 1905, pp. 479–493. Bourdieu had discussed this kind of example at greater length the previous year (lecture of 9 November 1982, in *Habitus and Field*, pp. 109ff).

10 These acronyms denote the grade of the workman's job: OS *'ouvrier spécialisé'* (specialist workman); OP *'ouvrier professionnel'* (professional workman); OQ *'ouvrier qualifié'* (qualified workman).

11 Bourdieu returns to this question of titles in his analysis of the broadcasts devoted to the strikes of 1995 (in the programme 'Arrêts sur images', France 5, 20 January 1996, and in *On Television and Journalism*, trans. Richard Nice (London: Pluto Press, 1998 [1996]).

12 Max Weber, 'Lay Justice and Corporative Tendencies in the Modern Legal Profession', in *Economy and Society*, pp. 892–895.

13 Huret, *L'Enquête sur l'évolution littéraire*. At the time, Jules Huret was working for *L'Écho de Paris* (later for *Le Figaro*, from 1892).

14 Bourdieu has in mind the study that he had started on the Impressionist revolution of which he gave a first airing in his lectures the following year (1984–1985). He deals with the Salon des refusés in detail in *Manet: A Symbolic Revolution*.

15 The term 'Impressionism' seems to have been first used by an art critic (Louis Leroy) who was ironic and hostile towards Claude Monet's painting *Impression, soleil levant* (Impression, Sunrise) of 1872.

16 The sense, if not the exact wording, of this quotation, is no doubt taken from the following: Georg Wilhelm Friedrich Hegel, *Philosophy of Right*, trans. T. M. Knox (Oxford: Clarendon Press, 1952 [1820]), pp. 3, 5: 'As to nature, philosophy, it is admitted, has to understand it as it is. The philosophers' stone must be concealed somewhere, we say, in nature itself, as nature is in itself rational. Knowledge must, therefore, examine, apprehend and conceive the reason actually present in nature. Not with the superficial shapes and accidents of nature, but with its eternal harmony, that is to say, its inherent law and essence, knowledge has to cope. But the ethical world or the state, which is in fact reason potently and permanently actualized in self-consciousness, is not permitted to enjoy the happiness of being reason at all . . . On the contrary, the spiritual universe is looked upon as abandoned by God, and given over as a prey to accident and chance. As in this way the divine is eliminated from the ethical world, truth must be sought outside of it. And since at the same time reason should and does belong to the ethical world, truth, being divorced from reason, is reduced to a mere speculation.'

17 A probable allusion to the use made of this term by philosophers, in particular in the wake of the publication of Jacques Derrida's book, *Of Grammatology*, trans. Gayatri Chakravorty Spivak (Baltimore: Johns Hopkins University Press, 1997 [1967]).

18 Known as an actress, rather than a writer.

19 *Gault et Millau* is a gastronomic restaurant guide created in 1972 by two journalists.

20 Bourdieu uses this formula in reference to Weber who defines the state through its 'monopoly of legitimate physical violence': Max Weber, 'The Profession and Vocation of Politics', in *Political Writings*, trans. Ronald Speirs (Cambridge: Cambridge University Press, 1994), pp. 310–311. See also Bourdieu's later lectures on the state, published as *On the State*.

21 P. Bourdieu, *On the State*.

22 A reference to the etymology of the word 'collusion', formed from the Latin verb *ludere*, 'to play'.

23 That is, the suspension of judgement, the practice of systematic doubt.

24 Plato often analyses human activities, and especially philosophy, as serious games. Philosophy is 'the old men's rational pastime': *The Laws*, trans. Benjamin Jowett, The Internet Classics Archive, book 6; it requires us to 'treat (doctrine) seriously' despite enjoying 'amusement': *Theaetetus*, trans. Robin A. H. Waterfield (London: Penguin, 1987), §168d–e).

25 In 1984, Mardi Gras (Shrove Tuesday) was on 6 March, and Bourdieu's lecture was given on 8 March.

26 Catherine Clément was a well-known philosopher, novelist and critic. She may have been in the news because of an enthusiastic defence of bullfighting she had published in 1981. She is an ideal 'writer-journalist' for Bourdieu's purposes.

27 Émile Durkheim, *The Elementary Forms of Religious Life*, trans. Carol Cosman (Oxford: Oxford University Press, 2001 [1912]). The following phrase too is often quoted: 'In the world of experience I know of only one being that possesses a richer and more complex moral reality than our own, and that is the collective being. I am mistaken; there is another being which could play the same part, and that is the Divinity. Between God and society lies the choice [. . .] I myself am quite indifferent to this choice, since I see in the Divinity only society transfigured and symbolically expressed': Durkheim,

'The Determination of Moral Facts' in *Sociology and Philosophy*, trans. D. F. Pocock (Abingdon: Routledge, 2010 [1906]), p. 52.

28 A reference to the etymological origin of the word 'verdict' ('spoken in truth', 'tell the truth').

29 The problem of the relations between sociology and artists was a long-standing and permanent concern for Bourdieu. He regretted that sociology did not dispose of the same freedom as artists to resort to different artistic forms to help broaden the appeal of sociology. From 1975, with the creation of *Actes de la recherche en sciences sociales*, Bourdieu introduced into the world of the academic social science journal a freedom that gave his journal an avant-garde edge. His analysis of Flaubert's *Sentimental Education* in 'L'Invention de la vie d'artiste', *Actes de la recherche en sciences sociales*, no. 2, 1975, pp. 67–94, constituted an approach midway between sociology and literature. But it was *The Weight of the World* (Cambridge: Polity, 1999 [1993]) that made a decisive move towards the artistic world, as Bourdieu conceived this volume of interviews as a series of short stories enabling a wide public to project or identify and accede to an understanding of sociological analyses. The book was later given theatrical expression: the interviews were acted on stage for several years. Bourdieu continued this collaboration with artists for the rest of his life. He replied positively to Daniel Burin's offer to dedicate a room for his exhibition in the Pompidou Centre planned for March 2002. This project remained as a sketch, being interrupted by Bourdieu's death in January 2002.

30 Jean-Paul Sartre, *Search for a Method*, trans. Hazel Barnes (New York: Vintage, 1968 [1960]), p. 18: 'It was at about this time [1925] that I read *Capital* and *German Ideology*. I found everything perfectly clear, and I really understood absolutely nothing. To understand is to change, to go beyond oneself. This reading did not change me.'

31 'A "hierocratic organization" is an organization which enforces its order through psychic coercion by distributing or denying religious benefits ("hierocratic coercion"). A compulsory hierocratic organization will be called a "church" insofar as its administrative staff claims a monopoly of the legitimate use of hierocratic coercion.' Max Weber, *Economy and Society*, vol. 1, p. 54. This definition goes together with the definition of the 'state' as 'a compulsory political organization with continuous operations [which] successfully upholds the claim to the monopoly of the legitimate use of physical force in the enforcement of its order' (ibid.).

32 Bourdieu is probably thinking of an article by Maurice Blanchot, 'Notes sur un roman', *La Nouvelle revue française*, no. 3, 1955.

33 Bourdieu had to give details of the state of the philosophical field at the time when he launched into his self-analysis. In particular, he compared the case of Bachelard with that of Georges Canguilhem, who was 'consecrated, with Gaston Bachelard, as the *maître à penser* of philosophers more remote from the heart of the academic tradition, such as Althusser, Foucault and some others. It was as if his at once central and minor position in the university field, and the entirely rare, even exotic dispositions that had predisposed him to occupy it, had designated him to play the role of a totemic emblem for all those who sought to break with the dominant model': *Sketch for a Self-Analysis*, trans. Richard Nice (Chicago: University of Chicago Press, 2008), p. 11.

34 Claude Lévi-Strauss, *Introduction to the Work of Marcel Mauss*, trans. Felicity Baker (Abingdon: Routledge, 1987 [1950]). Bourdieu himself commented on

this preface in his analyses of the gift – see, in particular, *The Logic of Practice*, trans. Richard Nice (Cambridge: Polity, 1990 [1980]) – and on other occasions – see, in particular, 'Les conditions de la circulation internationale des idées', *Actes de la recherche en sciences sociales*, no. 145, 2002, p. 6.

35 Matthew, 25–29.

36 Pierre Bourdieu, 'Postface', in Erwin Panofsky, *Architecture gothique et pensée scolastique* (Paris: Minuit 1967 [1951]), pp. 133–167.

37 The scholastic philosopher Jean Buridan's paradox presents an ass, placed midway between a stack of hay and a pail of water, which died of hunger and thirst because it could not decide which to start with.

38 A brasserie in the Latin Quarter in Paris, 200 metres away from the Collège de France, frequented mostly by academics and writers.

39 This example refers implicitly to the research undertaken by Bourdieu and his team, in particular in the 1960s (in a centre which, after 1968, was to assume the significant title of 'Centre for the sociology of education and culture'), one of whose characteristics was the simultaneous analysis of cultural practices and education; on this point, see, for example, Pierre Bourdieu, Alain Darbel and Dominique Schnapper, *The Love of Art: European Art Museums and their Public*, trans. Caroline Beattie and Nick Merriman (Cambridge: Polity, 1997 [1966]).

40 An allusion to the congresses of the International Sociological Association, which, since 1950, have taken place every three (and now four) years. Although Bourdieu, with some members of his research centre, attended the 7th Congress of the ISA at Varna in Bulgaria in 1970, he did not return in later years. The Association is organized into thematic 'research networks' (sociology of education, work, etc.) and, apart from the 'plenary sessions', the congresses follow this arrangement.

41 Bourdieu is drawing an analogy with Mendeleev's periodic table of elements.

42 These baccalaureate options were in place between 1968 and 1995 (Options C and D were scientific baccalaureates).

43 'Anyone who has breathed the air of the École is impregnated with it for life. His brain retains its dull, musty professorial odours; these are, and forever will be, sterile aspirations, the rule of the rod, and the unspoken, impotent desires of the confirmed bachelor who has missed out on women. If ever these brave men are bold and witty enough to have a bright idea, which does sometimes happen, they cut it up into so many pieces or distort it so much with their pedagogical turn of mind that they make it indigestible. They are not, and never can be, original, because they have been nurtured in a very singular manure. If you sow professors, you will never reap creators': Émile Zola, 'Notre École normale', *Le Figaro*, 4 April 1881, reprinted in *Une campagne* (Paris: Charpentier, 1882), pp. 247–259.

44 Pierre Bourdieu, *The Political Ontology of Martin Heidegger*, trans. Peter Collier (Cambridge: Polity, 1991 [1975]).

45 Although Durkheim may not have used this particular expression, he did write that 'this [religious] delirium . . . is well founded': *The Elementary Forms of Religious Life*, pp. 171–172.) He develops the idea at greater length in a passage at the start of the conclusion to the book. He explains that sociology owes it to itself to pose the 'postulate that this unanimous feeling of believers across time cannot be purely illusory . . . religious beliefs rest on a specific experience whose demonstrative value is, in a sense, not inferior to that of scientific experiments, while being quite different . . . But, given the fact that, if you will,

"religious experience" is grounded in some way – and what experience is not? – it does not in the least follow that the reality that grounds it must objectively conform to the idea that believers have of it' (ibid., p. 312).

46 Bourdieu had developed this point at greater length during the first year of his teaching at the Collège de France (in the lecture of 26 May 1982).

47 Raymond Aron died a few months before this lecture, on 17 October 1983.

Lecture of 15 March 1984

1 The book had just been published at the time of the lecture: Jacques Bouveresse, *Le Philosophe chez les autophages* (Paris: Minuit, 1984), p. 164.

2 Ludwig Wittgenstein, *Philosophical Occasions 1912–1951*, ed. James Carl Klagge and Alfred Nordmann (Indianapolis: Hackett Publishing, 1993), ch. 7, 'Remarks on Frazer's *Golden Bough*', p. 133.

3 See above, lecture for 1 March 1984, pp. 21–2.

4 Sigmund Freud, *Jokes and their Relation to the Unconscious*, trans. James Strachey (Harmondsworth, Penguin, 1976 [1905]), p. 228.

5 The theme of social suffering is at the heart of the collective work that Bourdieu published under the title *The Weight of the World*, which also underlined the possibility for the sociologist to assume functions normally reserved for the psychoanalyst.

6 Pierre Bourdieu, 'La maison kabyle ou le monde renversé', in *Esquisse d'une théorie de la pratique* (Paris: Droz, 1972), pp. 45–69; partly reproduced in 'The Dialectic of Objectification and Embodiment', in *Outline of a Theory of Practice*, pp. 87–95.

7 An allusion to the influence exerted by the theories of the social contract developed in the seventeenth and eighteenth centuries, of which Grotius, Hobbes, Locke and Rousseau were the principle representatives.

8 This phrase, often quoted by Bourdieu, is inspired by the following passage: 'A truly philosophical criticism . . . does not however consist . . . in discovering the concepts of logic at every point; it consists in the discovery of the particular logic of the particular object': Karl Marx, 'Critique of Hegel's Doctrine of the State', in *Early Writings*, trans. Rodney Livingstone and Rodney Benton (London: Penguin, 1992 [1843]), pp. 158–159. One French translation is closer to the wording quoted by Bourdieu: 'Ce n'est pas la Logique de la Chose mais la Chose de la Logique qui est le moment philosophique': Karl Marx, *Critique du droit politique hégélien*, trans. Albert Baraquin (Paris: Éditions sociales, 1975), p. 51.

9 Bourdieu quotes this in *The Logic of Practice*, pp. 39–40. 'Consider the difference between saying "The train is regularly two minutes late" and "As a rule, the train is two minutes late . . . There is a suggestion in the latter case that the train being two minutes late is as it were in accordance with some policy or plan . . . Rules connect with plans or policies in a way that regularities do not . . . To argue that there must be rules in the natural language is like arguing that roads must be red if they correspond to red lines on a map': Paul Ziff, *Semantic Analysis* (Ithaca: Cornell University Press, 1960), p. 38.

10 Willard Van Orman Quine, 'Methodological Reflections on Current Linguistic Theory', in Gilbert Harman and Donald Davidson (eds), *Semantics of Natural Language* (Dordrecht: D. Reidel, 1972), pp. 442–454.

11 Émile Durkheim did define sociology as being the 'science of institutions': 'In fact, without doing violence to the meaning of the word, one may term an institution all the beliefs and modes of behaviour instituted by the collectivity; sociology can then be defined as the science of institutions, their genesis and their functioning': Preface to the second edition, in *The Rules of Sociological Method*, p. 45.

12 'The universal predominance of the market consociation requires on the one hand a legal system the functioning of which is *calculable* in accordance with rational rules': Max Weber, *Economy and Society*, vol. 1, p. 337. 'In a developing market economy, the calculability of the functioning of the coercive machinery constitutes the technical prerequisite as well as one of the incentives for the inventive genius of the cautelary jurists (*Kautelarjuristen*), whom we find as an autonomous element in legal innovation resulting from private initiative everywhere, but most highly developed and most clearly perceptible in Roman and English law': Max Weber, *Economy and Society*, vol. 2, p. 757.

13 For this example, see Pierre Bourdieu, 'Parallel-Cousin Marriage', in *Outline of a Theory of Practice*, pp. 30–71; 'The Social Uses of Kinship', in *The Logic of Practice*, pp. 162–199.

14 Spinoza says of *obsequium*: 'Obedience is the constant will to execute that, which by law is good, and by the general decree ought to be done': *Tractatus politicus*, trans. R. H. M. Elwes (New York: Dover, 2004), p. 298. Alexandre Matheron presents *obsequium* and respect for justice as 'the end product of the conditioning which the state uses to shape us to its ends and enable its preservation': *Individu et communauté chez Spinoza* (Paris: Minuit, 1969), p. 349.

15 See in particular the first part of the *Discourse on the Arts and Sciences*, trans. G. D. H. Cole (Zurich: ISN/ETH, 1993 [1750]): 'Politeness requires this thing; decorum that; ceremony has its forms, and fashion its laws, and these we must always follow, never the promptings of our own nature.'

16 *The Political Ontology of Martin Heidegger*, pp. 70–71.

17 Max Weber, *The Sociology of Religion*, trans Ephraim Fischoff (Boston: Beacon Press, 1993 [1922]), p. 66: 'Every prophecy by its very nature devalues the magical elements of the priestly enterprise, but in very different degrees . . . Thus, tensions between the prophets and their lay followers on the one hand, and between the prophets and the representatives of the priestly tradition on the other existed everywhere.'

18 *Émile Durkheim, Montesquieu and Rousseau. Forerunners of Sociology*, trans. Ralph Manheim (Ann Arbor: University of Michigan Press, 2016), p. 136.

19 Jean Wahl, *Du Rôle de l'idée d'instant dans la philosophie de Descartes* (Paris: Vrin, 1953 [1920]), p. 18.

20 In the *Theodicy*, written in French for a relatively wide readership, Leibniz says of the universe that 'God orders all things at once beforehand': *Theodicy* (Whithorn: Anados Books, 2019 [1710]), p. 10. In a discussion in Latin of the theses of a German Cartesian, Johann Sturm, he argues: 'It is not sufficient to say that in creating things in the beginning, God willed that they should observe a certain law in their progress, if his will is conceived to have been so inefficacious that things were not affected by it and no lasting effect was produced in them': 'On Nature in Itself', in *Philosophical Works of Leibniz*, trans George Martin Duncan (New Haven: Tuttle, Morehouse & Taylor, 1908 [*Ipsa Natura*, 1698]), §6, p. 123.

21 'He [Johann Sturm] repels as an unjust imputation on the part of his opponent

the thought that God moves things as a wood-cutter does his two-edged axe, or as a miller governs his mill by retaining the waters or by turning them loose on the wheel': Leibniz, 'On Nature in Itself', §5, p. 122.

22 See, for example, Henri Bergson, *Creative Evolution*, trans. Arthur Mitchell (Project Gutenberg eBook #26163, 2008 [1911]).

23 'On Nature in Itself', §13, p. 129.

24 Bourdieu may be thinking of a passage like the following: 'The three forces operative within the laity with which the priesthood must come to grips are: (a) prophecy, (b) the traditionalism of the laity, and (c) lay intellectualism. In contrast to these forces, another decisive factor at work here derives from the necessities and tendencies of the priestly enterprise as such': Max Weber, *The Sociology of Religion*, p. 65.

25 On the difference between body and field, see Pierre Bourdieu, 'Effet de champ et effet de corps', *Actes de la recherche en sciences sociales*, no. 59, 1985, p. 73. Later, Bourdieu was to discuss this difference at greater length in his lectures on Manet (*Manet: A Symbolic Revolution*).

26 'For I ask if this volition or this command, or, if you prefer, this divine law, decreed originally, attributed to things only an extrinsic denomination; or if, in forming them, it created in them some permanent impression, or as Schelhammer, remarkable as well for his judgment as for his experience, well calls it, an indwelling law (although it is most often unknown to the creatures in whom it resides), whence proceed all actions and all passions' 'On Nature in Itself', §5, p. 122.

27 See *The Logic of Practice*, esp. book 1, ch. 7, 'Symbolic Capital', pp. 112–121.

28 See *The Logic of Practice*, book 1, ch. 6, 'The Work of Time', pp. 98–111.

29 A translation of this text by Max Weber appeared with the title 'Enquête sur la situation des ouvriers agricoles à l'Est de l'Elbe. Conclusions prospectives', trans, Denis Vidal-Nacquet, *Actes de la recherche en sciences sociales*, no. 65, 1986 [1892], pp. 65–68. ['The Situation of Rural Workers in Germany East of the Elbe River' in 'Condition of Farm Labour in Eastern Germany'.]

30 In case this example should puzzle the British reader, I should point out that in Bourdieu's France general practitioners are not public servants as in Britain, but self-employed professionals. (Translator)

31 On the notion of personal loyalty, or *fidès*, see Émile Benveniste, *Dictionary of Indo-European Concepts and Society* (Chicago: Hau Books, 2016), pp. 75–90. Bourdieu develops this analysis in his lectures for 1985–86, lecture of 24 April 1986.

32 Bourdieu is no doubt referring to Georges Duby's book *The Three Orders. Feudal Society Imagined*, trans. Arthur Goldhammer (Chicago: University of Chicago Press, 1982 [1972]).

33 Benveniste, *Dictionary of Indo-European Concepts and Society*, p. 278.

34 Bourdieu, *In Other Words*, p. 93.

35 A reference to 'labelling theory', which was developed in the framework of interactionist sociology and which draws attention to what an individual's behaviour owes to the identity that others credit them with. Two famous expositions of this theory have been made by Erving Goffman – at least in *Stigmata: Notes on the Management of Spoiled Identity* (New York: Simon and Schuster, 1963), and *Asylums: Essays on the Social Situation of Mental Patients and Other Inmates* (London: Routledge, 1961) – and Howard Becker, *Outsiders. Studies in the Sociology of Deviance* (New York: The Free Press, 1991 [1963]).

36 Kenneth Arrow is often cited as the person who, at the end of the 1960s and the beginning of the 1970s, introduced the theme of trust into economics. He insists on the importance of 'mutual trust' in hierarchical relations and in economic exchanges. According to an oft-quoted formula, 'the agreement to trust each other' is part of the 'invisible institutions: the principles of ethics and morality' that govern economic development: *The Limits of Organization* (New York: W. W. Norton, 1974), p. 26.

37 Bourdieu mentions this 'disenchantment' with work observed starting in the 1960s in *Distinction*, in particular pp. 144–146.

38 'But it is not only outside the sphere of contractual relationships, but also on the interplay between these relationships themselves that social action is to be felt. In a contract not everything is contractual. The only undertakings worthy of the name are those that are desired by individuals, whose sole origin is this free act of the will. Conversely, any obligation that has not been agreed by both sides is not in any way contractual. Wherever a contract exists, it is submitted to a regulatory force that is imposed by society and not by in individuals: it is a force that becomes ever more weighty and complex': Durkheim, *The Division of Labour in Society*, pp. 165–166.

39 Bourdieu and other researchers of the Centre de sociologie européenne were working on publishing in the 1960s. Bourdieu was to return to these points in an article titled 'Une révolution conservatrice dans l'édition', *Actes de la recherche en sciences sociales*, no. 126–129, 1999, pp. 3–36.

40 Georges Dumézil (1898–1986) was a French comparative philologist best known for his analysis of sovereignty and power in Proto-Indo-European religion and society. He is considered one of the major contributors to mythography, in particular for his formulation of the trifunctional hypothesis of social class in ancient societies (*Wikipedia*). Bernard-Henri Lévy, born on 5 November 1948, is a popular French intellectual. Often referred to in his country simply as BHL, he was one of the leaders of the '*nouveaux philosophes*' (new philosophers) movement in 1976. In 2015, the *Boston Globe* said that he is 'perhaps the most prominent intellectual in France today'. His opinions, political activism and publications have also been the subject of several controversies over the years (*Wikipedia*). Bourdieu clearly wants to distinguish between someone he sees as a scientist and someone he sees as a mere 'essay writer'. (Translator)

41 In his analyses of May 1968 in the university field, Bourdieu notes the break in the doxic relation to the social world provoked by the crisis. See *Homo Academicus*.

42 An example might be: 'Our whole aim can only be to translate religious and political problems into their self-conscious human form. Our programme must be: the reform of consciousness not through dogmas but by analysing mystical consciousness obscure to itself, whether it appear in religious or political form': Karl Marx, 'Letters from the *Franco-German Yearbooks*', in *Early Writings*, p. 209.

43 Bourdieu, 'Espace social et genèse des classes'.

44 Francis Ponge, 'Natare piscem doces', *Proèmes* (Paris: Gallimard, 1965 [1924]), p. 148.

45 For further reading, see Bourdieu and de Saint-Martin, 'La sainte famille', esp. p. 44.

46 Romain Rolland, *Jean-Christophe*, trans. Gilbert Cannan (New York: Henry

Holt and company, 1911 [1904–12]), p. 17: 'He was also a magician. He walked with great strides through the fields, looking at the sky and waving his arms. He commanded the clouds. He wished them to go to the right, but they went to the left. Then he would abuse them, and repeat his command. He would watch them out of the corner of his eye, and his heart would beat as he looked to see if there were not at least a little one that would obey him. But they went on calmly moving to the left. Then he would stamp his foot, and threaten them with his stick, and angrily order them to go to the left; and this time, in truth, they obeyed him.'

47 Bourdieu, 'Rites of Institution'.

48 Thomas Kuhn, *The Copernican Revolution* (Cambridge, MA: Harvard University Press, 1990 [1957]), and *The Structure of Scientific Revolutions* (Chicago: University of Chicago Press, 2012 [1962]).

49 Isidore Isou, 1925–2007, was an avant-garde French-Romanian writer, artist and film director who launched the 'Lettrism' movement, inspired by Dada and Surrealism.

50 'The scientific revolution is not the business of the most deprived, but on the contrary the most scientifically endowed of the newcomers': Pierre Bourdieu, 'Le champ scientifique', *Actes de la recherche en sciences sociales*, no. 3, 1976, p. 99. In his work on Flaubert and Manet, Bourdieu draws attention to the same phenomenon affecting the symbolic revolutions in the literary or artistic fields (see *The Rules of Art* and *Manet: A Symbolic Revolution*).

51 On these points, see the introduction to *Homo Academicus*, in particular pp. 6–7.

52 'Taking as his guide the old empirical adage *Nihil est in intellectu quod non ante fuerit in sensu*, he [the German philologist Max Müller] applies it to religion and declares that there can be nothing in faith that was not first felt by the senses. Here we have a doctrine that seems to escape our serious objection to animism. From this viewpoint, religion appears not as a vague and confused reverie but rather as a system of ideas and practices well grounded in reality': Émile Durkheim, *The Elementary Forms of Religious Life*, p. 64.

53 On prediction in politics, see Pierre Bourdieu and Luc Boltanski, 'La production de l'idéologie dominante', *Actes de la recherche en sciences sociales*, no. 2/3, 1976, pp. 3–73; republished by Raisons d'agir/Demopolis, 2007.

54 This example refers to the debates that started in France in 1982 around the economic and monetary political choices of the socialist government of the time. The French franc had by that time been devalued several times. Some of the political authorities pleaded for France to leave the European monetary system (a modified form of the European currency snake established in 1972), but this option was to be rejected a few months after this lecture, with the arrival in summer 1984 of a new government led by Laurent Fabius.

55 See, in particular, Karl Popper, *The Poverty of Historicism* (London: Routledge, 2002 [1957]).

56 This is an allusion to Michel Serres (number 20 in the *Lire* 'hit parade'), who explained, for example: 'What is good is mixture. What is horrible is separation. I am at the moment writing a philosophy of mixture. We have always been taught that to be rigorous we must separate, and in fact this does bear fruit up to a point. But it is a religious gesture, banishing the impure': 'Michel Serres ou la philosophie du mélange', *Le Matin de Paris*, 12 janvier 1982, p. 28, quoted

by Bouveresse, *Le Philosophe chez les autophages*, p. 63. See Michel Serres, *The Five Senses. A Philosophy of Mingled Bodies*, trans. Margaret Sankey and Peter Cowley (London: Continuum Books, 2008 [1985]).

57 See Pierre Bourdieu, 'La force du droit', *Actes de la recherche en sciences sociales*, 1986, no. 64, pp. 3–19.

58 'But I am quite disgusted [. . .] with the difficulty that there is in general to write ten lines of common sense on the facts of language. Since I have been preoccupied for a long time with the logical classification of these facts, and the classification of the viewpoints from which we approach them, I increasingly see [. . .] the immensity of the task we face if we want to show the linguist *what he actually does*': Ferdinand de Saussure, letter to Antoine Meillet, 4 January1894, quoted by Émile Benveniste, 'Saussure après un demi-siècle', *Cahiers Ferdinand de Saussure*, no. 20, 1963, p. 13.

Lecture of 22 March 1984

1 See the lecture of 2 November 1982, in *Habitus and Field*, pp. 82–86.

2 Albert O. Hirschman, *The Passions and the Interests. Political Arguments for Capitalism Before its Triumph* (Princeton: Princeton University Press, 2013 [1977]).

3 Bourdieu must be thinking of the kind of analysis that Weber develops in the section 'The Disintegration of the Household: The Rise of the Calculative Spirit and of the Modern Capitalist Enterprise', in *Economy and Society*, vol. I, pp. 375–380.

4 Gary S. Becker, *The Economic Approach to Human Behavior* (Chicago: University of Chicago Press, 1976), ch. 11, 'A Theory of Marriage'; A *Treatise of the Family* (Cambridge: Harvard University Press, 1981).

5 Gaston Bachelard, *The New Scientific Spirit* trans. A. Goldhammer (Boston: Beacon Press, 1986 [1934]).

6 See Pierre Bourdieu, 'La délégation et le fétichisme politique', *Actes de la recherche en sciences sociales*, nos 52–53, 1984, pp. 49–55.

7 German for 'as'.

8 Bourdieu went on to devote a whole series of lectures – to be published in due course – to the economic field in the 1992–93 academic year.

9 Pierre Bourdieu et Monique de Saint-Martin, 'Le patronat', *Actes de la recherche en sciences sociales*, nos 20–21, March–April 1978, pp. 3–82.

10 See, for example, its formulation in Leibniz's *Monadology* (1714): 'Our reasonings are based on two great principles: the principle of contradiction, on the strength of which we judge to be false anything that involves contradiction, and as true whatever is opposed or contradictory to what is false.' 'And the principle of sufficient reason, on the strength of which we hold that no fact can ever be true or existent, no statement correct, unless there is a sufficient *reason why* things are as they are and not otherwise – even if in most cases we can't know what the reason is': G. W. Leibniz, *The Principles of Philosophy known as Monadology*, trans Jonathan Bennett, www.earlymoderntexts.com, 2017, §§31, 32.

11 'The soporific quality of opium' is an example of a tautologous explanation delivered by one of Molière's characters, a bachelor of medicine, in *Le Malade Imaginaire* (Act III, scene 14): '*Mihi a docto Doctore / Domandatur causam*

et rationem, quare / Opium facit dormire? / A quoi respondeo, / Quia est in eo / Virtus dormitiva.'

12 Freud's German term *Besetzung* is generally translated into French as *investissement* (English 'investment'), but can also be translated as *occupation* (English 'cathexis'), which is closer to the German sense and has fewer economic overtones.

13 This alludes to the etymology suggested by Johan Huizinga when he writes that the spoilsport 'robs play of its *illusion* – a pregnant word which means literally "in-play" (from *inlusio, illudere*, or *inludere*)'. Johan Huizinga, *Homo Ludens. A Study of the Play Element in Culture* (London: Routledge, 2003 [1949]), p. 11.

14 On this point, see the previous lecture, p. 85.

15 Max Weber, *The Protestant Ethic and the Spirit of Capitalism*, trans Talcott Parsons (London: Routledge, 2001 [1930]), p. 140.

16 On these points and on the limits of the politics of cultural democratization of the 1960s and 1970s, see, in particular, Bourdieu, Darbel and Schnapper, *The Love of Art.*

17 Alain Peyrefitte, a graduate of the École normale supérieure and the École nationale d'administration, was both a politician and a man of letters (he finished his career in the Academy). In the 1970s, his books *Quand la Chine s'éveillera . . . le monde tremblera* (1973) and *Le Mal français* (1976) were both best sellers.

18 Bourdieu is no doubt thinking of the ways that most psychoanalysts were using it, or its use by Gilles Deleuze and Félix Guattari (whose *Anti-Oedipus* of 1972 claimed to offer a 'new concept of desire').

19 Georg Wilhelm Friedrich Hegel, *The Philosophy of History*, trans. John Sibree (New York: Prometheus Books, 1991 [1837]), ch. II, §2, 'The Ruse of Reason', p. 23. Bourdieu had already mentioned and commented on this quotation in his lecture of 2 November 1982 (see *Habitus and Field*, pp. 85).

20 On all these points, see Pierre Bourdieu, *Algerian Sketches*, trans. David Fernbach (Cambridge: Polity, 2013 [2008]).

21 This is a reference to the distinction between 'micro-economics' (whose unit of analysis would, rather, be individual economic agents, consumers or producers) and 'macro-economics' (which studies aggregates, such as consumption or employment considered at the national level). The distinction is somewhat confused, in particular because it is sometimes confused with theoretical considerations, meaning that a 'micro-economic' character may be ascribed to individualistic approaches such as those that have arisen from neoclassical theory (which may moreover develop a 'macro-economics with micro-economic foundations'), and a Keynesian analysis can become associated, for reasons other than the sheer scale of its objects, with 'macro-economics'. In addition, some economists identify a 'meso-economics', midway between 'micro-' and 'macro-economics', associated with the level of a branch of activity, a sector of the economy or a region.

22 See in particular the lecture of 23 November 1982, in *Habitus and Field*, pp. 152–175.

23 An allusion to Jean-Paul Sartre, *The Family Idiot: Gustave Flaubert 1821–1857*, 5 vols, trans. Carol Cosman (Chicago: University of Chicago Press, 1971–1993).

24 Karl Marx and Frederick Engels, 'Manifesto of the Communist Party', in Karl

Marx, *The Revolutions of 1848. Political Writings*, vol. 1 (Harmondsworth: Penguin, 1973 [1850]), p. 98. (Translator)

25 Bourdieu and de Saint-Martin, 'Le patronat'. And on a later occasion Bourdieu returned to these questions in his work on private housing – 'Un placement de père de famille. La maison individuelle: spécificité du produit et logique du champ de production', *Actes de la recherche en sciences sociales*, n°o. 81, 1990, pp. 6–33) – and in his article on the economic field – 'Le champ économique', *Actes de la recherche en sciences sociales*, no. 119, 1997, p. 48–66) – which were republished together in *The Social Structures of the Economy*, trans. Chris Turner (Cambridge: Polity, 2005 [2000]).

26 Bernard Guibert, Jean Laganier and Michel Volle, 'Essai sur les nomenclatures industrielles', *Économie et statistique*, no. 20, 1971, pp. 23–36. On the nomenclature of the CSP that Bourdieu mentions in the following sentence, see another study made by the administrators of INSEE (and presented in the 1970s in Bourdieu's seminar): Alain Desrosières and Laurent Thévenot, *Les Catégories socio-professionnelles* (Paris: La Découverte, 'Repères', 1982).

27 An allusion to Kant's procedure in the *Critique of Pure Reason*: to determine what we can know, we should investigate our faculty of knowledge, which is involved in setting up the categories of knowledge.

28 As for the studies previously cited, this research was linked to INSEE. François Eymard-Duvernay was the administrator of INSEE (assigned to the 'enterprise' division) when he drew up, with Daniel Bony from the same division, the article mentioned here: 'Cohérence de la branche et diversité des entreprises: étude d'un cas', *Économie et statistique*, no. 144, 1982, p. 13–23.

29 An allusion to the need, often emphasized by Bourdieu, to 'make a name for oneself' in order to exist in the field of cultural production. He writes, for instance, in the case of the scientific field '[. . .] accumulating capital is "making a *name* for oneself", a proper name (and for some, a first name, a known and recognized name, a brand that immediately distinguishes its holder, wrenching him away from the undifferentiated, invisible, obscure background in which the common mortal is lost, into visible form [. . .]': 'Le champ scientifique', esp. p. 93).

30 The 1970s and 1980s saw the arrival in the 'sociology of organizations' and, especially in political science and in management studies, quite a number of often very descriptive case studies were devoted to decisions. For a frequently quoted example, see Graham T. Allison, *The Essence of Decision: Explaining the Cuban Missile Crisis* (Boston: Little Brown, 1971).

31 Probably a reference to the 'scandal' surrounding the decision of the public authorities in the 1950s and 1960s to redevelop the abattoirs of the la Villette neighbourhood in the north-east of Paris. This 'scandal' gave rise to a parliamentary enquiry in 1970. Bourdieu's lecture was given in the period when the site of the old abattoirs was being reconstructed with a park and cultural facilities, whose construction, and in particular its Centre for Music, had been decided by the socialist government that came to power in 1981.

32 Bourdieu had already referred to this kind of thinking in a previous lecture, that of 9 November 1982 (see *Habitus and Field*, pp. 107–109).

33 An allusion to Gaston Bachelard, *The Formation of the Scientific Mind*.

34 In other places Bourdieu points out that this ironic formula ('beyond the beyond') comes from the comic strip *Achille talon* (Achilles Heel) created by the illustrator Greg in the 1960s.

35 Pierre Bourdieu, 'Officializing strategies' in *Outline of a Theory of Practice*, pp. 38–42.
36 See the lecture of 30 November 1982, in *Habitus and Field*, pp. 165–166.
37 'Jemand mußte Josef K. verleumdet haben, denn ohne daß er etwas böses getan hätte, wurde er eines Morgens verhaftet' / 'Someone must have been telling lies about Joseph K., for without having done anything wrong he was arrested one fine morning': Franz Kafka, *The Trial*, trans. Willa and Edwin Muir (Harmondsworth: Penguin, 1953 [1925]), p. 7.
38 Émile Durkheim, *The Elementary Forms of Religious Life*, pp. 42–45.
39 'An ideal-type is one formed by the one-sided *accentuation* of one or more points of view and by the synthesis of a great many diffuse, discrete, more or less present and occasionally absent *concrete individual phenomena*, which are arranged according to those one-sidedly emphasized viewpoints into a unified analytical construct [*Gedankenbild*]. In its conceptual purity, this mental construct cannot be found empirically anywhere in reality. It is a *utopia*. Historical analysis faces the task of determining in each individual case, the extent to which this ideal-construct approximates to or diverges from reality': Max Weber, ' "Objectivity" in Social Science and Social Policy', in *Methodology of Social Sciences*, trans Edward A. Shils and Henry A. Finch (Abingdon: Routledge, 2017 [1949]), p. 90.
40 Erving Goffman says that he takes the expression used in psychiatric hospitals to describe some of the inmates, where some patients are said to be 'asylumized' and suffering from 'hospitalitis'. For Goffman, 'asylumization', along with the tactics of 'situational withdrawal' and 'the intransigent line', is one of the strategies through which individuals can undertake to adapt themselves to a totalitarian institution. 'The sampling of the outside world provided by the establishment is taken by the inmate as the whole, and a stable, relatively contented existence is built up out of the maximum satisfaction procurable within the institution': *Asylums*, p. 62.
41 Before the war, in the scientific preparatory classes, the term 'bizut' designated a first-year student. Hence the verb *bizuter*, to 'rag'. Bourdieu develops the analogy in the following lines: a '*bica*' was a pupil taking the second year, the '*taupe*' year, for the third time.
42 The advocate is called Dr Huld.
43 Kafka, *The Trial*, p. 197.
44 This is the title that Bourdieu gave to his article on Kafka ('La dernière instance', in *Le siècle de Kafka* (Paris: Centre Georges Pompidou, 1984), pp. 268–270).
45 '. . . if a morality, or system of obligations, exists, society is a moral being qualitatively different from the individuals it comprises and from the aggregation from which it derives. The similarity between this argument and that of Kant in favour of the existence of God will be noted. Kant postulates God, since without this hypothesis, morality is unintelligible [. . .] Between God and society lies the choice [. . .] I myself am quite indifferent to this choice, since I see in the Divinity only society transfigured and symbolically expressed': Émile Durkheim, 'The Determination of Moral Facts', in *Sociology and Philosophy*, trans. D. F. Pocock (Abingdon: Routledge, 2010 [1906]), p. 51–52.
46 See Bourdieu's lecture of 28 April 1982, in *Classification Struggles*, esp. pp. 12–14.
47 This may be a reference to the following fragment: 'So we must follow the

common (*logos*), yet the many live as if they had a wisdom of their own': Heraclitus, *Against the Mathematicians*, VII, 133. quoted by Sextus Empiricus.

48 J. L. Austin, *How to Do Things with Words*.

49 In particular, Mary Douglas, ed., *Witchcraft, Confessions and Accusations* (New York & London: Tavistock, 1970).

50 See *Homo Academicus*, pp. 14ff.

51 Joachim Unseld, *Franz Kafka. A Writer's Life*, trans. Paul F. Dvorak (Riverside: Ariadne Press, 1994).

52 Bourdieu took this observation as the point of departure of his analysis of publishing in 1999: 'The publisher is the person who has the absolutely extraordinary power to ensure *publication*, that is to make a text and an author accede to public existence [*Öffentlichkeit*], known and recognized': 'Une révolution conservatrice dans l'édition', p. 3.

53 Basing himself in particular on the analyses of Levin Ludwig Schücking, a specialist in British literature, Bourdieu had insisted on the importance of 'mutual admiration societies' in the avant-garde in 'Champ intellectuel et projet créateur', *Les Temps modernes*, no. 246, 1966, p. 872.

54 *Letter to my Father* is a text that Kafka wrote to his father, without sending it to him, in 1919. It was published in the 1950s. Franz Kafka, *Letter to his Father*, trans. Ernst Kaiser and Eithne Wilkins, bilingual edition (New York: Schocken Books, 1966).

Lecture of 29 March 1984

1 'Interest' comes from the Latin interest, an impersonal form of *interesse*: 'being in', 'being in between', 'being among', 'being present', 'taking part'.

2 On Huizinga, see lecture of 22 March, note 13.

3 Giambattista Vico, *The New Science*, trans. David Marsh (London: Penguin, 1999 [1725]); for Hegel on the atheism of the moral world, see the lecture of 8 March 1984, note 16.

4 Written in 1866, *The Gambler* presents both rich and impoverished people in the framework of a bathing resort called Roulettenburg. The narrator, a tutor at the start of the book, does at first win money at the casino, but finishes up as a domestic servant.

5 A saying current in the French army from the nineteenth century, expressing the possibility for any soldier to gain promotion.

6 Bourdieu, *The Logic of Practice*, pp. 42–47.

7 Leibniz uses the phrase on several occasions. For example: 'It is one of the rules of my system of general harmony, that *the present is big with the future,* and that he who sees all sees in that which is that which shall be': *Theodicy*, trans, E. M. Huggard (Project Gutenberg EBook #17147), §360.

8 Bourdieu is no doubt thinking of this passage: 'The manufacturer who in the long run acts counter to these norms will just as inevitably be eliminated from the economic scene as the worker who cannot or will not adapt himself to them will be thrown into the streets without a job': Max Weber, *The Protestant Ethic and the Spirit of Capitalism*, p. 19.

9 See Pierre Bourdieu, 'Structures sociales et structures de perception du monde social', *Actes de la recherche en sciences sociales*, no. 2, 1975, pp. 18–20.

10 See Pierre Bourdieu and Luc Boltanski, 'La production de l'idéologie

dominante', *Actes de la recherche en sciences sociales*, no. 2/3, 1976, pp. 3–73.

11 In Latin, *habitus* is the past participle (passive) of the verb *habere* (to have).

12 'Nor indeed must one imagine that the democratic representatives are all shop-keepers or their enthusiastic supporters. They may well be poles apart from them in their education and their individual situation. What makes them representatives of the petty bourgeoisie is the fact that their minds are restricted by the same barriers which the petty bourgeoisie fails to overcome in real life, and that they are therefore driven in theory to the same problems and solutions to which material interest and social situation drive the latter in practice': Karl Marx, *The Eighteenth Brumaire of Louis Bonaparte*, trans. Ben Fowkes (Harmondsworth: Penguin, 1973 [1852]), pp. 176–177.

13 Émile Durkheim, *Pragmatism and Sociology*, trans. J. C. Whitehouse (Cambridge: Cambridge University Press, 1983 [1914]), ch. 20, 'Are Thought and Reality Heterogeneous?': 'The initial state is a multiplicity of germs, of ways and means, and of different activities which are not only intermingled, but, as it were, lost in each other, so that it is extremely difficult to separate them. They are indistinct from each other ... In social life, that primitive undivided state is even more striking. Religious life, for example, contains a rich abundance of forms of thought and activities of all kinds. In the field of thought, these include myths and religious beliefs, an embryonic science,' and a certain poetry. In the sphere of action we find rites, a morality and a form of law', and arts (aesthetic elements, songs and music in particular). All these elements are gathered up into a whole and it seems extremely difficult to separate them. Science and art, myth and poetry, morality, law and religion are all confused or, rather, fused. The same observations could be made about the early family, which is at one and the same time, for example, a social, religious, political and legal unit.' See also Durkheim, *The Division of Labour in Society* and *The Elementary Forms of Religious Life*.

14 Moses I. Finlay, *The Ancient Economy* (Berkeley: University of California Press, 1973).

15 Karl Marx, *A Contribution to the Critique of Political Economy*, trans. S. W. Ryazanskaya (Moscow: Progress Publishers, 1999 [1859]): 'The anatomy of man is a key to the anatomy of the ape.' (One of the conclusions that Marx draws from this aphorism is precisely that: 'Bourgeois economy thus provides a key to the economy of antiquity.')

16 Karl Marx, *Grundrisse. Foundations of the Critique of Political Economy*, trans. Martin Nicolaus (Harmondsworth: Penguin, 1993), pp. 157–158.

17 See Norbert Elias, *On the Process of Civilisation (The Collected Works of Norbert Elias*, vol. 3), trans. Edmund Jephcott (Dublin: University College Dublin Press, 2012). See also Pierre Kamnitzer and Jeanne Étoré, *La Société de cour* (Paris: Calmann-Lévy, 1974 [1969]). On sport, see Norbert Elias, 'Sport et violence', *Actes de la recherche en sciences sociales*, no. 6, 1976, pp. 2–21, and, published after Bourdieu's lectures, Norbert Elias and Eric Dunning, 'Sport and Civilisation: Violence Mastered? From Civilising Functions to Pacifying Functions', *International Journal of the History of Sport*, vol. 31, no. 16, November 2014.

18 'In the past, the most diverse kinds of association – beginning with the clan – have regarded physical violence as a fairly normal instrument. Nowadays, by contrast, we have to say that a state is that human community which (suc-

cessfully) lays claim to the *monopoly of legitimate physical violence* within a certain territory, this 'territory' being another of the defining characteristics of the state. For the specific feature of the present is that the right to use physical violence is attributed to any and all other institutions or individuals only to the extent that the *state* permits this to happen. The state is held to be the sole source of the "right" to use violence': Max Weber, 'The Profession and Vocation of Politics', in *Political Writings*, pp. 310–311.

19 See the first year of the course of lectures, in *Classification Struggles*, esp. pp. 12–23.

20 In his lecture of 30 November 1982 (see *Habitus and Field*, p. 177), Bourdieu had already dealt with the topic of the 'inertia-violence of institutions' that Sartre had referred to on the subject of colonialism: 'The old violence is reabsorbed by the inertia-violence of the institution': Jean-Paul Sartre, *Critique of Dialectical Reason*, trans. Alan Sheridan-Smith (London: Verso, 2004 [1960]), vol. 1, p. 723.

21 See *The Logic of Practice*, esp. pp. 122–140.

22 Ibid., p. 125.

23 See lecture for 8 March 1984, note 38.

24 Bourdieu returned to the domestic economy in 'The Family Spirit', in *Practical Reason. On the Theory of Action* (Cambridge: Polity, 1998), pp. 64–74.

25 Georg Lukács, 'The Changing Function of Historical Materialism', in *History and Class Consciousness. Studies in Marxist Dialectics*, trans. Rodney Livingstone (London: The Merlin Press, 1971 [1923]), pp. 224–253.

26 Bourdieu returned to the topic of amorous relations in 'Postscript on Domination and Love', in *Masculine Domination*, trans. Richard Nice (Cambridge: Polity, 2001 [1998]), pp. 109–112.

27 On the gift, see *The Logic of Practice*, pp. 98–111. Bourdieu had developed the question of time in the gift in the previous year of this course. See lecture of 19 October 1982, in *Habitus and Field*, pp. 53–54.

28 Karl Marx and Frederick Engels, 'Manifesto of the Communist Party', p. 70: 'The bourgeoisie, historically, has played a most revolutionary part. The bourgeoisie, wherever it has got the upper hand, has put an end to all feudal, patriarchal, idyllic relations. It has pitilessly torn asunder the motley feudal ties that bound man to his "natural superiors", and has left remaining no other nexus between man and man than naked self-interest, than callous "cash payment". It has drowned the most heavenly ecstasies of religious fervour, of chivalrous enthusiasm, of philistine sentimentalism, in the icy water of egotistical calculation.'

29 Norbert Elias, 'Etiquette and Ceremony', in *The Court Society. The Collected Works of Norbert Elias*, vol. 2, trans. Edmund Jephcott (Dublin: University College Dublin Press, 2006), pp. 86–126.

30 On this topic, see Bourdieu, *Outline of a Theory of Practice*, pp. 213–214, note 109. Bourdieu had previously referred to this quotation in the framework of a development on symbolic capital (see *Classification Struggles*, p. 93)

31 Elias, 'Sport and Violence'.

32 This film by Shohei Imamura, which won the Palme d'or at the Cannes film festival, had been shown in Paris a few months before these lectures, in September 1983. It is situated in a poor village in nineteenth-century Japan. The main character, a sixty-nine-year-old woman, bows to a custom whereby old people must go up to the top of the mountain to let themselves die when they reach

the age of seventy, after which the community regards them as unproductive creatures, and a liability.

33 On distant marriages in Kabylia, see Bourdieu, *The Logic of Practice*, pp. 179–187.

34 See *The Political Ontology of Martin Heidegger*.

35 On the phenomenon of the devaluation of educational qualifications, see chapter 2 of *Distinction*, esp. pp. 132–135, 142–143.

36 Groucho Marx says that at the end of the 1940s he replied to an invitation from a club for celebrities, saying: 'I don't want to belong to any club that will accept me as a member.' Groucho Marx, *Groucho and Me* (New York: Da Capo Press, 1959), p. 321.

37 On the space of the disciplines, see *Homo Academicus*, and also the lecture of 23 November 1982, in *Habitus and Field*, pp. 152ff.

38 A *sous-préfecture* in the Cantal, one of France's most sparsely populated departments [and therefore not a prestigious teaching appointment].

39 *Distinction*, p. 141.

40 The rue du Faubourg Saint-Honoré was the traditional centre of the haute couture industry; the rue du Faubourg Saint-Antoine, near the Bastille, was traditionally populated by cabinetmakers and the like.

41 An allusion to the 'master–slave dialectic' developed by Hegel, which shows that the master is also a slave to the slave because he depends on him: Georg Wilhelm Friedrich Hegel, *The Phenomenology of Mind*, trans. Terry Pinkard (Cambridge: Cambridge University Press, 2018 [1806–7]), pp. 102–135.

42 Weber, *The Protestant Ethic and the Spirit of Capitalism*; *Economy and Society*, vol. 1, pp. 587–588.

43 On the notion of 'care' or 'concern' (*Fürsorge*) in Heidegger, see Bourdieu, *The Political Ontology of Martin Heidegger*.

44 'The same stale platitudes would be brought out again either to delude him with vague false hopes or to torment him with equally vague menaces': *The Trial*, p. 208.

45 In the two previous years, Bourdieu had developed his argument on the mechanism of the *numerus clausus*. See *Classification Struggles*, pp. 90–92; *Habitus and Field*, p. 201.

46 Bourdieu is no doubt thinking of the research by Victor Karady that he quoted on this subject during the first year of his lectures – particularly, Victor Karady and Istvan Kemeny, 'Antisémitisme universitaire et concurrence de classe: la loi du *numerus clausus en* Hongrie entre les deux guerres', *Actes de la recherche en sciences sociales*, no. 34, pp. 67–97.

47 The exact sentence was quoted by Bourdieu in the previous lecture: 'Any man can call himself great, of course, if he pleases, but in this matter the Court tradition must decide': F. Kafka, *The Trial*, p. 197.

48 Ibid., p. 216.

49 On this point and the argument that follows, see Bourdieu, *Homo Academicus*, in particular the section 'Time and Power', pp. 90–105.

Lecture of 19 April 1984

1 This book appeared in November 1985 in the series 'Le sens commun' edited by Bourdieu: Anna Boschetti, *Sartre et 'Les Temps modernes'. Une entreprise*

intellectuelle (Paris: Minuit, 1985) / Anna Boschetti, *The Intellectual Enterprise: Sartre and 'Les Temps Modernes'*, trans. Richard C. McLeary (Evanston: Northwestern University Press, 1988).

2 See Bourdieu, 'Le champ scientifique', esp. p. 95.

3 See Pierre Bourdieu, 'La société traditionnelle: attitude à l'égard du temps et conduites économiques', *Sociologie du travail*, no. 1, 1963, pp. 24–44. This article was republished in *Esquisses Algériennes* (Paris: Seuil, 2008), pp. 75–98, and as 'Traditional Society's Attitude towards Time and Economic Behaviour', in *Algerian Sketches*, pp. 52–71.

4 Thorstein Veblen, *The Theory of the Leisure Class* (Oxford: Oxford University Press, 2009 [1899]).

5 An allusion to Claude Lévi-Strauss, *Tristes Tropiques*, trans. John and Doreen Weightman (London: Penguin 2009 [1955]). (Translator)

6 Ockham's razor (cited by analytical philosophers in particular) designates the principle of simplicity advocated by the English Franciscan William of Ockham in the fourteenth century in debates between nominalism and realism. Without claiming to have invented the term, he argued that it is pointless to use a greater number of factors to explain something that can be explained with fewer – thereby dispensing with an appeal to universals. William of Ockham, *Theory of Terms*, Part I of the *Summa Logicae*, trans. Michael Loux (South Bend: St Augustine's Press, 2011 [1323]). See *The Cambridge Companion to Ockham*, ed. Paul Vincent Spade (Cambridge: Cambridge University Press, 1999), ch. 5, 'Ockham's Nominalist Metaphysics', pp. 100–117.

7 Pierre Bourdieu, 'Les trois états du capital culturel', *Actes de la recherche en sciences sociales*, no. 30, 1979, pp. 3–6.

8 Bourdieu will return later to this notion of information capital on several occasions, especially in *On the State*, pp. 212–215, and *Pascalian Meditations*, trans. Richard Nice (Cambridge: Polity, 2000), p. 78.

9 We should remember that when Bourdieu was speaking, in 1984, there was no internet or email. If he were writing now, he would no doubt be speaking of 'software' and 'apps' and 'algorithms'. (Translator)

10 As he explains a little later, it was in his work on education at the beginning of the 1960s that Bourdieu began using notions close to those of 'cultural capital' such as 'cultural heritage' and 'culturally privileged'.

11 The notion of human capital was developed from the end of the 1950s by neo-classical economists, in particular Jacob Mincer, 'Investment in human capital and personal income distribution', *Journal of Political Economy*, vol. 66, no. 4, 1958, pp. 281–302; Theodore W. Schultz, 'Investment in human capital', *The American Economic Review*, vol. 51, no. 1, 1961, pp. 1–17; another important work was the book by Gary Becker published in 1964 that Bourdieu cites in the next paragraph.

12 Bourdieu is thinking of Alain Girard's research at INED – in particular, 'Enquête nationale sur l'orientation et la sélection des enfants d'âge scolaire', *Population*, vol. 9, no. 4, 1954, pp. 597–634.

13 See *Homo Academicus*, esp. pp. 77–84.

14 See *Distinction*, pp. 295–317.

15 This caveat applies not only to the concept of profit in Bourdieu, but also to the concepts of strategy', 'distinction' and 'interest', all of which need to be understood in Bourdieu's usage in their objective sense without necessarily implying any subjective intent by the social agents.

16 The word 'naivety', often used by Bourdieu, has a technical rather than a polemical meaning and designates nonreflexive, first-degree attitudes or behaviour, which consists in accepting things at their face value.

17 See, for example, Theodore Schultz's theory of growth.

18 On these points, see Pierre Bourdieu and Jean-Claude Passeron, 'La comparabilité des systèmes d'enseignement', in Robert Castel et Jean-Claude Passeron (eds), *Éducation, développement et démocratie* (The Hague: Mouton, 1967), pp. 21–33.

19 In 1984, when Bourdieu was giving these lectures, the baccalaureate was still awarded to barely 25 per cent of the relevant age group. It was not until the following year, 1985, that the ministry of education announced the (long-term) aim of bringing 80 per cent of the age group up to the level of the baccalaureate. [The target was achieved in 2018; see *L'Express* of 5 January 2018. (Translator)]

20 Marginalism is a theory of economics that attempts to explain discrepancies in the value of goods and services by reference to their secondary, or marginal, utility. (Translator)

21 This was a Catholic-inspired movement that appeared in the interwar years. It placed the individual at the heart of a religious reflection with progressive intentions. Its principle theorist was Emmanuel Mounier (1905–50) who founded the journal *Esprit*.

22 See *Distinction*, p. 75.

23 No doubt an allusion to the radio broadcast 'La tribune des critiques de disques' (France Musique).

24 'The accumulation of cultural capital demands an incorporation which, insofar as it supposes a work of inculcation and assimilation, *costs time*, time that must be invested *personally* by the investor (just like suntan, it cannot be acquired by proxy)': Bourdieu, 'Les trois états du capital culturel, pp. 3–4.

25 Ernst Hartwig Kantorowicz, *The King's Two Bodies. A Study in Mediaeval Political Thought* (Princeton: Princeton University Press, 1957).

26 According to one (uncertain) etymological tradition, the 'imbecile' is someone who walks without a stick (*in-bacillus*) and thus takes the risk of falling.

27 Bourdieu had developed this theme in his lecture of 19 October 1982, in *Habitus and Field*, pp. 47ff.

28 An allusion (also made in *Pascalian Meditations*, pp. 13, 226) to a witticism recounted by Socrates in the *Theaetetus*: 'While [Thales] was studying the stars and looking upwards, he fell into a pit, and a neat, witty Thracian servant girl jeered at him, they say, because he was so eager to know the things in the sky that he could not see what was there before him at his very feet. The same jest applies to all who pass their lives in philosophy': Plato, *Theaetetus*, trans Harold North Fowler (Cambridge MA: Harvard University Press, 2006), §174a, p. 121.

29 See 'Postscript: Towards a "Vulgar" Critique of "Pure" Critiques', in *Distinction*, pp. 485–500.

30 In *Distinction*, pp. 296–304, see the developments on the relations between the holders of economic power in the firm and the holders, such as the engineers and the executives, of the cultural capital enabling them to take charge of instruments such as machines.

31 'When a man who is happy compares his position with that of one who is unhappy, he is not content with the fact of his happiness, but desires some-

thing more, namely the right to this happiness, the consciousness that he has earned this good fortune, in contrast to the unfortunate one who must equally have earned his misfortune. Our everyday experience proves that there exists just such a need for reassurance as to the legitimacy or deservedness of one's happiness, whether this involves political success, superior economic status, bodily health, success in the game of love, or anything else. What the privileged classes require of religion, if anything at all, is this psychologic reassurance of legitimacy'. This theodicy of 'good fortune' is opposed to a 'theodicy of disprivilege': Max Weber, *The Sociology of Religion*, pp. 107, 113.

32 On this point, and more generally on the whole of this second part of the lecture, see the developments that Bourdieu had devoted during the previous year to the analysis of working-class youth, in *Habitus and Field*, pp. 87–88; for a sketch of the themes broached here (and in particular the comparison between the characters of Beckett and certain social experiences), see Pierre Bourdieu, 'Préface', in Paul Lazarsfeld, Marie Jahoda and Hans Zeisel, *Les Chômeurs de Marienthal* (Paris: Minuit, 1982), pp. 7–12, as well as the interview (dating from after this lecture) titled 'Those Were the Days', in *The Weight of the World*, pp. 427–440.

33 These are probably the lectures for 1 and 8 March 1984.

34 André Gide, *The Journals: 1939–1949*, trans. Justin O'Brian (London: Secker and Warburg, 1951), under 2 September 1940, p. 44.

35 What Bourdieu calls the 'discourse of authority' or 'importance'; see *Language and Symbolic Power*, p. 76.

36 Samuel Beckett, *Waiting for Godot* (New York: Grove Press, 1954).

37 The two main characters in *Waiting for Godot*, Vladimir and Estragon, are both tramps.

38 Bourdieu develops this theme in the last chapter of *Pascalian Meditations*, pp. 206ff.

39 Bourdieu had discussed this theme at greater length the previous year, in particular in the lectures of 30 November 1982 and 25 January 1983, in *Habitus and Field*, pp. 182, 266–267. On the 'morality of *ressentiment*' that Nietzsche opposes to 'noble morality', see, in particular, his *On the Genealogy of Morals* (1887).

40 In one of La Fontaine's fables inspired by Aesop ('The Fox and the Grapes'), this is the reason given by the fox when he realizes that the grapes he wants to eat are too high for him to reach: 'Bah! Fit for boors! Still green!': *The Complete Fables of Jean de La Fontaine*, trans. Norman R. Shapiro (Urbana: University of Illinois Press, 2007 [1668–94]), p. 67.

41 David Hume, *A Treatise of Human Nature* (Oxford: Clarendon, 2011 [1739–40]), p. 5: 'We are no sooner acquainted with the impossibility of satisfying any desire, than the desire itself vanishes.'

42 Martin Heidegger, *Being and Time*, trans. John Macquarrie and Edward Robinson (Oxford: Blackwell, 1962 [1927]), §40: 'The basic state-of-mind of anxiety as a distinctive way in which Dasein is disclosed', pp. 228–235.

43 See Pierre Bourdieu, 'Les sous-prolétaires algériens', *Les Temps Modernes*, no. 199, 1962, pp. 1030–1051; republished as 'The Algerian Sub-Proletarians', in *Algerian Sketches*, pp. 146–161. See also Bourdieu, 'La société traditionnelle. Attitude à l'égard du temps et conduite économique'.

44 Norman Cohn, *The Pursuit of the Millennium. Revolutionary Millenarians and Mystical Anarchists of the Middle Ages* (London: Secker & Warburg, 1957).

45 Bourdieu is thinking of Paul Willis, 'The Motorbike Club within a Structural Group', *Working Papers in Cultural Studies*, no. 2, 1971, pp. 53–70; *Profane Culture* (London: Routledge & Kegan Paul, 1978).

46 See Heidegger, *Being and Time*, Division Two, ch. I, §§46–53: 'Dasein's Possibility of Being-a-whole, and Being-towards-death', pp. 279–312.

47 *Being and Time*, §75, pp. 439–444.

48 'Putting a letter in the mailbox, I expect that unknown people, called postmen, will act in a typical way, with the result that my letter will reach the addressee within typically reasonable time': Alfred Schütz, 'Common Sense and Scientific Interpretation of Human Action', in *Collected Papers*, vol. 2 (The Hague: Martinus Nijhoff, 1964), p. 17.

49 Bourdieu will return to this point later in the first lectures of 1985–86 and in 'L'illusion biographique', *Actes de la recherche en sciences sociales*, no. 62, 1986, pp. 69–72.

50 *Agenda* is a form of the Latin verb *agere* meaning literally 'things to do'. Bourdieu had already remarked on this the previous year: see lecture of 19 October 1982, in *Habitus and Field*, pp. 67–68.

51 Max Weber, *Economy and Society*, vol. I, p. 507.

52 Bourdieu evokes this aspect of the sociologist's profession in *Sketch for a Self Analysis*, p. 66.

53 'In phenomenological research, *épochè* is described as a process involved in blocking biases and assumptions in order to explain a phenomenon in terms of its own inherent system of meaning. This is a general predisposition one must assume before commencing phenomenological study. It is different from bracketing, which is to acknowledge any personal bias or contextual assumptions of the researcher. This involves systematic steps to 'set aside' various assumptions and beliefs about a phenomenon in order to examine how the phenomenon presents itself in the world of the participant' (*Wikipedia*). Generally, the Greek word *épochè* means 'suspension of judgement' or 'withholding of assent'. (Translator)

54 J. L. Austin, in particular, enumerates the 'conditions of felicity' that must be met to ensure the successful function of a performative: *How to Do Things with Words*, pp. 42–45. In 1986, Bourdieu published an article by Erving Goffman, 'La condition de félicité', in *Actes de la recherche en sciences sociales*, no. 64, pp. 63–78 and no. 65, pp. 87–98.

55 Erich Fromm, *The Fear of Freedom* (London: Routledge & Kegan Paul, 1942).

56 An allusion to Leibniz's saying, 'The present is big with the future', which Bourdieu had quoted in the previous lecture.

57 See the chapter 'Irresistible Analogy' in *The Logic of Practice*, pp. 200–270.

58 Hesiod, *Works and Days*, trans. A. E. Stallings (London: Penguin, 2018).

59 Alfred Schütz, 'Making Music Together: A Study in Social Relationship', *Social Research*, vol. 18, 1951, pp. 76–97 (also in his *Collected Papers*, vol. 2, pp. 159–178).

60 E. Durkheim, *The Division of Labour in Society*.

61 On this point, see the lecture of 19 October 1982, in *Habitus and Field*, p. 64.

62 See Weber, *Economy and Society*, vol. 1, pp. 80–82.

63 Michael Pollak, 'Des mots qui tuent', *Actes de la recherche en sciences sociales*, no. 41, 1982, pp. 29–45.

64 Gerhard Botz, 'Survivre dans un camp de concentration. Entretien avec

Margaret Glas-Larsson', *Actes de la recherche en sciences sociales*, no. 41, 1982, pp. 3–38.

Lecture of 26 April 1984

1 On the break operated by the journal *Actes de la recherche en sciences sociales* in the presentation of the results of research, see the text that introduces the first issue: Pierre Bourdieu, 'Méthode scientifique et hiérarchie sociale des objets', Actes *de la recherche en sciences sociales*, no. 1, 1975, pp. 4–6.

2 See above, lecture for 1 March, note 41.

3 An allusion to a reflection by Aesop that Jean de La Fontaine refers to; see 'La vie d'Ésope le Phrygien', in *Oeuvres complètes*, vol. I (Paris: Gallimard, 'Bibliothèque de la Pléiade', 1991): 'Language is "the best of things", because it is "the bond of social life, the key to the sciences, the organ of truth and reason", and the worst of things, because it is at the same time "the mother of all disputes, the nurse of all legal proceedings, the source of division and war, the organ of error, and, worse still, of calumny".'

4 Bourdieu is thinking of the research that developed after the Second World War, using the statistical analysis of the tables of mobility mapping the social position of men against that of their fathers. *Distinction* contains several passages critical of this branch of research (see, in particular, pp. 102–106).

5 While engaged in research in Algeria, Bourdieu, who had reflected on the effects of the passage from oral to writing (see, in particular, *Outline of a Theory of Practice*, pp. 186–187), also had published, in 1979, in his series 'Le sens commun', the French translation of an important book on the topic: Jack Goody, *The Domestication of the Savage Mind* (Cambridge: Cambridge University Press, 1977).

6 A few years before these lectures, the translation of a book dealing with the distribution of musical competence in African and European societies had been published in 'Le sens commun' series: John Blacking, *How Musical is Man?* (Seattle: University of Washington Press, 1974).

7 This formula (which makes us think of what economists call 'non-competing goods') is no doubt not to be found verbatim in Spinoza. In *Distinction*, pp. 227–228, Bourdieu makes a connection between the 'love of art' and the 'intellectual love of God', which suggests that he has in mind the following passage: 'This love towards God is the greatest good which we can desire according to the dictate of reason, and it is common to all men, and we desire that all should enjoy it. And therefore it cannot be stained by the emotion of envy, nor again by the emotion of jealousy; but, on the other hand, it must be cherished the more, the more men we imagine to enjoy it': Baruch Spinoza, *Ethics*, trans. Andrew Boyle, Part V, proposition 20, 'Concerning the Power of the Intellect or Human Freedom' (London: Dent, 1986), p. 211.

8 Saussure, for instance, sees language as 'a storehouse filled [treasure deposited] by the members of a given community through their active use of speaking, a grammatical system that has a potential existence in each brain, or, more specifically, in the brains of a group of individuals. For language is not complete in any speaker; it exists perfectly only within a collectivity': Ferdinand de Saussure, *Course in General Linguistics*, trans. Wade Baskin (New York:

McGraw-Hill, 1959 [1916]), pp. 13–14. On the 'illusion of linguistic communism', see Bourdieu, *Language and Symbolic Power*, esp. pp. 43–44.

9 Bourdieu refers to these reading scenarios in the preface to *The Rules of Art*, pp. xiv–xviii.

10 Probably an allusion to Bourdieu's work on culture in the 1960s and the objections that he had encountered.

11 An allusion to the collective work by Louis Althusser et al., *Reading Capital*, trans. Ben Brewster and David Fernbach (London: Verso, 2006 [1965]). In 1975, Bourdieu had published 'La lecture de Marx ou quelques remarques critiques à propos de *Lire "Le Capital"*', *Actes de la recherche en sciences sociales*, no. 5, 1975, pp. 65–79; republished as 'Le discours d'importance', in *Langage et pouvoir symbolique*, pp. 379–396 (*Language and Symbolic Power*).

12 See Pierre Bourdieu, Jean-Claude Passeron and Monique de Saint-Martin, 'Les étudiants et la langue d'enseignement', in *Rapport pédagogique et communication* (Paris-The Hague: Mouton, 1965), pp. 37–69.

13 Bourdieu is referring here to research he was engaged in when he was in Lille teaching two days a week in the Arts Faculty (he held a post there from 1961 to 1964 and one of his close colleagues was the philosopher Éric Weil). Mrs Malaprop is a character in the play *The Rivals* (1775) by the Irish playwright and politician Richard Brinsley Sheridan, which gave birth to the neologism *malapropism* – 'abuse of language'.

14 The first test presented a series of sentences; the candidates were asked to 'underline the words that seem to you to be incorrectly used [. . .]. Some sentences may not contain any terms wrongly used. [. . .] Here is an example: "Modern science proves that phenomena are subject to a random determinism." The word "random" is not suitable here.' The second test is presented as follows: 'Define as rigorously as you can the following terms: Antinomy; Land register; Epistemology; Extension (of a concept); Manichaeism.'

15 This notion is used in particular in Pierre Bourdieu and Jean-Claude Passeron, *Reproduction in Education, Society and Culture*, trans. Richard Nice (London: Sage, 1977).

16 These remarks on the novels of Pierre Daninos are developed in Pierre Bourdieu (ed.), *Photography: A Middle-brow Art*, trans. Shaun Whiteside (Cambridge: Polity, 1990 [1965]), and in 'Différences et distinctions', in Darras, *Le partage des bénéfices* (Paris: Minuit, 1966), pp. 124–125.

17 See Bourdieu, *Photography: A Middle-brow Art*.

18 'Instruments are nothing but theories materialized': Gaston Bachelard, *The New Scientific Spirit*, trans. A. Goldhammer (Boston: Beacon Press, 1986 [1934]), p. 13.

19 On the opposition between material appropriation and symbolic appropriation, see *Distinction*, in particular the chapter 'The Sense of Distinction', pp. 257–317 (where the modes of symbolic appropriation developed by those fractions rich particularly in cultural capital appear, at least in some aspects, as a substitute for the material appropriation permitted by their economic capital).

20 Bourdieu had developed analyses along these lines the previous year (see lecture of 12 October 1982, in *Habitus and Field*, pp. 24ff).

21 These allusions recall Bourdieu's comments on the subject of Jacques Derrida; see 'Parerga and Paralipomena', in *Distinction*, pp. 494–498.

22 Daniel Dessert and Jean-Louis Journet, 'Le lobby Colbert: un royaume ou une affaire de famille?', *Annales*, vol. 30, no. 6, 1975, pp. 1303–1336.

23 'Constant capital' in Marx designates: 'That part of capital therefore, which is turned into means of production, i.e. the raw material, the auxiliary material and the instruments of labour, [which] does not undergo any quantitative alteration of value in the process of production.' Whereas 'variable capital' corresponds to 'that part of capital which is turned into labour-power [and] does undergo a alteration of value in the process of production. It both reproduces the equivalent of its own value and produces an excess, a surplus-value, which may itself vary, and be more or less according to circumstances': Karl Marx, *Capital*, vol. I, trans. Ben Fowkes (London: Penguin, 1990 [1976]), ch. 8, p. 317.

24 Bourdieu had already raised this issue (which he also deals with in *Distinction*, pp. 280, 467) in his lecture of 19 April.

25 This allusion may perhaps refer to what Kenneth Arrow simply calls 'knowledge' in the article where he sets out the principle of 'learning by doing' ('The Economic Implications of Learning by Doing', *The Review of Economic Studies*, vol. 29, no. 3, 1962, pp. 155–173), which Bourdieu cites on other occasions (see *The Logic of Practice*, pp. 76, 294). In his article, Arrow insists on the fact that knowledge grows over time, and he underlines the role of experience in the growth of knowledge and productivity.

26 On these points, see Bourdieu, Darbel and Schnapper, *The Love of Art*, esp. pp. 69–76.

27 On these points, see the lecture of 12 October 1982, in *Habitus and Field*, pp. 39ff, and a later artcicle, 'Piété religieuse et dévotion artistique. Fidèles et amateurs d'art à Santa Maria Novella', *Actes de la recherche en sciences sociales*, no. 105, 1994, pp. 71–74.

28 'The Code of Hammurabi is a well-preserved Babylonian code of law of ancient Mesopotamia dated to about 1754 BC (Middle Chronology). It is one of the oldest deciphered writings of significant length in the world. The sixth Babylonian king, Hammurabi, enacted the code. A partial copy exists on a 2.25-metre-tall (7.5 ft) stone stele. It consists of 282 laws, with scaled punishments, adjusting "an eye for an eye, a tooth for a tooth" (*lex talionis*) as graded based on social stratification depending on social status and gender, of slave versus free, man versus woman' (*Wikipedia*). (Translator)

29 Max Weber's *The Protestant Ethic and the Spirit of Capitalism* contains a number of developments – for instance on the notion of the 'calling' (*Beruf*), which Weber describes as a 'product of the Reformation' that 'comes from the Bible translations' (pp. 39–40) – or notes on these points: 'Luther read the Bible through the spectacles of his whole attitude' (p. 43).

30 See P. Bourdieu, 'La société traditionnelle. Attitude à l'égard du temps et conduite économique'.

31 Erving Goffman, who offers a typology of total institutions, also includes old people's homes and orphanages, psychiatric hospitals, penitentiaries, ships, colonial forts, etc.; see *Asylums*, p. 5.

32 In Greek, the word *metanoia* indicates a change of sentiment. Bourdieu uses it with reference to its religious usage, associated with the idea of conversion.

33 This sixth-century text aimed to define the organization of monastic life. It has continued to be widely read until the present day. Erving Goffman refers to it on several occasions when, in *Asylums*, he analyses the 'universe of confinement'.

34 Michael Pollak, 'Des mots qui tuent', *Actes de la recherche en sciences sociales*, no. 41, 1982, pp. 29–45.
35 At the time of these lectures, most of the male population would be familiar with the barracks, since military service was compulsory in France until 1997 (at the beginning of the 1980s the government thought of reducing the period of service by half, to six months, but did not pass the legislation).
36 Cournot draws our attention to 'the double sense of the word probability, which sometimes refers to a certain degree of our knowledge, and sometimes a degree of the possibility of things, independently of the knowledge that we have of them [. . .] It is from the language of metaphysics that I have shamelessly borrowed the two epithets of objective and subjective [. . .] to distinguish radically between the two meanings of the term probability': Antoine-Augustin Cournot, *Exposition de la théorie des chances et des probabilités* (Paris: Vrin, 1984 [1843]), pp. 4–5. He also speaks of 'the fundamental distinction between the probabilities which have an objective existence and measure the degree of probability of things, and subjective probabilities, partly dependent on our knowledge or ignorance, variable from one intelligence to another, according to their capacities and the data that they have available' (ibid., p. 106), and mentions that subjective probability 'will cease to express a relation existing really and objectively between existing things; it will assume a purely subjective character, and will be liable to vary from one individual to another, depending on the degree of their knowledge' (ibid., p. 288). On the notion of probability, Bourdieu later published Michel Dufour's French translation of Ian Hacking, *L'émergence de la probabilité*, in his 'Liber' series (Paris: Seuil, 2002 [1975]). The English title is *The Emergence of Probability. A Philosophical Study of Early Ideas about Probability, Induction and Statistical Inference* (Cambridge: Cambridge University Press, 2006 [1975]).
37 The legal retirement age was lowered to sixty in 1982. This was one of the reforms of the socialist government that came to power in 1981.
38 On this question, see Pierre Bourdieu, 'Youth is Just a Word', in *Sociology in Question*, pp. 94–102.
39 The age of majority, including the right to vote, had been lowered to eighteen in 1974.
40 See above, lecture of 29 March, note 5.
41 Charles Tilly, Louise Tilly and Richard Tilly, *The Rebellious Century, 1830–1930* (Cambridge: Harvard University Press, 1975).
42 Eric Hobsbawm, especially *Primitive Rebels* (London: Abacus, 2017 [1959]), and The *Age of Revolution* (London, Abacus, 1988 [1962]); Edward E. Thompson, *The Formation of the Working Class in England* (London: Penguin, 2013 [1988]).
43 Bourdieu is no doubt thinking of the riots and demonstrations that took place in Iran in 1978 and that helped to topple the Shah and bring the Ayatollah Khomeini to power.
44 The problematic of 'awakening consciousness' and its critique had been discussed during the previous years (see *Classification Struggles*, pp. 71–72, 102–103, 114–115, 123).
45 A reference to the importance attributed in Durkheim's analyses of religion to the sacred and the profane (see *The Elementary Forms of Religious Life*).
46 For the analysis of May 1968, see Bourdieu, 'The Critical Moment', in *Homo Academicus*, pp. 159–193.

47 Raymond Aron had used the word 'psychodrama' in his articles in *Le Figaro* in May and June 1968, articles reprinted in *La Révolution introuvable* (Paris: Fayard, 1968).

48 See the lecture of 19 April, p. 178 and note 48.

49 This formula, attributed to Mallarmé (here by Bourdieu, but also by other authors) appears neither in the poet's works nor in his correspondence. It is no doubt an apocryphal remark, like so many attributed to the poet.

50 Lubomir Doležel, 'Proper names, definite descriptions and intensional structure of Kafka's "The Trial"', *Poetics*, vol. 12, no. 6, pp. 511–526.

51 Ibid., p. 523.

52 'When Joseph K. asks Titorelli the name of the judge whose portrait he is painting, Titorelli replies: "*Das darf ich nicht sagen*" ("I'm not allowed to tell"). This reply indicates that the names of the judges are taboo. It is because the Court in *The Trial* is an alien, separate, unknown and inaccessible world': ibid, p. 523.

53 *Flatus vocis* are mere names, words, or sounds without a corresponding objective reality – a term used in the Middle Ages by the nominalists to criticize universals. (Translator)

54 This reminiscence dates no doubt from the 1972–1973 academic year that Bourdieu spent as a visiting fellow at the Institute for Advanced Studies in Princeton.

55 Bourdieu may be thinking of the places where Max Weber insists on the fact that social regularities are based less often on obedience to norms or customs than on what participants take to be their 'normal interests'. 'Many of the especially notable uniformities in the course of social action are not determined by orientation to any sort of norm which is held to be valid, nor do they rest on custom, but entirely on the fact that the corresponding type of social action is in the nature of the case best adapted to the normal interests of the actors as they themselves are aware of it . . . The more strictly rational their action is, the more they will tend to react similarly to the same situation. In this way there arise similarities, uniformities, and continuities in their attitudes and actions which are often far more stable than they would be if action were oriented to a system of norms and duties which were considered binding on the members of a group': Weber, *Economy and Society*, vol. I, p. 30.

56 See the lecture of 15 March 1984, p. 71.

57 See P. Bourdieu, *Outline of a Theory of Practice*, especially pp. 17, 20, 27.

58 A reference to the justice that Sancho Panza metes out on his island, and to the judgement of Solomon and probably, more generally, to a phrase by Max Weber: 'The ideal example of this type of rational administration of justice is the "kadi-justice" of the "Solomonian" judgement as it was practised by the hero of that legend – and by Sancho Panza when he happened to be governor': *Economy and Society*, vol. II, p. 845. Bourdieu returns to kadi-justice, Sancho Panza and Solomon at greater length in the lecture of 10 May 1984: see p. 249.

59 The passage that Bourdieu refers to is no doubt the one on 'Administration by Notables', in *Economy and Society*, vol. 1, pp. 290–292. Weber explains that the notable 'is able to live *for* politics without living from politics' and draws a parallel with the position of the 'annually elected head [*Rektor*] of the German University, who administers academic affairs only as a sideline'.

60 Bourdieu developed this point in 'Modes of Domination', in *The Logic of Practice*, pp. 122–134.
61 'Space and time are not separable. But what is time in our perception? When we represent to ourselves the extent of things, we are representing our power over things, that is, the power we have to acquire sensations that we lack at present, and doing this by passing through certain means or intermediaries. It is then the possibility of the movement of the self that is not represented by space. Space is the sign of my power. Time is the sign of my powerlessness. It expresses the necessity that links these movements from me to all the other movements of the universe': Jules Lagneau, 'Cours sur la perception', in *Célèbres leçons* (Paris: PUF, 1964), pp. 175–176.
62 'God is and has all that man has, but in an infinitely greater measure. The nature of God is the nature of the imagination unfolded, made objective . . . God is a being conceived under the form of the senses, but freed from the limits of sense, – a being at once unlimited and sensational. But what is the imagination? Limitless activity of the senses. God is eternal, i.e., he exists at all times; God is omnipresent, i.e., he exists in all places; God is the omniscient being, i.e., the being to whom every individual thing, every sensible existence, is an object without distinction, without limitation of time and place': Ludwig Feuerbach, *The Essence of Christianity*, trans. George Eliot (Walnut: MSAC Philosophy Group, Mt. San Antonio College, 2008 [1841]), p. 272.
63 An allusion to an incident related in the *New Testament* where the apostle Peter denies Jesus. See Luke 22: 54–62.
64 Weber, *Economy and Society*, vol. 1, pp. 246–254.
65 On power and time management in the academic world, see Bourdieu, *Homo Academicus*.

Lecture of 3 May 1984

1 See 2 Corinthians 3: 6. Bourdieu had already briefly used the formula the previous year (see his lecture of 11 January 1983, in *Habitus and Field*, p. 275).
2 Jean-Paul Sartre, *The Family Idiot. Gustave Flaubert 1821–1857*, vol. III, trans. Carol Cosman (Chicago: University of Chicago Press, 1989), p. 40: 'Consequently, living thought as a surpassing is at once advanced, aroused and retarded by that opacity to be surpassed which is precisely the idea as written, "thing-a-fied".'
3 'Written words are stones. Learning them, internalizing their combinations, we reintroduce into ourselves a mineralized thought that will subsist in us by virtue of its very minerality, until such time as some kind of material labor, acted on it from outside, might come to relieve us of it': ibid., p. 38.
4 'Enclosed in writing, it (the multiple and contradictory comprehension of our species) has become canned thought': ibid., p. 40.
5 On this point, see Pierre Bourdieu and Jean-Claude Passeron, 'Sociologues des mythologies et mythologies des sociologues', in *Les Temps Modernes*, no. 211, pp. 998–1021.
6 Plato's critique of poetry is developed in *The Republic* (in particular in books III and X), but can also be found in other dialogues (*Ion*, 533d–534b; *The Apology of Socrates*, 22a–c; *Phaedrus*, 245a, etc.).

7 Eric A. Havelock, *Preface to Plato* (Cambridge: Harvard University Press, 1963).

8 On the theme of poetic enthusiasm, Plato writes for example: 'For all good poets, epic as well as lyric, compose their beautiful poems not by art, but because they are inspired and possessed': Plato, *Ion*, trans. Benjamin Jowett, §533e (Project Gutenberg Ebook #1635, 2013).

9 'First, the instinct of imitation is implanted in man from childhood, one difference between him and other animals being that he is the most imitative of living creatures, and through imitation learns his earliest lessons; and no less universal is the pleasure felt in things imitated': Aristotle, *Poetics*, trans. S. H. Butcher (Internet Classics Archive, Section I, Part IV, 1448b).

10 The verb to 'produce' comes from *pro* ('before') and *ducere* ('to lead', 'to bring').

11 'Consequently, living thought as a surpassing is at once advanced, aroused and retarded by that opacity to be surpassed which is precisely the idea as written, "thing-a-fied"': *The Family Idiot*, p. 40.

12 'I started my life as I shall no doubt end it: amidst books. In my grandfather's study there were books everywhere': Jean-Paul Sartre, *The Words*, trans. Bernard Frechtman (New York: Vintage, 1981 [1964]), p. 40.

13 All of which is in *The Family Idiot*, p. 40.

14 For example: 'Descartes's dictum that everything in which there is the least uncertainty is to be doubted might have been better and more accurately formulated in the precept that we must consider the degree of assent or dissent that a matter deserves or, more simply, that we must look into the reasons for every doctrine [. . .] I wish however that he had remembered his own precept or rather, that he had understood its true force [. . .] So if Descartes had wished to carry out what is best in his rule, he should have worked at the demonstration of scientific principles and thus achieved in philosophy what Proclus tried to do in geometry, where it is less necessary. But our author seems sometimes to have preferred applause rather than certainty': G. W. Leibniz, 'Critical Thoughts on the General Part of the Principles of Descartes' (1692) in *Philosophical Papers and Letters. A Selection*, trans. Leroy E. Loemker (Dordrecht: Kluwer Academic Publishers, 1976), Part III, §42, pp. 383–384.

15 Bourdieu is probably thinking of a passage like the following: 'The idealist's question would be something like: "What right have I not to doubt the existence of my hands?" (And to that the answer can't be: "I know that they exist.") But someone who asks such a question is overlooking the fact that a doubt about existence only works in a language-game. Hence, that we should first have to ask: "What would such a doubt be like?", and don't understand this straight off': Ludwig Wittgenstein, *On Certainty*, trans. Denis Paul and G. E. M. Anscombe (Oxford: Wiley, 1991 [1969]), §24.

16 Edmund Husserl, *Logical Investigations*, trans. J. N. Findlay (London: Routledge, 2001 [1900]), vol. II, Investigation IV: 'The Distinction Between Independent and Non-Independent Meanings', pp. 47–76. 'He (the philosopher) must surely also know that it is precisely behind the obvious that the hardest problems lie hidden, that this is so much so, in fact, that philosophy may be paradoxically, but not unprofoundly, called the science of the trivial' (p. 76).

17 Graphic signs, for instance, must be subjected to 'reactivation' (*Reaktivierung*): 'Written signs are, when considered from a purely corporeal point of view,

straightforwardly, sensibly experienceable; and it is always possible that they be intersubjectively experienceable in common. But as linguistic signs they awaken, as do linguistic sounds, their familiar significations. The awakening is something passive; the awakened signification is thus given passively, similar to the way in which any other activity which has sunk into obscurity, once associatively awakened, emerges at first passively as a more or less clear memory. In the passivity in question here, as in the case of memory, what is passively awakened can be transformed back, so to speak, into the corresponding activity: this is the capacity for reactivation that belongs originally to every human being as a speaking being': Edmund Husserl, The *Origin of Geometry*, trans. David Carr (University of Lincoln: Press, 1989), p. 164.

18 See, among others, Karl Popper, 'Epistemology Without a Knowing Subject', in *Objective Knowledge. An Evolutionary Approach* (Oxford: Oxford University Press, 1979), pp. 106–152, in particular the section of 'The Objectivity and the Autonomy of the Third World' where Popper rejects the idea that 'a book is nothing without a reader': although the objective third world is a human product and creation, it creates in its turn, as do other animal products, its own realm of autonomy' (p. 115).

19 A reference to formulae by Spinoza such as '*verum index sui*' or 'He who has a true idea, knows at that same time that he has a true idea, nor can he doubt concerning the truth of the thing, and cannot doubt the truth of his knowledge': *Ethics*, trans. Andrew Boyle (London: Dent, Everyman's Library, 1986), Part II, Proposition 43, p. 69.

20 For the reference see the lecture of 29 March 1984, note 8.

21 Lecture given in 1967 and published in 1969: Ernst H. Gombrich, *In Search of Cultural History* (Oxford, Oxford University Press, 1969.) Bourdieu had mentioned this book the previous year (see his lecture of 9 November 1982, in *Habitus and Field*, p. 117).

22 Bourdieu may be thinking of the analyses that Hegel devotes to illusion in art: 'Art liberates the true content of phenomena from the pure appearance and deception of this bad, transitory world, and gives them a higher actuality, born of the spirit. Thus, far from being a mere pure appearance, a higher reality and truer existence is to be ascribed to the phenomena of art in comparison with [those of] ordinary reality': Georg Wilhelm Friedrich Hegel, *Aesthetics. Lectures on Fine Art*, vol. I, trans. T. M. Knox (Oxford: Oxford University Press, 1975 [1818, 1829]), p. 9.

23 Bourdieu is alluding to work by Claude Lévi-Strauss, in particular his book *The Savage Mind* (London: Weidenfeld & Nicholson, 1994 [1962]). See Bourdieu, *Habitus and Field*, p. 155, note 10.

24 See the lecture of 19 April 1984.

25 For example: 'Do you believe that if France, instead of being governed ultimately by the mob, was in the hands of the mandarins, we would be in this state? If, instead of wanting to enlighten the lower classes, we had busied ourselves with educating the higher . . .' (Letter of 3 August 1870 to Georges Sand, in Gustave Flaubert, *Correspondance*, vol. III (Paris: Gallimard, 1975), p. 389.

26 Flaubert, *Correspondance* (Paris: Gallimard, 'Bibliothèque de la Pléiade', 5 vols, 1971–75). The book by Hippolyte Taine is *Les Origines de la France contemporaine* (1875).

27 François de Malherbe, 'Consolation to M. du Périer on the Death of his

Daughter', 1598: 'The poor man in his hut, with only thatch for cover, / Unto these laws must bend; / The sentinel that guards the barriers of the Louvre / Cannot our kings defend.'

28 An allusion to the syllogism: 'All men are mortal; Socrates is a man, therefore Socrates is mortal.'

29 See Ferdinand de Saussure, *Course in General Linguistics*, Part IV, 'Geographical Linguistics', pp. 191–211.

30 Bourdieu had used this term earlier in the first year of his course (see his lecture of 5 May, in *Classification Struggles*, p. 28).

31 A reference to a poem by Horace: 'I've raised a monument more durable than bronze, one higher than the Pyramids' royal towers, that no devouring rain, or fierce northerly gale, has power to destroy: nor the immeasurable succession of years, and the swift passage of time': Horace, *The Odes*, Book III, 30, trans. A. S. Kline, *Poetry in Translation*, https://www.poetryintranslation.com.

32 'From the same shelf he has just taken another book, whose title I can make out upside down: *The Spire of Caudebec, Norman Chronicle*, by Mademoiselle Julie Lavergne. The Autodidact's reading matter always disconcerts me. All of a sudden the names of the last authors whose works he has consulted come back to my mind: Lambert, Langlois, Larbalétrier, Lastex, Lavergne. It is a revelation: I have understood the Autodidact's method: he is teaching himself in alphabetical order': Jean-Paul Sartre, *Nausea*, trans. Robert Baldick (London: Penguin, 2000 [1938]), p. 48.

33 On this point and the ideas developed in this paragraph, see Bourdieu, *The Political Ontology of Martin Heidegger*, and *Classification Struggles*, pp. 118–119.

34 Although the welfare state has always been attacked by liberals, it attracted at the beginning of the 1980s a much stronger criticism, which has been summed up by Pierre Rosanvallon in *La crise de l'État-providence*. The arguments attacking these 'privileges' were backed up by the essay of the journalist François de Closets, *Toujours plus!*, published by Grasset in 1982, which sold more than a million copies.

35 Bourdieu often quotes Raymond Aron's *The Opium of the Intellectuals* as an illustration of the disingenuous lucidity of the 'right-wing intellectuals', and Simone de Beauvoir's article, 'La pensée de droite, aujourd'hui', as an example of the resistance of intellectuals to objectification. He sees there two obstacles to a 'sociology of the intellectual'. See, in particular, the lecture of 12 May 1982, in *Classification Struggles*, p. 43.

36 On this point, see the end of the previous lecture.

37 Louis Pinto, '"C'est moi qui le dis". Les modalités sociales de la certitude', *Actes de la recherche en sciences sociales*, no. 52, 1984, pp. 107–108.

38 See, in particular, Durkheim, *The Rules of Sociological Method*, ch. 1, 'What is a Social Fact?', pp. 50–59.

39 'Nor does every person have the capacity to achieve the ecstatic states which are viewed, in accordance with primitive experience, as the preconditions for producing certain effects in meteorology, healing, divination, and telepathy. It is primarily, though not exclusively these extraordinary powers that have been designated by such special terms as "*mana*", "*orenda*", and the Iranian "*maga*" (the term from which our word "magic" is derived). We shall henceforth employ the term "charisma" for such extraordinary powers': Max Weber, *The Sociology of Religion*, p. 2.

40 C. Lévi-Strauss, *Introduction to the Work of Marcel Mauss*, esp. pp. 53–57.
41 From *Aeneid*, Book 3, 57. Later quoted by Seneca as '*quid non mortalia pectora coges, auri sacra fames?*' ('What do you not force mortal hearts [to do], accursed hunger for gold?'). (Translator)
42 See Weber, *The Protestant Ethic and the Spirit of Capitalism*, p. 21, and the entire chapter 'The Spirit of Capitalism', pp. 13–38.
43 I remind you of Max Weber's definition of charisma: 'The term "charisma" will be applied to a certain quality of an individual personality by virtue of which he is considered extraordinary and treated as endowed with super-natural, superhuman, or at least specifically exceptional powers or qualities. These as such are not accessible to the ordinary person, but are regarded as of divine origin, and on the basis of them the individual concerned is treated as a "leader" [Führer]': *Economy and Society*, vol. 1, p. 241.
44 10 June 1940 was the date when the French government, after its military collapse, left Paris. General de Gaulle broadcast his appeal for resistance on the BBC on 18 June 1940. This followed the previous day's broadcast of Marshal Pétain's speech announcing France's capitulation and his decision to 'offer up [his] body to France to attenuate her misfortune'.
45 An implicit reference to Marx's analysis, 'The Fetishism of the Commodity and its Secret', in *Capital*, Vol. I, ch. 1, sect. 4, pp. 163–175.
46 'As against this, the commodity form, and the value-relation of the products of labour within which it appears, have absolutely no connection with the physical nature of the commodity and the material relations arising out of this. It is nothing but the definite social relation between men themselves which assumes here, for them, the fantastic form of a relation between things. In order, therefore, to find an analogy we must take flight into the misty realm of religion. There the products of the human brain appear as autonomous figures endowed with a life of their own, which enter into relations both with each other and with the human race. So it is in the world of commodities with the products of men's hands. I call this the fetishism which attaches itself to the products of labour as soon as they are produced as commodities, and is therefore inseparable from the production of commodities': ibid., p. 165.
47 Jean-Paul Sartre calls 'seriality' a 'mode of coexistence, in the pratico-inert milieu, of a human multiplicity each of whose members is at once interchange-able and other by Others and for himself': *Critique of Dialectical Reason*, vol. II (London: Verso, 2006), p. 459. See also *Classification Struggles*, pp. 102–103, 124.
48 Bourdieu returns to the structure of the novella *A Rose for Emily* (1930) in 'A Theory of Reading in Practice', in *The Rules of Art*, pp. 322–329.
49 This example, which some of Bourdieu's audience found amusing, alludes to the numerous and wide-ranging foreign visits made by Pope John-Paul II, elected in 1978, compared to his predecessors.
50 Georges Séguy was Secretary General of the CGT from 1967 to 1982. Henri Krasucki succeeded him in June 1982.
51 See *Classification Struggles*, pp. 111–114 and *passim*.
52 Bourdieu, 'La délégation et le fétichisme politique', p. 49.
53 The journalist Ferdinand Lop (1891–1974) was noted for his practical jokes, particularly in the Latin Quarter in Paris.
54 In the passage that follows, Bourdieu plays on the double meaning of the French word *appareil*, which designates the administrative structure of a politi-

cal organization but is also used by Pascal – in his *Pensées* 44 (82) – to refer to 'display'; that is, the ceremonial dress (wigs and gowns, etc.) that judges and doctors, repositories of 'imaginary sciences', need in order to earn respect. See Bourdieu, *Pascalian Meditations*, pp. 168, 171.

55 Bourdieu makes two allusions to the Société *des agrégés* and the standpoints adopted by its president (Guy Bayet) in May 1968, in *Homo Academicus*, pp. 10, 192.

56 Bourdieu is no doubt thinking of the divisions within the French Communist Party. In 1978, for instance, a 'Manifesto of the three hundred' contested a report by the Secretary General of the PCF and, in 1981, a manifesto, signed notably by ex-members of the Central Committee of the PCF, attacked its leadership ('The party cannot be confiscated by a restricted group of leaders', *Le Monde*, 27 February 1981).

Lecture of 10 May 1984

1 Perhaps in his lectures at the Collège de France in 1954–55, entitled 'L'"institution" dans l'histoire personnelle et publique'; transcription in Merleau-Ponty, *L'Institution, la passivité. Notes de cours au Collège de France (1954–1955)* (Paris: Belin, 2003), pp. 31–154.

2 Durkheim, *The Elementary Forms of Religious Life*; Marcel Mauss and Henri Hubert, 'Esquisse d'une théorie générale de la magie', in Mauss, *Sociologie et anthropologie* (Paris: Presses universitaires de France, 1997 [1950]), pp. 1–141.

3 See the lecture of 8 March 1984, note 1.

4 Describing 'the purest type of exercise of legal authority' that is 'dominance by means of a bureaucratic administrative staff', Max Weber notes that 'in the most rational case [candidates] are tested by examination or guaranteed by diplomas certifying technical training, or both': *Economy and Society*, vol. 1, p. 220. He points out that 'the role of technical qualifications in bureaucratic organizations is continually increasing' (p. 221).

5 'Bureaucratic dominance' implies above all 'the dominance of a spirit of formalistic impersonality: *Sine ira et studio*, without hatred or passion, and hence without affection or enthusiasm. The dominant norms are concepts of straightforward duty without regard to personal considerations. Everyone is subject to formal equality of treatment, that is, everyone in the same empirical situation' (ibid., p. 225).

6 Weber distinguishes three types of legitimate dominance, according to whether the legitimacy of the regime is based on 'rational', 'traditional' or 'charismatic' grounds (ibid., pp. 215ff).

7 'The problem of succession' presented by 'the disappearance of the personal charismatic leader' is studied by Weber in the section 'The Routinization of Charisma and Its Effects', in ibid., pp. 246–254.

8 In the case of the 'purest type' of rationality, 'the official works entirely separated from ownership of the means of administration and without appropriation of his position' (ibid., p. 221).

9 See for example, *Classification Struggles*, p. 80; *Habitus and Field*, p. 324.

10 See the lecture of 26 April 1984; Bourdieu, *Outline of a Theory of Practice*, pp. 201, 209.

11 See the lecture of 26 April 1984, p. 209.

12 Jack Goody, *The Domestication of the Savage Mind.*

13 Eric A. Havelock, *Preface to Plato.* Here, Bourdieu is repeating points some aspects of which he had developed at greater length in his lecture of 3 May 1984.

14 Jean Cavaillès, *Méthode axiomatique et formalisme. Essai sur le problème du fondement des mathématiques* (Paris: Hermann, 1938), p. 94.

15 The name of the author is not audible. It might be a reference to Lucien Lévy-Bruhl, *L'Expérience mystique et les symboles chez les primitifs* (Paris: Alcan, 1938).

16 Bourdieu had already developed his thoughts on this word during the first year of his lectures (see, in particular, *Classification Struggles,* pp. 40–41, 45–46).

17 Bourdieu himself, at any rate, used the expression to designate a 'contract' of the type: 'Why not say "tu"?', 'Don't you think it would be easier if we used our first names?'; see 'L'économie des échanges linguistiques', *Langue française,* no. 34, 1977, p. 29.

18 On this point, see the first year of lectures, in particular *Classification Struggles,* p. 106.

19 On this definition of academicism, see also *Manet: A Symbolic Revolution,* esp. pp. 195, 240.

20 These chapters did not figure in the French edition of *Economy and Society,* and have still not been translated into French. Max Weber borrowed the term *Kadijustiz* from one of his contemporaries whom he met at Freiburg university (Richard Schmidt) to designate an 'empirical justice'; in the English edition, there is a section specifically devoted to the notion 'Excursus on Kadi Justice, Common Law and Roman Law' (*Economy and Society,* vol. 2, pp. 976–978). As for the notion of 'rational law' that Bourdieu refers to in the following pages, it is expressed no doubt in the following passage: 'Present-day legal science, at least in those forms which have achieved the highest measure of methodological and logical rationality, i.e., those which have been produced through the legal science of the Pandectists' Civil Law, proceeds from the following five postulates: viz., first, that every concrete legal decision be the "application" of an abstract legal proposition to a concrete "fact situation"; second, that it must be possible in every concrete case to derive the decision from the abstract legal propositions by means of legal logic; third, that the law must actually or virtually constitute a "gapless" system of legal propositions, or must, at least, be treated as if it were such a gapless system; fourth, that whatever cannot be "construed" rationally in legal terms is also logically irrelevant; and fifth, that every social action of human beings must always be visualized as either an "application" or "execution" of legal propositions, or as an "infringement" thereof.' *Economy and Society,* vol. 2, pp. 657–658

21 See the phrase by Max Weber quoted in the lecture of 26 April, note 58. The reference to Don Quixote refers to chapter 45 of the second part, entitled 'How the Great Sancho Panza Took Possession of his Island'.

22 An allusion to the 'Judgement of Solomon' that Bourdieu will refer to again later on.

23 'In the purely empirical conduct of legal practice and legal training one always moves from the particular to the particular but one never tries to move from the particular to general propositions in order to be able subsequently to deduce from them the norms for new particular cases': Max Weber, *Economy and Society,* vol. 2, p. 787.

24 Durkheim, *The Division of Labour in Society*.
25 Robert Blanché, *Axiomatics*, trans. G. B. Keene (London: Routledge, 1962 [1955]), pp. 49–50.
26 Bourdieu, *Outline of a Theory of Practice*, pp. 16–17, 199–200.
27 Language is 'a system of signs in which the only essential thing is the union of meaning and sound images': Ferdinand de Saussure, *Course in General Linguistics*, p. 15.
28 Bourdieu had developed this example in his lectures of 19 and 26 April 1984. See above pp. 178, 208.
29 See Heidegger, *Being and Time*, pp. 163–168.
30 An allusion to the 'judgement of Solomon': to distinguish between two women who both claim to be the mother of a newborn baby, the King of Israel, Solomon, proposes to have the infant cut into two halves, in order to identify the mother (who objects to the sacrifice of the infant) (1 Kings 3: 16–28).
31 The question in *The Meno* – 'Can you tell me, Socrates, is virtue something that can be taught? Or does it come by practice. Or is it neither teaching nor practice that gives it to a man but natural aptitude or something else?' (70a) – is to be understood thus, if the Greek term [*arete*], often translated as 'virtue', is translated as 'excellence' (see *Classification Struggles*, p. 92).
32 Themistocles' son, Cleophantus, benefits from his father's instructions to be 'well trained in horsemanship', but in other areas, he is not a 'good and wise man in the way his father was' (Plato, *The Meno*, 93d.)
33 On Leibniz's critique of Descartes, see 'Meditations on Knowledge, Truth and Ideas' (1684) and 'Critical Thoughts on the General Part of the Principles of Descartes' (1692) in G. W. Leibniz, *Philosophical Papers and Letters*, vol. 2 (Amsterdam: Kluwer Academic Publishers, 1989), pp. 291–295, 383–412.
34 For example, 'All is therefore certain and determined beforehand in man, as everywhere else, and the human soul is a kind of *spiritual* automaton': *Theodicy*, trans. E. M. Huggard (Project Gutenberg ebook # 17147, § 52). Leibniz borrows the term 'spiritual automaton' from Spinoza's *On the Improvement of Understanding*, trans. R. H. M. Elwes (London: Forgotten Books, 2008), §85: 'The soul acts according to fixed laws, and it is as it were an immaterial automaton'.
35 For the second aspect, his theme is 'The disenchantment of the world'. 'The fate of our age with its characterization by rationalization and intellectualization and above all the disenchantment of the world is that the ultimate, most sublime values have withdrawn from public life, either into the transcendental realm of mystical life or into the brotherhood of immediate human relationships': Max Weber, *Science as a Vocation*, ed. Peter Lassman and Irving Velody, with Herminio Martins (Abindgdon: Routledge, 2015), p. 30.
36 Plato, speaking through Socrates, reproaches the Sophists (who, unlike him, were not sons of the Athenian aristocracy) with receiving payment for all their teaching. See, for example, *Hippias Major*.
37 Frances A. Yates, *The Art of Memory* (London: Penguin, 2014).
38 Milman Parry, *The Making of Homeric Verse. The Collected Papers of Milman Parry* (Oxford: Oxford University Press, 1971). Albert Lord, who was Parry's assistant, published a study of the bards of southern Yugoslavia [now Bosnia]: *The Singer of Tales* (Cambridge: Harvard University Press, 1960).
39 Initials of the École nationale d'administration. Bourdieu refers to it ironically

as a school that teaches the art of entering politics, since many of the alumni of this school are recruited directly into ministerial cabinets.

40 The tape recorder was in general use by the French public, and particularly by sociologists, from the 1950s onward.

41 On this point, see Bourdieu's interview with Franz Schultheis on the subject of the photographs that he took during his research in Algeria between 1958 and 1961: 'Photographies d'Algérie', in *Images d'Algérie. Une affinité elective* (Paris: Actes Sud, 2003), pp. 17–45. See also *Actes de la recherche en sciences sociales*, no. 150, December 2003, devoted to 'L'anthropologie de Pierre Bourdieu', which gives prominence to the role of photography in ethnography. We could also recall Bourdieu's use of photography both in this journal and in *Distinction*.

42 Antoine Compagnon, *La Troisième République de Lettres* (Paris: Seuil, 1983).

43 Gustave Lanson (1857–1934), who was Director of the École normale supérieure, was a leading figure in the reform of the university and of literary criticism. He took social influences into account, and opposed Taine, who represented the traditionalist tendency. He was also interested in pedagogical questions like the dissertation and the textual commentary.

44 See, in *Homo Academicus*, which offers an analysis of the university world in the 1960s and 1970s, the references to the fight over the 'new Sorbonne' (esp. pp. 117–118).

45 On this topic, Bourdieu refers in a later lecture (30 May 1985) to research by Francis Haskell.

46 See Bourdieu, Darbel and Schnapper, *The Love of Art*; Pierre Bourdieu, 'Piété religieuse et dévotion artistique. Fidèles et amateurs d'art à Santa Maria Novella'.

47 Erwin Panofsky, *Architecture gothique et pensée scolastique* (Paris: Minuit, 1967 [1951]), esp. pp. 89–95 [translated from the original into French by Pierre Bourdieu].

48 Bourdieu is thinking of a page that Panofsky had inserted into the postface of the French edition, p. 155 (Panofsky's commentary on the introduction of the division into chapters is on p. 93).

49 Bachelard, *The Formation of the Scientific Mind*.

50 Thomas Hobbes, *Leviathan* (London: Penguin, 2017), p. 180.

51 'In Homer this *skeptron* is the attribute of the king, of heralds, messengers, judges, and all persons who, whether of their own nature or because of a particular occasion, are invested with authority. The *skeptron* is passed to the orator before he begins his speech so that he may speak with authority': Émile Benveniste, *Dictionary of Indo-European Concepts and Society*, p. 325.

52 During the first year of his lectures, Bourdieu had already dealt with the crown with reference to Percy Ernst Schramm's book, *A History of the English Coronation*, trans. Leopold G. Wickham (Oxford: Clarendon Press, 1937). See the lecture of 9 June 1982, in *Classification Struggles*, p. 115.

53 See the passage on 'apparel' in the fragment 'Cause and Effects', in *Pensées and Other Writings*, pp. 29–34.

54 Immanuel Kant, 'Religion Within the Boundaries of Mere Reason', *in Religion and Rational Theology*, trans. Allen W. Wood and George di Giovanni (Cambridge: Cambridge University Press, 1996), p. 186.

55 The word *minister* in Latin denotes a 'domestic servant', or an 'aide' or 'assis-

tant'. It is formed from *minus* ('less'); *magis* ('more') has given us the word *magister* ('he who commands', the 'master').

56 An allusion to the numerous 're-readings' of Marx in the 1970s on which Bourdieu had written an article, 'La lecture de Marx ou quelques remarques critiques à propos de *Lire "Le Capital"*'.

57 Nietzsche, *'The Anti-Christ'*, in *Twilight of the Idols and The Anti-Christ*, trans. R. J. Hollingdale (London: Penguin, 2003 [1895]), §44, p. 169.

58 Ibid.

59 Ibid., 2003, §11, p. 134.

60 Ibid., 2003, §12, p. 135.

61 Ibid., 2003, §44, p. 169.

62 Ibid., 2003, §47, p. 175.

63 Ibid., 2003, §55, p. 187.

64 Ibid., 2003, §44, p. 170.

65 Ibid., 2003, §44, p. 171.

66 See, in particular, Lucien Lévy-Bruhl, *La Morale et la science des moeurs* (Paris: Alcan, 1903); Émile Durkheim, 'Introduction à la morale' (1917), in *Textes, II. Religion, morale, anomie* (Paris: Minuit, 1975), pp. 313–331.

67 See especially Durkheim, *The Rules of Sociological Method*, trans. W. D. Halls (New York: The Free Press, 1982), ch. 3, 'Rules for the Distinction of the Normal from the Pathological', pp. 85–107.

68 The Proletarian Left was an organization claiming allegiance to Maoism that was formed in May 1968. In the years following 1968, it was the rival on the far left of the 'Trotskyites' of the Revolutionary Communist League.

69 On these points, we could also read the developments in the second year of lectures, *Habitus and Field*, pp. 299–301, 308–309.

70 On this point, see the lecture of 15 March 1984, p. 79.

71 '"How do you mean?", asked Dauber. "There are volumes of reminiscences which show very clearly that he was a man out of the common rut." "Name me the man who, in your view, is the ideal of mediocrity", said Neurasthenic. "Perfect; now place him at the head of our Union. Leave him there for ten years. And he'll begin to turn out such amazing material that you'd be able to publish a collection of the best aphorisms of this cretin. If a complete mediocrity feels that his hands are untied, he'll begin to behave as if he was a genius. And through the efforts of enormous numbers of people, an illusion of genius will be created"': Alexander Zinoviev, *The Yawning Heights*, trans. Gordon Clough (London: Bodley Head, 1979), pp. 397–398.

72 'The impression is of being up against an extraordinarily insignificant force, which, by virtue of this very fact, is invincible' (ibid., p. 399).

73 See the study of the episcopate that Bourdieu had recently completed (Bourdieu and de Saint-Martin, 'La Sainte famille'). Bourdieu used the notion of the 'oblate' in the study of the academic world that he had recently published: *Homo Academicus*, pp. xxiv, 44, 100–101.

74 Bourdieu and de Saint-Martin, 'La Sainte famille'.

Lecture of 17 May 1984

1 P. Bourdieu and J.-C. Passeron, *Reproduction in Education, Society and Culture*, esp. pp. 5-11, 15-16.

2 Max Weber, 'Discipline and Charisma', in *Economy and Society*, vol. 2, pp. 1148–1157.

3 The concept of a 'total' (or 'totalitarian') institution that Bourdieu had already used in earlier lectures is developed by Goffman in *Asylums*, where he makes explicit reference to rules and discipline: 'A total institution may be defined as a place of residence and work where a large number of like-situated individuals, cut off from the wider society for an appreciable period of time, together lead an enclosed, formally administered round of life': *Asylums*, p. 1.

4 'The first and most basic rule is to consider social facts as things': Durkheim, *The Rules of Sociological Method*, p. 60.

5 If he heeds only his reason, the moral subject in Kant obeys the 'moral imperative' without further consideration.

6 An 'imperative' is 'a rule indicated by an "ought", which expresses objective necessitation to the action and signifies that, if reason completely determined the will, the action would without fail take place in accordance with this rule.' Kant distinguishes between hypothetical imperatives and categorical imperatives. The former 'contain mere precepts of skill' which 'determine the conditions of causality of a rational being as an efficient cause merely with respect to the effect and its adequacy to it'. The latter 'would be categorical and would alone be practical laws ... The latter must sufficiently determine the will as will even before I ask whether I have the ability required for a desired effect or what I am to do in order to produce it': Immanuel Kant, *Critique of Practical Reason*, trans. Mary Gregor (Cambridge: Cambridge University Press, 2015 [1788]), pp. 16–17.

7 No doubt Bourdieu is thinking of the end of the lecture of 19 April 1984.

8 For Kant, action can only be moral if it is founded on duty: 'To be beneficent where one can is one's duty, and besides there are many souls so attuned to compassion that, even without another motivating ground of vanity, or self-interest, they find an inner gratification in spreading joy around them, and can relish the contentment of others, in so far as it is their work. But I assert that in such a case an action of this kind – however much it conforms with duty, however amiable it might be – still has no true moral worth [. . .]; for the maxim lacks moral content, namely to do such actions not from inclination, but *from duty*': Immanuel Kant, *Groundwork of the Metaphysics of Morals*, trans. Mary Gregor and Jens Timmermann (Cambridge: Cambridge University Press, 2012 [1786]), pp. 13–14.

9 The title of a section of *Sodom and Gomorrah*, volume 4 of Marcel Proust's *In Search of Lost Time*, trans. John Sturrock (London: Penguin, 2002).

10 Weber, 'Discipline and Charisma', pp. 1150–1155.

11 'The above considerations show that there is a type of suicide the opposite of anomic suicide, just as egoistic and altruistic suicides are opposites. It is the suicide deriving from excessive regulation, that of persons with futures pitilessly blocked and passions violently choked by oppressive discipline. It is the suicide of very young husbands, of the married woman who is childless. So, for completeness's sake, we should set up a fourth suicidal type. But it has so little contemporary importance and examples are so hard to find aside from the cases just mentioned that it seems useless to dwell upon it. However it might be said to have historical interest. Do not the suicides of slaves, said to be frequent under certain conditions [. . .] belong to this type, or all suicides attributable to excessive physical or moral despotism? To bring out the ineluc-

table and inflexible nature of a rule against which there is no appeal, and in contrast with the expression "anomy" which has just been used, we might call it "fatalistic suicide"': Émile Durkheim, *Suicide*, trans. John A. Spaulding and George Simpson (New York: The Free Press, 1979 [1897]), p. 276, note 25.

12 The term *'pathologisch'* in Kant is not connected with disease; it designates what relates to negative passions and feelings (as opposed to the 'moral feeling'). See *Critique of Practical Reason*, p. 63.

13 See the arguments based on *Waiting for Godot* and Paul Willis's research in the lecture of 19 April 1984, as well as the arguments on the experience of time in 'total institutions' in the lecture of 26 April 1984, and, at the end of the same lecture, on the relation between time and power.

14 For Kant, the individual who acts morally neutralizes their 'pathological self'. 'Now, however, we find our nature as sensible beings so constituted that the matter of the faculty of desire (objects of inclination, whether of hope or fear) first forces itself upon us, and we find our pathologically determinable self, even though it is quite unfit to give universal law through its maxims, nevertheless striving antecedently to make its claims primarily and originally valid, just as if it constituted our entire self': *Critique of Practical Reason*, p. 62.

15 A reference to the type of communal organization that Charles Fourier wanted to develop, known as a *'phalanstère'*.

16 The myth of the Abbey of Thélème (from the Greek *thelema*, 'will', 'desire') is to be found in Rabelais's *Gargantua*. Thélème is based on the inversion of monastic discipline, or on the rule that consists in having no rules. 'All their life was regulated not by laws, statutes, or rules, but according to their free will and pleasure. They rose from bed when they pleased, and drank, ate, worked and slept when the fancy seized them. Nobody woke them; nobody compelled them either to eat or to drink, or to do anything else whatever. So it was that Gargantua had established it. In their rules there was only one clause: Do What You Will': François Rabelais, *The Histories of Gargantua and Pantagruel*, trans. J. M. Cohen (Harmondsworth: Penguin, 1963 [*c.*1534]), 'The Rules According to Which the Thélémites Lived', ch. 57, p. 159.

17 The 'invisible hand' is the expression that Adam Smith uses on several occasions to defend the idea that the free play of individual interests would satisfy the general interest by itself, without any need for intervention such as that of the state. 'The individual [. . .] generally, indeed, neither intends to promote the public interest, nor knows how much he is promoting it. [. . .] He intends only his own security; [. . .] and [. . .] his own gain; and he is in this, as in many other cases, led by an invisible hand to promote an end which was no part of his intention. [. . .] By pursuing his own interest, he frequently promotes that of the society more effectually than when he really intends to promote it': *The Wealth of Nations* (Middletown: Shine Classics, 2014 [1776]), Book IV, ch. 2, pp. 242–243.

18 Bourdieu returns to this notion of competence, especially in 'The Ambiguities of Competence', in *The State Nobility*, trans. Lauretta C. Clough (Cambridge: Polity, 1996), pp. 116–123.

19 The previous year, Bourdieu had commented on Hegel's analyses of bureaucracy and developed the points arising there (see lecture of 19 October 1982, in *Habitus and Field*, pp. 55–60).

20 On the distinction between formal and substantive rationality, see Weber, *Economy and Society*, vol. 1, pp. 85–86.

21 Bourdieu's reflection on the 'universal' will be amplified over the following years and take an important place in the 1990s, in the lectures on the state (*On the State*) and in his texts on the 'corporatism of the universal'.

22 Robert Blanché, *Axiomatics*, trans. G. B. Keene (London: Routledge, 1962 [1955]), pp. 49–50.

23 Bourdieu had used the example of language in the previous lecture (see lecture of 10 May, p. 250).

24 In the previous lecture, Bourdieu illustrated the quotation from Blanché with the example from the game of draughts: the adoption or rejection of the rule allowing a piece to be 'huffed' (taken, for not having taken an available piece) has, for a long time, divided players and federations.

25 Émile Durkheim, *Textes, III: Fonctions sociales et institutions* (Paris: Minuit, 1975), p. 192 [trans. Peter Collier]. This was an oral contribution by Durkheim to a 'debate on the relationship of officials to the State' in 1908.

26 See note 11 above.

27 Max Weber tackles this point on a number of occasions. For instance, in medieval Florence: 'First the household ceased to exist as a necessary basis of rational business association. Henceforth, the partner was not necessarily – or typically – a house member. Consequently, business assets had to be separated from the private debts of the partners. Similarly, a distinction began to be made between the business employees and the domestic servants. Above all, the commercial debts had to be distinguished from the private debts of the partners': *Economy and Society*, vol. 1, p. 379.

28 On 7 May 1984, ten days before this lecture, Bourdieu had invited Aaron Cicourel to his seminar at the École des hautes études en sciences sociales. He published the transcript of this interview the following year in his journal: Aaron V. Cicourel, 'Raisonnement et diagnostic: le rôle du discourse et de la compréhension clinique en médecine', *Actes de la recherche en sciences sociales*, no. 60, 1985, pp. 79–89; fifteen years later, Bourdieu published a collection of articles by Cicourel in his 'Liber' series: Aaron V. Cicourel, *Le Raisonnement médical*, ed. Pierre Bourdieu and Yves Winkin (Paris: Seuil, 2002).

29 See *Le Raisonnement médical*. For instance: 'The medical appointments and the reviews of clinical history that they occasion reveal the characteristics of two forms of knowledge: the doctor re-codifies the often ambiguous and disjointed information that he draws from the interviews into abstract categories that facilitate the solution of the problem and specify the conditions of an effective resolution; while the patients resort to a personal or restricted semantic field to translate what they believe about their illness – which is often diametrically opposed to the doctor's opinion' (p. 66).

30 See Max Weber, *The Rational and Social Foundations of Music*, trans. D. Martindale, J. Riedel and J. Neuwirth (Carbondale: Southern Illinois University Press, 1958 [1921]).

31 See the second sessions of the lectures of 19 and 26 April (above, pp. 183 and 201).

32 In fact, Bourdieu is here referring above all to the content of his lectures of 9 and 16 November 1982, which focus on the habitus (see *Habitus and Field*, pp. 100ff.).

33 Here Bourdieu is referring to the last six lectures of the second year of his teaching (lectures of 30 November 1982 and after, in *Habitus and Field*, pp. 176ff.).

34 See the lecture for 14 December 1982, in *Habitus and Field*, pp. 244–246.
35 Georges Canguilhem, *La Connaissance de la vie* (Paris: Vrin, 1965 [1952]), pp. 129ff. Bourdieu had used and commented on this reference in his lecture of 14 December 1982, in *Habitus and Field*, p. 245.
36 See the lectures for 22 and 29 March 1984 (above, pp. XXX and XXX).
37 'But I prefer Helleu. – There's no connection with Helleu, said Mme Verdurin. – Yes there is, it's eighteenth-century febrile. He's a *Watteau à vapeur*, and he started to laugh. – Oh, heard it, heard it a hundred times, I've been having that served up to me for years, said M. Verdurin, who had indeed once been told it by Ski, though as his own creation': Marcel Proust, *Sodom and Gomorrah*, p. 335. The joke was so popular that its origin was attributed to several authors (Degas, Léon Daudet, and anonymous sources). [*Watteau à vapeur* is a pun on *bateau à vapeur* (a steamship), alluding perhaps to such paintings as Manet's *Gare St. Lazare*, or the general haziness of Impressionist painting. (Translator)]
38 Bourdieu may be thinking of Proust again (Françoise is the first name of the narrator's governess in *In Search of Lost Time*).
39 Around 1900, Charles Seignobos – for whom 'the "social fact", as accepted by several sociologists, is a philosophical construction, not a historical fact': Charles-Victor Langlois and Charles Seignobos, *Introduction aux études historiques* (Paris, Hachette, 1909 [1898]), p. 188 – and the Durkheim school are in disagreement. Seignobos and Durkheim themselves debated the issue: see 'Débat sur l'explication en histoire et en soiologie', *Bulletin de la société française de philosophie*, no. 8, 1908, pp. 229–245, 347, reprinted in Durkheim, *Textes, I*, pp. 199–217. See also François Simiand, 'Méthode historique et science sociale' [1903], *Annales*, vol. 15, no. 1, 1960, pp. 83–119.
40 'Again, the elements will not be even knowable; for they are not universal, and knowledge is of universals. This is clear from demonstrations and from definitions; for we do not conclude that this triangle has its angles equal to two right angles, unless every triangle has its angles equal to two right angles, nor that this man is an animal, unless every man is an animal': Aristotle, *Metaphysics*, trans. W. D. Ross (Internet Classics Archive), vol. II, 1086b, 33–38.
41 Bourdieu takes the example of the 'critical moment' that he had analysed in *Homo Academicus*, pp. 159–193.
42 'Ours [i.e. our butler] insinuated that Dreyfus was guilty, the Guermantes' that he was innocent. They behaved in this manner not to hide their convictions, but out of shrewd, hard-headed competition. Our butler, who was not sure that there would be a retrial, wanted to compensate in advance for not winning the argument by denying the Guermantes' butler the satisfaction of seeing a just cause crushed. The Guermantes' butler thought that if a retrial was refused, ours would be more incensed by the continued detention of an innocent man on Devil's Island': Marcel Proust, *In Search of Lost Time*, vol. 2, *The Guermantes Way*, trans. Mark Treharne (London: Penguin, 2003), p. 294.
43 Christophe Charle, 'Champ littéraire et champ du pouvoir: les écrivains et l'Affaire Dreyfus', *Annales ESC*, vol. 32, no. 2, 1977, pp. 240–264. See also Christophe Charle, *Naissance des 'intellectuels', 1880–1900* (Paris: Minuit, 1990).
44 An allusion to the controversy between the academic Raymond Picard, a specialist in Racinian theatre, and Roland Barthes, following the publication by the latter of *Sur Racine* (Paris: Seuil, 1963), considered as the flagbearer of the 'new criticism' that had emerged during the 1960s and that Picard had attacked

in *Nouvelle critique ou nouvelle imposture?* (Paris: Pauvert, 1965). See Bourdieu, *Homo Academicus,* pp. 115–118.

45 'Robert was chiefly preoccupied at this time by the Dreyfus case. He said very little about it, because he alone of the party at table was a Dreyfusard; the others were violently opposed to a fresh trial, apart from my neighbour at table, the new friend whose opinions seemed less fixed': Proust, *The Guermantes Way*, p. 105.

46 See Bourdieu, *Homo Academicus,* pp. 117–118.

47 Émile Faguet (1847–1916), a literary critic much attached to the defence of the classical tradition, was elected to the Académie française in 1900.

48 An allusion to attacks in the name of classical culture, inspired by Maurras, against the new Sorbonne by Henri Massis and Alfred de Tarde under the pseudonym of Agathon in *L'Esprit de la Nouvelle Sorbonne* (1911) and *Les Jeunes Gens d'aujourd'hui* (1913).

49 Compagnon, *La Troisième République des Lettres.*

50 Probably a tongue-in-cheek reference to a line from Mallarmé's poem 'Le tombeau d'Edgar Poe': *'Calme bloc ici-bas chu d'un désastre obscur'*; see Stéphane Mallarmé, *Oeuvres completes* (Paris: Gallimard 'Pléiade', 1945), p. 189. (Translator)

51 See Bourdieu, *The Rules of Art*, especially 'Foundations of a Science of Works of Art', pp. 177–282; 'How to Read an Author', in *Pascalian Meditations*, pp. 85–92.

52 An allusion to Heraclitus. In Plato's *Cratylus*, Socrates says: 'Heraclitus is supposed to say that all things are in motion and nothing at rest; he compares them to the stream of a river, and says that you cannot go into the same water twice': Plato, *Cratylus*, trans. Benjamin Jowett (project Gutenberg Ebook #1616, 2008), 402a. (Translator)

Situating the Third and Later Volumes of *General Sociology* in the Work of Pierre Bourdieu

1 Lecture of 28 April 1982, in *Classification Struggles*, p.11

2 Ibid.

3 'The notion of habitus means that there is a sort of information capital that structures and is structured, which functions as a principle of structured practices without these structures that can be found in the practices having existed before the production of practices in the form of rules.' (10 May 1984).

4 A formula employed in Bourdieu, Chamboredon and Passeron, *The Craft of Sociology*, p. 35.

5 Bourdieu would certainly have revised the text as was his habit, but an aside ('Besides, this exists in book form, or will do, I hope', 25 April 1985) as well as later indications ('This chapter . . . tends to leave aside the specific logic of each of the specialized fields . . . that I have analysed elsewhere and which will be the subject of a forthcoming book': *The Rules of Art*, p. 380; see also *On the State*, p. 367) indicate that he envisaged publishing one or several volumes. The 'Course in General Sociology' is perhaps one of the projects that was not published for lack of time; on this point, see Pierre Bourdieu and Yvette Delsaut, 'L'esprit de la recherche', in Yvette Delsaut et Marie-Christine Rivière, *Bibliographie des travaux de Pierre Bourdieu, suivi d'un entretien sur*

l'esprit de la recherche (Pantin: Le temps des cerises, 2002), p. 224. *Pascalian Meditations* (like the volume on the 'theory of fields' that he had nearly finished) was an opportunity to publish some developments from the lectures.

6 The reflections delivered during this first year 1981–82 were to furnish the substance of an important later article: 'The Social Space and the Genesis of Groups', *Theory and Society*, vol. 14, no. 6, November 1985, pp. 723–744.

7 'And if I rework the same themes and return several times to the same objects and the same analyses, it is always, I think, in a spiralling movement which makes it possible to attain each time a higher level of explicitness and comprehension, and to discover unnoticed relationships and hidden properties': *Pascalian Meditations*, p. 8.

8 See Bourdieu and Delsaut, 'L'esprit de la recherche', p. 193.

9 As noted earlier, this incident explains why the first year of lectures, published in the previous volume, *Classification Struggles*, is shorter than the following four (and perhaps also why the second year, *Habitus and Field*, is the longest: Bourdieu had probably envisaged a greater number of sessions in 1982–83 to make up for the sessions that he had not been able to provide in spring 1982).

10 Bourdieu, *Classification Struggles*, p. 4.

11 On the other hand, he is sometimes very pleased with this (see, for example, the lecture of 2 May 1985).

12 'The questions are very useful to me psychologically because they give me the feeling that I understand your expectations better' (23 May 1985).

13 As a result, the lectures published in this volume all last more or less two hours, whereas in 1982–83 some lectures lasted considerably longer than the time allotted.

14 Between the two sessions Bourdieu observed a formal break (or an 'interval', as he somewhat ironically calls it, perhaps to remind us of the objectively rather theatrical nature of the occasion).

15 Pierre Bourdieu, 'L'institutionnalisation de l'anomie', *Les cahiers du Musée national d'art moderne*, nos 19–20, 1987, pp. 6–19; 'La révolution impressioniste', *Noroît*, no. 303, 1987, pp. 3–18.

16 *Manet. A Symbolic Revolution.*

17 See the indications given on this subject in the lecture of 14 March 1985.

18 Pierre Bourdieu and Erec R. Koch, 'The Invention of the Artist's Life', *Yale French Studies*, no. 73, 1987, pp. 75-103.

19 'The Hit Parade of French Intellectuals, or Who Is to Judge the Legitimacy of the Judges?'.

20 'Un jeu chinois. Notes pour une critique sociale du jugement', Actes *de la recherche en sciences sociales*, no. 4, 1976, pp. 91–101, and as 'Associations: A Parlour Game', in *Distinction*, pp. 546–559.

21 'I'm rather like an old doctor who knows all the diseases of the sociological understanding': Interview with Pierre Bourdieu by Beate Krais (December 1988), in *The Craft of Sociology*, p. 256.

22 Ibid., pp. 256–257.

23 We may note that it was in 1985 that Bourdieu ceased to direct the Centre de l'éducation et de la culture.

24 In fact, between 1983 and 1997 Bourdieu's graduates completed only half as many theses as between 1970 and 1983 (fourteen as opposed to twenty-nine).

25 Bourdieu and Koch, 'The Invention of the Artist's Life'.

26 Bourdieu refers more briefly to Dostoevsky's *The Gambler* (29 March 1984).

During this period, he also published an article on Francis Ponge: 'Nécessiter', in 'Francis Ponge', *Cahiers de L'Herne*, 1986, pp. 434–437.

27 Bourdieu, 'La dernière instance'.

28 *Images d'Algérie*, p. 42.

29 The index of the two volumes of *General Sociology* confirms this: Marx, Durkheim and Weber are the authors Bourdieu refers to most often (they are followed by Sartre, Kant, Hegel, Flaubert, Lévi-Strauss, Plato, Goffman, Kafka, Foucault and Husserl). Weber is cited the most (116 citations against 86 and 81 for Marx and Durkheim), particularly in 1983–84.

30 'N'ayez pas peur de Max Weber!', *Libération*, 6 juillet 1982, p. 25.

31 In 1962–63, when Bourdieu was teaching at Lille, he devoted a lecture course to Max Weber and invited his students to read and translate passages from *Economy and Society*. In the 1960s, he made copies of selected passages for his students and researchers. It was only in 1971 that Plon published a partial translation of the book.

32 Bourdieu, 'The Force of Law'.

33 *On the State*.

34 'La domination masculine', *Actes de la recherche en sciences sociales*, no. 4, 1990, pp. 2–31; *Masculine Domination*.

35 On this reflection (preceded by 'L'évolution des rapports entre le champ universitaire et le champ du journalisme', *Sigma*, no. 23, 1987, pp. 65–70), which includes an analysis of journalism in terms of field, see in particular 'L'emprise du journalisme', Actes *de la recherche en sciences sociales*, nos 101–102, 1994, pp. 3–9; 'Journalisme et éthique' (Communication à l'ESJ Lille, 3 June 1994), *Les Cahiers du journalisme*, no. 1, 1996, pp. 10–17; 'Champ politique, champ des sciences sociales, champ journalistique (lecture at the Collège de France, 14 November 1995)', *Cahiers du Groupe de recherche sur la socialisation* (Lyon: Université Lumière-Lyon 2, 1996), republished in English in Rodney Benson and Erik Neveu (eds), *Bourdieu and the Journalistic Field* (Cambridge: Polity, 2005) pp. 29–47; *On Television and Journalism* (1996); 'Return to Television', in *Acts of Resistance: Against the New Myths of our Time*, trans. Richard Nice (Cambridge: Polity, 1998), pp. 70–77; 'À propos de Karl Kraus et du journalisme', *Actes de la recherche en sciences sociales*, nos 131–132, 2000, pp. 123–126.

36 Patrick Champagne, 'Sur la médiatisation du champ intellectuel. À propos de *Sur la télévision*', in Louis Pinto, Gisèle Sapiro and Patrick Champagne (eds), Pierre *Bourdieu, sociologue* (Paris: Fayard, 2004), pp. 431–458.

37 During the period of these lectures, Bourdieu participated in two sessions of 'Apostrophes' (for *Language and Symbolic Power* and *Homo Academicus* and then for the report by the Collège de France on education) and presented two of his books (*Language and Symbolic Power* and *Homo Academicus*) on two television news programmes (one 'regional' and the other 'night-time').

38 Drawing on his analyses of the fields of cultural production, he introduces a sociological reflection on the themes of the disaffection of 'the young' for the press and on the relations between journalism and the educational institution. See Philippe Bernard, 'Exercice illégal de la pédagogie', *Le Monde*, 16 May 1985.

39 See *Pierre Bourdieu et les médias. Rencontres INA/Sorbonne (15 mars 2003)* (Paris: L'Harmattan, 2004.) In the years following the seminar (and therefore after the growth of the private channels in France), Bourdieu was one of

the instigators of the movement 'Pour que vive la télévision publique' ('Long live public television'); see Pierre Bourdieu, Ange Casta, Max Gallo, Claude Marti, Jean Martin and Christain Pierret, 'Que vive la télévision publique!', *Le Monde*, 19 October 1988.

40 Remi Lenoir, 'Duby et les sociologues', in Jacques Dalarun and Patrick Boucheron (eds), *Georges Duby. Portrait de l'historien en ses archives* (Paris: Gallimard, 2015), pp. 193–203.

41 Although the socialist François Mitterrand remained President of the Republic, legislative elections in 1986 compelled him to share power with a right-wing prime minister, Jacques Chirac.

42 *Propositions pour l'enseignement de l'avenir. Rapport du Collège de France* (Paris: Minuit, 1985), a forty-eight-page pamphlet; see also *Le Monde de l'éducation*, no. 116, May 1985, pp. 61–68).

43 On the origins, drafting and reception of the project, see the research in progress by P. Clément (for a first draft: 'Réformer les programmes pour changer l'école? Une sociologie historique du champ de pouvoir scolaire', doctoral thesis in sociology, université de Picardie Jules-Verne, 2013, ch. 2, pp. 155–240).

44 Bourdieu, *Sketch for a Self-Analysis*, pp. 78-81.

45 Bourdieu mentions this ceremony in *Manet. A Symbolic Revolution*, pp. 318–319.

46 Bourdieu, 'Le plaisir de savoir', *Le Monde*, 27 June 1984; 'Non chiedetemi chi sono. Un profilo di Michel Foucault', *L'indice*, October 1984, pp. 4–5.

47 For a detailed analysis of the philosophical field at the time of the lecture course, see Louis Pinto, *Les Philosophes entre le lycée et l'avant-garde. Les métamorphoses de la philosophie dans la France d'aujourd'hui* (Paris: L'Harmattan, 1987).

48 See also Pierre Bourdieu, 'Sartre', *London Review of Books*, vol. 2, no. 22, 1980, pp. 11–12.

49 By this time, this intellectual recognition already included American universities. In Foucault's case, for instance, there was a wave of translations in 1977 in the United States. At this time, Bourdieu, who was slightly younger and the only one not to call himself a 'philosopher', lagged behind rather in this respect.

50 See Bourdieu, *Homo Academicus*, pp. 105–112.

51 Luc Ferry and Alain Renaut, 'La Pensée 68': Essay on contemporary antihumanism, published in November 1985 by Gallimard.

52 On this point see Benoît Peeters, Derrida (Paris: Flammarion, 2010), pp. 369–380.

53 This model is that of the academic combining genuinely intellectual recognition with notoriety for a fairly broad educated public. The beginning of the 1980s (which corresponds, for instance, to the moment when François Maspero sold his publishing house) was a period when publishers started to deplore the scarcity of scholarly authors able to sell in quantity, in a context where academic specialization seemed to be increasing.

54 Collectif Les Révoltes logiques, *L'Empire du sociologue* (Paris: La Découverte, 1984).

55 We can also refer to his remark on the 'slightly cubist' character of his sociology (9 May 1985).

56 Bourdieu, *Sociology in Question*.

57 Alain Accardo, *Initiation à la sociologie de l'illusionnisme social. Invitation à la*

lecture des œuvres de Pierre Bourdieu (Bordeaux: Le Mascaret, 1983); republished Marseille: Agone, 2006. This book was followed by a collection of texts edited by Alain Accardo and Philippe Corcuff: *La Sociologie de Bourdieu* (Bordeaux: Le Mascaret, 1986).

58 On the opposition between methodology and epistemology, see *The Craft of Sociology*, pp. 6–7, 11–12. On Bourdieu's relation to Paul Lazarsfeld's enterprise, see Bourdieu, *Sketch for a Self-Analysis*, pp. 72–75. On the 'methodological imperative' that tends to unite the different stages of Raymond Bourdon's sociology, see Johan Heilbron, *French Sociology* (Ithaca: Cornell University Press, 2015), pp. 193–197.

59 Bruno Latour and Steve Woolgar, *Laboratory Life: The Social Construction of Scientific Facts* (London: Sage, 1979).

60 *Science of Science and Reflexivity.*

61 On the public positions adopted by Bourdieu during this period, see *Interventions 1981–2001*, pp. 157-187.

62 See, for instance, *Acts of Resistance*, p. 40.

63 Jean-Pierre Chevènement was minister of education under prime minister Laurent Fabius from 1984 to 1986. He hoped to revive the original mission of the Republican school, which, in addition to promoting civic and lay values, was to level out social inequalities. (Translator)

64 In 1986, activists belonging to Solidarność, the Polish Workers' Trade Union, demonstrated in favour of the release of political prisoners and organized strikes, which defied the regime of General W. Jaruzelski and paralysed the country. Bourdieu and some colleagues signed a petition protesting against the French government's lack of supporting action. (Translator)

65 *On the State.*

66 *Manet. A Symbolic Revolution.*

67 *Science of Science and Reflexivity.*

Index